Thoughts for Sundays

Thoughts for
Sundays

Handley C. G. Moule, D.D.

AMG
PUBLISHERS
Chattanooga, TN 37422

Thoughts for Sundays
© 1997 by AMG Publishers
All rights reserved.

ISBN: 0-89957-216-2

Library of Congress Catalog Card Number: 97-071385

Thoughts for Sundays is a compilation of three books by Dr. Moule: *Thoughts for the Sundays of the Year* (4th edition, Religious Tract Society, London: 1907); *From Sunday to Sunday* (Isbister & Company LTD, London: 1903); and *The Sacred Seasons* (Seeley & Company LTD, London: 1907).

Printed in the United States of America.
02 01 00 99 98   –R– 6 5 4 3 2

Contents

BOOK ONE
Thoughts for the Sundays of the Year

BOOK TWO
From Sunday to Sunday

BOOK THREE
The Sacred Seasons

Foreword

Thoughts for Sundays is a collection of devotional readings taken from three different works by Dr. Moule: *Thoughts for the Sundays of the Year, From Sunday to Sunday,* and *The Sacred Seasons.* These inspiring meditations were originally designed for Sunday reading, but can be read throughout the week according to the readers' desires. Each brief reading takes readers deep into the Word of God, and since the readings are based on the Sundays of the calendar, readers may find them an excellent way to prepare themselves for worship on the Lord's Day.

In combining three volumes into this single edition, we at AMG Publishers have made some minor changes to the original works to help make their content more clear to modern readers: We have updated spelling and some archaic terms in accordance with how our language has changed over the years; in some cases, unusual forms of punctuation have been simplified in order to eliminate confusion. We have also added scripture references; these are placed in brackets in the text. Readers should also note that points of history cited by Dr. Moule are from the early 1900's.

BOOK ONE

Thoughts for the Sundays of the Year

To the heart-uplifting memory
of my friend, now resting in God,
G. H. C. MacGregor

Preface

Of the following short chapters the larger number were originally contributed in monthly succession to the *Sunday at Home*, as "Thoughts for the Day of Days." The remainder have been written since, to complete a series for the Sundays of the Year.

As the opening of the New Century coincided, in my work of periodical contribution, with that of the New Year, I made reference to it, as a matter of course. When revising my "Thoughts" for the present volume, I decided to leave that reference as it stands; it will recall to my readers a memorable epoch, whose messages do not pass away with its occurrence.

Readers to whom the traditional sacred Seasons of the Year are, as they are to myself, a help to faith and hope, will find them here recognized in their succession. But I hope that this feature of the book will be found to be so managed as to be no intrusion on the attention of other Christians.

The preparation of this simple work has been a refreshment to my own heart and soul. Happy shall I be if in some humble measure its brief chapters may serve, under the blessing of the Lord of the Sabbath, to magnify His Name to His believing servants, and to endear to them more than ever that "Day of rest and gladness," the loving and reverent observance of which is of such inestimable value to the Church.

Handley C. G. Moule
St. Beatenberg, Switzerland,
July 9, 1907

1

My Presence Shall Go with Thee

My presence shall go with thee, and I will give thee rest—Ex. 33:14.

This is the first Lord's Day of a New Year. It is more; for it is
the first of a new century [first printing in 1899]. The transition is
strange and moving as we pass such a boundary of time. Last Sunday
we could still think of the "seventeen hundreds" as "last century."
The reign of Anne, the Pretenders' wars, the work of Wesley, the
British conquests in India and Canada, the independence of the
United States, the French Revolution, all still were grouped to our
minds within that "last century." Now our long familiar "eighteen
hundreds" take that place. The imagination feels it. It is as if the
past had moved abruptly further off, and the unknown future stood,
in its solemn veil, closer at hand before us.

To be sure it is *imagination* which has most to do with this experience. But imagination is not nothing. It is a peculiar grouping of
facts to our inner eye. And in this case the grouping is one which
may deeply influence both thought and will, as it brings so vividly
before us the swift march of the things temporal towards the things
which are eternal.

The first Sunday of the twentieth Christian century is a fitting
day on which to listen to this great promise, spoken by the living
Lord to His servant Moses, at a great crisis: "My presence shall go
with thee, and I will give thee rest" (Ex. 33:14).

We well remember the occasion and the conditions. Moses was
on the eve of a great and serious "new departure." The sin of the
golden calf had darkened the whole scene, and he was looking

forward to the future of his leadership of the unfaithful and restive people with a sinking heart. As a fact, though he did not know it yet, he had before him not merely a few difficult weeks or months, but years upon years of toil and care. The great Wandering would soon begin, of whose sorrowful annals we hear so little, but which must have put immense demands upon the prophet's patience and strength. Just now it is that he cries to his Heavenly Master in the sore need. He thinks of the future, and he cannot face it, except on one condition; the Lord must send with him His own supernatural aid. He must be allowed to "know the Lord" and enjoy the blessings of access and friendship. He must be sure of His mighty favor; "show me now Thy way, that I may know Thee, that I may find grace in Thy sight" (Ex. 33:13).

Then came the answer: "My presence shall go with thee, and I will give thee rest."

How pregnant, how profound, are the terms of that assurance! The anxious man, encountering the difficult and the unknown, is to have with him in it the eternal Presence, and is to enjoy not only support and assistance but a wonderful Rest.

"*My Presence*"; literally, "*My Face*." He was to have always with him a personal Companionship. He was to hold converse face to Face, eye to Eye, with One who was strong enough to meet all his demands for guidance, succor and strength. What he should enjoy should be no mere superintendence, as from a distant heaven. An everlasting Friend should travel with him along the desert, and sit with him in his tent, and accompany him to the council, and to the seat of justice, and amidst the rebellious concourse, and to the field of battle with heathen foes, giants and others, when the time should come. He should experience the infinite difference of never being alone, never without a personal Presence, perfectly sympathetic, and at the same time almighty.

"*I will give thee Rest.*" There are two possible sorts of rest. One is rest *after* toil, the lying down of the weary, at the end of the march, on the morrow of the battle, on the summit of the hill. The other is rest *in* toil, the internal and deep repose and liberty of a spirit which has found a hidden refuge and retreat, where feeling is calm and disengaged, while the march, the battle, the climb, are still in full course. This last was the promise to Moses. Another day, a distant day, was to come when he should taste the endless rest *after* toil, when he should sink down on Pisgah in the arms of the Lord, and (to quote the beautiful legendary phrase) should die—if death it could be called—by His kiss. But now he was to taste the wonderful rest *in* toil. He was to traverse that last long third of his vast and memorable life, thinking, ruling, guiding, bearing, under the divine enabling condition of the inward rest of God, the peace of God, passing understanding.

Today, looking out upon the new year and the new age, let us humbly claim the promise of Moses for ourselves. We may do so. For "he that is least in the kingdom of heaven" has, in the Lord Jesus, a guaranteed assurance of nothing less. "Lo, I am with you all the days" (Matt. 28:20). "We have access into the holiest" (Heb. 10:10). "The peace of God shall keep your hearts and minds in Christ Jesus" (Phil. 4:7).

"E'en let the unknown tomorrow bring with it what it may," while that promise is in our grasp. It may bring with it surprises of earthly joy, personal or domestic. It may bring unlooked for clearings away of dark public prospects, in state or in church. Or it may bring clouds, and storm, and conflict, and what looks like confusion. But if the Presence goes with us we shall, in either event, have the Rest. Our life's week will have at its heart a perpetual Sabbath, on the way to the great and perfect "Sabbath-keeping which remaineth for the people of God" (see Heb. 4:9).

2

The Lord's Day

The Lord's Day—Rev. 1:10

It is already the second Sunday of the New Year. Before we go another step along the holy days thus in prospect, let us pause to think a little of what is given to us in the gift of them, and to make before God some resolves about our use of the gift.

Think of our Sundays in advance. If (heart-solemnizing *if!*) we are permitted to see this new year through, it has some fifty of them still to bring us. They will come in their faithful and holy succession; the Sundays of the winter, short days and long evenings, with inclement skies not seldom, and biting frosts and driving rains. Then the Sundays of the opening spring, with their deep parables and bright memorials of resurrection-life and hope. Then the Sundays of the summer, glorious with the full life of the year, perhaps also, to some, trying and tiring, as their heat is felt in hours of labor in church, or school, or by the wayside. There will be the Sundays of our normal periods of life and work. There will be the Sundays of our intervals of holiday, precious in their opportunities, yet also bringing their temptations to neglect and to misuse.

What shall we think of them as we look forward? We will, in the first place, solemnly recollect the inestimable value of the gift of them. Whatever differences there are (and they are many) between one life and another, as to the possibility of full Sabbath rest, at least there is this gift in the Sabbath for all Christian lives, that once every seven days recurs this great monument of "the better things." Each Lord's Day is as it were a pillar on the path, where the path

10

rises to a hilltop. And the pillar is inscribed with the eternal truths of God, of Christ, of Resurrection, of Holiness, of Worship, of the Word. And the hilltop commands a fresh prospect of "that blessed Hope" (Titus 2:13). Like the pilgrims on the Delectable Mountains, we can look from it and see from its vantage-ground "something like the gate, and also some of the glory of the place" where the Christian is forever with the Lord.

Aye, the Lord's Day, the First Day of the Week, is itself a pledge and earnest of that coming glory. For why do we keep now the first day, not the seventh? For one reason, and one only because "Jesus died, *and rose again*" (1 Thess. 4:14). And is not that resurrection the inalienable warrant that all His promises are true, and so that He shall come again, and His saints with Him? "Till He come" is an inscription fit alike for the holy Table and for the holy Day.

Therefore we will personally resolve, the Lord helping, that we will be, to the best of our real power, keepers of the Lord's weekly Festival of rest and worship. It is no part of my duty here to lay down an impossible uniformity of rule for this in detail. Very tenderly would I think of the many Christians whose lives, under our difficult modern conditions, are so circumstanced that their Sabbath observance is, in this respect or that, sorrowfully hindered and limited by causes which are *really* out of their control. "To their own Master they stand" (Rom. 14:4). But I may, without fear of seeming uncharitable, or unduly stringent, appeal to every Christian reader to see to it, before God, that the hindrances to the full observance of the Day in his case *are really* out of his control. Let no lightly admitted reason of mere personal liking or comparative convenience come between him and a *diligent* attendance at Sabbath worship, remembering the evening as well as the morning. Let nothing short of a very real and grave necessity, I dare to say it, justify to him the use of public conveyances on the Sunday. I say this the more earnestly since an occasion when, addressing a gathering of railway men, I remarked passingly that I never used the train on Sunday; their delight, loudly expressed, I shall never forget. Let nothing make us careless, those of us who employ domestic service, about the call that lies upon us to lighten the work of our households on Sunday in every way reasonably possible. Let us not lightly fall into the fast-advancing fashion of

11

making no difference between our Sunday reading and that of the weekday. For myself, I cannot express the benefit, mental as well as spiritual, which I have derived from a life-long adherence, very "narrow" as some might think it, to a careful rule of difference. Let anyone who pleases use the word "Sabbatarian" as a reproach. Profoundly sure I am that a "Sabbatism," not harsh nor gloomy, nay, the delightful opposite to such ideas, yet real and careful, is rich in manifold blessings for the man, for the home, for our whole society. Let us put ourselves upon its side.

I read not long ago, in a book where I had looked for nothing of the kind, an appeal for loyal reverence towards the Lord's Book and the Lord's Day. The appeal was based on national grounds. The writer affirmed that the Book and the Day are still *the* two sacred institutions in the English nation's view, and that it is of priceless benefit to the nation to foster and sustain that thought. Be it ours to aid the process, and more than ever so this coming year. But not for the nation only. For our own soul's sake, for our very life's sake, let us love, reverence, *and use,* in public, private, secret, the Lord's Holy Book, and also the Lord's ever-blessed Day.

3

Earnest Expectation and Hope

According to my earnest expectation and my hope—Phil. 1:20

Still early as we are in the year, it seems natural and fitting to direct our Lord's Day thought to what lies in front, to what is sought, hoped for, worked for, in the future. Today and next Sunday let us think a little of certain *ambitions* of the Christian man, some of the aims and desires after success and achievement with which he should look forward.

"Ambition" is a word which has been so much "soiled with all ignoble use" that it seems at first sight out of place in Christian thought. Yet the word is used by the great Apostle, once and again. *Philotimia,* "love of honor," that is to say, ambition, is Paul's chosen word in, for example, (2 Cor. 5:9). There our Authorized Version reads, "We labor to be accepted of Him." But the Greek is, literally, "We are ambitious to be accepted." Nor is there any wonder in this, when we come to reflect upon it. "Honor" may be "loved" with widely different motives. It may be sought on grounds merely selfish, as selfish as possible; the one thought may be *my* success, *my* fame, *my* gain, *my* power. It may be sought on the other hand on grounds which, practically speaking, are pure and unselfish; certainly we can *conceive* such a seeking of it. Look at the ardent student at the University, striving for intellectual distinction that he may lay his honors at the feet of parent, or of schoolmaster. Look at the soldier in the field, resolved to "distinguish himself" for England's sake, or so that his beloved and admired commander may win another victory with his aid.

13

May not the believer "seek honor," the honor which cometh, ultimately, from God only, "the praise of the glory of His grace," with the pure desire that fresh laurels may be added to the wreath of his victorious Lord? If so, he may be, nay he is called to be, ambitious.

The verse from the Philippian Epistle, at the head of this chapter, is exactly in point. Here the Apostle discloses to us his ambition; and what is it? It is, that "*Christ should be magnified* in my body, whether it be by life or by death." (Phil. 1:20) He is ambitious—for Him. He seeks success, he seeks honor. He is all alive with the hope of living, and dying, so that notice shall be taken of his life and of his death. He is ambitious of a course of action or suffering that shall be, in one important aspect, anything but commonplace, for it shall be seen to have God in it. But why? That the world may think that Paul is great? No rather, that it may see that Christ is glorious. Paul's ambition is to be as the lens which "magnifies" the heavenly body to the astrono-mer; he wants to bring Christ nearer, and to show Christ more resplendent, to the eyes of men around him. In order to do this, he desires *himself* to live and die in no common way. He is ambitious. But it is for his Lord.

Reader, I earnestly call you, as before God I call myself, to this "ambition" in view of our New Year. Think of the possibilities for this purpose which the months to come contain, if we will but watch them, and use them. Who shall attempt to calculate the ways, and the occasions, for the "magnification of Christ in our body," which this year will develop for us as we go on? What moments for the display of His presence in us, in the common things of common life, will it not bring? For the life we are ambitious of, while it is to be so far from commonplace, may have to be lived in the pathway of common things. Not so much in the doing of conspicuous deeds, as in the doing of all deeds in the sweet grace of God, is He to be magnified in us. What beautiful victories of patience, of self-denial, of love, may not the Holy One win in us this year! What lovely achievements of faithful service, of unselfish painstaking! What winning testimonies may be born for Him, in which we shall so confess His Name as *obviously* to be, not advertising ourselves, but disclosing what He has become to us!

14

Perhaps the year may bring us some "great thing" to do, or to suffer, for His name's sake. If we are wise, if we are near to God, we shall not *ask* for such "great things," as if we would rather have them for our lot than the little things which often test us more. But He may choose them for us. If so, we shall be best prepared for them by being found "faithful," faithfully ambitious for His sake, "in that which is least" [Luke 16:10]. And we will remember all along that the whole process must be carried out not only in our spirit but "in our *body*"; that is to say, not in sentiment only, however spiritual and beautiful, but in action and communion, in whatever way these may be conditioned. It is through *the body,* and the body only, that we serve others, and influence others, as we shall soon realize upon reflection. So we must, in a holy ambition, "present *our bodies* a living sacrifice, for a reasonable service" (see Rom. 12:1).

So we pass onward into the year, "loving honor," full of ambition, in quest of success, for the sake of Him "who loved us, and gave Himself for us" (see Eph. 5:2).

4

More and More

More and more—1 Thess. 4:1

Last Sunday we meditated a little upon the ambition of a Christian. Let us give the subject a little further thought today, that our New Year, for it is still new, may be the better used for our ambitious purposes.

Here is a phrase full of ambition: "More and more." It suggests at once the familiar fact of the eager and grasping character of ambition. Who does not know how proverbially the ambitious are never content? It is a familiar story, that of the young Romanist student who was asked what his hopes and wishes were. He looked forward ere long to the priesthood. Then, quite possibly, his diligence and devotion would lead him up in due season to the bishop's miter. Was that enough? No; he was bold enough to think of the arch-episcopal dignity as another step that might be taken. Was that enough? No; it was conceivable that the Pope might call him to the peculiar honors of a cardinal. And then? Why then, it was the cardinals' function, when the Pope died, to elect one of their number to be his successor; and who could tell—? And then? Then, says the story, the young man held his peace, and thought, and sighed. And another version of it adds that he died at twenty-five.

Here is indeed "the vanity of human wishes." But I quote it now to illustrate not the vanity, but the wishes, the human instinct of desire for "more and more." That instinct is not in itself evil, though it may be as evil as possible in its application. In itself, it is no more than one indication, among many others, that man was made for boundless development and growth in the scope and use of his life. There is that in him which by nature, not necessarily by sin, tends to look ever onward and to ask for more. The sin comes in only when the tendency is ruled by self-will and self-love, and seeks its object for ends divorced from the will of God. "Grace," it has been well said, "does not destroy our natural instincts, but glorifies them." So it is with this instinctive asking for "more and more."

How often the thought, "more and more" meets us in the Word of God! "The path of the just shineth more and more unto the perfect day" (Prov. 4:18). "The Lord shall increase you more and more" (Ps. 115:14). Here, in the chapter of our text, we have it twice over: "We exhort you by the Lord Jesus, that as ye have received of us how ye ought to walk and to please God, so ye would abound more and more" (1 Thess. 4:1); "Ye love one another . . . but we beseech you, brethren, that ye increase more and more" (vv. 9, 10). And where this precise phrase is not used, its equivalents continually occur, as for instance in all the many passages where we are called to be always "growing," "growing in grace, and in the knowledge of our Lord," and where we read of advances "from faith to faith," "from glory to glory," (2 Pet. 3:18) and the like. The Bible is full of the promise, and of the ambition, of growth.

It is a deep law of the spiritual life. A merely stationary spiritual condition is hardly conceivable; to be stationary must imply something already of loss and decline. "The man who says *enough*," remarks Augustine, "is a lost man." Awful words, which must be read with some obvious qualifications. But they point us to a real danger signal, though they do so with a stern grasp upon our arm.

Let us, for our own soul's sake, as well as for our Lord's, and for our brethren's, be ambitious of "more and more." Let us be always grasping, covetous, unsatisfied, in the desire for a growth which means nothing if it does not mean more of Him.

> O Jesus Christ, *grow* Thou in me,
>   And all things else recede;
> My heart be daily *nearer* Thee,
>   From sin be daily freed.

What, after all, is the great requisite to this "more and more," and what accordingly will be its manifestations? To answer the last

17

question first: it will show itself above all, as this passage of 1 Thessalonians reminds us, in a deeper desire "to walk and to please God," and in a truer, warmer "love one to another"; words equally simple and profound, as we look into them with prayer. It may or may not show itself in enlarged outward influence and enterprise. Nay, the day will come, if we live long, when in *that* respect the experience will be "less and less." Brain, eyes, tongue, hands, feet, will "less and less" serve us. Perhaps at length we shall be shut up to a sick-room, to a sick-bed, quietly to fade and die. But the spiritual "more and more" may be, and shall be, a prospect of immortal growth. "The outward man doth perish, but the inward man is renewed day by day" (2 Cor. 4:16). Which of us has not known the aged saint who, bodily, could scarcely totter, but, spiritually, "mounted up with wings like the eagle," loving, praising, manifesting Christ, "more and more," till the immortal spirit passed upward to the immortal scene?

To such a "more and more," what is the grand requisite? It is simply the divine secret; more of Christ. What will secure the blessed ones in Heaven, through their endless life, from the very possibility of decay, and enable them for an eternal "more and more" of love, and joy, and service? Simply, the being "forever *with the Lord,*" who is their life. That same secret, in its measure, is the talisman here below for the "more and more" of holy ambition in His name. "Beholding His glory, we are being transformed from glory to glory, as by His Spirit" (2 Cor. 3:18). We shall never decline, we shall ever grow, in the deep life of grace, unto the end, if we are faithful to our call to grow in the knowledge of Him who lives for us and in us, to grow in closeness of communion with Him, to "press towards the things which are still before" in the bright depths of His Person, Work, and Love.

5

Adorning the Doctrine

That they may adorn the doctrine of God our Savior in all things—Titus 2:10

The connection of these words is noteworthy. Paul is instructing Titus what to say to that element in the Cretan mission congregations which consisted of slaves. No one can read the Epistles without realizing how considerable that element was all over the rising Christian world; again and again Paul devotes special instructions to the slave-converts, notably when writing to Corinth, to Ephesus, to Colossae. Peter, in his First Epistle, addresses them in a passage full of the most tender sympathy and deepest spiritual truth (1 Pet. 2:18–25). But of all these allusions to the slaves none is more striking in some respects than this in the Epistle to Titus. For these slaves were Cretans, or living in Crete, and Paul himself reminds us how bad a reputation Crete bore for the low type of its national character, untruthful, cruel, selfish, indolent (Titus 1:12). A Cretan master, like other slave owners of the ancient world, was the almost irresponsible despot of his slave; a formidable despot he too often must have been. Legree, in *Uncle Tom's Cabin*, probably represents the Cretan character not unworthily, at least in its ferocity and selfishness. And even a Legree, in the former slave states of America, had heard of the Lord Jesus, and inherited some influences, however faint, from Christianity—an inheritance unknown to the pagan Cretan.

How impressive, when we remember this, is this appeal to "adorn the doctrine of God our Savior in all things" (Titus 2:10)! The Apostle calls upon them, not only to do right, to tell the truth, to be faithful in every trust, to see that their answers, even to harshest speech, were modest and Christian. The right deed was to be done not rightly only, but beautifully. It was to be done so as to show that the divine principle of life was not only strong but lovely. They were to "adorn the doctrine."

It was a great demand. It was an appeal to people whose walk always led them through the busiest and stoniest paths of life, to walk there with dignity and grace. It asked the slave-Christian to find a secret which should enable him so to rise above himself and his surroundings that there should be something in him and about him positively winning. He was to live so that others should wish to be like him, because they should be so impressed by the comeliness of his character, and, through it, by the comeliness of his creed.

It is hardly necessary to point out at any length the moral of this simple but most noble passage. It speaks for itself. If the Cretan slave, himself quite recently as little Christlike as his heathen owner, was called upon to live a beautiful life on gospel principles, how much more are we, with all our English circumstances, called upon so to live! Let it lie then prominent among our Christian ambitions to do so; let us covet, day by day, to "adorn the doctrine."

I remember hearing an old friend, long ago, speaking (in no uncharitable strain) of a neighbor, say, "I am sure he is a Christian, but he is a rather disagreeable one." He meant, I gathered, that this person took no pains at all to "adorn the doctrine." He worshiped God in Christ; he recognized his own sinfulness and need; he trusted his Savior for pardon, and strove in His name to lead a pure and honest life. But it never occurred to him—at least it did not seem to do so—that part of his duty to his Lord was to learn at His feet the kindliness, the gentleness, the sympathy, the considerateness, which win and are attractive for Him. Let us see to it that we are not classed, by fair criticism, among "disagreeable Christians."

If we recognize, as we should do, that the blessed gospel is intended not only to rescue us, but to mold us, to impart a noble impress to our character, we shall surely give a leading place in our thoughts to this call so to live as to "adorn the doctrine." We shall take loving pains about it; we shall think and pray about it. Perhaps above all things, in this direction, we shall study the blessed art of considerateness in the common things of the common day. We shall remember that two obvious items of Christian duty are to take trouble and to save trouble. We shall pray for the gift and grace to "look upon the things of others," and to look at them, in an important sense, through the eyes of others, putting ourselves in their place.

This, as we well know, was "the mind that was in Christ Jesus" (Phil. 2:5). And they will soonest catch it who, believing in Him, live much with Him.

6

The Master's Scrutiny of His Servants

For we must all appear before the judgment seat of Christ; that every one
may receive the things done in his body, according to that he hath done,
whether it be good or bad—2 Cor. 5:10

A slight change or two in translation will help us the better to
grasp the bearing of these words. "We must all appear" may better
be read, "we must all be displayed," or "manifested." The thought
is not merely that of attending at a summons, of putting in an appearance. It is that of being disclosed, examined, under a broad
light, so as to seem just what we are. Again, "the things done in his
body" should rather be read, "the things done through the body";
this is the only literal rendering of the Greek. The thought is of the
body as the implement of action, the vehicle of faculties and energies, the talent, so to speak, which has been laid out and used.

Thus translated, and put into connection with the previous verse,
our passage stands out with a distinctive message of its own. The
Apostle has just expressed a deep purpose of his life; it is that,
"whether present or absent," (2 Cor. 5:9) that is to say, whether out
of the body or in it, when the Lord calls him to examination, he
may be "accepted of Him," or again to render more literally, may
"meet with His approval." This is his "ambition." For this is one of
the passages where the Greek equivalent to "ambition" occurs;
"wherefore we are ambitious," is the precisely literal translation.
Now he expands that prospect and its conditions in the verse before us. He anticipates a definite occasion on which may be expressed the "approval" of which he is "ambitious." There is coming

a time when his Lord will summon him, as He will summon all who serve Him, to a "judgment seat," where a scrutiny will be conducted into what has been "done through the body," and at which the Lord will express His opinion of the doing, and will award accordingly.

If I interpret this passage correctly, it does not refer to the great general judgment, but to what we may describe as a domestic court, concerned not with a nation but with a household, and which conducts its solemn business within the walls of home. It does not refer to the all-important question of the Christian's acceptance before the Holy One in his Redeemer's merits; that is another matter, and is, I think, taken for granted all through this context. Rather it refers to the saved servant's use of his Master's gifts in his Master's service; to the inquiry into what, during his allotted span of life here below, he has "gained by trading." The person is a genuine member of the family and household of salvation. He is saved by faith. But as he was saved, not only to be safe, but to serve the purposes of his Savior, he has to be examined about his works. And so his ambition is that he may have the joy, the bliss, of the great Examiner's approval; "Well done, good and faithful servant" (Matt. 25:21).

Thus viewed, the passage finds a striking parallel in 1 Corinthians 3:11–15. There we have the thought of a fiery test to be applied hereafter, not to the persons but to the works of laborers for God. All are supposed to have "built upon the foundation." All are supposed to be "saved." But how they have worked, what they have done as builders for the King, is, nevertheless, put to test. Have they piled up a structure of precious metal and precious stones, or have they reared what is only fit to be food for the fire? "Of what sort" has been their work? Accordingly as "the fire" answers that query, so does the worker, as a worker, "receive" or not receive a "reward"; he hears or he does not hear, "Well done, good and faithful."

What shall he say to these things? Humbly, thankfully, lovingly, we will first remember that the Master who will preside at the scrutiny is at the same time the Lord who loves us and who gave Himself for us. To Him His unworthiest workman is unspeakably dear, with that love which springs unbought in a Savior's heart. He will never be harsh, He will never be unfair. He will forget no extenuation, He will have understood every difficulty. Nevertheless, His eyes will

23

be quite open, and He will express His entire opinion upon what we have done through the body.

And His opinion will be followed, assuredly, by results which will somehow affect the experiences of the servant even in the world of light and immortality. So, in Paul's words just following, literally rendered, "we know the fear of the Lord" (2 Cor. 5:11). We recognize, we realize, the solemnity of the prospect of that scrutiny. We recall it when we are tempted to misuse "the body," to forget the responsibility we have with these lips, and eyes, and hands, and feet, and brain. But our last thought, as we remember how our passage stands connected, shall not, after all, be one only of "fear." Rather it shall be full of a bright "ambition." Delightful call, to use these bodies, in which we live and move, so happily, so habitually, *for Him,* by His grace alone, that "Well done, good and faithful" shall be the voice of the beloved Master when He holds His domestic court.

7

Eternal Service

Thou hast been faithful over a few things, I will make thee ruler over many things—Matt. 25:21

We thought last week of that examination of our work for Him which is to be held hereafter by the Lord Jesus Christ our Master. We studied that prospect in the words of one of the greatest of His servants. Today we take up a prospect closely connected with that other, and it is opened to us in words of the Master's own.

The scrutiny is supposed to have taken place. "The Lord of the servants" has ascertained what they have "done through" the property He has entrusted to them, the golden "talents," the wealth of faculty and opportunity, whatever it has been. And the man in this case has "met with His approval." His employment of the means for service has been satisfactory. Now comes the allotment of reward.

And that reward takes two remarkable aspects, deeply connected, yet distinct. The man is to enter "into the joy of his Lord." And also he is to continue in his Master's service; he is to serve Him forever, and to serve Him more than ever; "I will make thee ruler over many things."

So one side of the prospect of the eternal life is this; it is to be a life of serving God. And this, not only in the sense of the service of worship, which we see referred to in the glorious words, "they serve Him day and night in His temple" (Rev. 7:15). No, the allusion here is to the service of active, positive, responsible labor. The man who has "traded with the talent" on earth is somehow to have his Master's interests entrusted to him in heaven. "I will make thee ruler over many things" [see Matt. 25:21-23].

Wonderful prospect, with its contrast between "few" and "many." Perhaps the servant had to do with what seemed "a few things"; he was perhaps weak, indigent, unintelligent, limited in a hundred ways, set to work in an area bounded, it may be, by the walls of a cottage, or of a poor and bare sick-room. On the other hand, "the things" may have seemed to be by no means "few"; the servant may have had to administer a province, a kingdom, to lead a mighty movement for God, to influence generations by his words. Or again, his place may have lain somewhere in the midst; there may have been nothing at all remarkable, this way or that, in his lot and in his scale of service. But in every case such shall the future be that the heavenly work shall be thus described relatively to the earthly; it shall be concerned with "many things." The feeblest worker shall now have much, gloriously much, to do for his beloved Lord. The seemingly mediocre life shall be expanded magnificently in its conditions and employments for the King. And even an Apostle shall be so employed that his mighty labors and their fruits below shall look narrow and scanty by comparison.

We are lost, of course, when we try to go into details. In the companion parable, that of the Pounds, we have an allusion to "cities" as the future field of service. We ask ourselves what, in eternity, will correspond to that word, and all we can say is that "it doth not yet appear" (1 John 3:2). All is yet hidden from us which can answer the question, how precisely shall we find scope for enterprise, action, government, in the life to come; what shall we achieve there; what is at all akin to the well-understood service here in which the Christian seeks to watch, and toil, and win conquests for his Lord, carrying light where there is darkness, purity where there is pollution, love where there is enmity, joy where there is sorrow, knowledge where ignorance yet reigns. We do not know, but we can abundantly believe; and in a measure we may illustrate the unknown by one glorious fact which we know already, namely, the fact of the ministry of angels. Those blessed "elder brethren" of ours, from one point of view, "do always behold the face of our Father" (Matt. 18:10), and always "stand in His presence" (Luke 1:19). Yet they are always also "being sent forth to minister" [Heb. 1:14], in countless ways, amidst the conditions of this world of sin and sorrow. Somehow, their heavenly bliss and their earthly ministries find a perpetual and beautiful harmony in their holy experience.

So for us also, in our Master's mercy, it shall be possible to experience simultaneously the many-sided life to come. Scripture depicts it now as a rest, now as a feast, now as a song, now as a garden, now as a home. It also depicts it, as we have just remembered, as a scene of loyal and veritable work for God. And these all are sides of one life; they will be harmonized forever by the unveiled presence of the Lord.

8

The Tempted Christ and His Secret of Victory

Then the devil leaveth him, and, behold, angels came and ministered unto him—Matt. 4:11

The record of our Lord's Temptation in the Wilderness is one of the great mysteries of Scripture. It is a large demand on faith to take it as it stands. What do the Evangelists ask us to believe? That our Lord's sinless and perfect humanity was yet capable of temptation, real and terrible; that He was, as a fact, assailed by such temptation; that He was approached by a personal lord and chief of evil, an existence and will as real as His own; that one of the assaults of this great power upon Him was conveyed through a claim on the tempter's part to have a certain authority over the kingdoms of the world. And that claim, whatever falsehoods may have surrounded it, is surely recorded by the Evangelists in a way which suggests a mysterious element of fact within it.

All this is difficult of belief. But that only means that we want exceptional ground here for our reliance. And surely here we have it. For how did Matthew and Luke get the narrative at all? One Person, and one only, could be the original informant. The Lord Jesus Christ Himself must have said that it happened thus and thus.

Taking then this great mystery as a great fact, let us ask over it one or two solemn questions, for our own warning and our own comfort.

First, however, let us ask what were *the forms* in which temptation assailed the Lord. In every case, evil was presented to Him hidden deep under good. He was invited to satisfy the pangs of famine by a direct act of miraculous power; to assume the empire of the world, doubtless to the world's own vast benefit; to entrust Himself in the air to the arms of angels. What a parable for us is here! To many a nature the most dangerous temptation is that which comes through avenues made of things that are good. The love of beauty, the delights of bodily or mental strength and skill, the sweetness of home, may all be made vehicles of evil if they are so treated by the will as to take, in the affections, the place of God and Christ. The process may be very subtle, the end of the wedge may be exquisitely thin, BUT if it actually is inserted so as to divide our will from God's will, the victory of the tempter has begun. Let us watch and pray, particularly that we may have a conscience, not morbid indeed, but really awake. Above all let us cultivate communion with God; a hundred "cases of conscience" will solve themselves if we live near Him.

Next, let us look at our blessed Lord's *secret of victory*. It seems to divide itself into three elements or aspects. First, we observe that He met the evil spirit in the power of the fullness of the Holy Spirit. Fresh from His baptism He went to the wilderness. The eternal Dove was upon Him when, in that dread solitude, He met the serpent. Let that be a message direct to us. "Not by might, nor by power, but by my Spirit" (Zech. 4:6). We will not dare to meet Satan in our own name. We will seek nothing short of that wonderful fullness which means, in brief, the Holy Ghost in full possession of our will. And that precious gift is an open secret for all believers who will ask it. It is set forth not only in promise, but also in precept: "*Be ye* filled with the Spirit" (Eph. 5:18). Let us not rest without that filling.

Next, we solemnly note the Lord's use of the written Word of God. Three times the awful enemy was upon Him. Three times He beat him off by the incantation, "It is written." Is our faith in the Scriptures getting slack and faint amidst the chatter of many criticisms? Let us go apart sometimes, to remember that the Bible, in the hands of the Man Christ Jesus, proved valid as a weapon in the world of spirits. Mysterious Book! If it availed there then, let us be sure it avails there now. Let us learn to know that sword; let us learn to use it.

Lastly, let us remember the Lord's great Fast in the wilderness. What is its message to us? We may or may not feel led by it to dedicate special times to special abstinence from food. But most surely

29

it says to every Christian, Live a life always abstinent from self-indulgence, from weakening habits; live a perpetual Lent of holy self-control in the name of Jesus, and for His sake; be found, like Standfast in the *Pilgrim's Progress,* keeping wakeful upon the Enchanted Ground. "Gird up the loins of your mind" (1 Pet. 1:13), and of your will, and of your life; not that you may after all win the battle by yourselves, but that you may consciously, and always, keep hold upon your victorious Savior, so that He may "tread down your enemy" (see Ps. 60:12).

9

Cause Me to Hear It

Thou that dwellest in the gardens, the companions hearken to thy voice;
cause me to hear it—Song 8:13

The Song of Songs has been in all ages of the Church a peculiar treasure to hearts which have had experience of divine communion. Of recent years, literary criticism has sometimes seemed as if it would rob them of this treasure. Critical students have largely tended to deny all inner and mystical meaning in the Song, and to represent it as no more than a beautiful idyll of human love. It seems obvious to ask how, if so, the Song ever found its place in the sanctuary of the holy Books, so jealously reverenced by Israel. For it is amply clear from the Bible itself that Israel possessed a considerable literature beyond that enshrined in the Scriptures; a book needed to be more than a book, even more than a book by a famous author, to find admission there; it needed to have a sacred prestige about it. But now, apart from this consideration, literary criticism itself is helping to give us back this book as a spiritual treasure. Some recent students have been pointing out how oriental poetry outside the Bible, the Persian poetry, for instance, is full of hidden and mystical meanings conveyed under the images of human love and human festival. Why not then the Song of Songs?

I allude to this matter before approaching our text, as just possibly some of my readers, in these days of many questions, may have been deterred a little from the spiritual use of the Song of Solomon. Let us not fear to approach the beautiful region again. It is no dream of visionaries that in it is shadowed out "the spiritual marriage and unity that is betwixt Christ and His Church," aye, and betwixt the Lord and the soul which knows and loves Him. All through Scripture, in the Prophets as well as in the Apostles, runs the thought of that wonderful unity. It only shines out with a more special beauty and detail here.

So we listen as the divine Bridegroom (it is the Bridegroom who speaks in this verse) calls to His Bride, and asks to hear her voice. Let us attend to what He says.

"Thou that dwellest in the gardens." So she is addressed. He has introduced her into His paradise of peace, beauty and delight; no mere visitor, soon to be conducted to the gate, but the dweller there, moving in and out habitually in the fair place which He has prepared. It is a fit and delightful image of the Lord's intention that His Church, that His servants, even here and now, shall abide satisfied and glad. "*Christus ist mein Paradies*," says the German hymn writer, Novalis, "Christ is my Paradise"; rightly intimating that we are not meant to wait till the other side of death for *all* our realization of joy and singing, rest and leisure of soul, amidst "the beauty of the Lord our God" [Ps. 90:17]. In this Paradise, here on earth, walked Paul, Peter, and John, with their disciples: "We joy in God through our Lord Jesus Christ" (Rom. 5:11); "With joy unspeakable and full of glory" (1 Pet. 1:8); "Our fellowship is with the Father and with His Son Jesus Christ" (1 John 1:3).

But now it appears that even in this Paradise the Bride may still need to be reminded and invited to a fuller communion. "The companions hearken to thy voice." In that fair place there is company, loving and congenial. And she is assuredly not blamed for communion with them, with "the companions" who share the same blessings, and see the same landscape, and understand the dialect of "the gardens." No, we trace no reproof in the sacred Voice among the trees and flowers. Yet we hear in it a desire, an appeal, a royal request, for more communion directly with HIMSELF. "The companions hearken to thy voice" (or, perhaps, as in the margin of the Revised Version, "hearken *for* it," BUT the import will be much the same); "*cause Me to hear it*." She has been expressing and exchanging thought freely elsewhere. Will she not do the same with Him?

32

The lesson for our Christian life is manifest. And it is one which is conveyed, in one form or another, by a multitude of other Scriptures, nay, by the whole drift and burden of the Bible, which is the Lord's Word to His people inviting their responsive word to Him. Shall we lay it to heart, in holy attention, prayer and love?

"The companions hearken to thy voice"; yes, and it is well that they should do so. Sometimes in the public worship of the believing company, sometimes in more private hours, when we talk over the Word, or when we "speak to one another in psalms, and hymns, and spiritual songs" (Eph. 5:19), sometimes a pair of friends together, conferring or discussing—we "hearken to the voice of the Bride," through one another. And all this is well. But even this must not be a substitute for that communion with the "Lover of the soul" which is for Him alone, with Him direct, and which here, as it beautifully appears, He condescends to covet and to enjoy.

In our busy and sometimes bustling modern Christian life, this is the very word to listen to, to take apart with us and act upon. Have our prayers been hindered at all by our work? Have we been leading a life so gregarious, so public (even on its most Christian sides), that we are a little strange with ourselves? Are we insensibly getting, even in His work, a little strange with the Lord? Then let us not delay. Let us go aside in "the gardens," with His Book, His Promises, His own blessed Spirit ready to "cry" in our hearts. And let us "cause" our eternal Friend "to hear," nothing between, that poor voice, for which, in His wonderful grace, He listens.

10

The Un-Upbraiding Giver

God giveth to all men liberally, and upbraideth not—James 1:5

James says this in the course of an appeal to us to make much of the privilege of prayer. The man who "lacks wisdom," especially (such is the evident reference) the holy wisdom which sees and acts aright in things spiritual, let him go directly to the Giver, and ask. He will have One to deal with who is the ideal Person for a needy applicant's approach. For in the first place He giveth liberally. And then, He upbraideth not.

We are familiar with the words, and perhaps we let them pass over the heart (like too much of Scripture in general) leaving only a vague impression. We will attempt, in this brief and simple study, to do something better with them today. We will, with all reverence, but in a practical spirit, seeking results, take them and turn them over in our hands. The words mean what they say. And what a saying it is!

First then, "He giveth liberally." This, according to the Apostle, who knew his Lord's mind, this is the character, the way, the habit, of the heavenly Giver. He is great, and rich, and mighty. He has large gifts to give, if He will. But will He? Is it His liking to bestow? Perhaps we shall have to expend much power in asking, and then the infinite Will may consent to a very small movement in response, graduated to the minute scale of our character and position. It might be so, but it is not. "He giveth liberally."

Let us take that fact with us, in a conscious grasp, to the very foot of the throne of grace. We remember there, with reverent wonder, all the provision made in Christ for our access and acceptance. We adore the grace which has sprinkled the way in with the blood of Calvary, and has established the High Priest over the house of God. But having remembered this, let us clasp anew this perfectly simple assurance, "He giveth liberally." Not only is our access and welcome secured to some sort of mercy, to some possibilities of blessing. We are ushered in by our Mediator to the presence of Him who, to sinners coming so, is delighted to give, and to give with both hands. "He giveth liberally."

> Thou art coming to a King:
> Large petitions with thee bring;
> For His grace and power are such
> None can ever ask too much.

Yes, and His habit, His blessed character, of which the grace and the power are but expressions, is such that the act of giving is His joy. "He giveth liberally." In His inmost eternal nature, which is Love, He is naturally communicative of good and bliss.

The sacred provision of atoning blood, of propitiation, of mediation, of advocacy, what is its purpose? Not to persuade a secluded and unwilling Power, under special circumstances, to yield something. No, but to set free along a channel of holiness the glorious "liberality" of "the Father of mercies and the God of all comfort" (2 Cor. 1:3), flowing down upon His dear children in His dear Son.

So let us come freely, boldly, simply, outspokenly, without reserve, without shame. "What wilt thou that I should do unto thee?" (Mark 10:51). The voice is not that of the unjust judge, but of the liberal Giver.

And now secondly, "He upbraideth not." This is a sort of development of the first statement; it is in a sense included in it. Yet it has a perfectly special import and value of its own. It tells us some things about the character and (may I dare again to say?) the habit of our blessed God which are inestimable, when we take them as they are revealed.

We all know, in human relationships, that it is possible for a gift to be given, or a service done, which may be in itself large, beautiful, momentous, while yet the glory and the joy is sadly taken off from it in the sequel by some sort of "upbraiding" on the giver's part.

He has given, he has served. But he somehow makes us feel that he is keenly conscious of the claims set up by the action, and that he is not at all satisfied with the way in which we have met or used it; and so it becomes to us far more of a debt than a possession. The donor is to us rather a creditor and a critic than anything else.

Now I need not say at any length that the gifts of our blessed God do, in deepest reality, set up incalculable claims upon us; may that fact sink ever deeper into our wills. Yet those claims are so presented to us in His Word as not for a moment to obscure the brightness of this utterance, "He upbraideth not." For the payment He asks is the payment of love. And that request can only be made by a Love which itself delights to go out freely to its object. His gifts might, if He pleased, be set before us in the aspect of so much gratuity calling for so much obedience. As a fact, they are set before us as the expression of His own yearning lovingkindness, which asks us, not for a "tally of bricks," but, as for heart answering heart, to give Him our love and all it contains in reply.

The Roman historian, Tacitus, noted long ago that it is characteristic of the basest and meanest natures "to hate the man whom they have hurt." It is the blessed Characteristic of the Supreme Nature, our God and Father in Christ Jesus, to love the being whom He has blest. Poor the use, at best, that we have made of His precious gifts. But He has given them to us sinners. And He loves His beneficiaries, as such, with a persistent love. "He upbraideth not."

11

The Indweller's Home and Habitation

I will dwell in them, and walk in them—2 Cor. 6:16

Paul is quoting here; he introduces the words with, "As God hath said." For him indeed, as for his Lord before him, the spiritual Word of God, through whatever human messenger they might come. As a fact, he is using here more than one such message, and blending them all into one. He takes one clause from Exodus (29:45), and another from Leviticus (26:12), and, in the immediate sequel goes on to Jeremiah (31:33), and Ezekiel (11:20), and Zechariah (8:8). But all alike is one thing as to its ultimate origin. It is, "as God hath said."

We notice one further point about the words. They are quoted from passages whose first reference is to "Israel according to the flesh"; they bear upon the national community of the race of Abraham, Isaac and Jacob. But Paul is writing to the Greeks of Corinth, who had recently come out of a debasing paganism to the Lord Jesus Christ. Yet he has no misgiving about his application. His converts, simply and solely because "they were Christ's," because, that is, they belonged in living faith to the great Messiah of the promises, were now, "the Israel of God" (Gal. 3:29; 6:16). So to them belonged, not by a mere uncovenanted concession, but "according to promise," the deepest blessings lodged first in covenant for the elder Israel. Even so, the Lord Jesus Himself. Jeremiah has much to say of a "new covenant, with the house of Israel and with the house of Judah" (Jer. 31:31); and it proves, when we read his words about it, to be just the glorious gospel of pardon and of holiness. Jesus our Lord institutes

His precious Supper, for all His disciples of every race forever. And He calls the cup, "The New Covenant in My blood" (Luke 22:20 [NIV]). So it is for us all, be we Jew or Greek, Scythian, barbarian, bond or free.

Ancient, national Israel has still a place most special in the heart of God, and in His purposes. We cannot read Romans 11 and doubt that. But not even that fact must obscure to us Gentile believers the glory of our own covenanted part and lot "with Abraham, Isaac, and Jacob in the kingdom of God." We are "heirs according to promise," lawful heirs, of the great blessings of the Word.

But this is by the way. It is a clearance of our thoughts in order to the simpler exercise of our faith and obedience. Come let us read our text over again. "I will dwell in them, and walk in them." Such is the promise of the God of grace to the community of His faithful ones. Such surely is the promise also to the faithful member of that community, to the Christian who watches, prays, believes, obeys. Few are those promises to the Church which have not also their assured reference to the individual disciple's soul.

"I will dwell in them." It is a wonderful word, when we take it aside and look at it anew in the light. Here is "the high and lofty One, that inhabiteth eternity" (Is. 57:15). He is the sovereign Cause and Basis of existence. The universe is large. But relatively to Him, in order and mode of being, it is "a very little thing" (Is. 40:15). The persons alluded to in the promise are inhabitants of a sand-grain on the seashore of His vast creation. Moreover, they are beings who have misused a mysterious moral and personal relation to Him so as to turn away from Him, and sin. Nevertheless, they are so much to the eternal Heart (for the First Cause is also the eternal Heart) that, coming to bless them, He cannot say less than this, "I will dwell in them." Would it not be enough that He should pass them by on the roadside of the universe, and command His angels to spare and to tend them, while He is absent in greater scenes? Nay He selects them for His personal abode. He is to be in residence and keep His court in them. "I will dwell in them."

Does my reader need to be reminded how full the whole Scripture is of that surprising promise? Read again Isaiah 57, and John 14, and Ephesians 3, and Revelation 3 and 21, and then explore the parallels they suggest. Let him follow up the study with an act of definite faith and appropriation, receiving afresh, and for deeper effects, the indwelling of his God.

But now the promise proceeds, and borrows from Leviticus this beautiful addition, "I will walk in them." What has this to say to the disciple's heart, in a special message of its own?

It indicates on the one hand, under striking imagery, the delight and repose of the gracious Indweller, His being indeed *at home* in His abode. On the other hand, it has a precious intimation for the disciples as to what his Lord looks for in the heart-welcome given Him there.

"I will walk in them." We seem to see the King in His mansion and its gardens. He is not merely there; He is there possessing and enjoying. At His will, at His leisure, He traverses the chambers, He surveys the points of view, He paces the alleys and the lawns. The place is His dear home, in which He "lives *and moves*." Oh what benedictions to that "home" are conveyed by that traversing Presence!

"I will walk in them." Yes, and therefore to Him every gate and avenue must be perpetually open. What would the lord of some fair domain say if he was constantly barred and hindered in his home walks by doors which his own servants had carelessly left locked against him? But the King eternal, who thus mysteriously delights to make room for His own abode in His creature's heart, too often, by our grievous fault, finds it so. This chamber and that, a department of the will, of the affections, of the imagination, is not quite open to Him today. Neglect, prayerlessness, self-indulgence, have left it locked; sin is in that corner, using it for itself. But it belongs to the King! And He is in residence! And hark, His step is at the door! (Rev. 3:20).

Lord, in Thy name we will keep the avenues open. Be pleased to walk in them all, and fill the whole place with Thyself.

12

Every Mouth Stopped

That every mouth may be stopped, and all the world may become guilty before God—Rom. 3:19

What a silence! Here is a hush in which there is a great cessation of that large amount of human utterance which is expended in self-justification. The Apostle sees, in idea, a "world" of human hearts and souls, prostrate under a sense of guilt, and having come to the very end of explanations, extenuations, recriminations.

There is silence. Every mouth is stopped.

How obstinately strong is the inward impulse to say one word more for self! In the very first scene of human sin that impulse appears. Primal man and woman, amidst the trees of the garden, are confronted by their Maker, and questioned about their manifest guilt. The facts are patent. But the mouths are not stopped. "The woman whom Thou gavest to be with me, she gave me of the tree, and I did eat"; "The serpent beguiled me, and I did eat" (Gen. 3:12, 13). So it is again and again, in the picture gallery of the Bible. Aaron after the sin of the golden calf (Ex. 32), Saul after the halting vengeance upon Amalek (1 Sam. 15), the man of the one talent in the parable (Matt. 25)—these mouths are not stopped. They must extenuate, and explain, and throw the blame, in part at least, elsewhere.

But there are some great contrasts to this. There are cases where the convincing Spirit's work has penetrated "to the joints and marrow"; and then the man's mouth is stopped. So it is with David, when Nathan comes to him, and drives the long, keen point of the story of the ewe-lamb deep into his conscience. "I have sinned against the Lord" (2 Sam. 12:13); that is all, and then the mouth is stopped. So it is with Job. He has fought a long battle with his friends over the awful mysteries of Providence, dark then, and dark today, to our short and aching sight. Then the Lord answers him, and shows him His glory, till he begins to realize something of what it is for the creature to arraign the Creator. Behold, Job's mouth is stopped. "I am vile; what shall I answer Thee? I will lay my hand upon my mouth. Mine eye seeth Thee; wherefore I abhor myself, and repent in dust and ashes" (Job 40:4; 42:5, 6). So it is with the Publican: "God, be merciful to me a sinner" (Luke 18:13)—that, and not a word more.

Not one of these men need have been at a loss for specious self-justifications, or at least for extenuating explanations. David might easily have turned upon Nathan, and said a hundred things about a sudden temptation, an unguarded moment, and then about an infinitely difficult situation for a king in the blaze of popular observation. Job might have fallen back with obstinate and weary reiteration upon his fearful temptations to doubt, his shocking personal sufferings, contradicting apparently a host of promises, and the needless cruelty of the suspicions and accusations of his friends, making his spirit bitter beyond bearing. The Publican had a great resource for self-defense, in the way of the world, in his training and surroundings, and in the ruthless and hardening contempt of the Pharisees.

But then, every one of these men had really, not fictitiously, heard the voice of the Lord convincing him of sin. His soul had passed through a "time of finding" (Ps. 32:6). His "inmost rudiment" had been exposed to the consciousness of what it is to be at variance of will with the living, infinite, holy Maker of his being. "The law," in Paul's words here before us, that is to say, the very voice of the awful, blessed will of the eternal King, had spoken to him, as under the law. And the Holy Spirit of the Lawgiver made the man's spirit fully responsive, in its penitent depths. So, his mouth was stopped.

For us today it needs to be the same. Man's heart in the twentieth century needs, more than ever, if that is possible, to be brought under divine conviction of sin. It is all too rare a thing in our modern world. This is so, if I see the matter correctly, very much because of the countless hindrances we have gathered around us to bar the way to real self-knowledge, and to real listening to the deeper voices of eternal truth. Our inner ears are beset with the clatter and the hum of endless theories of morals and conduct. We get only too easily accustomed to such catchwords as heredity, environment, evolution, falling upward, and the like. Certainly for one cause or another, man finds himself all too rarely now in the attitude of spirit which really hears "the Law" speak, and then really shuts the mouth before God.

But the experience is not out of date, nor will it ever be, while God endures, and deals in justice and mercy with the being which He made in His own image, and which cast himself down from Him in the fall. O dread and still reality, when the Holy One deals so with His creature, in some hour when conscience lies awake in the dark! Extenuating circumstances may have seemed to be many, before that hour. We may have been able quite easily to urge that this incident, and that person, had really a great deal to do with our regrettable failure, our prolonged indecision, our unfaithfulness to God or man. But when "our eye seeth Him," then, whatever *He* may think about extenuations, *we* think nothing about them. Our "mouth is stopped." Our whole consciousness is concentrated upon the awful difference between the actual condition of our will—and Him. We have not a word to say about others, and only this to say about ourselves, "Be merciful, to me a sinner."

13

The Message of the Lord's Resurrection: Part One

If we believe that Jesus died, and rose again—1 Thess. 4:14

We have reached the period of the year connected forever in the Christian's thought with the Resurrection of the Lord. We may or may not be keepers of the traditional seasons observed by so large a part of the universal Church; Christmas, Epiphany, Lent, may or may not be points in our religious almanac. But the memory of the Resurrection stands outside such questions of the calendar in this respect, that we know the season at which it occurred, as marked in *the Jewish* Year. It was just after Passover that "Christ our Passover" (1 Cor. 5:7) was raised again, in the power of an endless life. So, within limits. we know that with the sweet spring season is immortally linked that great triumph over sin and death. The time of the Lord's Birth is, and probably will remain, a question impossible to answer with certainty. The time of His Death and Resurrection we know. It is this time of opening Spring.

It is needless to point out in any detail the beautiful fitness of the season to the event. It expounds itself to every heart that thinks, believes, and feels. The Lord's return from death is indeed "the harbinger of everlasting spring"; a spring ever rising towards that "golden summer of the endless year of years" of which Paul Gerhardt sings, yet never losing its first freshness and eternal youth. He who rose again has not *aged* in this long tract of subsequent time, nor will He *age* through the coming ages. And the fact of His rising again is, like Himself, never old; it springs up new eternally. Well then is its anniversary accompanied by vernal beauties in garden, and wood, and field, as "the flowers appear on the earth"; and "the time of the singing of birds is come" (Song 2:12).

Spend a little time with me this Lord's Day on some quite simple thoughts over that blessed Resurrection. What are the restful certainties which should come to us today, as we recite the words, "If we believe that Jesus died, and rose again"?

Very briefly then, we will recollect the weight of fact which lies behind that "if." Paul writes it in no doubtful mood, as indeed his Greek construction indicates. It is the "if" not of conjecture but of logic, as when we say that such and such results are certain *if* two straight lines cannot enclose a space. He brings the Thessalonians, anxious about their buried dear ones, back to a certainty of hope by appealing to this certainty of accomplished fact. *They knew* that Jesus had died and risen. Well then, granting that, "*if so*," with equal fullness of knowledge were they to say, "*Even so* them also which sleep in Jesus will God bring with Him" (1 Thess. 4:14).

Was it a certainty to them that He had risen? Yes; and why? Because on the one hand adequate testimony attended the assertion, the testimony not only of the words of many witnesses, but of the moral miracle which those witnesses themselves were; *they were transfigured men* compared to what they had been before Jesus rose. On the other hand the Thessalonians had themselves made proof of the transforming power of Him who was presented to them as risen again; *they were themselves transfigured men,* knowing God, loving God, at peace with Him now, and looking with indescribable assurance of hope for His glory hereafter.

Was it a certainty to them, about the year 52? I dare to say that it should be an even deeper certainty to us, in this present year. True, the vast lapse of time is on one side a trial, with the delay of the promised Return of the Risen One. But there is another side. These nineteen ages have shown us, among other things, the immortality of the gospel. They have been strewn all over with proofs that its "word liveth and abideth forever," both in the revivals and the progress of the Church, and in the new birth and new life of innumerable individual souls. Now, the gospel was once buried—in the grave of Jesus. His death (as a thousand artless touches in the pages of the Evangelists show us) was the death also of His disciples' hopes in Him. But the gospel lives, and grows, and conquers, today. Therefore it had a resurrection. And of that resurrection there is only one adequate account to be given, alike to reason and to faith; it is, the Resurrection of the Lord. The great universal Church today descends in unbroken historical continuity from the little group who could do nothing but "mourn and weep" (Mark 16:10) when their Master died, and who met the first assertions of His Resurrection with a derision infinitely pathetic. They rose out of that depth to be what they were, a few weeks later, to the then world, and to be what they are to us today, not by any force generated among themselves. One power only was equal to that immense moral and mental miracle. It was the power to which, from the first and to the last, they assigned it, the Resurrection, or rather the Risen One; the life, the love, *the words,* of Him whom they had seen die and whom they saw risen again.

Next Sunday, we will carry on a little further our reflections on the glory of the fact of the Resurrection. For today let us close with this brief meditation upon the fact in itself. Clasping it afresh, till its power passes into all our thought, and all our life, let us step on into "the unknown tomorrow" with a quiet assurance that all is well, for He is risen. The statement is simple, BUT it is a radiating point from which results of infinite hope and reassurance spring forever. "The Lord is risen indeed."

14

The Message of the Lord's Resurrection: Part Two

If we believe that Jesus died, and rose again—1 Thess. 4:14

"I am not clear what you mean by spiritual experience; I am bewildered by the conflicting thoughts of our time. But I try, amidst them, to keep my mind settled on the fact of the Resurrection." So said an able and highly cultivated layman, long years ago, to his friend, my dear father. They were partners in many thoughts and plans for the material help and benefit of the needy around them, and my father could not rest without seeking to secure their partnership also in the living faith of the gospel. The words I quote were spoken in a conversation thus occasioned. And the reply to those words was this, as I remember the report; "Keep your mind settled on that fact, and you are straight on your way to spiritual experience."

We looked a little while last week at the simplest and also, as I think, the deepest element of the evidence for the fact of the Resurrection. Today let us move onward from it, or rather with it, to some of the great matters of the spiritual experience of the believer, that is to say, his personal and conscious contact with the things unseen and eternal. True, the fact of the Resurrection cannot merely by itself work the deep inward miracles of spiritual experience. But He who does and will work them, "the Holy Spirit of the Promise" (Eph. 1:13) can and will use the fact of the Resurrection, the fact of the Risen One, in the blessed process.

First, then, let us, with great simplicity, take the sacred fact as our vast, our all-sufficient assurance that in this universe of ours, after all, spiritual power is the conquering power. "Sophist may urge his cunning proofs" against all beliefs and hopes that transcend the routine of materialistic theory. Or, if a mere materialism is not in question (and we note with thankfulness how much a *mere* materialism has disappeared from much of the most acute and deepest thought of our time), the reasoner may take a line which by no means leads the anxious spirit towards the light which gathers around supreme Personal Holiness and Love, working freely for our spiritual salvation, with gifts of grace now and hopes of glory beyond the veil. Now we may be quite unable to follow, still less able to meet, one subtle speculation or another. Like my father's friend, we may often find ourselves very seriously "bewildered by the conflicting thoughts of our time." But, like him, let us at least "keep our minds settled on the fact of the Resurrection." Let us, if I may again use the better phrase, keep them settled upon the fact of the Risen One. For never be it forgotten that "the Resurrection" means, not an isolated story of *some man's* escape from death, but the victory over death won by "*this* Man," the Jesus Christ of the Gospels, this mysterious, glorious Personage, the more supernatural the more you study Him; impossible to be invented by a Luke, aye, or by a John; certain, by the deepest sort of self-evidence, to have been really such as they depict. Keep your mind settled upon the fact of *His* victory over the inexorable grave, the seemingly omnipotent grave. Watch Him down, and watch Him up. See Him, on His return, passing on into a life which must now indeed be endless, "indissoluble" (Heb. 7:16); identically "this same Jesus," (Acts 1:11) in His love, in His holy sympathies, in His witness to His Father, in His witness to His Father's Word, in His promise of His own Return from heaven. Let all this sink into the mind, as it considers, as it accustoms itself to take in, the greatness of the fact. Then look back again at the thoughts which would stifle, or at least muffle, all our hopes in the folds of the material, or the cosmic, or the unknowable; or which, on the other hand, would chill them to the heart with the ice of a mere literary criticism of religion. Do not these things look less formidable now, "if we believe that Jesus died, and rose again"?

One thing assuredly results. Some immense premises must have been left out of the logic which would discredit or minimize the faith of the soul which can only say, "I know whom I have believed." For here as a fact is He, the Friend of sinners, the Son of Man, vindicating Himself as "the Son of God, with power, according to the Spirit of holiness, by the resurrection from the dead" (Rom. 1:4). Whatever else is or is not true, He, in His mighty work and victory, is unalterable fact. Whatever else can or cannot take place, this has taken place—Jesus has overcome death, and is alive evermore. He stands beside us, yet on the other side of the grave, saying, "I was dead, and am alive, and have the keys of death" (see Rev. 1:18).

A thousand subsidiary questions of the mind, and of the soul, may remain still unanswered. But "if we believe that Jesus died, and rose again," the great primary questions are answered in Him forever. There is indeed an eternal life, able to swallow up death in victory. There is indeed a Redeemer, mighty to save, no mere inspiring memory of the past, but "He that liveth." And such is He seen to be, in His victory, that it needs must be eternally true that He, accessible to us in His living love, "is able to save them to the uttermost that come unto God by Him" (Heb. 7:25).

15

The Message of the Lord's Resurrection: Part Three

If we believe that Jesus died, and rose again—1 Thess. 4:14

Our last Lord's Day meditation led us to this great first inference from the fact of the Resurrection—that if we may be sure of a Risen Savior, we may be sure, in Him, of the bright realities of eternal life. God, heaven, prayer, immortality, are not dreams which have to fade away "when one awakes" in the light—a light without a sun— of a hopeless philosophy. "If we believe that Jesus died, and rose again," this at least is certain now and forever, that "we have not followed cunningly devised fables" (2 Pet. 1:16). We are not chasing a rainbow from field to field, to find nothing, where it seemed to be, but the common earth. We are not speaking to the void air when we pray. We shall not melt into a vaster void when we die.

> Every skeptic fear is vain:
> Jesus died—and rose again.

Today let us take up one or two lines of reflection more definite and particular, and belonging more to the interior of our faith, if we may put it so; thoughts not occupied with the bulwarks of the gospel, but with its home and shrine.

(1) Consider the witness of the Resurrection of the buried Lord to the nature and to the glorious efficacy of His atoning sacrifice. For this, we turn to 1 Corinthians 15, the great passage of all passages upon the hope and character of our own promised resurrection day. In the earlier paragraphs of the chapter, before coming to his main subject, the Apostle gives us, as in passing, some inestimable

49

treasures of truth. He writes down a remarkable summary of evidences for the fact of the Lord's Resurrection, and then offers some profound intimations of its place among the foundation-stones of our salvation. In this latter connection he writes, in verse 17: "If Christ be not raised, your faith is vain; ye are yet in your sins."

This verse has seldom received the attention it claims, unless I am much mistaken. To the reverent inquirer after the true nature of the Atoning Work, it seems to me to be of the first importance, supposing the inquirer to accept Paul as indeed a teacher who had "received his Gospel not of man, but by the revelation of Jesus Christ" (see Gal. 1:12). What does it say? In effect it says this, that the dying work of the Lord, had it not been crowned by His Resurrection, in other words, had it failed of its intended purpose, had it been abortive, would have left the Corinthians "yet in their sins." But in what sense "in their sins"? The meaning cannot be, in this place in the argument, that they would have been still in moral bondage, still in heathen vice, unreformed, unconverted. For they *were,* actually, different beings from their old selves. As a patent fact, they *had* received an emancipation, somehow, from the slavery of evil. Whatever the reason of the matter might be, the fact of it was this; whether or not the Lord had risen, they were better men (See note on p. 51). It is evident then that the Apostle refers not to the power of evil upon their wills, but to its guilt upon their heads. For him here, the phrase "in your sins" means, involved in their tremendous consequences, snared and chained in their dread liability, lying under their doom. And the implication is that the one thing which could remove that bond and burden was the Lord's work of death and resurrection, and that this had removed it. They were pardoned, they were accepted, justified, adopted, on account of a fact sublimely outside them in itself, though grace had put them now into living contact with it. Upon the head of Another their load had been laid—wholly and alone upon Him; with it He had sunk into the depths; without it He had risen again; therefore they were no longer "in their sins."

So, for Paul, and if for him then for me, and for thee, the Lord's all-precious Work is our ONE, because our all-sufficient, rest and refuge from "the curse of the Law" (Gal. 3:13). He, in His mysterious Passion, certified and crowned forever by His Resurrection, is "the great rock-foundation." Christ *for* us is our peace *with* God, that Christ *in* us, by the Holy Ghost, may be our peace *of* God, in life and death.

(2) Consider next the radiant message of the Resurrection of the Lord in its bearing on the reality and certainty of our own. It is in this connection, as I hardly need remind my reader, that Paul writes the words which head our portion for today. "If we" so "believe," then, "*even so,* them also which sleep in Jesus," (or in the beautiful literal rendering: "them which were laid asleep through Jesus") "will God bring with Him" (1 Thess. 4:14), with Jesus when He comes.

This is the precise point; "even so." As the Lord's Resurrection was not merely a revival of His influence, not merely the recovered permanence of His spiritual presence, but the actual renewal of His life embodied—"even so." We could conceive of His Resurrection as being designed after all only to assure us in a supremely evidential way of His own everlasting and victorious life. It does this. But with regard both to Him and to us it does more. It is a divine sanctification of the function and place of the body in the life of immortality. The Apostle is guided to press its witness upon us in this direction above all, when thus writing to the bereaved Thessalonians. Have you, for certain, a Risen Savior—not only an immortal Savior, but a Risen one? Then your own prospect, as you are His members, is not only immortality; it is resurrection. Mysteries unfathomable may surround the fact, but they leave the fact untouched in the midst. Not in figure, not in parable, but in deed, the believer's body as well as spirit shall inherit the bliss of heaven. "Wherefore comfort one another with these words" (1 Thess. 4:18).

NOTE—It has been objected, by a friend, to the remarks on p. 50 (line 22, etc.) that they seem to ignore the absolute necessity of the finished work of Christ not only for our acceptance but for our sanctification. All that I mean is to say that *in the argument* Paul appears to put only the question of our acceptance into view. Had he been thinking of our sanctification, would he not have said, "Ye *would be* yet in your sins"?

16

The Three Great Resurrection Interviews

Being seen of them . . . and speaking—Acts 1:3

These words, quoted as a fragment, are part of Luke's remarkable introduction to the Acts, where he expands his earlier and compressed account of the Lord's communion with His disciples after the Resurrection. To that paragraph we owe some most precious details of that sacred time, particularly, that it lasted nearly six weeks altogether.

But I am not about to dwell upon the passage now, for it deals more with the Ascension than with the Resurrection. I only take this brief extract from it to be a guiding title to a few thoughts on the "sights" and "speakings" of the Resurrection day itself. With these which we may close this short series of meditations on the Risen One and His Glory.

We have then three recorded manifestations of the Lord Jesus, leading and outstanding, vouchsafed by Him on the day of His Resurrection. They were certainly not the only ones which that day witnessed, but they are the only ones given to us in detail; and the details are such that each has a significance all its own, while all combine in some messages of supreme importance. To Mary in the garden of the sepulcher, to the two friends on the Emmaus road, to the gathered company at evening in the chamber—these are the three manifestations in our view today. We owe the narratives to Luke and to John.

The Manifestation to Mary needs no re-telling (John 20:11–18). Who has not followed every step, the steps that walked and the steps that ran, till at last all was quiet in the garden, and the weeping woman, turning from the sympathy of angels, addressed herself to the imagined gardener, and found that it was her Lord? There forever shines the scene before us, radiating the immortal light of both the majesty and the tenderness of Jesus. Never was His bearing and His speech more kingly than when He sent Mary back to "His brethren" with the message of His coming exaltation, "unto My Father and your Father, unto My God and your God" (v. 17). Never was His shepherd-heart more tender in its individual sympathies than when He found out Mary's heart through her name, and devoted to her, altogether to her, that first communication of His immortal life, as if she were the one charge upon His hands.

Let the Christian, seeking a fresh realization of the Lord in His holy communion with the individual soul, often walk in thought to Joseph's garden, and listen to that colloquy by the empty cavern, while the morning sun smiles upon Mary at the Master's feet. What He was then, He is now. He knows the individual name which belongs to the individual heart. He can reveal to the solitary disciple, now as then, His glory and His grace. He can send us also away, sure at least of this, that we have seen the Lord, and He has spoken to us, all alone.

Then came the afternoon, and the Emmaus-walk (Luke 24:13–32). Cleopas and his friend travel out to the country, and talk as they go; an uncommon thing with Orientals, who do not usually chat upon the road; only urgent matters break their silence then. Behold, a Stranger joins them, courteous as a friend. Within a few minutes He is deep in their confidence; soon He has led them into a long, continuous, detailed Bible study. They follow His guidance from Genesis to the latest pages of their ancient Scriptures. Strangely moving the exposition proves; their hearts are burning; their whole being is awakening to the mysterious, blessed glory of a foretold Sufferer who was to save and to reign through death. Then the sun sinks, and the three friends sit down to the evening meal, and eyes are opened, and lo, it is the Lord. Wonderful story, self-evidencing in its matchless simplicity! As an invention, I dare to say it with decision, it is beyond the skill of human genius. As a record of fact alone is it intelligible.

Walk often to Emmaus, Christian friend, or rather, Christian friends. For here is the Lord giving His blessed company *to companions.* "They spake to one another," those two, and they spake about Him. "And the Lord hearkened, and heard it" (Mal. 3:16), and struck in to bless them. Friends in Christ, do you talk of Him? Do you, perhaps anxiously, converse together about His Person, His Work, His Salvation, His Book, difficulties of belief, mysteries and doubts? Be sure to carry on your talk upon the road to Emmaus. You know that you may expect Jesus near you there. Welcome His company. Remember what He said there long ago, about the Bible, and about Himself, and about His Cross, and His Glory. We may be very sure that His opinion on all these things, the Bible included, is now what it was then. Look out for Him, listen for Him, as you think and talk together.

Then later, on that Resurrection day, the night falls, and the Paschal moon is full and glorious in the sky (John 20:19–23). The disciples are gathering now in the Chamber, and shutting themselves in. Yes, they are gathering now, not walking away from one another, this way and that; for it is rumored that He is risen; and a Risen Savior is evermore a mighty magnet of union to His disciples. They gather, and gather. Apostles are there, and holy women doubtless; and now Cleopas and his friend knock and come in with their story; and voices rise in joyful mutual witness, "The Lord is risen." Then, behold, the Risen One Himself! Jesus is in the midst, speaking peace, showing His hands and His side, breathing on them the Spirit, sending them to the world. And oh how glad are the disciples, for they see the Lord.

Here is a scene meant indeed to live in the hearts of Christians as they meet in their congregations. "There am I in the midst of them" (Matt. 18:20). This evening meeting, the Risen Lord with His disciples, is like a visible seal upon that promise, a heaven-given help to realize and appropriate its blessing. Not in the mode and manner of that blessed evening, yet with an equal reality, "where'er His people meet," there, in a wonderful speciality, the eternal Master is. He is there to breathe His peace, and to breathe His Spirit, to manifest His glories to the soul, and to animate His servants, as they have met in His name, so also in it to part, to be witnesses and ministers of His salvation to the world.

17

The Heavenly Mind

Seek those things which are above, where Christ sitteth on the right hand of God—Col. 3:1

The ascension of our dear risen Lord into heaven is an event which ranks among the earliest and the greatest certainties of our faith. It is expressly recorded in two Gospels, Mark and Luke, and in the Acts. John makes the Lord Jesus twice over refer to it in prospect; "What if ye shall see the Son of Man ascend up where He was before?"; "I ascend unto My Father and your Father" (John 6:62; 20:17). In the Acts and the Epistles it is everywhere taken for granted that Jesus, though out of sight, had left His people (only for a while) by a definite step upward to the heavenly throne; "received up in glory" (1 Tim. 3:16). His had been no vague vanishing away, no mysterious disappearance they know not how. At such a time, from such a spot, He had quitted the ground, He had mounted in the air, He had climbed the visible sky, in glorious symbol of His return to the supreme state of majesty in the invisible.

No wonder that in the very earliest beginnings of anything like an "Apostles' Creed," in the second century, we find the Ascension among the primary facts of faith. "The Church, though dispersed through all lands," writes Irenaeus, in that early age, "holds, as the teaching of the Apostles, the bodily Ascension into the heavens of the beloved Jesus Christ, our Lord."

The Ascension is, from one point of view, a supreme miracle, an act and fact of the supernatural order in the highest degree; and, as such, it gathers a thousand unanswerable questions around it.

From another point of view, it is a help to the simplest thought and faith. Did that blessed Lord, that "beloved Jesus Christ," ascend "bodily" into the heavens? Then there is given to me a point of rest and light in my thoughts about that invisible world. About it I know almost nothing else in detail. "It doth not yet appear." But I know this; it is where He, "bodily," is gone. The latitude and the longitude of my eternal hope and home are given me in this: it lies "where Christ sitteth on the right hand of God."

Shall I puzzle myself, till reason almost swims, with the mysteries of time, and space, and place? Shall I ask unanswerable questions about what the throne is, and what is "the right hand of the majesty on high" (Heb. 1:3)? No; I will rather cultivate, cherish, and develop this blissful certainty, which will one day throw its light over a million mysteries; the region of my coming happy life is "where Christ, the ascended Christ, sitteth, at the right hand of God."

Very practical is the use made by Paul of this fact about heaven, this localization of the state of glory. He is writing to believers. He tells them that as such, as men and women, whose faith, sealed by their baptism, has joined them to the Lord, they are "risen with Christ" (Col. 3:1). One with Him, in His Death they died, receiving all the precious benefits of Calvary as truly as if the members had been crucified themselves, instead of the Head having suffered for them. One with Him, in His Resurrection they had risen, sharers of His "endless life," living with a vitality which rose above all death, a life "hidden with Christ in God" (Col. 3:3)—He in them, they in Him, in the wonderful bond bound by the Holy Ghost. Well, let them now remember that their dear risen Lord and Life was "seated on the right hand of God." And let their oneness with Him take this further range; let them yield their being to the magnet of the fact that their Head had thus gloriously "out-soared the shadow of our night." His blessed Presence, bodily, was nowhere lower than *there*, "on the right hand of God." Then let the drift of their thought and love take that direction too. Let them cultivate "the heavenly mind."

Two phrases are used by the Apostle in this connection. The first is, as we have seen, "*seek* those things which are above." In other words, set the helm of the life that way; make for that blessed shore, by the heavenward use of thought, love, and will. "Seeking" may mean either of two very different processes, according to context. It may mean a weary quest of a lost thing, or of a thing uncertain, as when year after year brave men "sought" in vain the relics of Sir John Franklin's company in the awful North, or earlier, when Raleigh sought in vain the fabled golden city of Manoa in the West. But "seeking" may also mean the following of a sure clue to a certain though as yet invisible boundary, as when Columbus "sought," on solid grounds of reason, a shore beyond what seemed the boundless Ocean. Such is our "seeking." We have the latitude and the longitude. We do not yet see the shore. But it is there, there; "where Christ sitteth."

The other phrase of the Apostle is, "*set your affection* on the things above." That is to say, looking at the Greek, "let your bias go that way." "Affection" is here used by our translators in the large old sense, including much more than mere fondness. It imports tone of mind, drift of interests, cast of disposition. Well, this is to be *our* "bias." We are to ponder our Treasure, and His place of rest and power, till the whole set and drift of our "heart" is there also (Luke 12:34). We are to dwell upon and develop our information (in Christ) about heaven, till it colors our purpose and our conduct all through. And this *can* be done, as surely as we *can* "abide in Him, and He in us" (John 15:4). For heaven is, for us, "where Christ sitteth."

Let Christians deliberately covet and acquire "the heavenly mind." It is perhaps not now so common a spiritual characteristic as it once was, so importunate around us is this present scene. But the heavenly mind, in Christ, is as possible now as ever, and as practical. And it is wholly for practical ends that Paul here dwells upon it. For he goes on directly from it, and with it, in the paragraph that follows, to the subject of the Christian's triumph over very real sins, in very real life, in the power of the heavenly mind.

18

The Ten Days before Pentecost

Wait for the promise of the Father—Acts 1:4

Taking the narrative of the Acts as our guide, we have reason to think that about ten days intervened between the Ascension of the Lord Jesus and the Descent of the Holy Spirit upon the disciples. "Pentecost," as we know, is only the Greek word for "fiftieth," the fiftieth day from Passover. At Passover the Lord died and rose again, and for some forty days remained with His followers below (Acts 1:3). Thus His Ascension took place about ten days before Pentecost; a broad interval. Then, on that "fiftieth day," the mighty shower of blessing fell upon the waiting church, the fire and the wind of God, the baptism of the Eternal Spirit.

Amidst the many wonders of the Christian Pentecost, not the least is this fact of the interval between the up-going of the Savior and the down-coming of the Comforter. I venture to say that no mere inventor of a legendary story of redemption would have put that interval into his narrative; it carries its own truth upon its face. Well, what may we gather to be the meaning, the message, of this marked and deliberate pause? Why did the disciples thus need to be sent away by their ascending Lord to "*wait* for the promise of the Father" (Acts 1:4)?

At first sight, surely, we might well ask whether they were not already fully equipped for their work. Think how vastly much they knew, and how truly and how deeply they loved. As regarded their knowledge, they were now, all of them, perfectly and forever sure of that vast foundation fact, that "Jesus died and rose again"

[1 Thess. 4:14]. Yes, and not so only; they had been permitted for nearly six weeks to have one interview after another with the crucified and risen Lord. Added to the three wonderful years of their "coming in and going out" with Him, before He suffered, that long season of absolutely unique opportunity and blessing, they had now enjoyed this period after His Resurrection, when of course every previous impression must have been divinely deepened, and a thousand new immortal lights shed upon their knowledge of the Lord. Then further, they had already greatly grown in their devotion to Him, and trust in Him. Dear as He was to them before, was He not dearer now? That one scene beside the lake, in John 21, seems in a way quite new to take us into the depths of mutual love between Master and disciple. That moment where Thomas, in the upper chamber, says on a sudden, after all his doubts, "my Lord and my God" (John 20:28), seems to carry us to the highest heights of adoring devotion.

Was not all this enough? Were they not adequately equipped, with such knowledge and such loyalty, for going out into the world, and calling it to come to Jesus, and to be blest in Him? What, must they wait, and wait, day after day, a week, eight days, ten, for the power which was to "endue" them, clothe them, "from on high" (Luke 24:49)?

Yes, they must, according to their Lord's wise love. And the after story of the Acts, and the words of the Epistles about the Holy Ghost, and the language of the Gospels too, recording (as in John 15, 16) the thoughts of the Lord Himself about the Holy Spirit, all help us to grasp something of the reason. Let us reflect upon it; it is a message for our own inmost hearts.

The Apostles had much indeed, but they wanted more. They possessed treasures sacred, indispensable, vital. But in order to the fullness of their life and witness they wanted more. They had, in a supreme degree, *historical knowledge* of the Lord Jesus, in all the wonderful unfolding of His life and work on earth. They had come, especially since the Resurrection, to see deep into the boundless blessings which that life and work were to bring to believing man. And they had *personal devotion* to Him, strong and true, glowing in their hearts, the stronger and the truer because of the discoveries which they had all made of their own sin and weakness. But they needed still, speaking broadly, and allowing for many gracious beginnings and foretastes before Pentecost, the deep working of the eternal Spirit, to put the Lord Christ and them into full, supernatural spiritual contact; "I in them, and thou in Me" (John 17:23). I dare to say that, till Pentecost, the entire meaning of the words, "that Christ may dwell in your hearts by faith" (Eph. 3:17), would not have been recognized by them as within their experience. But *then,* those words would exactly express what they knew, what they had, what they could use, in a strength not their own.

Their knowledge of the blessed facts, their devotion to the blessed Person, had to be touched from above by a power which made it work in them, under the very hand of God. The Spirit needed to "take of the things of Christ, and show them unto them" (John 16:15); to "strengthen them in the inner man, that Christ might dwell in their hearts, by faith" [see Eph. 3:16], Then, and not till then, were they fully ready to move the world for Him.

"As then, so now." Nothing is more profoundly needed now in the Church, and in the soul, than a new development of the power of Pentecost. Let the blessed Comforter be welcomed in His benignant power, humbling us, exalting Christ, bringing Him anew to dwell in our hearts by faith. Let Him in His grace and love respond to the "truthful call" of the disciples of today. And behold, a thousand obstacles will melt around us, and we, whatever obstacles remain, shall be ready, amidst them, for a witness and a work full of joy, full of force, full of the Lord Jesus Christ. Even so, come, gracious Spirit, come quickly, and in power.

19

The Spirit and the Christ

He shall glorify Me—John 16:14

Last Sunday we thought a little on that impressive object-lesson, the ten days' gap between the great Ascension and the great Descent. Its message to us is surely this, that the full presence and power of the blessed Spirit of God is not only important, but supremely important, nay, vital, in the work and witness of the Christian and of the Church.

Now let us approach the holy subject a little nearer. Rather less generally, though it is but in outline after all, let us think of the promised work of the Holy Ghost in one supreme aspect of it. That aspect is the connection of the work of the Spirit with the glory of Christ.

Nothing is more noteworthy than this connection. It appears everywhere in the Bible. The great prophecies of Messiah in Isaiah are full of it. "The Spirit of the Lord shall rest upon Him" (Is. 1:1—11:2; 61:1); "The Holy Ghost shall come upon thee" (Luke 1:35). It comes up at once in the gospel history. The Spirit is the divine Worker in the Birth of the Lord Jesus. He descends upon Him at His Baptism (Luke 3:22). He leads Him into the wilderness (Luke 4:1). He leads Him to His work in Galilee. The Son, "through the eternal Spirit, offers Himself without spot to God" (see Heb. 9:14). "Through the Holy Spirit" He "gives commandment to the Apostles" (Acts 1:2). In the Master's own words when the Spirit comes, His "conviction of the world about sin, and righteousness, and judgment," is all to be connected with Christ; "because they believe not

61

in Me"; "because I go to the Father" (see John 16:8–11). The Spirit is to be given only "when Jesus is glorified." Out of Jesus as the fountain are to flow the "rivers of living water" "which they that believe on Him should receive" (John 7:38, 39). And when that great blessing comes at last in its fullness, the result is just this, that the Spirit-filled Church pours out a glorious testimony to the fullness of her Lord. So it is even to the closing Book of the Bible, where we have, in one of the seven Epistles after another, the two Voices blent into one in their infinite connection. Each begins with "thus saith" JESUS CHRIST, under one glorious title or another. Each ends with "hear what the Spirit saith unto the Churches" (Rev. 2, 3).

Let this be well remembered. There is no separate "Gospel of the Holy Ghost." The plan of God assuredly is not to teach us about Christ, as a first lesson, and then, as a more advanced lesson, to lead us on into truth about the Holy Ghost, apart from Christ. We do indeed, and to the last, need teaching about the blessed Spirit. But the more we learn about Him the more surely we shall learn this from Him, that His chosen and beloved work is just this—to glorify the Lord Jesus Christ.

So let us lay our poor hearts more and more simply in His way for that work, that He may do it in us. Let us carry with us the recollection we spoke of last Sunday. Was it necessary that He should come to the Apostles, even after they had eaten and drunk with the risen Savior, and by His inward power make Christ Jesus a divine Reality in their hearts, present and powerful? Assuredly He is at least as necessary so to us. Let us not fail to plead the promise of the Father, in the name of the Son. Let us remember that we may have a complete historical knowledge of the Lord Jesus, and even a deep loyalty to His Person, and yet fail to be in divine union, spirit to Spirit, with Him. We may "know Him after the flesh," (2 Cor. 5:16) but not after the Spirit. Come then, Thou Holy One. Take this heart in hand, and glorify Christ to me. Show Him to me as being consciously "all my salvation and all my desire" (2 Sam. 23:5). Grant me to know, consciously, that He and I are "joined, one Spirit" (1 Cor. 6:17). Make me able, in all my soul's weakness, to welcome Him every day into my heart, by faith, to dwell and to rule. Teach me every day to "call Him Lord," (1 Cor. 12:3) for Thou only canst do it; to "call Him

Lord" with a divinely given sense of His greatness, His love, His mastership, and His full salvation. Make Thou the blessed twofold motto of my life to be ever this—"in the name of the Lord Jesus, and by the Spirit of our God" (1 Cor. 6:11); joining Him and Thee together in one secret of power and peace. O glorify Christ to me, that Christ may be glorified, in some humble measure, through me.

Turning for a few closing moments to our text, let us notice how intensely *personal* are its terms. Nothing is more characteristic of the Gospel than its holy way of giving all its truths a personal aspect. No, nothing in it is merely abstract; all is alive, with "He," and "Him," and "Thou," and "Thee."

"HE shall glorify ME." It is a Person who is to work. Let us grasp afresh the living Personality of the Holy Ghost. He is the heavenly Wind, the heavenly Water, the heavenly Fire. But that Wind, that Water, that Fire, is not It, but He. As truly as Christ the Son is not a mere notion, or force, or principle, but our own beloved Savior, so truly is the Spirit of eternal Love no mere power, but our own almighty Friend; *loving* the soul He teaches, loving (with the love of God for God) the Lord who is His Lesson. And then, and indeed, it is a Person who is the Matter of the Spirit's work. O happy fact of salvation! The supreme Teacher draws nigh to teach us. And He throws His exalted light not first, or most, or last, upon an eternal principle, though eternal law does lie so deep in all He has to say. He sheds an illuminating glory upon a Heart, a Face, an Embrace; "the beloved Jesus Christ, our Lord."

20

The Blessed Trinity

The name of the Father, and of the Son, and of the Holy Ghost—
Matt. 28:19

Very simply, and briefly, and in a spirit of worship and love, let us think a little this Sabbath morning upon the Holy Trinity.

> Holy, holy, holy, Lord God Almighty,
> > Early in the morning our song shall rise to Thee;
> Holy, holy, holy, Merciful and Mighty,
> > God in Three Persons, Blessed Trinity.

The word Trinity does not occur in the Bible. But it expresses, by its meaning ("Threeness," or "Threefoldness"), with a wonderful fullness in brevity, a mass of Bible truth about our God. It is thus a word which Christians may prize and use, although they freely own that the word is not itself divine.

What two grand truths, on the whole, does the Book set forth about the Being of that Blessed GOD whom it reveals? First, an unspeakable and supreme Oneness. Then, we affirm it without misgiving, an equally wonderful and sublime and mysterious Threeness.

All down through the many books of that "Divine Library," the Bible, we have the ever-repeated assertion of the eternal Oneness of the true God. "Hear, O Israel; the LORD Thy God is One LORD" (Deut. 6:4), or, let us render it, "JEHOVAH is Thy God, JEHOVAH is One." Before and beside Him there is no divine power. There may be, there are, other *superhuman* powers, "gods many, lords many." But they are immeasurably different from Him. "There is no God beside Me; I know not any" (Is. 44:8). And all this is carried over

64

into the New Testament, and reaffirmed as by the very voice of Christ.

But then, this same Book has another side to its account of GOD. Even in the Old Testament this appears. A mysterious Person, "the Angel of Jehovah," is often mentioned. He is a sublime enigma. As "Angel" He is, of course, for He appears as a Messenger. But He continually speaks of Himself also as Master; as for example when He says to Abraham, "Thou hast not withheld thy son *from Me*" (Gen. 22:12). Not to dwell on many a similar mystery in the Prophets, we come to the Evangelists and Apostles. And there we find references, scattered all about, to—not two, nor five, nor twenty, but—Three Persons (we can only call Them so) for whom is claimed divine, eternal, honor. Everywhere appears the FATHER, in His unchallenged glory. But then also there is the SON, the WORD, of whom it is written, "Thy throne, O God, is forever" (Heb. 1:8); "The Word was God" (John 1:1); and who, though also Man with men, says, "No one knoweth the Son but the Father" (Matt. 11:27); "I and my Father are One." And then there is also the SPIRIT, the PARACLETE, of whom it is written, "Your body is the temple of the Holy Ghost" (1 Cor. 6:19). And who inhabits a temple, if not its God?

How shall we harmonize these two sacred strains of truth into one? Surely, by the doctrine of the Blessed Trinity. Let us hold to the uttermost the Eternal Oneness of the Divine Being. Let us reverently own, because the messengers of God's own revelation bid us do so, that *within* (not outside, but *within*) that Oneness, within that bright Depth, within that most holy Sanctuary, unchangeable and eternal, there is a Life which is More-than-Oneness. Within the One Being there is no solitude, but the unspeakable Companionship of Love with Love. The One God moves and glows within with relations and responses of infinite love. There, "before the foundation of the world" (John 17:24), the FATHER loved the SON. There, eternally, the eternal Spirit of life and of love is with Them, is One with Them.

All that thought can do, at this holy height, is just to recognize what revelation says, and then to kneel down side by side, with faith and love. Thought can recognize. Thought can see that we are called not to believe against reason, but above it, which is another thing.

And then thought can come down to the plain, as it were, and follow out some of the results of its view of that Great Glory.

Of those results, take today just this one. We have recollected how the Godhead, revealed in Scripture, is a Godhead of glorious inward Love. It is no sublime solitude. It is infinite and eternal Fellowship. Well, how divinely fitting then that from it should flow forth a Stream true to that Fountain! "God is Love" (1 John 4:8, 16). That is, after all, the true message of the doctrine of the Holy Trinity. And lo, the whole Trinity pours Itself forth, in love, for the salvation of sinners. The Father gives the Son. The Son unites Himself to the sinner. The Spirit opens the sinner's soul to his Redeemer's glory. It is a Trinity of saving love.

The great lake of Central Africa, the deep Victoria Nyanza, is one exhaustless reservoir of waters, clear and pure, its surface flashing to the equatorial sun, and a thousand currents far beneath stirring its massy volume. At its northern border the shores open, and the lake issues, thundering, in a river; that river is the Nile. Forth goes the wonderful stream on its journey of fertility and blessing, till it pierces the Nubian hills, and floods with its benignant overflow the plains of Egypt. And, all along, it is but the great Lake, extended into the great River; the Nyanza mirrors the Pyramids, the Nyanza gives the harvest to the Delta, and bears European commerce on its breast at Alexandria.

All similes are altogether inadequate to set forth the glory of the Trinity of Love. But just a step or two upwards they may help our thoughts. The blessed Deity is essential, everlasting, internal Love;

> A sea of light and love unknown,
> Without a bottom or a shore.

And Redemption is but that Love in overflow and outflow. God in Three Persons is true to His Eternal Nature in the sinner's salvation from death and sin.

21

Concentric Circles

These things I have spoken unto you, that in me ye might have peace. In the world ye shall have tribulation: but be of good cheer; I have overcome the world—John 16:33

These words are part of the closing sentences of our dear Lord's last address to His disciples, on the eve of His death. He did indeed speak again, immediately afterwards, and in their presence. But that was an utterance not to them, but for them; it was what the Germans beautifully call the great High-priestly Prayer, the prayer of John 17, in which He solemnly entrusted His disciples to His Father, closing His requests for them with that supreme expression of desire, whose very manner is divine: "Father, I will that they whom Thou hast given Me, be with Me where I am, that they may behold My glory" (John 17:24). That Prayer is, may we not say? the Holy of Holies of the Bible.

But our words for this Sabbath's meditation are found not in that Sanctuary, but on its threshold. They are spoken straight to weak and troubled human hearts, in their mortality, their mistakes, their fears. They tell of a life "in the world," which the disciples must inevitably live, and of the strife, the pressure, the "tribulation," which that life must involve. Yet the precious words, while they stand just outside the sanctuary, reach their hands as it were within it, to bring out its treasures. Their promises are for earth, for time, for the Christian's needs today. But the reasons of the promises lie deep in eternity, in glory, in the Lord of glory, even Jesus Christ, who is our life.

"In the world": "in Me." Here are two contrasted conceptions—
one would say at first sight, two irreconcilable conceptions. The matter treated of is the life and experience of the disciple of Jesus, his
field and sphere of existence. This, in one breath, is described as
"in Me"; in the next, nay, in the same, as "in the world." What a mea-
sureless difference! Can these two positions, these two *locations,* belong to the same being, at the same time? At best, must not the man
be supposed to fly to and fro, and take his residence up now in one,
now in the other, now in the blessed Paradise, now in the desert of
the world?

Not so, according to the Lord's manifest meaning. The two positions are intended, in His thought, to be simultaneous and com-
bined; the contrasts are all to be harmonious; the opposites are to
be poles of one sphere. "In the world ye shall have tribulation; in
Me ye shall have peace."

A very simple simile may illustrate the truth. This is a matter of
concentric circles. The central point, all along, in respect of experience, is the Christian man. Around him rolls, as the necessary
outer circle of his life, the world; that is to say, the present current
of human things, disordered by sin, with its countless interests, its
manifold communications, its light and music, its strife and storms,
its shocks of change and death, its dreadful drifts of temptation, its
alienation from the holy will of God. Yes, around him moves this
great "world," this *cosmos,* with its winds and its clouds. Nay, like the
physical atmosphere, it not only revolves around him; it enfolds
him, and enters into him. Whether he will or no, whether he likes it
or no, he is in it, as man is in mid-ocean, though he may be borne
along by the great "liner," above the depths.

But then, this same disciple is also, such is the blessed promise,
"in Me," in Christ. A concentric circle, closer and nearer, is about
him in the midst of the tumult; and it is the Lord. The same being,
the same conscious, feeling, needing, personality, is the center of
both. But while the outer circle rolls around that center with all its
agitation, the inner circle is the peace of God Himself. For it is the
presence, the embrace of Him who has overcome the world, and
has now overcome the man, "subduing all things unto Himself" (see
Phil. 3:21).

Let's revert for a moment to the imagery of the ocean-voyage. The traveler is far from land; the Atlantic is his horizon, his scenery, rolling, heaving, perhaps wild with the tumult of the storm. But then, if he is in the midst of the sea, he is, in a far more immediate sense, in the midst of the ship. Humanly speaking, he is safe—in the inner circle. So with the world's "cold ocean." It is treacherous, deep, restless; it is the scene of innumerable deaths. But you are no more asked to meet it *exposed* than the traveler is asked *to swim* the Atlantic waves. The Lord offers Himself to be our mighty, our almighty, transport vessel, which cannot lose its reckoning, and cannot founder. We take refuge in Him by faith, and lo, the troubled sea is around us still, we feel its heaving, we hear its voices. But He is around us, much nearer, and in that respect much more. "When thou passest through the waters, I will be with thee" (Is. 43:2); "My presence shall go with thee, and I will give thee" (Ex. 33:14)—not only after the strife, but in it—"rest."

It was true of old. *In* Rome, *in* Corinth, the saints were yet more *in* Christ; and their lives were luminous with Him. It is true today. *In* China, aye, *in* murderous Shansi, *in* Africa, *in* England, *in* toil, *in* sorrow, *in* withering pain, *in* hatred of opposition, *in* manifold temptation, the children of God do still, abiding *in* Christ, prove "more than conquerors" (Rom. 8:37). In the world, but not of it, they are therefore the truest blessing for it; embodiments and conveyers, amidst its "tribulation," of their Master's "peace."

22

The Two Coal Fires

A fire of coals—John 18:18; 21:9

Very interesting is the likeness and then the contrast of the two scenes indicated by these two identical phrases. The likeness consists in several points. There is first, of course, the incident, common to both, of the fire and its fuel. Further, there is the occurrence, beside each fire, of conversation, an interchange of questions and answers, in each case most pointed and memorable. Further, one principal speaker, the answerer, is the same on both occasions; it is Simon Peter, who is drawn on, in succession, to make assertions about his relation to the Lord Jesus Christ. Lastly, the Lord Himself is both times present, though on the first occasion it is only as an observer in the background, who, probably from the wide-open chamber where He is placed before the unjust judge, "turns" His sacred face to the courtyard, "and looks upon Peter" (Luke 22:61), as Peter stands by the fire of coals. On the second occasion He is the central Figure of the scene.

The contrasts, on the other hand, are at least equally remarkable. The coals for the first fire were gathered and kindled by "the servants and officers," the domestics and the constables, who were so busy that cold passover-evening, and felt the keen air the more as the night wore on, and the proceedings indoors before the Priests were protracted. The coals for the second fire—who laid them, and who lighted them? Was it not the work of the Lord Himself, in the mystery, in the reality, of His resurrection body? Again, the scenes of the two kindlings were strikingly contrasted. The first was the central

70

quadrangle of the high-priestly palace, thronged with a miscellaneous concourse of officials and lookers-on, while the bearer of Aaron's office was busy close by, hastening the doom and the death of the true Melchizedek. It was night; it was the hour of the power of the darkness of the eternal night. The second scene was the fair margin of the Galilean lake, deep in its genial valley, in the season of flowers, and under the light of the rising day; and the only company was the risen Jesus, and those seven favored men who "knew that it was the Lord." From around him forever had died away the contradiction of sinners. He sat now, quiet and serene, in the loving majesty of His victory for us, to bless, to command, to empower His happy followers for their glorious work for Him. Lastly, on the one occasion, Peter's voice, now (as we seem to hear it) in half-stifled accents, now rising, in its despair, in loud appeals to heaven, in "anathema and adjuration," is heard denying all connection with Jesus, all knowledge of Him, as one rude inquirer and another, man and woman, challenges him to confess. On the other occasion that same voice is heard again, and once more in three successive utterances. This time it is the Lord who questions. And all that the Apostle has to say is, "Thou knowest all things, thou knowest that I love thee" John 21:17.

It is a moving contrast, all along. Let it speak to us, this Lord's Day, some of its manifold messages. We will look at Peter first, then at the Lord.

Consider the Apostle, first by one fireside, then by the other. Is it possible that we have the same person? This abjectly-frightened denier of his best, his glorious Friend, can he be identically the same with the man who sits by the side of that Friend and Master, calm, humble, entirely devoted, sparing of all exuberant expression, afraid now only (so it surely appears) of himself, simply affirming, in terms profound in their brevity, his love? Yes, it is the same. The being which experienced by the one fireside that terrific moral collapse is the very being which, by the other, sits at peace by the feet of Jesus, "clothed" with the beauty of holiness, "and in his right mind" for life and death. Something has wrought an inconceivable revolution, which yet is actual. The ruin has been more than rebuilt. Old things are passed away, behold all things are new, and all things are of God.

It is the same man. But it is a new creation. And while the ruin passes, the new creation stands. To the end, Peter is the man not of the first fireside, but of the second. "Thou knowest that I love Thee" is the account now of his whole life, till he stretches out his hands upon the Roman cross, and by death glorifies God.

But then—the Lord. Here is the secret of the wonderful contrast between the Peter of the first fire of coals, and the Peter of the second. It is, that JESUS is the same, yesterday, on the first occasion, and today, on the second. The heart of the wonderful Master is identical in both scenes. He who "turned and looked on Peter" in his terrible fall, so that Peter did not throw himself away, but wept, is only *the same* when He approaches the man with that inquiry which opens up His own unalterable heart of love, "Do you love Me?"

And we, dear reader, you and I, in ourselves, are just mirrored in Peter's weakness in himself. And for us, for you and me, this same Jesus is still the same, at the side of either fire of coals.

23

Faith in the Open Air

But I will remember the years of the right hand of the most High—Ps. 77:10

This Psalm, like very many others, is a record of spiritual conflict and victory. It is attributed in the ancient title to Asaph, to whom the like authority assigns that wonderful Psalm, the seventy-third, one of the most significant pictures of doubt and deliverance in the whole Bible. Certainly there is this "family-likeness" between the two Psalms, that in each of them we see first a heart eating itself away, as it were, with inward questioning, with awful misgivings about eternal things, under the perplexities of Providence, and then that same heart finding a wonderful solution and repose in going out of itself to look upon God.

In the seventy-third Psalm the troubled believer gets to rest again by "going into the sanctuary" (v. 17). That is, as I should suppose, by a literal visit to the Temple, and a solemn meditation on its significance as the vast sacramental seal and sign, so to speak, of the faithfulness of the God of the covenant and the promise. In view of this, his inner eye clears and brightens, and he is again able to look at things in their true proportions; and so the mysterious "prosperity of the wicked" is seen to be but a partial and fleeting incident in view of the eternal certainties of the righteousness of Jehovah.

In this seventy-seventh Psalm Asaph (if we may use his name) finds himself again in darkness; "stretching out his hand in the night, refusing to be comforted" (see v. 2). Nay, from one point of view, when he "remembers God," evidently in the awfulness of His holiness, in the dread rigor of His eternal law, his soul is "troubled"; he "cannot speak" (vv. 3, 4). Do we know anything of this? Is it with an awestruck dread that, remembering ourselves, we remember God, feeling for the while as if we would, if we could, creep away from Him, and hide among the trees? If it be so, may Asaph's happy after-experiences be ours. And that it may be so, let us make experiment of Asaph's way.

What did he do? If I may put it very boldly, very simply, he left the close and foul smelling chamber of mere self-consideration, and walked into the open air. And what, for him, was the open air? It was God, seen in the great field of human life, in the large history of redemption. He looked, for the time, away altogether from Asaph, and "remembered the years of the right hand of the Most High" (v. 10). By those "years," evidently, he means not his own past experiences of mercy, in individual life, but the story of the people of God. He recalls, in fact, the deliverance of Israel from Egypt. Before him, as a Hebrew believer, there rises up that sublime historical event, to whose mighty reality every page, well nigh, of the Old Testament, from Exodus onward, bears witness to us. He sees the people in their dire perplexity, hemmed in by Pharaoh this way and by the Red Sea that way. And lo, the very waters have to yield to the *command* of the great Deliverer; "the waters saw Thee, the depths were troubled; Thine arrows went abroad; the voice of Thy thunder was in the heaven; Thy way was" (so surely we must read; "*was*," not "*is*") "in the sea, and Thy path in the great waters, and Thy footsteps were" (not "*are*") "not known." So Thou didst take a path open only to Thine own omnipotence. So "Thou leddest Thy people like a flock, by the hand of Moses and Aaron" (vv. 16–20).

No result is recorded of that walk into the open air, by that Red Sea shore which saw the great deliverance from trouble. But how impressively the result is suggested by silence! Asaph has no more to say, for his spirit is at rest in God.

Is there not a true message here for certain states of the Christian's mind? Are we tempted to stay too much indoors, so to speak, and muse, and brood, and mourn, and fear? Is it our own soul that occasions the trouble? Is it the state of the Church, or of the world, just in our own time? Whatever it is, is it something that shuts up our view, as it were, within four dark walls? If our own soul's state really calls for explicit confession to God, let us make it; in *that* sense let us do anything rather than get away from the facts. If in the troubles of a troubled time we can *do* anything, however little, let us do it; in *that* sense let us not look away from them. But, with that proviso, let us as promptly as possible open the door and walk out, spiritually, into the open air. Let us "remember the years of the right hand of the Most High." Let us look out, and look up, to some great fact, objective and sublime, which witnesses to Him.

To take examples; let us go to our Bible, and get once more, quite fresh and at first hand, some grand specimen of its witness to Jesus. Read a great paragraph of the Gospels again, above all, the paragraphs of the Cross and Resurrection. "Never in my young manhood," wrote the late Lord Chancellor Hatherley to me, "were my doubts so solved as by reading over again, from time to time, the closing chapters of John." Do not trouble yourself, for this purpose, with critical details. Look at the forest, not at the trees. Let the impression of the gospel portrait of the Lord Jesus come on you with its inexpressible weight of truthfulness and majesty. Let the effects of the Resurrection, seen in the transfigured disciples, and in the upspringing Church, tell with simple power upon your reason. And then ask yourself, is not there basis enough here for a calm, large, hopeful "remembrance of the years of the right hand of the Most High"?

Then take a walk out in the broad fields of Christian history; the annals which give us an Augustine, a Bernard, a Huss, a Luther, a Ridley, a Bunyan, a Fenelon, a Wesley, a Moody. Take a walk out over the vast brotherhood which is in the world, scattered under every sky, speaking every language. There they are, on the Arctic ice, under the tropic palms, in the cities, the islands, the wildernesses; all one in Christ Jesus. It will be a bracing exercise to travel so. And we shall return to find the chamber of our own life the airier, and to set to work afresh within, in a new, bright, blessed consciousness of God, full of the power of the years of His right hand.

24

Holy Converse in Bad Times

Then they that feared the Lord spake often one to another; and the Lord hearkened—Mal. 3:16

The Bible is rich in special encouragements for the dark and difficult day. Scattered all over its biographical pages are the portraits of the good men of unfavorable periods, made strong by grace to meet their trying surroundings, and not only to meet them, and endure them, but to illuminate and to bless them. The Psalms, in far the larger number of them, are, from the human side, just the "good thoughts in bad times" of sorely tried and tempted children of God. And the writings of the Prophets and of the Apostles may often be described, from the same human side, in the same terms. Here, in the last page of the Old Testament, we have not the Prophet's own utterance of this sort, but a very beautiful allusion to many such utterances around him; an allusion full of cheer, and full of teaching, for ourselves.

Truly the days were dark around Malachi and his pious friends. We need not here laboriously inquire into his date. Whatever that date was, it marked a period in the history of Israel when iniquity abounded and love waxed cold; a depressing, saddening time. One curious feature of the current, popular, Jewish mind of the time was, apparently, a sort of surly skepticism, a habit of angry and irreverent questioning of the ways of God. Malachi records a whole sheaf of such questions. "Wherein hast Thou loved us?" "Wherein have we wearied Thee?" "Wherein have we robbed Thee?" "What have we spoken so much against Thee?" "Wherein have we despised Thy name?" In the passage just preceding the sentence before us today, we have the angriest outburst of all; "It is vain to serve God; and what profit is it that we have kept His ordinance, and that we have walked mournfully before the Lord of Hosts? And now we call the proud happy; yea, they that work wickedness are set up; yea, they that tempt God are even delivered" (3:14, 15). All the while, be it remembered, these were the people who had been, after the captivity, in a wonderful course of loving providence, restored to their land, their city, their temple. The hand of God had been almost visible for them. Yet already they were talking the dialect of infidelity.

Is there not much in all this to remind us of some features of our own time? Spoken out, or compressed into gloomy silence, there is a great deal now of this arrogant questioning of God, the God of the Word, the God of Providence, the God of Christ. Shocking are the loud outbreaks sometimes. "We will listen to Jesus Christ, if He will behave Himself," was actually said a few years ago, and it expressed ten thousand less articulately rebel thoughts. Only too often (does the Christian never know it in his own heart?) there swells up, very near the surface of even a religious mind, some fierce questioning of His messages, or of His actions, till the thought hovers in a wretched ambiguity between half-censure of His Character and half-denial of His Being. In distress and perplexity, sometimes, the Christian is driven to ask whether reverence and submission are vanished from (not only the world but) the Church. This may be, nay, it is, a hasty asking, based on very partial data. But the data are terribly prominent, though there is indeed, in the mercy of God, another side.

Certainly, if there ever really has been an "age of faith," in the sense of a time when eternal truths were accepted and cherished generally without misgiving, that age is not our own. Nor was it the age of Malachi either.

How beautiful against this dark background is the small but vivid picture of this verse! In those bad times, in poor, ungrateful, skeptical Jerusalem, there was an undying "holy seed." Living within sound of the godless questioning and defiance were found "they who feared the Lord." Doubtless the Prophet was one of them, their center and support. But they were each, individually, a man, a woman, in contact with God, through faith and fear, and therefore *alive,* amidst the stifling malaria of unbelief, and thanklessness, and scorn. Aye, and they were not content with individual contact with God, and personal spiritual life. They knew the blessing of communion, of converse, of strengthening one another's hands. So they often met for holy conference and conversation. Perhaps it was under the Prophet's roof; perhaps it was on the slopes of Olivet, or looking down from its further side upon the Bethany which, centuries later, was to be the locality of Jesus. But, however, somewhere, somehow, they "spake often one to another."

We can almost overhear them. They would "speak often" of the glorious past of the ways of God; they would lead one another out into that "open air" of His historic dealings of which we thought last week. They would remind one another of the troubled saints of other evil days, believing, suffering, triumphant. They would speak of the boundless proof of the mighty being and unchangeable purpose of the God of Abraham, and Moses, and David, and the Prophets. They would solemnly remind one another of their present personal certainty and experience of Him. Would not one say to another, "Whom have we in heaven but Him? There is none upon earth that we desire beside Him" (Ps. 73:25). And then they would dwell upon the Promise and the Hope; Messiah would fill their souls, and kindle their words; and they would go out to live above the miserable level of the scorn and doubt around them.

Christian brother, let us do the like if we think the times are evil. We have all the topics of Malachi and his friends—and Jesus Christ, glorified and coming back, besides. Let us speak often one to another; the Lord is listening still.

25

Happy Alone with Christ

And he went on his way rejoicing—Acts 8:39

This was the Ethiopian eunuch, the man of great authority under Candace the queen, who had charge of all her treasure. We know well his memorable, his most beautiful story. All the way from Abyssinia, down the Nile, through the Egyptian cities, across the wastes, up the rising land to mountainous Jerusalem, he had traveled to worship. At Jerusalem, apparently, he had seen no Christian; he had heard no word, certainly no friendly word, about Jesus. But he had worshiped, assuredly in spirit and in truth, and he possessed at least Isaiah as a written Word of God; perhaps he had procured the scroll in the city, and was now exploring his new treasure. There he sat, in his traveling carriage, moving along the solitary road, and reading, reading aloud, as Orientals commonly do. As he read the fifty-third chapter, the chapter of the Cross, a voice accosts and surprises him; "Do you understand what you read?" It is Philip, sent by his Lord to that unlikely spot, with an unerring choice of place and time. So follows the conversation, the faith, the joy, the baptism in the wayside pool. And then—suddenly, in mystery, Philip is gone, and the new Christian is alone. "The Spirit of the Lord caught away Philip, that the eunuch saw him no more; and he" the Ethiopian traveler, "went on his way rejoicing."

It was a strange close to that blessed interview. And part of the strangeness is the new convert's joy as he goes on, pursuing the vast journey homeward, to meet whatever might meet him there when he arrived, and to meet it alone.

Was it nothing to him to be left alone by his suddenly-found friend and teacher? We may be sure it was not. The very last thing the true gospel does is to blunt human sensibilities and sympathies; it deepens them. We may modify the words of the grand song of the seventeenth century, and say, with a deep meaning:

> I could not love thee, dear, so much,
> Loved I not Jesus more.

And oh, how deep and tender are the human sympathies which are the immediate creation of the gospel! Strong is the bond between the teacher and the taught, the helper and the helped, the human instrument of conversion and the convert, in the gospel life. Most sure we may be that when Philip and the eunuch ascended from the pool and prepared to remount the carriage, they felt their hearts one with a oneness which had never stirred the being of the African treasurer before. May we not lawfully imagine him preparing now to carry his beloved and loving teacher homeward with him, and to learn from him all along the way more of this wonderful, this blessed, Jesus, "glad theme of rapt Isaiah," the Bearer of our sins, and who sees the travail of His soul in our salvation?

Then on a sudden—Philip was gone. "The Spirit caught him away." We can only note the phrase; God only knows all it means. It may have been an actual rapture through the air. It may have been a removal by steps along the ground, but taken with superhuman speed. However, Philip was gone, and the eunuch has to make his way homeward, orphaned of him, probably forever on earth.

Does not the experience of that moment come home? Who, that is no longer quite young, has not somehow lost a Philip? It may be the dear instructor who actually first led you to Jesus; perhaps a blessed parent, perhaps your teacher in Sunday School, or in the Bible Class; your pastor, perhaps, or your college friend, or your aged neighbor, young with the love of God. Perhaps it is some helper further on upon your path; you felt a powerful "lift" in your soul's life in that conversation with him, in that address, that sermon he delivered, that letter he wrote to you. Or perhaps it has been simply the "sweet influences" of his (or her) life, in and for the Lord, which have been used to bless you. Anywise, this friend has become very, very much to you, both in nature and in Christ. You love that face, that voice, that fellowship; and you justly love it. Then, the Spirit of the Lord has caught the friend away, perhaps to a distant place of life and duty, perhaps to the world to come. Alas, the blank which that going leaves! Life is lonelier all over for that one absence from it.

But now, look once more at the traveler. He is not weeping and wailing, and calling for Philip back again. Behold, the carriage, the cavalcade, is moving. They are off again for Abyssinia. And the new-baptized man beams in every look with joy. "He went on his way rejoicing":

> For Philip indeed flies, but Jesus stays
> And travels with His friend.

Yes, he has found the Lord, he possesses the Lord. Yesterday he had never heard of Him; today He is His happy servant's all in all. He has Him in the Book, revealed as his Sacrifice of peace, his Life of life. He has Him in the Ordinance, sealed to him as his own forever. He has Him in his converted heart, living there, dwelling there, by faith. The dear Lord Jesus Christ is traveling with him all the way to the court of Candace, and is going to live with him there. Philip is gone, BUT he has Jesus; and, what is noteworthy, in Jesus he has Philip still.

We need not elaborately point the moral. The Lord knows what the bitterness of our partings is. He has tasted the like griefs Himself. "He knows, He knows." But then, let us boldly say it to the silent earth and skies, "He lives, He lives." We have Him, and in Him all things, our blessed ones included. Come, let us go on our way, in our turn, rejoicing.

26

Saved to Serve

All things are lawful for me, but all things are not expedient; all things are lawful for me, but all things edify not—1 Cor. 10:23

If I read these words correctly, they are a sort of dialogue. The Corinthian convert makes an assertion of his liberty; the Apostle meets it, not with a contradiction, but with a caution and counter-balance. "All things are lawful for me; I have not to carry the burden of seeking to earn my acceptance with God by a process of elaborate and regulated abstinence. I am an accepted child, in Christ, out and out. The whole liberty of the home life is mine." So says the Corinthian, founding his claim upon the teaching of Paul. And Paul recants not one word of his teaching, any more than he does in (Rom. 6:1), where he similarly calls up a supposed partner in conversation, who asks why, with so free a salvation, we may not go on sinning. He only bids his friend take another point of view, and look at the glorious truth in its proper perspective. "Yes, all things are, in that respect, lawful to you. You say it, and you say it again, and it is true. But then, the fact of freedom is one thing, the purpose and the use of it is another. You are placed amidst the delightful liberties and resources of your Father's home, without grudging and without doubt. But you are placed there not to enjoy only, but to use; not to be free only, but to have the privilege of contributing to the freedom around you. You are free—but as the child of a Father, and as the member of a family. And such freedom would be only the harsh parody of itself if it were not a freedom to love, to be loyal, to serve, to share. Your rights are given you as bright implements to promote the highest right. You are saved to be serviceable; you are saved to build up other lives. And not all things are serviceable. And not all things build up the lives of others. So, back to liberty, but not to license. Live out the noble freedom of freely fulfilled mutual duty. Let no man seek his own, but every man another's wealth, another's well being."

This sort of dialogue, which may be thus expanded for exposition, meets us once and again in this Epistle. There is a striking example, in my view, in the sixth chapter, where the Apostle in the same way takes up an assertion, as made by a disputant or correspondent, and meets it with a counterpoint. "All things are lawful unto me"—"But I will not be brought under the power of any." "Meats for the belly, and the belly for meats; appetites are as natural as the supply which feeds them, but God shall destroy both it and them; we are made for an ultimate life above material appetites; for that life let us live" (see 1 Cor. 6:13). In fact, the great Epistle is, in its substance, one long series of apostolic answers to questions, more or less wise, from the agitated Mission Church; and these are specimens.

Let us return to the questions and answers before us. In these short phrases we have set out, as tersely as possible, two profoundly contrasted views of the Christian life. And their contrast is the more remarkable because in a certain sense, the disputants stand on common ground, and feel their footing on it. That ground is the grand Pauline truth of free salvation, in virtue, solely and entirely, of the finished work of Christ. This the Corinthian has learned, and learned eagerly, from Paul. And this truth is as dear as ever, and as vital and as strong as ever, for Paul himself. But the Corinthian takes it as if its purpose were to turn him loose upon the field of personal enjoyment, to give him an unencumbered license to live as he pleases, to assert his rights, and be a man. The Apostle takes it as above all things an emancipation from—himself, a buying of him *out* of the self-slavery which is the inevitable inmost condition of unforgiven and unregenerate man, and a buying of him *in* to a service which is perfect freedom, for it is the service of a beloved, welcomed, transformed, congenial son of the home. No one can assert the liberty of the justified and the regenerated more absolutely than Paul does. But never for a moment does he view it as liberty, so to speak, in the abstract, in the air. It is liberty in Christ. It is liberty with a law, the royal law of love, the law which means just the living out of the fact that I am no more my own, but the dear-bought property of the eternal Love.

Let us ponder these opposing views, which, from their common ground, point in opposite directions, the one to the eternal night, the other to the eternal day. And let our whole Christian being be placed, more deliberately than ever, upon the side of the apostolic truth. Yes, we are free indeed. But in our freedom we exist for purposes which alone are worthy of that sacred word, freedom. We exist to be of service. We exist to build others up, to help others on, in the blessed life. Not a day, not an hour, of our lives lies outside that law. Not one personal habit, nay, not one personal habit of our most solitary and secret times (for everything tells upon character, which is our great implement for service), lies outside that law. Not an action of our wills, not an utterance of our lips, not a look of our eyes, but may have something to do with being serviceable, with building up, or with their opposites. Let us remember it, and welcome it, and love it, and live it out. It will be a life not of bondage at all, but of perfect freedom—on one condition, that we are keeping in pure personal contact with Him who is at once our Liberty and our Law; "whom to know is to live, whom to serve is to reign."

27

Peace, Perfect Peace

The peace of God, which passeth all understanding, shall keep your hearts and minds, through Christ Jesus—Phil. 4:7

This is indeed a passage of beauty. There is a music, as of the spheres, about its very phrase. And it connects itself with moments, full of the beauty of holiness. Often we have heard it spoken at the close of our Sabbath worship, where the lamps have been lit, and the disciples have been gathered together, to praise, to pray, to hearken, and to go forth the calmer and the stronger for the week. Often we have heard it as we prepared to quit the precious Table of the Lord, when

> Too soon we rise; the symbols disappear;
> The feast, but not the love, is past and gone;
> The Bread and Wine depart, but Thou art near,
> Nearer than ever, still my shield and sun.

Yes, the words and their connections are full of a most peculiar charm,

> Like setting suns, or music at the close.

But we return to them with the question, are they as strong as they are beautiful? Are they made for wear? Are they good not only for the Lord's Day evening, or for the hour of the divine feast of the slain and risen Redeemer, but also for Monday morning, and the clamor of the street, and the hurry of the shop, and the labor of the study, and the cares of the pastor or the master, and the woe of the mourner, and the last gaze of the dying?

It is easy to talk of that peace; it is easier to write about it. Is it easy to possess it, in the light of the perfectly common day, and of perfectly real trial?

Is it easy? Yes, and no. No, just so far as the call to surrender and to trust, seeing Him that is invisible, in this visible world of sin, is so far from easy to obey that no man can do it but by the Holy Ghost. But also yes, because the Holy Ghost is able to "make all grace abound towards us" (2 Cor. 9:8), that we may quite simply surrender, and quite simply trust. Yes, because He is able to glorify Jesus Christ to us, to present Him to us so that He is indeed a living, bright Reality to us. Peace is easy when its almighty Reason is full in our spiritual sight.

It may be helpful to us to look at this promise of peace, in the Philippian Epistle, as illustrated by the personal example, at the time, of the writer of the Epistle. Apparently without the least intention of doing so, Paul gives the Philippians, from his own experience, just then, at least three noble illustrations of the heart-keeping power of the peace of God. And in each case we see that the secret of the realization is simply this—Jesus Christ in full possession of the soul. Let us take them, one by one.

Two of the three experiences appear in the first chapter (Phil. 1:15–18). The first has to do with an exquisite personal pain, caused by the trying and sinful conduct of an anti-Pauline clique among the Roman Christians. Sad as it is, it is yet true, that at that early date already the spirit of separatism was active in the Church. And certain persons were misguided enough to take such advantage of Paul's imprisoned position, and consequent total inability to move about among the disciples, as to work a propaganda of their own, not only independent of him, but hostile; "preaching Christ of envy and strife; supposing to add affliction to his bonds." It needs no unusual imagination to realize, in some measure, the extreme trial of such a circumstance, to see how it must have struck, through the personal sensibilities, deep at the root of peace. Paul was a Christian, not a Stoic, and he felt the pain, and quite clearly saw the wrong. But pain and peace are not necessarily contradictions. And the pain appears to have left Paul's divine peace unruffled, in the sense of wholly failing to produce in him that miserable "worry" which *is* the contradiction to peace, for it is the white flag of surrender to trouble, the confession that we are *not* overcoming in our Lord. He rises over the trial to a serene contentment, nay, to a tranquil joy. "What then? notwithstanding, every way, whether in pretense or in truth, Christ is preached; and I therein do rejoice, yea, and *shall* rejoice" (Phil. 1:18). Paul is "more than a conqueror."

Then emerges another assault upon peace (Phil. 1:21–25). It is a very grave one. It is the dubious prospect of the issue of his trial in the Roman courts; it is the question of life or death. He does not yet, from his then permitted viewpoint, "see how it will go with him." He may be soon acquitted, released, and sent back to his beloved work. But he may be capitally condemned. The death warrant may be handed in, almost any day. Is he thrown off the equilibrium of peace by this dread ambiguity of his lot? Far from it. He indulges himself in the luxury of an elaborate comparison of the two sides of his double wealth, his embarrassment of blessings! Life and death— each has for him an immense charm. And in each case the charm is Christ. "To live is—Christ" [v. 21]. To die is—"to be with Christ, which is far better." [see v. 23]. Paul is "more than a conqueror" [see Rom. 8:37].

Lastly, in the fourth chapter, we have another problem. It is, the experience of financial need. That is a less heroic trial than the trial of a possible sentence of death. But who does not know something of its penetrating power, its awful temptation to a loss of peace? There is a weird story told, of a man who besought the wizard to call forth the great Enemy in visible form before him. He did so, and there fell upon the floor—an empty purse! But Paul has a peace unbroken by the shrinking of his little store. And he lets us into the secret: "I can do all things through Christ which strengtheneth me" (Phil. 4:13).

Reader—and writer—the peace of God is made for wear. Its texture is such that it needs not be torn, even by the toothed wheels of this world. And it shall not be torn by them, if for us its secret is not an abstraction but a Person, the Savior and Master of Paul; Jesus, our Peace.

28

The Express Image

The brightness of His glory and the express image of His person—Heb. 1:3

Here is set before us the Son, the blessed Son of the Father. "In" Him the Father has, "in these last days, spoken to us," and He has, "by Himself, purged our sins." He, being thus the brightness of the Father's glory and the express image of His person, has, after His great sacrifice for us, and in consequence of it, "sat down on the right hand of the majesty on high."

So opens the Epistle to the Hebrews. It is one long discourse upon the glory of Christ, and His all-sufficiency for the believer, above all as "our Priest, our great Melchisedek." This first chapter is occupied with the theme of His Godhead, the second with that of His Manhood; then opens and develops the sublime presentation of His offices of grace and love, till at length He stands before us, He walks amongst us, in all His risen power, with all His covenant blessings, as "the great Shepherd of the sheep" (Heb. 13:20).

But today, in our quiet Sunday meditation, we will not wander far afield in the rich Epistle, we will dwell upon one point only. That point is a star of the first magnitude in the heaven of Christian truth; it will well repay our undivided attention. It is the assurance given us here, that the holy Son of God, who for us men became Man, and forever now bears our nature as His own, is the brightness of the Father's glory, and the express image of His person.

Let us look into this wonderful assurance. I am not about to discuss its terms in critical detail. The Greek of the second clause, particularly the word rendered "Person," lends itself to such discussion in the proper place. But I do not think there is need for such inquiries here. Whatever be the result of verbal criticism in detail, the general effect of the words will be found to remain the same in this respect, that they are intended to tell us that in the Son we have the exact and adequate Representation of the Father. As regards "glory," as regards the light and splendor of divine Being and of Character, as is the Father so is the Son. In respect of what the Father is, the Son is His express image. The Greek word rendered "express image" means, properly, the impress left by a seal. The impress of a seal shows only, and exactly, and fully, what the seal is, as to its device. Even so the blessed Son, seen by us, shows us not partially but fully, not approximately but exactly, what the Father is. As is the Father, so is the Son.

This to be sure is obvious and primary Christian truth, confessed in one form or another by all orthodox people. But am I wrong in thinking that it is a truth which needs to be taken up sometimes, and looked at afresh, with a purpose deeply practical? If I judge correctly, if I guess truly at all at the minds of others from my own, it is so. It is known among Christians, to think, perhaps rather to *feel*, as if there were a certain difference between the character of the Father and the character of the Son. Such feeling sometimes takes the line of an emphasis upon the tenderness and gentleness of the blessed Son, with a certain forgetfulness of the side of stern and solemn power which He presents when in face of man's sin not repented of, above all of man's sin veiled under the mask of religion. Sometimes, on the other hand, this half unconscious feeling about a difference between the Son and the Father tends to emphasize the mystery, the invisibility, of the Father, till it seems, I had almost said, to be an "aloofness," an isolation, hiding within itself we know not what elements other than the revealed. And then thought fastens upon the Son less as the Way to the Father than as (may I dare to say it, without irreverence?) a preferable substitute for Him in our thought, and to our hearts. In the Son we behold a character which, in a sense, we know, we see, we can wholly rest in, we can embrace. In the Father, we seem to see, too often, more of an inscrutable Mystery than an eternal Heart; almost "the Unknown and Unknowable."

This is no mere modern aberration. In the early days of the Church some of the most subtle errors of thought took very much this line. To the "Gnostic," the ultimate eternal Being was entirely unknowable. "The Christ" was, in his view, one out of many sublime (but lower) existences who made man capable of some part and lot in the eternal world.

How entirely is the whole gospel of the grace of God in contradiction to such dreams! How nobly they are scattered by even this one ray of eternal daylight, this passage before us here! True, "no man hath seen God at any time" (John 1:18), in His essential glory. But then, "the only begotten Son, who is in the bosom of the Father, He *hath* declared Him." He *hath* told us exactly, fully, finally, His character; nay, He hath *displayed* it; for He is the "express image" of it, the true Impress of the celestial Seal.

Think it simply through, with rest and with thanksgiving. In the mystery of Eternal Existence there must be, forever and ever, depths unknown. But in the splendor of Eternal Character there is nothing which, in the Lord Jesus Christ, is not revealed. There is nothing concealed, different, alien, in the Father, which is not manifested in the Son. All the holiness of the Father, all His omnipotence, all His omniscience, is in the Son. And then, equally, all the love that is in the Son, all the compassion, all the tenderness, all the care for the weakest, and the most ignorant, and the most wandering, is in the Father. As absolutely as the Son, He loves to save, He yearns over the lost, He calls the wanderer to come. There is no colder central region behind the warmth of the Name of Jesus. He is the "own Son" (Rom. 8:32) of the Blessed. He is exactly like His Father, who loved Him before the foundation of the world. Our Father which art in heaven, hallowed, and also beloved, be Thy Name, revealed in Jesus Christ.

29

The Christian as Evidence to Christ

Glorified in His saints—2 Thess. 1:10

Some time ago I experienced one of those moments of mental trial which are known, if I mistake not, to most Christians, sooner or later, more or less. Perhaps I should use a more complex word than *mental* to describe what I mean. It was a trial to faith and hope, to conscious certainty about the things unseen and eternal, which was compounded of several elements besides the element of the understanding. Emotion had to do with it, no doubt, and some physical conditions too. However, it was, in the strictest sense of the word, a trying experience; it *tried* the spirit, by demanding answers to such questions as "Yea, hath God said?" "What is the reason of the hope?" "Where is the promise of His coming?"

One solemn comfort at such moments is the recollection that the very saints of God, in other days as in our own, have known such hours. Asaph knew them, as he tells us fully and candidly, in the seventy-third Psalm. Job knew them, and so did Jeremiah. I have little doubt that Paul knew them. In days much nearer our own, Payson knew them. "I have sometimes mounted the pulpit" says Payson, "while a dead whisper was heard in my heart, *Is there a God at all?*" Yet Payson was the means of innumerable conversions, during his ministry so weighted with physical suffering. And when he came to die, he affirmed with calm and beaming looks, that he almost literally saw the Holy City, and felt the fragrance of the immortal air around him, while death looked merely a narrow stream in the foreground, to be crossed by a single step.

Let us never, for one moment, *cherish* the experience of difficulty in belief, as if there were anything great or deep in it of itself. It always, necessarily, comes of knowing not too much but too little; of seeing as yet not deep enough. But if the experience is upon us, let us take the fact as *a trial*. And the Apostle tells us that "the trial of our faith is precious" (1 Pet. 1:7) in its effects, if it is rightly met.

I allude thus far to a personal incident of the soul only to give point to what seems to me to be the lesson of its sequel. About the time in question I had been reading some pages of a book by the late Dr. John Ker, one of my best-loved authors, a bright ornament not only of the Scottish Church, but of the Church of Christ at large; a deep, luminous thinker, a man of wide cultivation, and a believing witness to the Lord who had tasted deep of the trials of both physical and mental pain. I do not remember now what the topic was which he handled in the passages I had read. But I did, and do, remember the living impression left on me by the writer; the depth of insight, the large and tender sympathy, the practical wisdom, the admirable power of suggestion and counsel, and, shining through all, the presence in the man's entire mind of the influence of his Master, molding, animating, giving a character which raised and sanctified the whole.

Then the thought occurred to me that a man like this is, in himself, in what he is, a testimony to the existence and to the character of Christ, of God in Christ. He is no self-originated phenomenon. He is an effect, he is a product, he is a stream; and as the stream, so the fountain. To begin with, here is a person, a thinking, willing, purposing, understanding person. This stream flows then from a Spring which, whatever else it contains, contains at least this, which I observe under my eyes in the stream—personality. Ker, and such as he, great and beautiful as they are in their personality, are, with equal clearness and certainty, not the mere highest results of lower grades of being, with nothing above them, the crown and end of all things. Their very nature is to look up, and to know that "He hath made us, and not we ourselves." They come forth, and from a higher Source. They are evidences, by what they are, to It.

This reflection is of course at once extended and intensified when we think not only on the phenomenon of a rich personality, but on what we can only call the beauty of the holiness of a genuine and deeply taught Christian personality. This is a phenomenon which, we may be reasonably sure, in the deepest sense of the word "reason," points upwards to a supreme and *kindred* source. A John Ker is an enigma without an answer, a negation of the highest reason, except as the effect, the product, the child, of a Holy God, Himself beautiful in His holiness.

Take this thought out into the wide field of Christian history. We have looked at one instance of a vast phenomenon, isolated for the moment. But such a life is not isolated. It is part of an immense system of phenomena, which, to think of the Christian centuries alone for the moment, extends from Paul, and Polycarp, and Monica, and Augustine, to Anselm, Bernard, Tauler, Huss, and on to Luther, Melanchthon, Calvin, Ridley, and on to Herbert, Bunyan, Pascal, Guyon, Fenelon, and on to Watts, Wesley, Whitefield, Newton and Simeon, and on to Thomas Scott, Elizabeth Fry, Chalmers, Neff, Oberlin, McCheyne, Vinet, Monod, till we come to Patteson, and Hannington, and the martyrs of 1900 in the Far East. These, and the quite countless Christians whom they represent, the vast nebula behind the stars, with endless differences in other things, are alike in this, that they present themselves to us naturally, consistently, unanimously, as effects of a common Cause, the outcome of a Source infinitely higher but necessarily kindred. They bear traces of that Origin in their very existence. They are rays diffused from an Archetype, and they lead our eyes backward and upward towards its brightness.

As sure as the existence of the saints, so sure is the existence of their Savior. The Christ of the Gospel is at the same moment the Christ of history and the Christ of experience. Let us gird up the loins of our minds, be sober, and hope to the end (see 1 Pet. 1:13).

30

Onesimus

That thou shouldest receive him forever—Phile. 15

How beautiful is that miniature picture in the gallery of the New Testament, the Epistle to Philemon! Even non-Christian critics have praised its perfect literary charm. It has often been compared with a somewhat similar letter of intercession to an offended master, written some years later, by that perfect gentleman in the Roman sense, the younger Pliny. And the Christian Apostle cannot but come victorious out of the competition, so perfect is the tact, so fine the feeling, so large and deep the kindness, so kind the dignity, of his little letter to Philemon. Nor need we wonder, for he had over Pliny the immeasurable advantage of that education of the whole being, mind and feeling included, which comes with "knowing Christ, and the power of His resurrection, and the fellowship of His sufferings" (see Phil. 3:10).

But today we will not study the precious document; we will fix our thoughts upon one person, the most conspicuous person mentioned in it. We will consider Onesimus, and Onesimus as a lesson and a type.

Onesimus is to us now an immortal name. As long as the Bible lasts that name will live with it, and will live to be studied and to be loved. Yet Onesimus was once a being low among the degraded and the wretched of his time. He was a slave, in the old Greek slavery, which left the human chattel, as nearly as possible, to the mere mercy of his—of its—owner. And let the owner be never so good-natured, still the iron, or rather the cancer, of the chattel-character

94

would go deep into the slave's soul. And Onesimus was probably a Lydian by birth, and Lydian slaves were a proverb for exceptional badness, that is, for a full receptivity of the worst personal effects of slavery. No wonder that he proved (as it seems, v. 18) a dishonest servant, and at length a runaway.

This is no place to examine the problems raised by the attitude of the Apostles towards slavery. It must be enough to say here, as some critics by no means too orthodox have said, that this attitude showed a prescient wisdom of the highest kind. It absolutely and always declined to meddle with revolution, while it was incessantly teaching principles of the spiritual order which led to lasting and profound reform. Meanwhile, it tolerated the existing system of society; and so Paul evidently regarded it as Onesimus' duty to go back to his master, and "submit himself under his hands." Only, he sent, along with him, the Epistle to Philemon!

We seem to see the fugitive going back. He has had strange, probably terrible, experiences of human misery since he left Colossae. Somehow, he has found his way, through such adventures as an escaped slave might expect, to Rome; Rome, the moral sink of the known world. But at Rome, we know not how, he has found his way to Paul's chamber door, and there, in due time, he has found the Lord Jesus. The imprisoned Apostle has "begotten him" (v. 10); that is, he has been the means of the poor fellow's new birth by the Holy Ghost. Onesimus goes back to Colossae, because he is "a new creature in Christ Jesus," and because it is the law of the new creature's being to do right, to do the will of God in the next thing.

So he arrives. He is not exactly a prodigal son. Legally, he is an escaped slave, caught again (by his own conscience), and in his old master's power. Spiritually, however, he is a prodigal *brother,* yea, "a brother beloved" (v. 16). And if we read Philemon correctly, through the hints of his character given us by the letter addressed to him, he would meet Onesimus in a spirit very different from that of the elder brother of that other prodigal. He would grasp his hand, and welcome him *home;* and so would Apphia, and Archippus too.

But what would Onesimus feel, and what would he do? Here again we may turn with some confidence to "read between the lines" of the Epistle, and to read alongside of them that bright, beautiful phrase of the larger Letter to the Colossians, written at the same time: "Onesimus, a faithful and beloved brother, who is one of you" (Col. 4:9). Paul did not write lightly in such terms. Converted Onesimus must have risen into a noble Christian character, true and lovable. How would such a man, with exactly his past, go back to his injured master?

Most certainly to do anything but take airs, and pose as the representative of "fraternity, equality." He would have nothing to say for himself, everything against himself. He would long to be more than ever at the entire service of Philemon. To Philemon he now was joined by a spiritual bond strong as the Lord could make it, but therefore all the more, not the less, he recognized him as, *in Christ,* far more than in law, his appointed director and disposer. Nothing in daily duty would be too humble or too menial for his wishes. And what he did, menial or not, would be done in a totally new way; from the soul, as unto the Lord, "with good will doing service" (Eph. 6:6, 7); loving everything in the daily round, for Jesus' sake.

"We are all the Lord's Onesimi." So says blessed Luther, in his vivid way. Is it not so? The slavery of man to man is a condition impossible to reconcile permanently with God's will. The slavery of man to God in Christ, the absolute "belonging," the entire surrender, the supreme and irresponsible disposal, is a thing of eternal right, and is the condition forever precedent to man's noblest freedom. And we have run away. And we have been found again, and have somehow come back to our divine Colossae, to our divine Philemon. And He, blessed be His name, has not upbraided us, still less has consigned us to torture or the scourge. He has not been ashamed to call us brethren, and to treat us as such indeed. But meanwhile, if only for our own bliss, He cannot abdicate His master-character. He gives us the joy of "serving him forever" (See Ex. 21:6).

How shall we meet it, receive it, and taste its happiness? By loving everything about His household, and in His service, and the humblest things most, for His sake. By asking never, never again, to be allowed to run away into the wretched world from our dear Colossae. By seeking to live and serve every hour, thankful, faithful, perfectly possessed, perfectly free, under the very eyes of our divine Philemon.

31

Whence Came They?

And whence came they?—Rev. 7:13

The environment of this short question is as familiar as it is magnificent. It occurs in that great apocalyptic vision where John sees an uncounted multitude gathered before the throne, robed in white, and bearing the palms which to Hebrew thought would symbolize an immortal Feast of Tabernacles, the rest and triumph of the eternal Country, the better Canaan, after the desert and the river. There they stand, and there they sing to their Lord the great anthem of their salvation:

> Loud as from numbers without number, sweet
> As from blest voices, uttering joy; heaven rings
> With jubilee, and loud Hosannas fill
> The eternal regions.

Then did one of the glorified "Elders" ask the Seer this question, who they were, and whence they came; and went on to answer it himself. These happy singers had come "out of the great tribulation, and had washed their robes in the blood of the Lamb; therefore they were before the throne of God."

This vision, and so this question with its answer, have no doubt a first and particular reference. I am one of those who hold the Revelation of John to be just what it professes to be, no mere rhapsodical utterance (as some would make it) of the best thoughts of the Apostle, at a crisis of persecution, setting out in symbolical forms the general principles of Christian hope and courage. I hold it to be a veritable vision, divinely given, of the long future of the

Church, written down at the Redeemer's own bidding for our study, and faith, and prayerful expectation. And I take "the great tribulation" here to be thus, primarily, an awful foreseen time of trial, perhaps yet to come, and the white multitude with the palm and the song to be, primarily, the sufferers of that time.

Yet all through this book of mystery and light we may trace also another aspect. Through the primary and the particular may be seen the larger, the universal, which corresponds. Permanent facts of the kingdom of God are given to us all along under the types of the events foretold; so that the Revelation, apart from its predictive aspect, forms one of the richest of all the Biblical mines of moral and spiritual teaching. One example of this we certainly have here. The Elder's question we may quite lawfully take with a reference wide enough to touch all the lives, in all ages, which have reached a bright eternity. We may listen for the answer, as for a message for everyone, ourselves included, who prays, who hopes, who looks, to be with the Lord hereafter.

"Whence came they?" "They" are glorified spirits in heaven.

> Our knowledge of that life is small,
>   The eye of faith is dim.

"I cannot imagine what a spirit is," said Charles Simeon, on his deathbed, at Cambridge; "I have no conception of it; though I know that in a few days I shall, by the mercy of God, join the company of the redeemed above." It is even so; "we cannot imagine"; "we have no conception." One moment's happy experience will tell us, relatively, all. And the fact of the prospect is inestimably precious, and can be really grasped by loving faith because the essence of it is revealed in sublimely *personal* terms; it is just this, "to be *with Christ,*" in a sense conscious and supreme. But as to detail, we can only say, "it doth not yet appear." What it will be like, to be where the very causes of grief, of fear, of decay, of death, the very occasions of trial, above all the very possibility of sin, shall "be swallowed up of life," so that the *beata necessitas boni*, the blessed necessity of good, shall be the free law of joy forever—this, indeed, "doth not yet appear." We "look for the life of the world to come," but with the eyes not of imagination, but of faith, as faith sees the Person, the Word, and the Work of the risen and everlasting Christ.

So the *where* and the *whither* of the coming blessedness is hidden. But not so the *whence*. "Whence came they" to that infinitely desirable Land unseen? Here is our point. They came from earth, and time, and common human life, from scenes the most common, concrete, familiar; from all that makes up the poor annals of our mortality from the cradle to the grave. "Whence came they" to the City of the Hereafter? From precisely the things which we, their successors, find around us in the ordinary daylight here. From being children in their mothers' arms; from "youth's new years of many a fitful change"; from unheroic, unpoetic trials and temptations; from disappointments, and mistakes, and many a failure; from convictions of their own heart's sin; from pangs of repentance in which they saw themselves to be, in themselves, the very opposite of saints; from asking not, How shall I be glorified, and wear a halo, and bear a palm, but, What must I do to be saved? They came from discoveries of Jesus as their own, not in mere ecstasies of fitful emotion, but with an indescribable harmony of seriousness and wonder, and so as to see that in the act of being embraced by Him they passed into His absolute possession, to be His servants forever. They came from no dreamer's paradise of soft "religionism," nor from any brittle and unseemly pedestal of self-advertising excellence, but from a life given up humbly to do the next right thing rightly, in the Lord's strength, for His dear sake. They came from rising up in the morning not to try to be heroic, but to pray to be faithful, and most faithful in the most common hour; from living out the ordinary day as those who were indeed not ashamed to be known to love their Redeemer, and who could be seen to find in Him a law and a power which sweetened and uplifted the whole action of life, producing that great result, the Christian character, full orbed in humbleness, light and strength. They reached the summit a step at a time. Some of them sometimes found that the next step led them into great tribulation indeed, into agonies of personal grief, exquisite pangs of slander or contempt, or such violence of terror and death as thousands upon thousands of our fellow-Christians in China were called to only last summer (Written in 1901), while we were spending, perhaps, a pleasant holiday. But most of them, at most times, took the next step, in the name of Jesus, into commonplace duties, which yet all were occasions for loving and doing the will of God in the strength and freedom of the Spirit of His Son.

It is written of the Holy City that its "street" is "pure gold, like unto transparent glass" (Rev. 21:21); glorious image of a state of action and communion where the true and the beautiful come together absolutely and forever. The road to the City is often rough with flints, and clogged with mire, and dark with shadows of the valley. But when the road runs up to the gate at last, it passes on through it, in one line, into the golden street. No gulf divides them. It is a transfiguration. Grace, used humbly and in fear, is one in essence with the glory that is to be revealed.

32

The Robe and the Wearer

The Lord shall rejoice in His works. . . . I will be glad in the Lord—
Ps. 104:31, 34

A Holiday Meditation

Perhaps this Sunday finds my reader taking rest, seeking recreation, in the true sense of that word, a *re-creation* of the strength of body and mind for the will of God in common duty, amidst some grand or pleasant scene of His handiwork.

Is it by the English sea, or the English lake, or on the Scottish heather, or amidst the fair green hills of Ireland? Is it in the Norwegian fiord, or in the German forest, or near the ice-rivers of the Alps?

In any such case, the Christian will not be at rest if he does not take care that the holiday is also a holy day. He will remember to invite, very particularly, the presence of the Master in the most completely leisure moments of the faithful servant. For never, never, thanks be to the beloved Master, is the servant out of service, wherever he is; he carries with him, inseparably, and as part of himself, the service which is perfect freedom.

Today we will cherish and develop this recollection by some simple thoughts upon our double motto from the Word. Let us ponder its two parts, as they may be pondered amidst the glories of Nature.

(1) "The Lord shall rejoice in His works." Let this be remembered, let this sink into the soul, as we with our human eyes look upon those works today. Is it quiet beauty, the peaceful curve of "the far-foamed sands," or the mirror of the inland water, where the

101

woods and hills glass themselves? Is it majestic beauty, where the glacier winds between the black precipices, and the snowy summit lifts the eye half-way to heaven? Is it the glances of the sunrise, or the ineffable beauty of the after-glow, the *Alpengluth?* O Christian visitor to these fair scenes, do not be afraid to rejoice in them. Do not think that an intense, profound, soul-filling enjoyment of Nature need for one moment be the "nature-worship" which puts Nature in the place of God. Rightly entertained, that is to say, entertained with a full, tranquil recollection of Him, that enjoyment may be one form of close communion with the very thought of God. For what says our Scripture-word today? "The Lord shall rejoice in His works."

Yes, according to the Scriptures, which are full of the noblest passages on the splendor of creation, the beauty and the fullness of creation are a positive joy to the Creator. *"Verily, He hath taste!"* said Hugh Miller, finding on a mountain edge in the Grampians an exquisite flower, sown and nourished where no human eye, but by rarest accident, could behold it. He felt, with a flash of Christian intuition, that the eternal Observer had a joy in Nature all His own; that solitary flower was a pleasure to the Lord. His conviction was perfectly Scriptural. "The Lord shall rejoice in His works," with a joy personal and vivid, a joy to which our enjoyment is but as the dewdrop to the river.

Take a holy and unfearing pleasure, then, Christian friend, in the scene of light, and color, and noble line and form around thee. It is the robe of thy King and Friend, wrought by His hand, adjusted by His touch, pleasant to His eyes. True, a day will come when He will mysteriously change it; "as a vesture shalt Thou fold them up, and they shall be changed" (Ps. 102:26). But till then these heavens and this green earth *are His vesture,* as truly as the new heavens and the new earth will be His vesture hereafter. With Him, rejoice in them. Let their power of beauty flow through your soul. Make your holiday a holy day by entering into the rejoicing of the Maker in the thing that He has made.

And remember while you do so that "Nature" is the work not merely of God in the abstract, but of God in Christ. The fields, and hills, and woods, and waters, the sun and the changing moon, the stars and clouds, are Christian. For "unto the Son He saith" "and the heavens are the works of Thy hands" (Heb. 1:8, 10); "without Him was not anything made that was made" (John 1:3).

(2) But then there is the other side. "I will be glad in the Lord." We have seen how freely the Christian may rejoice in Nature without one unwholesome tinge of a false and pagan "nature-worship" in the joy. But this is on one condition, namely, a "joy in the Lord" which rules and hallows the other. The robe is glorious, nay, it is dear with a wonderful lovableness, because it is wrought and is worn by Him. But that means, of course, that there is something to His servant infinitely more glorious, and more dear, than the robe; that something is, the Heart that lives behind it.

So let us return to our joy in Nature through the avenue of a renewed and deepened joy in the Lord. "My meditation of him shall be sweet: I will be glad in the LORD" [Ps. 104:34]. (Perhaps the Hebrew should be rendered there, "My meditation shall be sweet *unto Him*"; another side of truth, and a precious one.) Let us look for His glory in the face of Jesus Christ, and drink that blessed light deep into our thankful spirits. Then, all the more largely, and all the more safely, "in that light we shall see light," the light of a beauty which gives joy to God, in the river, in the shore, in the field of flowers, the field of snow, the sunset and the stars.

33

One in Christ

There is neither Greek nor Jew—Col. 3:11

The triumphs of the gospel are many and various, alike in the individual and in the world. Among them, how striking, how beautiful, how supernatural, is its triumph shown in the fusion of sympathies across all the barriers of race! Let us think a while of this, as we see it illustrated in this short sentence of Paul's remembering who wrote the sentence, and who they were to whom he wrote it.

Paul was the consummate example of "the Jew." By training, by tradition, by every influence which builds up character, he was out and out a Jew. Up to his conversion, the whole development of his life was an intensive development, towards the Law, and towards "the hedge of the Law," the traditions; towards every belief and every practice which was built into "the middle wall of partition" (Eph. 2:14) between a sacred Israel and a profane outer world. The practical issue in his thought and habits must have been remarkable. Peter was by no means so fully formed a zealot as Paul. Yet Peter, years after his conversion, long after his Lord's glorification, was still in such a mental position that never, till he entered the house of Cornelius, had he seen his way to take a meal with a Gentile (Acts 10:28). Think of the general state of non-sympathy which such a conviction (unknown to the Old Testament) surely indicates. What interchange in even superficial modes of friendship was there likely to be between a Simon, still more between a Saul of Tarsus, and human beings born and brought up in the very heart of Gentilism?

Now the Colossians were exactly such persons. They were, in the very broad sense of the word, "Greeks"; a race of Western Asia Minor, speaking Greek as at least the tongue of external communication, and pagan by quite immemorial tradition. By no faintest link of nationality, habit, sentiment, worship, had they any contact with Abraham, Moses, David, and the prophets. To them, what were the temple, and the law? Nothing; or at most the dimly-rumored peculiarities of another Asiatic people, who of course had a religion of their own.

Humanly speaking, in the order of nature, how unlikely was any close contact of heart between a developed Pharisee and a Colossian! Yet here is the phenomenon before us, an accomplished fact. This Epistle is the message of the Pharisee to the Colossians. And it is a message which does very much more than convey information, and state principles. It does much more even than affirm that "there is neither Greek nor Jew." It is itself a living instance of the fact. For the heart of the writer is in complete contact with the hearts of the readers. They perfectly understand one another. Their sympathies are fused into the most delightful unity. The Pharisee gives his whole self out to the Colossians. He not only loves them; he lives for them, he lives, as to his spirit, with them. All that they are, all that they think, all that may affect their life and their belief, is supremely important to him. And plainly he is writing as to those whose hearts are reciprocal to his own. They have come to know him with an intimacy more than brotherly. He writes to them as to extensions of himself, responses to himself.

I dare to say that a phenomenon like this was a new thing upon the earth in those days, and a most wonderful thing. And one reason, and one only, is adequate to account for it; the Lord Jesus Christ. Yes, the Apostle inevitably closes the sentence which begins, "there is neither Greek nor Jew," with the truth which makes it actual, "Christ is all, and in all."

That blessed victory over human isolation, in the name of the Lord Jesus, has been going on every since. It is in progress everywhere today. In India, it literally joins the Pariah Christian arm-in-arm in the street with the Brahman Christian. In Europe, at a gathering of Christian students, in 1895, at Wartburg, just at the moment when America and Spain were in mortal conflict, it clasped the hands of the American delegate and the Spanish delegate with a genuine brotherhood. It is a power which develops, to noblest results, all pure patriotism. But it transcends the restrictions of land and race with a heavenly force and ease in favor of the unity of souls in Jesus Christ the Lord.

Sacred, wonder-working gospel! Where man needs to learn how rightly to stand alone, there is no power like the gospel to enable him to do so, aye, against a world in arms. Putting the soul into absolutely direct contact with God in Christ, nothing between, it not only sets him upon the eternal Rock; it incorporates him with its living strength. But then, where man needs the largest fusion with his fellow men, where, strong in God, he is called to be at the service of his brother, the gospel is the secret for this also. The heart which has admitted Christ to dwell in it, already begins to dilate with His glory. Knowing Him, and in His light knowing itself, it knows other hearts too in a new way, a way at once penetrating and full of love. It is open, it is accessible, it is able to be united, under the touch of Christ. It gives itself out, in Him. And then there is neither Greek nor Jew; He is all and in all.

34

Stepping by the Spirit

If we live by the Spirit, by the Spirit let us also step—Gal. 5:25
(literally rendered)

So I would render this verse, rather than read it as in the Authorized Version, "If we live in the Spirit, let us also walk in the Spirit." That reading does indeed express eternal truth, but not quite the truth of the Greek original. The Spirit, in the Greek, is regarded as the instrument, the means, of the life and the walk, rather than as the sphere; it speaks of a life and action *by* Him, rather than *in* Him. And the Greek verb of motion is not that which denotes progress generally; it is that which denotes the taking of steps, the moving along step by step.

On this last point let us think today. What to us is the message of this precept, "by the Spirit let us also step?"

On the first great truth of the verse, "life by the Spirit," I hardly touch at all. Let that be largely taken for granted, as our faith, and our experience. "By the Spirit," by the eternal Spirit, the Spirit of life, the Spirit of grace, we, "dead in trespasses and sins," must be "quickened" (Eph. 2:1), brought to life, if we are to live in and to the Lord. "The Lord, the Life-Giver," as the Nicene Creed nobly calls Him, must give that life to man, by putting man into vital contact with Him who is our Life. Then, and only then,

> Our quicken'd souls awake and rise
> From the long sleep of death,
> On heavenly things we fix our eyes,
> And praise employs our breath.

107

But all this the Apostle takes for granted. He brings it in as a ground of argument, with the argumentative "if." It is the assumed fact on which is now planted the inference of conduct; "by the Spirit let us step," let us take step after step by Him.

Here are two messages for us, as practical as possible. One is, the sacredness of the details of life. The other is, the promise of nothing less than the Holy Spirit's power as our resource for a holy walk in detail.

(1) "Let us *step*." Do we Christians adequately remember the importance of the single steps of a life which in any sense worth naming calls itself Christian? The vast majority of the incidents of life are of the nature of steps; not leaps, nor flights, but steps. And not one of them, no, not one, in its moral importance, is nothing. The merest trick of habit is helping, more or less, to form character. The mere habit of carelessness about stepping is itself a series of steps which may conduct us with terrible precision to a goal of moral disaster. And look at it from another side; it is upon our little steps, more than on more general aspects of our life, that the observation of those around us is commonly engaged, consciously or not. Character, purpose, temper, the texture of the man's *morale,* is often much more surely indicated by his everyday steps than by some great feat of life in which he seems to spring or to fly. Christian friend, your minor life-movements are pretty sure to be noticed; your temper under petty trials, your fidelity under small engagements, your attention to simple claims of kindness, your habits at table, your activity or sloth in the morning, your use of the tongue in off-hours, particularly about other persons and their faults. Who shall reckon up the significance of steps? They are great things, in their littleness. They are great in power upon our own life. They are great in the impression they make upon those who surround our life, and see it.

(2) "By the Spirit let us step." The Apostle directs us to no lower secret. Do we want to do fully right in the little things of life? We may do something to modify the surface, imperfectly indeed, but something, by natural means. But do we want to do the fullness of right in the smallest things? Do we want to glorify God in the common hour? Do we ask that our steps may, in some humble measure, leave a track of Christian light and love behind them? Then noth-

ing short of the supreme secret will do. It must be by the Holy Spirit.

This means much for us in the way of recollection, and of purpose, and of the prayer of faith. It means that we must indeed awaken ourselves, and keep awake, with ever renewed persistency, to the momentousness of little things; not miserably, not morbidly, but seriously, so as to realize habitually that they are *worthy of* the help of God Himself. It means the cultivation of a habit of prayer, the prayer which is just faith expressing itself to its blessed Object, and expecting that He will be as good as His word, filling us with His Spirit. Yes, a life in which, "by the Spirit, we step," must be a life which is in earnest for the Lord, and willing to take pains for His sake.

But is it not infinitely worth the while? Is not this the only happy life after all? It is a life which moves along a path paved with the greatest promises that God has given. It walks, it steps, along that pavement in the companionship of the Holy One. It advances in the light, and to the light, "shining more and more unto the perfect day" (see Prov. 4:18). It is the true walk with God. And its end is an Enoch-translation, to walk and please Him, with faultless steps, in the land of life forever.

35

Communion Thoughts

Ye do proclaim the Lord's death, till He come—1 Cor. 11:26
(literally rendered)

Let us ponder together some of the simplest, sweetest, deepest messages of the precious Communion, the Supper of the Lord. Many controversies have gathered around that quiet place of peace and blessing, the holy Table. But today we will shut these all out, and ask our Master to meet us, as if within those chamber doors of old, where the disciples were gathered together, and suddenly they heard the voice of their Beloved, "Peace be unto you."

As the ages roll and gather, is not the Communion yet more and more desirable and full of blessing? Not least when the believer has had some special trial to belief, when the things unseen and eternal have seemed as if remote and shadowy, when the joy of Bethlehem and of the garden of the Resurrection has felt for the moment a chill from surrounding indifference or denial, when the love of many has seemed to be waxing cold—then has not the sacramental Ordinance met us as with the very touch of God? Again the glorious solidity of everlasting fact is conveyed, as it were, through our very senses to our souls. The Bread and the Wine are not a myth; nor is their history, up to its very origin, obscure for one single step. The first Lord's Supper lives, identical and immortal, in the Lord's Supper of this Sunday. And in it lives all He did, all He said, all He was, and is, and is to be; "the same yesterday, today, forever" (Heb. 13:8). If the shadows are really to deepen around the Church, as denials of the faith grow more frequent and open *within* the Church, will not the radiance of the blessed Table shine ever brighter to the believing, to those who in any measure know Him, till it is lost in the radiance of His Return?

And now to gather up some of its precious messages.

(1) "*Ye do proclaim* the Lord's Death." That is, as I believe, ye do proclaim it, ye do tell the tidings of it, to one another. I know that many Christians hold another meaning, and take the Apostle to teach us that we "proclaim" the death, pleading its merits in the Ordinance, before the Father's throne, and to Him. As I said above, I attempt no discussions here. All that I am now concerned to say is, that a "proclamation" to one another *is* assuredly one great end of the Ordinance, and a most precious end. As instituted, the holy Service is nothing if not social, mutual. Scripture knows nothing of a solitary Eucharist. Therefore the rite has a *mutual* significance; it has some sacred thing to say, all around the circle, Christian to Christian. By his presence, by his partaking, "each is then a herald to the rest," telling it out that Jesus did indeed die, to rise again.

(2) "Ye do proclaim *the Lord's Death*." That is the central message. The *mortal* is the *vital* here. It is not, He was born, was made Man, lived, wrought, taught, blessed the poor sinful world by the touch of His feet, and the look of His fair countenance, and the words such as man never spoke before. It is, that He died. It is, that Gethsemane and Golgotha were that for which, above all things, He came. "He gave His life a ransom for many" (Matt. 20:28). "He poured out His soul unto death" (Is. 53:12). He was "lifted up from the earth" (John 12:32). He "endured the Cross" (Heb. 12:2). "That He might sanctify the people with His own blood, suffered, without the gate" [Heb. 13:12]; "Without shedding of blood was no remission" (Heb. 9:22); He "washed us from our sins in His own blood" (Rev. 1:5). He came "again from the dead . . . in the blood of the everlasting covenant" (Heb. 13:20). "Worthy is the Lamb that was slain!" (Rev. 5:12).

This is what we "proclaim" at the divine Table. The broken Bread, the poured-out Wine, the *separation* of the one from the other (solemn symbolism of *death*), the occasion of the institution, the words of it, all take us to the Cross. All with one sweet voice proclaim that Jesus died. All say to each awakened, each seeking, each believing soul, "He hath given thee rest by His sorrow, and life by His death."

111

Yes, every Communion draws afresh the sacred line of atoning blood around all our hopes, all our life. "We do proclaim the Lord's death."

(3) By the very fact of so doing we proclaim also His glorious present life, His victory over the grave, His spiritual presence with His people, His gift of Himself to be their life indeed. Never—let us be quite sure of this—would the first believers have kept festival over their Master's death, had not that death been followed by a triumph over the grave which at once and forever showed His dying work to be the supreme achievement which it was. Only the Risen Christ can explain the joy of the Lord's Supper. Without Him it would have been a funeral meal, kept for a while by love in its despair, and then dropped forever. From the very first till now it has been a feast of life and of thanksgiving. It is a contemporary and immortal witness to the Risen One. And the Risen One is alive forevermore. And in His eternal life He is our life, here and now. Feed on Him as such, feed everywhere and always upon Him. Eat Him and drink Him, that you may live because of Him (John 6:57). Such is the message of the festal Meal of the Church, spoken straight from her Lord, to the heart of every member of His Body.

(4) "*Till He come.*" As the Supper is our witness to the past of the Finished Work, and to the present of the Risen Life, so it is our infallible prophecy of the coming Glory. It points forward, with its straight and unbroken line of light, into the shadows of the future, and assures us that within those shadows, somewhere, at an hour we think not, lies hidden, lies waiting, the Coming of the Bridegroom, the Return of the beloved Lord to His waiting people. Around that prospect a thousand mysteries gather. But the prospect lies unalterable amidst the mysteries. And the Ordinance is our contemporary and immortal witness to this also. We keep it "till He come."

Even so, come, Lord Jesus, adored and longed for! And until Thou comest, hastening down upon the mountains of separation, we will, more gladly, more confidently, more expectantly always, "proclaim Thy death" (Song 2:17).

36

Renewal Day by Day

The inward man is renewed day by day—2 Cor. 4:16

This is a record of personal experience. Paul is describing to his Corinthian converts his own ministerial life, just as it was passing at the time. This was one great aspect of it. His "outward man," his physical frame and system, in the wear and tear of the Lord's work, was "perishing," decaying; from the bodily point of view he was aging, he was gradually giving way. But from the other side, from the inner side, the opposite process was going on. His "inward man," his unseen world of will, affection, thought, under the living power of the Spirit of God, making Christ present in his heart by faith, was "being renewed," being made quite fresh and new. It was not only kept going, somehow maintained in some sort of tolerable working order, beating on like an old clock not quite worn out. It was "being made new"; filled ever afresh with a strong, bright life, quickened with a wonderful youth, from a source, a spring, "full of immortality." And this was taking place "day by day." It was not a matter of one great crisis, or of a few such times. He was not lifted intermittently into new life, and then allowed to sink slowly back to spiritual exhaustion, to be animated once again. It was a matter of "day by day." He lived a day at a time as regarded the work, the suffering, the battle, and a day at a time as regarded the "being made new."

This record of personal experience is a message of universal truth for the Christian believer, now and "to the end of the age" (see Matt. 28:20). Thanks be to God that His messages to us in His

Word do thus so often come through personal experience, reaching us not as utterances from the air, but as testimonies carried to us through human hearts, which have beat and have ached like our own. They are divine oracles, sure and certain, the voice of the Eternal Spirit, to be trusted, to be obeyed, in life and death. But they are sent to us, not anyhow, but thus, through the warm and living medium of the experience of men, who have passed them on to us because they have themselves proved them so wonderfully true, and would fain have us also enter into a blessed peace and power in God.

This was the one deep, longing aim of the holy writers, "that we might have fellowship with them" (1 John 1:3). We may, if we please, study for their own sake the great characters of such men as Paul and John. But that is the last thing Paul and John ask us to do. They ask us rather to hear what they have to say of their experience of the blessed greatness of Jesus Christ, and then, because He is great, to find great grace in Him, just the same great grace which they found, for ourselves today.

Let us sit down then and listen to this message carried to us by Paul, that we may "have fellowship with" him.

(1) "The inward man is *being made new.*" Here is a welcome word for us, in this mortal life of ours. Too often it is as if everything in us and about us were being "made old." True, there are "novelties" always in the air. Fashions, not of dress only, but of almost all aspects of life, are always changing. But the effect upon us of such "newnesses," after a time, is anything in the world but a renovating one. Before the man knows it, he is out of date, a survival, moving among "new faces, other minds." His "inward man" is only too conscious of change and of, not renewal, but decay, under the crude novelties of life.

But here comes the Apostle, and tells him a better, a blissful story. It is open to him to carry about within him a secret of perpetual and bright beginnings, a spring-head of waters of immortality, a youth which grows and develops in its capacity to enjoy and do, and yet becomes only the fresher as time goes on; even as the legends say that the angelic life grows always not older, but younger, through the heavenly ages. Here is the possibility of a bright and beautiful permanence in that inner world which so profoundly affects for us all the seeming of the outer world. It is a permanence which means no mere crystallization of the past, but an expansion of all the treasures of past and present in the light and warmth of a very blessed and a very real future. That future again is not a mere prospect in the distance; it is in living contact with this hour. For it will consist, when it comes, in the eternal enjoyment in glory of Him who is now, in the life of grace, actually dwelling in the heart by faith. Jesus Christ, in the heart and in the hopes, is the sure secret of an inner youth, a youth evermore "made new."

(2) *"Day by day."* Delightful closing words of the Apostle's message! Life is built a day at a time. And the Scriptures keep this constantly in view in their promises. "I am with you all the days" (Matt. 28:20); "His compassions are new every morning" (Lam. 3:22, 23); "Be Thou their arm every morning" (Is. 33:2); "Renewed day by day" [2 Cor. 4:16].

Christian, tired and somewhat disheartened, take not only life, but the Lord, a day at a time. Forbid your imagination to wander over vague spaces of the pilgrimage. Let the lifetime you deal with be just today, with its birth when you wake, its maturity in the working hours, and its quiet death when you retire at night to your bed. It is but today. And for today you possess nothing less than the whole Christ of God; Christ for you, Christ in you, Christ living, loving, keeping, coming. Let Him make you young again today.

37

The Believer's Life after Death

Today thou shalt be with me in Paradise—Luke 23:43
We are confident, I say, and willing rather to be absent from the body, and
to be present with the Lord—2 Cor. 5:8

Let us think a little together, this Lord's Day morning, of two bright aspects of the believer's life after death. That life is, to be sure, a subject on which the Word of God says comparatively little.

> Our knowledge of that life is small,
>   The eye of faith is dim.

And no doubt there is a purpose in this reserve. The Bible is God's oracle not only in what it says, but in the scale on which it says it. Where it has much to tell us, we may be sure that the topic is meant to stand in the very front of our faith. Where its words are few, the topic must be subordinate in our hearts to others which are more important. Yet a subordinate Scripture truth may be, in its proper place, and treated with proper care, a very precious one. And surely this is true of what we gather from the Word about the believer's prospect between death and resurrection.

The two verses before us here both bear quite distinctly upon that prospect. Neither of them can be taken to refer to the full glory of the final state, in which, in resurrection-life, our being will be complete again. "Today," the very day of his painful death, the "thief" was to be with the Lord in Paradise. And the Apostle was "of good courage," as the Revised Version has it, in view of "absence from the body," because the other side of that experience was to be this, "at home with the Lord."

116

So here are two precious glimpses into the blessed unseen life in which our holy departed ones are now actually living, and in which, before long, we too look to live, we, "who have fled for refuge to lay hold on the hope set before us." Let us take the two views each in turn, for the distinctive truth of each, and then remember the glorious element present in both alike.

(1) "*Today thou shalt be* in Paradise." Here first, the dying man is promised the perfect continuance, through death, of his personality. "Today thou shalt be." The sun would set, the mangled and broken body would be thrown into its wretched grave. But the man, the *ego*, would persist beyond it, above it, identical and profoundly living. As little as Jesus was about to be extinguished by His body's death, so little was the "thief" about to be by his; this is guaranteed by the voice of Him who was so soon to die, and then to rise again forever, "in the power of an endless life." Let us lay down all *á priori* difficulties about spirit-life at His dear feet; He has given us His personal assurance of the fact of it, and sealed it with His resurrection.

Then, next, we have the promise here that the conscious personality, passing from the body, enters in the name of Christ upon an experience of security, repose, and beauty. "*In Paradise,*" said the Lord. "Paradise" is an oriental word, meaning a royal pleasure-ground, a royal park or garden. It calls up ideas accordingly of all that is rich and fair in the way of cultured nature. It suggests to us the loveliness of wood, and lawn, and flowers, and waters, and also of the company which possesses and enjoys the charming scene, the friends, the guests, the family, of the King. They are there for delightful rest, or for delightful exercise. They have come from the battlefield, or the council, or the journey, to walk, to recline, to converse, to listen, where all is beautiful with a large, ordered, stately beauty. And all this is taken up by the Lord Jesus, in His use of the word Paradise, to set forth one side of the believer's unseen life after death. After the manner in which spirits enjoy and spirits see, the departed Christian "walks, by sight" (cf. 2 Cor. 5:6, 7), in a scene of glorious and restful beauty, in the garden of his King. "O my dear wife!" said an aged saint, no visionary, in the moment of his departure, putting his hand upon her arm. It was, she said, the very phrase, tone, and action, with which he had once called her attention to a sudden burst of beauty, an "earthly Paradise," as they turned a mountain corner in the Highlands.

(2) Now, in turn, let the Apostle Paul speak, telling us, in the Holy Ghost, what the prospect is to him, as he contemplates "absence from the body" in the hour of death. Rendering his words as literally as possible, they are; "We are deliberately willing *to leave home* in the body and *to get home* to the Lord." "To get home"; that is the thought. The heaven beyond death is home. It is not only rest, or refuge; it is nothing less than home. And home is more than a place of safety, or of repose. It is the scene where our whole being is in sweet and vivid harmony with surroundings. It is where affections both rest and expand; everyone and everything there is dear. It is where we are at the same time rocked in the arms of absolutely trusted love, and prepared and refreshed for all the work of life. This precious thing is taken up here as the shadow of that substance which lies just beyond the veil. To enter the unseen state, Christian, is not to totter out into the cold and void. It is to "get home."

(3) Lastly, note the divine element common to both prospects. "Thou shalt be *with Me*"; "At home *with the Lord*." After all, it is "not it, but He." Jesus is the glory of the immortal Garden. Jesus is the sacred hearth-fire of the immortal Home. Heaven, whether before resurrection or after, is just the bliss of His immediate presence. So heaven is possible for those only to whom His presence is bliss. But oh, for them, what will it not be? The Paradise will be not only a sweet new world of rest and beauty, not a scene only of "pleasures forevermore," (Ps. 16:11) nor even only a state of blissful and undisturbed communion with the blessed ones who have entered in before us. It will be all this, in a degree inconceivable to us now. But all this will be just the circumference around that one possible living and life-giving center; "thou shalt be with Me." The Home will be indeed a circle of blessed fellowship, a place of inconceivable interchange of love and joy among its inhabitants. But the supreme bliss of it, which will always spring up through everything else, and be first in everything, is this—we shall have "gotten home to the Lord."

38

Our Possessions

"We have"—Heb. 8:1

Here are two very simple words; in the Greek they are but one. Yet they enfold a wealth of truth and blessing, rightly taken, and rightly used.

In this particular text they take us into the delightful region of fact and possession with regard to our Lord Jesus Christ, in His character and office as our great High Priest, who, having sacrificed Himself as our sin-offering, is now for us upon the throne as our Mediator—"We have such an High Priest." But the words recur in many other passages of Scripture, in connections of inestimable value. As, for example, (Heb. 6:19); "Which hope *we have,* as an anchor of the soul." Or again, (Eph. 1:7); "In whom *we have* redemption through His blood, the forgiveness of sins." Or again, (Eph. 2:18); "Through Him *we both have* access by one Spirit unto the Father." And with such sentences we may of course group such as these, for they are practically identical in phrase—(1 Cor. 6:19); "Your body is the temple of the Holy Ghost, which is in you, which *ye have* of God"; and (2 Cor. 7:1); "*Having* therefore these promises, dearly beloved, let us cleanse ourselves from all filthiness of the flesh and spirit"; and (Heb. 10:19, 22); "Having therefore, breth-ren, boldness to enter into the holiest by the blood of Jesus . . . Let us draw near with a true heart in full assurance of faith, having our hearts sprinkled from an evil conscience, and our bodies washed with pure water"; and (1 John 5:12); "*He that hath* the Son *hath* the life.

What is the message of this class of passages, this rich and beautiful wealth of jewels of the Word, strung on this golden thread, "we have"? It is that there is a large and all-important place in our Christian life for the use of humble but most positive assertion of our possessions. There is indeed, and must be to the end, ample room for the soul's aspirations and petitions, its search and effort after things yet unattained. But even for these exercises of the spiritual life it is all-important that we, if we are Christians indeed, if we have really come to the Lord in our need, to touch Him, and to live by Him, should never forget the right sort of assertion of the possessions which we have.

If I do not mistake, many a time of secret devotion would immensely gain in power and blessing by more recollection of this. Have we ever been conscious, at such moments, of a certain weariness and disappointment, in the use, perhaps, of a familiar series of earnest petitions? Let us not give up petitioning; God forbid. Are not some of the very greatest promises which "we have" linked to the precept "ask"? But then "we have" the promises. And often and again our petitioning would proceed with a new and delightful life and expectation if we would lay it aside for a while in order to reaffirm to ourselves what the promises are, and to reaffirm further to ourselves not only that they are, but that "we have" them. Once at the feet of Jesus, once having touched, with fingers however cold and trembling, the hem of His garment (are not His promises His robe, for our touch by faith?), we have indeed boundless mercies still to ask. But we have at once one supreme mercy to give thanks for, because it is possessed, because "we have" it. It is the mercy of Himself for us.

Again and again would I press this home, first on my own soul. Take up, in illustration and application, just one of the "possession" texts quoted above. Look at Ephesians 1:7; "We have the forgiveness of sins." To ask for forgiveness is, from one point of view, the daily duty of the child of God. "Forgive us our trespasses," stands side by side with, "Give us this day our daily bread," as the child's petition at the Father's side. But from another point of view, and in order to the truer and surer use of the petition, it is all-important to affirm often to ourselves that "*we have* redemption through His blood, even the forgiveness of sins." By His most precious sacrifice of peace, by the blood of the Lamb, we, believing, have "received power to become the sons of God" (see John 1:12).

And the sons of God, in that blessed inner sense of sonship, (the sense on which, above all others, Scripture delights to dwell,) who are they? Forgiven sinners, welcomed as such to the life and love of a Father's home. Their wonderful forgiveness is embodied in just this, that they are children at home, assured of home-privileges and home-affections. They are transferred from the court of justice (where they, the guilty, for the sake of the Beloved, have been acquitted) into the palace-home of the grace of God. In that home they are under paternal discipline; they often need paternal forgiveness, and must often ask for it. But they are at home, securely there, welcome there, beloved there. They are the Lord's redeemed ones, in wonderful fact. "They have redemption even the forgiveness of sins." So they are to look in their Father's face, even when they ask their Father's pardon, and to affirm to themselves that, in the deep, antecedent sense, they are forgiven; they are not rebels on trial, but children welcomed home. Will they not ask fatherly pardon in detail with all the deeper tenderness, all the more self-reproach, all the more loyalty of love, because of that wonderful "we have"?

So we may go round the whole circle of the gems strung upon this thread, "we have." Are we wistful and weary over the question of communion with God? Are we mourning over intermittent and cold approaches? Let us reaffirm to ourselves our privilege of approach, our *entrée,* free and welcome, to His very heart: "we have access with confidence" (see Eph. 3:12); "we have entrance into the Holiest" (see Heb. 10:19). Are we longing for a fuller flow of the life of the Lord in our life, for a larger power of His Spirit in our spirit? Let us reaffirm the initial fact that, "having the Son, we have the life" (see 1 John 5:12); "we have the Holy Ghost from God" (see 1 Cor. 6:19). The treasure is here; we have but to get it out, by simple faith, and set it free for use. Are we troubled in any direction, about our souls, our work, our beloved ones? Let us begin every act of petition with that sublimely simple affirmation, "we have such an High Priest."

Is there one reader of these words who dares not yet say that he has "touched the hem" [Matt. 14:36]? Yet for you also it is possible to use this talisman, "we have." You too "have" at least one radiant promise for your own; "Him that cometh to Me I will in no wise cast out" (John 6:37).

39

Living Stones

To whom coming—1 Pet. 2:4

These words stand in a rich and fruitful connection. Peter is showing his disciples some of the great secrets of a growing Christian life. He takes them for granted as alive; therefore he is in earnest that they should grow. He is ambitious for them; he cannot rest in the thought of a stationary or stunted life in them. He must see them grow in personal holiness, grow in love and in strength, grow together in holy fellowship, grow in power to shine for their Lord, winning Him "glory" from those who watch them, and who see what He has done in them.

Two main thoughts appear in this important part of the Apostle's letter. The believers are to grow by larger use of the "word of God, which liveth and abideth forever" (1 Pet. 1:23). First Peter 2:2 says they are to crave for it, and drink it into their young Christian systems, as the milk of life. And they are to grow by perpetual approaches to the Son of God; they are to be always touching Him, always "keeping touch" with Him, that "virtue may go out," always, from Him into them. This is what our brief text is all about. "To whom coming, as unto a Living Stone, ye also, as living stones, are being built up, a spiritual house."

Here we have the Lord called a Living Stone. We note the phrase in passing; it is full of meaning, and it stands alone in the Bible. Often does Scripture call the Lord the Stone, the Rock, setting forth His might, and fixity, and capacity to be at once His people's Foundation to build upon and their Refuge to hide in. Often does it call

Him the Life, the Living One, setting Him forth in all His personal and active qualities of grace and love. Here only do the two thoughts beautifully converge, and we have the Stone, the Rock, the Living. The wonderful Stone has eyes, and lips, and arms, and heart. It lives to welcome, to embrace, to save, to keep. He lives to make alive.

Then, His disciples are described as so many results or repetitions, in their measure, of Him. "Ye also, as living stones." They too are to be, each of them, a stone, sure and steadfast, and living too, with warm and loving life. Individually, each is to be thus strong with His strength, and alive with His life. As a company, they are thus to draw together and cohere, "being builded" together into "a house spiritual," strong with the strength and living with the life of the Cornerstone. Each in himself, and all together, they are to grow in that strength, and to develop in that wonderful life, till the issue is full of glory.

Bright, deep, and full of meaning is the imagery. A living stone, a structure of living stones! What blessings may not flow from that ideal realized? What may not the family become, which numbers only one true living stone among its sons or daughters? What may not the congregation become, which contains a genuine nucleus of members, who, not in name only but in deed, are living stones, and are being builded as such together? The Lord of the spiritual House multiply their number in His mercy; it will be a multiplication which must, in His Name, go on and gather ever fresh materials in from the stones as yet dead which lie around the stones that live.

But now, what is the internal secret of the process to be? How am I to be indeed a living stone, fit to be part of such a structure, in respect of both strength and life? The Apostle gives us a divine prescription, equally simple and adequate, in those three words, "To whom coming." The absolute requisite for such assimilation to the Living Stone is personal spiritual contact with Him. The absolute requisite for a growth in such assimilation is more such contact, continually maintained. We, in our weakness and our death, must come to the Lord in the first place, to touch Him and be saved. And then, we must be ever coming, and coming, and coming again, in the sense of perpetual fresh acts of faith in Him, and reception from Him, all along our life.

For observe that the Apostle's language means just this: coming and coming again to Him. In the Greek, "coming" is expressed not in the past form of the participle, but in the present. It indicates therefore not a coming once done, a completed act, as if it referred only to our initial approach to Him, such as I and perhaps my reader remember, in a definite conversion. It indicates a coming which is always to be done, and done again, a series and process. It points to a use of the Lord which can be illustrated in a measure by our perpetually repeated "comings" to the vital atmosphere around our bodies, to take in its virtues all the day, breath by breath.

Such, O disciple, longing to get more strength in thy soul, and more love along with the strength, must be thy secret; "to Him coming." For renewed applications of His pardoning grace, to Him be coming. For full and happy deliverance from the tyranny of every temptation, to Him be coming. For the perpetually needed patience, purity, self-forgetting serviceableness, to Him be coming. For grace to shine bright and pure for Christ, to Him be coming. For courage to confess His dear name, for skill and will to labor for Him, for inward rest in life and in death, to Him be always coming. And as you come, and come, remember that great promise, to "him that cometh to Me" (John 6:37). There too the words, "him that cometh," represent a present participle in the Greek; "the comer," the man who comes, and comes, and comes again. And not only the first approach, but all the comings that follow, shall never be in vain; "I will in no wise cast him out."

Charlotte Elliott wrote "Just as I am" far on in her Christian life. It was the expression of a sudden and profound conviction that to the last, as at the first, this must be the simple secret for all peace, purity, victory, assurance, hope. In that sense let us too take up the immortal hymn always as our own;

> Just as I am, poor, wretched, blind,
> Sight, riches, healing of the mind,
> Yea, all I need in Thee to find,
>   O Lamb of God, I come.

40

Power from On High

Ye shall receive power, after that the Holy Ghost is come upon you, and ye shall be witnesses unto Me—Acts 1:8

Two slight changes may be made in the wording here, to bring it yet nearer to the Greek: "Ye shall receive power *by the coming of the Holy Ghost upon you;* and ye shall be *my witnesses.*" Thus read, the sacred promise seems to present two additional points of truth. First, the "reception of power" is practically identified with the "coming upon you of the Holy Ghost"; it is not merely its sequel, it is its other side. Then, the "witnesses" are not only, as of course they are, "unto Me"; they are also "mine." They belong to Him to whom they testify. They testify because they belong. They belong that they may testify.

This is the final promise spoken by the Lord Jesus while He yet trod our earth. Another moment, and He was ascending the skies. Truly it is a sacred "last word," meant to be dear to the disciple's heart as well as binding on his faith.

To whom was it spoken? Immediately, to the Eleven. But the after-story of the Acts assures us that through them it was meant for all believers. For in the primitive Christian Church we find all the disciples living as the Lord's witnesses, and we see them all receiving the power and fullness of the Spirit. "*Be ye filled with the Spirit*" (Eph. 5:18) is just as general a precept as, "Be not drunk with wine." "*Show forth the praises of Him* who called you out of darkness into His marvelous light," (1 Peter 2:9) is just as general a precept as, "Abstain from fleshly lusts, which war against the soul" [1 Pet. 2:11].

So to you, dear friend and reader, and to me, as truly as to John and to Peter upon Olivet so long ago, the Lord says, "You shall be my witnesses." We are all called to be good evidence for Jesus. It is our object of existence, as Christians, to be valid proof that Jesus Christ the Lord is real, is good, is the supreme Blessing, is Savior, is God. By word, surely, where God gives us opportunity, and always by life, we are meant to be this. We are saved—to witness. True, His love rests really upon *us;* the saved one is personally dear to Him beyond all words. But out from that center He wills to radiate the light of His love all around. We are loved—to witness, to be witnesses unto Him, to be His witnesses.

Let us be covetous to live that life. Away with a "religion" which *terminates* in the precious gift of personal salvation. Our call is to leave behind us, to shed now around us, some solid evidence for Him who bought us, who joined us to Himself, on purpose that we might help in the expression of His grace and glory to this dark world.

But now, "how shall this thing be?" The Lord implies that it is something wonderful for a sinful man to be one of His witnesses. For He tells us that we need to receive a supernatural Power that we may be so. But then, He tells us that this blessed Power is provided, is accessible, may be received by every true disciple, and that so this wonderful life may be lived by us indeed.

How can it be? "By the coming of the Holy Ghost upon you." By the blessed gift of Pentecost, shed forth from the exalted Savior. Without it (nay, rather without Him, for the Gift is an Eternal Person) we cannot really live the witness-life. But with Him, we can. The thing desired is a life whose conduct and whose testimony shall be such that God can use them for the divine end of glorifying Christ to men. That life cannot be lived on our own resources. But it can be lived in the gracious fullness of the Spirit.

What shall we do in view of such certainties? We will "ask, that we may have." We will take a great promise with us, and, as it were, kneel down on it, as the Muslim kneels down on his prayer-carpet. We will spread under our knees that word, "your Heavenly Father shall give His Holy Spirit to them that ask Him" (see Luke 11:13). And then, we will "ask Him," looking, not at our faith, but at the promise.

As we ask, or ere we ask, we will see that our motive is true. *Why* do we seek the Spirit's special power? Is it to lift *us* to a religious pedestal? Is it that "*my* work," "*my* influence," "*my* character," may be talked about? Take heed. Those thoughts go very near the sin of Simon the Sorcerer, who would fain receive the wonder-power of the Spirit that he might, more than ever, be thought "some great one" (Acts 8:18, 19). Let our one motive be that somehow, through the little lens of our life and word, Jesus may be "great" to hearts around us, while the lens is invisible (as it should be) to those who see through it. Yes, with a humble, simple motive we will kneel down on our "carpet," and ask the fullness of the gift of God. And we will not doubt that, so asked, He "giveth . . . and upbraideth not" [see James 1:5]. The answer may be a crisis, or it may be a process. But it is sure.

How shall we evidence our possession of the sacred "power"? In many ways. For one way, in a great "growth downward," in our own eyes. The fullness of blessing tends naturally to this. Peter, before Pentecost, had a strong element of self-assertion in his character. After Pentecost, who ever saw a trace of it? He was everyone's brother and helper, loving to sympathize and serve, ready to be sent, or to be sent for, just as he was wanted (Acts 8; 9:10).

The man "endued with power from on high" will show it in a strong dominion over self. He will be "sweet at home"; "gentle, easy to be entreated" (see James 3:17), watchful not to "stumble" others, meek and lowly, loyal to every little duty; a *winning* character.

Above all, the evidence, both to himself and to others, will lie in this, that "Christ is all the world to him." The blessed Spirit "takes of the things *of Christ*, and shows them." The man who has the Spirit fully on him will have Christ fully in him, "dwelling in his heart, by faith" (Eph. 3:17). Where He so dwells, He will look out of the window, He will speak from the door. It is the life in which Jesus "cannot be hid" that is the true witness-life for Him, in the power of the Holy Ghost.

41

Fear and Cheer

The night following the Lord stood by him, and said, Be of good cheer—
Acts 23:11

Very memorable and instructive is the *setting* of those last five words (only two words in the Greek). They are the utterance of the Lord Jesus Christ Himself, direct to His servant. Paul was indeed leading the witness-life of which we thought last Sunday. And here comes the Lord to give him His own gracious encouragement in the midst of it: "Thou hast testified of Me in Jerusalem; so must thou bear witness also at Rome." Delightful words are these to study. They remind us that while Paul was speaking on the stairs, Jesus was listening. Every word the servant said about his old unconverted life, and about his conversion, and all his Master's mercies to him, was overheard by the Master (Acts 21:40). The Master loved the witnessing servant, and came the next night to tell him so, and to cheer him on his way. So it is still, in the deep spiritual reality of it. Our poor unworthy words about Him, unworthy, yet spoken because we love Him, are overheard; Jesus is listening. Our sadly imperfect aim and labor to live to Him, to "witness" to Him in a life transformed by His Holy Spirit, is recognized by Him. He loves it, with His most generous love. It is not now His desire to pay us visits which are also visions; yet He has His own way of giving us the joy and power of His spiritual Presence, saying to our inner man, "Be of good cheer, thou shalt witness yet for Me."

But not only are these words memorable; their *setting* is full of divine instruction. "The night following." What night was it? It was the sequel to a very stormy day of Paul's life, and it was succeeded by a day of more silent but still more deadly peril. The day before, his frail body had been nearly "pulled in pieces" (v. 10) by the angry Pharisees and Sadducees in the council; only the prompt action of the Roman commandant had saved him. And "when it was day," (v. 12) next morning, "more than forty" fanatics bound themselves by oath to assassinate him; with excellent prospects of success. Was it not a dark setting? Could any moment have been much more helpless and hopeless, in a life already wearing out with toils and sufferings? Look at this man. He is imprisoned deep in the recesses of the huge Antonia, the great Roman keep which dominated the temple-courts. He has just escaped, with difficulty, from a wild personal outrage. His life is about to be threatened by a large gang of the most dangerous people in the world, religious fanatics, thinking they serve God by murder.

Just then and just there, "the Lord stood by him." Luke, in his majestic simplicity, makes no allusion to the *arrival* of the Lord. No, He simply *was there*, "standing by him." Massive walls, iron bolts, disciplined sentinels—what were they to bar out the King? Wild tumults of the Sanhedrin, merciless plots of the wretched zealots out of doors—what were they to the royal feet of Jesus, as He stepped over them all, and "stood by" the desolate, exhausted man who had confessed Him, and said, "Be of good cheer"?

To Him circumstances are *nothing*, even when the circumstances mean the dungeon, and the power of Rome, and the hatred of the Jews. Jesus transcends all, and "stands by him," (see 2 Tim. 4:17) omnipotent to love, to bless, to keep.

Is there not an abiding parable of promise in this scene? It is not alone in Scripture. A close and glorious parallel is that of John 20, where, "when the doors were shut, for fear of the Jews," and the little company knew not what fierce violence might at any moment burst them in, "Jesus Himself stood in the midst of them, and said unto them, Peace be unto you," (v. 19) and "showed them His hands and His side" (v. 20). "Glad" indeed they were, as John tells us, "when they saw the Lord." And glad assuredly was Paul, when *he* saw the Lord. For the sight was not only the Lord, but the Lord *there*. It was His ineffable Presence in the very midst of awfully adverse circumstances. It was visible proof that not only was He Lord of His servant, but supreme Sovereign of all that could seem most adverse to His servant, and most dreadful; "subduing all things to Himself" (Phil. 3:21).

Thus the scene becomes a parable of promise. It speaks to the believer now, as it has spoken to all believers, ever since that "night following." It places before us not only a Christ Jesus "altogether lovely," (Song 5:16) but indeed also "mighty to save," (Is. 63:1) immeasurably independent of all that appears to crush His people. Do their circumstances find any parable in the walls of Antonia, or in the rage and craft of the unhappy Jews? Are their circumstances actually akin to Paul's, awful dangers, sickening fears, perhaps in some dangerous point of the heathen or Islamic mission-field? Are they circumstances outwardly less dark, but inwardly dreadful to the spirit, in which, whether for himself or others, the Christian is "sore amazed and . . . very heavy" (Mark 14:33), and knows not what to do? Is it anything, known in its bitterness, to the secret heart, which walls life in as with a prison, or seems to attack its love and hopes as with a dagger? Oh remember "the night following," that dark and menacing night, when everything, humanly speaking, was a symbol of despair to a very, very weary and sensitive man, exquisitely susceptible of fear and care. The Lord was there then. The Lord transcended circumstances then. The Lord loved His servant then, and was omnipotent for him, as well as kind. He is the same today; He is the same tonight.

42

Steadfastness and Sympathy

Whom resist, steadfast in the faith; knowing that the same afflictions are accomplished in your brethren which are in the world—1 Pet. 5:9

Here again, as we did two weeks ago, let us make a few changes in the translation. Then we may the better ponder some precious treasures in the message.

"Whom resist, solid in your faith; knowing that the same aspects" (literally the same *things*) "of these afflictions are being carried to their goal for" (in the case of) "your brotherhood in the world."

This rendering, which borders on a paraphrase, accentuates some important matters in the text. "Solid" gives us the thought of "steadfastness" and *something more*. It presents to us the believer, and the believing company, as not only rooted to one position but internally sound and true. No "hollowness reverbs" to the enemy's assault; their heart is fixed, "trusting in the Lord," with a trust real to its depths. Again, "in *your* faith," is, in my opinion, a safer rendering than the more literal one, "in *the* faith." For in the general usage of the Apostles the word *pistis* ("faith") very rarely, if ever, means *the* "faith," in the sense of a creed of sacred truth. It habitually means "faith," in the sense of the personal reliance with which man rests upon God in His promises. Thus we get here the precious message that we, if we would be "solid" against the Adversary (v. 8), who means our utter and eternal ruin, must be so, very simply, "by faith." To be rock-like, we must lean upon the Rock. To be "solid" to the very heart, we must have Christ "dwelling in the heart, *by faith*." It is the old story. Salvation, in all its stages, is by faith. And what, practically, is saving faith? It is—a trusted Christ.

Then further, our new translation brings out a certain delicacy of phrase as to the "sameness" of the afflictions of believers. Peter does not say simply "the same afflictions." He says, precisely, "The same things of the afflictions." This gives us a message very helpful to the troubled heart. We may feel, perhaps quite correctly, "This affliction of mine, in many details, is unique. There cannot be a precise parallel to it in other cases." True indeed, if we insist upon a bare likeness of events or conditions in detail. But Peter leads us rather to see the "sameness" in "the things of the afflictions." He refers to types, and classes, and aspects. He reminds us that somewhere or other in the "brotherhood in the world" there is a Christian who is enduring, and blessedly enduring, not an identical trouble, but a similar *type* of trouble. There is enough sameness thus to tell you that He who is enabling your unknown fellow-pilgrim to "count it all joy" (James 1:2), to say, "It is not worthy to compare with the glory to be revealed in us" (Rom. 8:18), no, "It worketh out a weight of glory" (2 Cor. 4:17), can enable you to say the same.

Again, our new translation brings out the truth that these "afflictions" are not merely "being accomplished," getting to their close, soon to be over. The Greek word gives us the richer and stronger thought that they are being *"carried to their goal,"* by Him who not only permits but overrules. The Lord is leading them up to a result. He is manipulating them for the highest final blessing of His "afflicted" saints. It is not only a *succession;* first "the cross," then "the crown." It is a profound *connection.* The crown is the goal of the process of the cross, the issue of the discipline of trial. "*Les croix sont les marteaux pour forger la couronne.*" "Crosses are hammers for forging the crown." They have everything to do with the crown's adjustment for just *that* brow!

This is no contradiction to the truth of free grace. As to merit, as to title, all is mere and wonderful mercy, the gift of God, the purchase of the Lord Jesus, the Lamb of Calvary, for His people. But as for capacity to receive and to enjoy, it is a matter of discipline, of training, of processes "carried to their goal," by the Hand, strong and patient, which makes no mistakes.

Then, lastly, this is being done "for your brotherhood in the world." That thought is all-important for us in getting the full blessing of this message. Think what it is meant to do for the afflicted believer's soul. First, it is to carry him out, a very long way out, of himself, even all over the world. In soul, he is to circumnavigate the globe, to penetrate its continents, to visit innumerable hearts and homes, with the thought, "This is my world-wide brotherhood." Under a million differences of place, scene, history, language, character, there is this wonderful oneness; these believers in Jesus are all brothers and sisters; they are "the brotherhood." The troubled heart may reap a sweet blessing from the mere act of that excursion. It will breathe a grand open air. It will go out in love to the countless "brethren," each with his burden and his staff. In that measure, it will forget itself, and rest. But then, from the excursion it will delightfully come home, revived and strong. With new courage it will take up its own share of "the afflictions" again. Things at home will be seen under a nobler, happier, holier light for that sight of the kindred "things of others," the others who are "one, in Christ Jesus" (Gal. 3:28).

It is Sunday morning. The glory of the Sabbath sun, zone after zone, is stealing around the world. Let us "take the wings of the morning," and visit especially today "the brotherhood in the world." In love, in spirit, let us see the faces, and hear the voices, and watch "the types of afflictions carried to their goal." Our own Sabbath will be all the brighter, and it will last us all the week.

43

Like a Weaned Child

Surely I have behaved and quieted myself, as a child that is weaned of his mother: my soul is even as a weaned child—Ps. 131:2

This little "Psalm of Degrees," or "of Ascents," is one of the sweetest and most tender utterances of faith in the whole Old Testament. From the first of its few words to the last it is the voice of the child of God, deep at rest in the Father's mother-like arms, and only looking outward to say to others, to Israel, just at the end, "hope in the Lord." As if the thought were, "Here am I, in the place of peace; it is a good place; the peace passeth understanding; dear brethren, dear fellow-pilgrim, you cannot too simply, nor too long, trust the Giver of that peace."

Let us look a little closer at this happy witness to the deep and blissful content to be found within the mighty hands of God. This possessor of repose indicates to us, in a very instructive way, certain conditions of that repose, which have suggestions of their own for us, full at once of heart-searching and of love. We observe at once an allusion to a state which has preceded the present sacred happiness; "I have stilled and quieted my soul." So the soul, with its consciousness, its emotions, its depths and currents of feeling, had *needed* stilling and quieting. It had been in agitation. A storm had swept it, with a tumult, with strong crying. The present calm had come on by way of a contrast; in some wonderful way, the unrest had heard a voice saying, "Peace, be still," and had obeyed. The quiet was quiet heightened by the reminiscence of distress.

135

Still further, we find an indication of the kind of disturbance which had come—and gone. This is given us in that exquisitely tender simile, "like a weaned child." The trouble of the weaned child is the trouble of a deprivation; the loss, the unexplained loss, for it is too young to understand explanations, of the sacred sustenance of its newborn life. It is the pain and grief of "*having to do without.*" And the stillness and the quiet, the silent rest, "the low beginnings of content," are the results and symptoms of "*learning to do without.*"

Here is a simple but very fruitful lesson for you and me, Christian reader. Very various are life's troubles, BUT a large class under that large variety comes to just this, the troubles occasioned by "having to do without." They meet us everywhere. They range from the lightest, the smallest, to the deepest and most dark. Quite possibly your example of the species just now may be a thing in itself very small. It may be the call to do without some innocent pleasure of the hour, an eagerly expected but frustrated holiday, or interview, or visit, or the like. It may be some looked-for letter which the postman will not bring. It may be the schoolboy's, or schoolgirl's, missing of the prize; a pain to parents as well as child.

But then it may be something very much graver, in kind and in results. Perhaps you have to "do without" health. Some mischief of our mortality has touched you, and you cannot get well. The spring and buoyancy of life are gone, and there has come to you, perhaps, in the place of them, the presence of a stern incessant pain, or, what some sufferers know to be even worse, an incessant exhaustion, a chronic inward failure. It seems but yesterday that your step was strong, and your spirits young; today you have, for the season at least, to "do without."

Perhaps you have to "do without" scenes and surroundings so dear that they seemed to be part of your heart. Your old landscape is in sight no more. If you went now to the familiar and beloved door, you would have to ring the bell.

> Children not thine have trod my nursery floor,

says the orphan poet to "his Mother's Picture"; realizing afresh what it is to have to "do without" the dear scenes which cradled life in their love and beauty.

And for William Cowper, it was not the nursery, after all, but the mother that it was so hard to have to "do without." His immortal Elegy over that precious portrait does but put into perfect words the unutterable sighs of numberless hearts which have tasted deep of bereavement. You know all about it, you, dear orphan child, and you, childless parent, and you, widowed wife or husband in your desolation, and you, O friend, to whom the world can never be the same since you have had to "do without" that "half of your soul in the other body." Already upon you all has come the skirt of the great shadow, or rather, perhaps, the heaviest folds of it are wrapped about your heads. You are called to a sore and heavy experience of this mysterious "weaning," this having to "do without."

Beloved friends, experienced in loss, may I point you, with a sort of silence, (for print is very quiet), to the loss-stricken Psalmist's testimony? Do we not gather that he had just been called to some mysterious trial, akin to yours, and was just learning to be quiet about it, not to "exercise himself in great matters," seeking to look behind the holy will of God, and to understand it all before the time? He was just getting a glimpse of the secret blessedness to be found, under certain divine conditions, in "learning to do without." He was tasting a strange sweetness in the cup of grief. Falling back quite simply on a Father's love in the unexplained sorrow, he found himself, he knew not how, getting to rest; not to sleep, but to rest; a rest out of which he could say to others, like one who had *a right* to say it, "Let Israel, hope in the Lord" [Ps. 130:7; 131:3].

One little touch of suggestion tells us where the secret of the blessed change was to be found. He compares his soul to a child weaned, not "*from*," but "WITH his mother." The loss is there. The joy is taken away, and he must do without it. But the *parent* is there, more profoundly, more fondly, loving than ever. And that is a guarantee that ultimate happiness lies deep within the sorrow; nay, it has begun already, in the simple consciousness of the beloved presence. And even so it is with the "weaned" mourners and their God. "As one whom his mother comforteth, so will I comfort you" (Is. 66:13).

44

City and Paradise in One

In the midst of the street of the city . . . was there the tree of life—Rev. 22:2

Let us look upward this Lord's Day, even as we did on one of our September Sundays, and by faith, in the light of Scripture, "behold the glory to be revealed." It is both sweet and serviceable, in our Sabbath hours on earth, to ponder the revealed conditions of that long and happy Sabbath-keeping which awaits us, when we shall rest forever from all sin, and all sorrow, and all distress and failure in our service, and from all that is unworthy in our worship, but shall never rest from the delight of serving, and from the solemn joy of worshiping.

So we look through the telescope of this text today, and take an observation of the heavenly life. Behold it, as the Seer sets it before us. It is a double glory. It is a life lived in a City. It is a life lived in a Garden. And the two radiant aspects are blended wonderfully into one.

(1) The heavenly life is a life lived in a City. The Bible closes with the gorgeous vision of a city, "God's great town in the unknown land." Here and there, all along the pages of the divine Book, intimations and preparations for this have appeared. In the Psalms and in the Prophets we have words spoken about "the city of the Lord," which surely transcend in their tone and phrase the mere earthly Jerusalem, and point to an eternal object, a Jerusalem whose walls and bulwarks are salvation, and whose gates are praise (Ps. 87; Is. 33:20). Then come the Apostles, and they tell the believer that he is "fellow-citizen with the saints"; that his "city-home is in the heavens"; (so I would render Phil. 3:20); that already, in spirit, he has "come

unto the city of the living God, the heavenly Jerusalem" (Heb. 12:22); that his Lord will hereafter "write upon him the name" (Rev. 3:12) of that fair place, making him to be, legibly and actually, all that a citizen of the blessed Zion in idea is. So we ascend step by step to the final scene. It opens, and we see "that great city," "the Bride, the Lamb's wife," with the gem-foundations, and the street of crystal gold, and the gates of pearl. Therein is no night, nor tears, nor pain, nor anything that defiles, nor one place more sacred than another; "I saw no temple therein, for the Lord God Almighty and the Lamb are the temple of it" (Rev. 21:22). The eternal Presence makes it all one sanctuary.

None the less it is *a City*, vast and populous. Its inhabitants are "nations" (21:24). It overflows with human life, life glorified and immortal, but none the less human life. All of good which we associate with the thought of a city has there its fullness and its work. It is a scene of supreme organized order; "*the throne* of God and of the Lamb shall be in it" (22:3); all the innumerable circles of the multifold society move in perfect regulation and harmony around that blessed Center. It is a capital point, where are concentrated together all the splendors, all the dignities, which associate themselves with the idea of a city which is not only great in scale but metropolitan in position. Who does not know the indefinable distinction which attaches to *the* city of a country, the place which is the seat of government, the summit of society, the natural headquarters of thought and action? This "great city, the holy Jerusalem," is "the city of the great King." It is also a city of kings; "His servants shall serve Him, and they *shall reign* forever and ever" (22:3, 5). We know little as yet of the arena and the conditions of those kingships under the King Eternal. But may we not be sure that the citizen-kings of heaven will have real and far-extended functions to exercise in their eternal service? "Have thou authority over ten cities" (Luke 19:17).

So the great vision sets the civic aspect of glory before us. To be sure, it does so in symbol, in hieroglyphic; we are not to press the gems and gold into literal interpretations. None the less, the things signified by those hieroglyphics are signified truly. They are what they are indicated to be. The life of Heaven *is a city life*, a scene and state in which human beings in numbers numberless live, converse, cooperate, govern and are governed, and experience all the countless influences which members of a community exercise on one another, and always under the blissful conditions of the absence of sin, decay, and death. That civic life has assuredly its events, its history. It has its infinitely varying experiences of love and tenderness. It unites its members, all of them individual forever, in the common joy and work of the service of their King.

(2) Meanwhile, the life which on one side is a City, on the other side is a Paradise. Compare Revelation 22:2 with Revelation 2:7. "The tree of life," says the Lord to the angel of Ephesus, is "in the midst of the paradise of God." "The tree of life," says the Apostle in this last vision, is "in the midst of the street of it, and on either side of the river"; "*the tree*," that is, in this place, no doubt (by a Hebrew usage), "*the trees*," the bowers and avenues of trees all belonging to the one celestial sort.

We need not dwell on this aspect of the picture; our previous meditation on the Intermediate State makes this unnecessary. But we may at least remember that we have here a beautiful symbol of the assurance that out of that holy city and its life will be forever banished all that defaces and defiles the cities of time. No deformity shall mar the scene; there shall be no place for want and vice. The life, with all its metropolitan dignity, order, and force, shall be forever pure, sweet, and beautiful, with the fruit and the foliage of the Paradise in which God shall walk with men.

45

The Spirit against the Flesh

The flesh lusteth against the Spirit, and the Spirit against the flesh—
Gal. 5:17

Here is a message full of divine encouragement. It can prove a perfect mine of treasure to the heart of the believer, conscious of spiritual conflict, and longing for a victory which shall be victory indeed. It is no fiction, but a bright and strong experience, that this short utterance can even make a spiritual crisis, and send the Christian on his way with a lasting accession of conscious peace and power.

But is it so indeed? Quite possibly the reader asks the question with a genuine sense of surprise and doubt. Surely this text is precisely one of the Scriptures which speaks most distinctly of a conflict in the soul. Scarcely does Romans 7 lead us more directly than this short verse to the consideration of the presence of discordant elements, or conditions, in the life of the regenerate man. Is it not a witness to the fact that "the flesh" is present always in the disciple, be he who he may, be he the oldest and most experienced of saints? And is not "the flesh," in the inspired vocabulary of Paul, no mere synonym for the body, as if it meant merely that in us which feels fatigue, and decay, and death? Is it not that aspect or element of our being which "is not subject to the law of God, neither indeed can be" (Rom. 8:7)? Is it not well said that its best popular equivalent is the word "self"? And, if so, is not the passage good Scriptural evidence that the Christian is deluded if he ever allows himself to say, "I have come to the end of myself"? Does it not warn him that he must reckon with the presence of that peril, "self," even to the end

141

of his chapter here on earth, yea, till he "receives the adoption, to wit, the redemption of his body" (see Rom. 8:23)? As surely as world and devil have to be treated, to the last, as present enemies, must we not so treat "the flesh" as well?

It is so. To everyone of these successive questions, in all conviction and solemnity, we answer, Yes. The Apostle's words are clear in their reference. He is writing to regenerate believers as such, to Christians as Christians. He gives not one hint that he is viewing them here as in a lower stage of divine endowment than need be. And he bids them all remember, as a factor in their spiritual condition, that "the flesh lusteth," desireth, liketh, tendeth, "against the Spirit."

But, then, another aspect of the passage has to be remembered. We first note that it contains also the words, "the Spirit lusteth against the flesh." We have next to note that this is the main, leading, ruling assertion; it is on this, not on the other and opposite side of things, that Paul lays stress. The whole context proves this; for the Apostle's obvious purpose all through it is to bring his readers into the secret of a life of liberty and holiness. "Walk in the Spirit" (Gal. 5:16), he has just written, "and ye shall not fulfill the lust of the flesh"; and he couches that last promise, in the Greek, in a specially energetic form; "you shall not fulfill them, *you shall not indeed*," would be a fair paraphrase. Then, lastly, we take careful notice that "the Spirit" here is not the spirit of man, but the Spirit of God dwelling in the believing disciple. This is abundantly clear again from the context. You have but to read from verse 16 to the end of the chapter and you will see that it is the Holy Spirit who is in view throughout. Compare verse 18 with Romans 8:14: "If ye be *led of the Spirit,* ye are not under the law"; "As many as are *led by the Spirit of God,* they are the sons of God."

Now therefore, is there not ground for saying that in this utterance upon the flesh and the Spirit, we have "everlasting comfort and good hope through grace"? Here is no mere affirmation that there must be a conflict. Here is rather a grand assurance that with, and in, the true Christian, resides the secret which can transform that conflict into a continuous victory, and more than victory.

Is "the flesh" present with you, and is it a strong enemy? Yes, but it is equally true that the Holy Spirit is present with you, dwelling within you, and He (not it, but He) is an almighty Friend, "stronger

142

than the strong." Does "the flesh" lust against the Spirit? Yes. But then, with all His divine antagonism to evil, the Spirit, dwelling in you, "lusteth against the flesh." His eternal "tendency," personal and intense, is "against the flesh." What chameleon aspect is "the flesh" in *you* taking? Is it felt as vanity, as pride, as defiled desire, as wrath and jealousy, as untruthfulness, unfaithfulness, unkindness? Is it masked as sloth, as greed, as anything which contradicts the life of love and the life of temperance in Christ? Remember, against all and several of these iniquities, "the Spirit lusteth." And He is in you, templed in your being, the gift of God in Christ, divinely set in profound contact with you. You need not *ask* Him to "lust against" your sin; He does so, as only the Lord can do. But you can, calling upon God, open your spirit to the eternal Spirit, place yourself, as it were, deliberately and consciously in the path of that mighty "tendency," give yourself to be borne along in sympathy with Him. And so He in you, and you in Him, shall be conqueror indeed. A force not your own shall lift you into a lasting victory, with your foot upon the foe. Led by the Spirit, you shall "mortify the deeds of the body," (Rom. 8:13) and "walk at liberty, seeking Thy precepts" (see Ps. 119:45).

46

As for Me

As for me—Josh. 24:15

This short phrase occurs again and again in Scripture. "As for me, I" (unlike the enemies of God) "will come into Thy house, in the multitude of Thy mercy" (Ps. 5:7). "As for me, I" (unlike those whose portion is in this life) "will behold Thy face in righteousness" (Ps. 17:15). We might add to such quotation many others where the same or similar Hebrew occurs, but is otherwise rendered in the King James Version. Such a passage is Psalm 73:28, where it could be rendered, "As for me, nearness to God for me is good." Others may, if they will, go wandering from Him, devoting themselves to the world, to self, to sin, as their life and choice. My preference and resolve are otherwise. "Nearness to God for me is good."

The phrase thus tends to put before us a certain contrast and separation. The speaker places himself, in some respects, aside and apart. He looks around him, and sees other men following this or that line of thought and action. Their numbers are large. Their action, their spirit and sentiment, have all the weight and force of a fashion, perhaps of a well-nigh universal fashion. He cannot help it. He must take another line. However singular he may make himself, so must it be. "As for me," I will serve the Lord; I will come into His house; I will behold His face; I will keep close to Him.

It was precisely in this spirit, we remember, that Joshua spoke the "as for me" which stands at the head of this chapter. There, at Shechem, the old leader of Israel sat, in the quiet power of faith, looking the nation in the face. He put before them the problems of loyalty to Jehovah, and of the obligations of that loyalty. He challenged them to a choice, which choice must be their own; not even Joshua could make it for them. Would they be the true worshipers and vassals of the Lord? Or would they prefer the service of Baal, or of Chemosh? "Choose you this day whom you will serve" (v. 15). Quite conceivably they might waver in their choice, even then, as all too certainly and sadly they not only wavered but broke away from their Redeemer in the next generations, till in Gideon's youth we find that, in Ophrah anywise, it was a capital crime to deny Baal (Judg. 6:30)! But whatever the nation of Israel might do, Joshua's choice was made. "As for me and my house, we will serve the Lord."

Those words have had a long and active life. Not only are they enshrined imperishably in the Book of God: they are frequently to be seen as a watchword in our modern homes, amidst the stir and movement of our life today, inscribed perhaps on plaque or framed tablet, and hung where the visitor cannot help seeing them, in an entrance hall, in a dining-room, or where not: "As for me and my house, we will serve the Lord." The way of the world may run otherwise, and my choice may be out of the mode altogether. It does not matter; this is my choice; "we will serve the Lord." Happy the house where that motto is realized in the household life. And happy the heart and character where it lies deep at the springs of individual thought and action, everyday.

Need we remind ourselves what "as for me" should *not* mean? Never for a moment is the Christian called to isolation, peculiarity, opposition, *for their own sake.* "Let every one of us *please his neighbor* for his good to edification" (Rom. 15:2). It is the believer's business to be the most considerate, sympathetic, courteous, and companionable of people, within the lines of the will of God. Let this be well remembered, with reflection, and sanctified good sense, and prayer. Otherwise, we may be merely disagreeable, and mistake this for fidelity to principle. We may be justly avoided for our own sakes, and think that this is "bearing the reproach of Christ," and "going forth to Him without the camp" (see Heb. 13:13).

But when all this is said, how great and sacred is the place in our hearts and wills which must be kept for "as for me!" Considerateness and sympathy are as different as possible from drift and compromise. They should be, and often are, most conspicuous in lives which are all the while governed absolutely by personal surrender to the will of God, such surrender as can lay quietly down at His feet all that is most cherished in reputation and ease, when it comes to a real alternative between Him and the world. By His grace, let us write such an "as for me" large and legible upon our hearts. Let fashions of thought and practice go as they will. Let a whole society, a whole period, drift into indifference to His Word, His Worship, His Day. Let even those who bear His name ignore His express commands as to common duty, personal self-discipline of habits, careless use of the tongue, and such-like things. Let it be out of fashion in even well-meaning circles to witness definitely for Christ, to seek the genuine conversion of souls, to labor for the extension of the gospel kingdom. "As for me," it must be otherwise. Without the least trumpet flourish, I must take another line. I am not my brethren's judge. But I am my Master's servant.

47

Notwithstanding, the Lord

Notwithstanding, the Lord—2 Tim. 4:17

These words are broken out of the record of the last known incident in the life of Paul. He is writing to his dear Timotheus, from the Roman dungeon which was now soon to give him up to execution. He has much to say, of the Church, the gospel, the eternal life, and also of the sorrows of the human heart. The criticism, ponderous yet shallow, which can question the Pauline genuineness of this Epistle, has first to ignore the fact that the pages come to us almost wet with the tears of a loving soul, pierced to its depths by grief; and such matters did not lie much in the line of fabrications in the second century.

But now, last among these many things, Paul lets in the light upon his trial at the Roman bar. We gather that the letter was dated between two stages of the process. There had been a "first answer," (2 Tim. 4:16) and then came a *comperindinatio,* an adjournment before the next. Of that second "answer" we know nothing now, except through the eloquence of the grave. But of this first we know that it was seized by the accused as an occasion for one more proclamation of his Lord, so delivered that all the hall could hear. "By me the preaching might be fully known, so that all the Gentiles might hear" (2 Tim. 4:17).

Would that we were told how he there struck the theme of Christ, and developed its glory! Never at Athens, surely, nor Caesarea, nor Jerusalem, was Paul more magnificently himself. But he had to act against tremendous odds; "no man stood with me; all men forsook

147

me; I pray God it may not be laid to their charge" [v. 16]. No, in the terror of that time, when to be a Christian was to pass for atheist and anarchist, no one cared to hold a brief for this leader of the abominated sect, and he had to plead alone. Ah, but not alone. Then, yet once more, he tells us, the Presence came, and overshadowed him. "Notwithstanding, the Lord stood by me"; "notwithstanding, the Lord."

The great martyr's experience has repeated itself in all the ages. For the Person who caused it is the same yesterday and also, blessed be His name, today. Just lately a missionary friend, from the remote western region of China, was recounting to me the last scenes of the missionary massacres of 1900 in Shan-si, in China. There a whole family, Mr. and Mrs. Pigott, and their dear child, dragged to the provincial capital, were led out one after another in public, and slain with the sword. To the last, on the road and in the city, Mr. Pigott "made the preaching known," to the unfeigned amazement of "the Gentiles." "What, will you say this now, when you will die for saying it tomorrow?" But his secret was that of Paul; "Notwithstanding, the Lord."

In that same lurid summer a missionary lady, Mrs. Atwater, loving her work, her neighbors, her scholars, her husband, happy in her noble calling, found herself confronted with death. She wrote fragmentary letters, one by one, and gave them to native friends, who, after her martyrdom, got them to the coast. Some sentences in those letters may well be inscribed as margins to the text of the Apostle:

> I am preparing for the end, very quietly and calmly. The Lord is wonderfully near, and He will not fail me. I was restless and excited when there seemed a chance of life, but God has taken away that feeling. The pain will soon be over, and O the sweetness of the welcome above! I cannot imagine the Savior's welcome.

"No man stood with them; notwithstanding, the Lord."

It is well for us thus to recollect that the ancient victories of faith repeat themselves today. Our Christian life is in many respects so traditionally easy that it is in grave risk of becoming merely routine. And at the heart of a perfunctory religion there sets in, only too often, the mortification of unbelief. But then comes across our view some glorious example of sacrifice, of suffering, in the Lord's name, bearing His inimitable impress. And it tells us, among other things, that supreme thing, that He liveth. "*Son culte se rajeunira sans cesse*"—"His worship shall renew its youth forever," said poor Renan, out of his profound agnosticism. It is even so, and in a sense which Renan could not know. He thought only of an idyllic memory, the Galilean peasant-prophet. We adore the Son of God, who liveth and abideth forever. He "renews His youth forever" in His true followers, living in them. "Notwithstanding, the Lord."

It may seem a sort of anti-climax to come from the martyrs of Rome, and of China, to the level of our common life. But it is not really so. The truest training for "some great thing" for God comes through fidelity to Him in the next little thing. And *full* fidelity to God in ordinary life is a thing which demands for its achievement nothing less than the secret of the saints, "notwithstanding, the Lord."

For this the glorious annals of holy suffering are given us. Not only, not most, to win our loving wonder for the sufferers; still less to set us upon imagining how we ourselves, in their circumstances, might show their spirit; such thoughts are much more likely to weaken than to brace the true courage of the soul. No, the supreme lesson of these scenes is another. It is the lesson of the sufficiency of Jesus Christ, in *all* the necessities of His people.

> I ask them whence their victory came;
>   They with united breath,
> Ascribe their conquest to the Lamb,
>   Their triumph to His death.

The witness of the saints is all to Him. Everything in them, as well as around them, would have failed and forsaken them. "Notwithstanding, the Lord." Their glory is to accentuate His Name. They will "see of the travail of their souls" [see Is. 53:11], if they can but write this large for us in their sacred life-blood, "Notwithstanding, the Lord."

We in England today are threatened neither by a Roman Nero nor by an Oriental Empress-Dowager. But we *are* threatened, day and hour, by all the forces of that darkness into which it is more awful to be led away than to follow the King of Saints to any Calvary outside the gate. Around us are the powers of the Triple Alliance of the pit [ed. The Triple Alliance was a pre-World War I European military alliance consisting of Germany, Austria-Hungary and Italy]. Within us is the weakness of the sometimes bewildered mind, the poor ambiguous will, the listening, the parley, the silent invitation to the tempter to come in. And no man can redeem his brother from such hours. And before the crudest temptation, often, the finest culture, the largest knowledge, the most endearing ties, the pleading of even maternal love, can fly like dust in the wind.

But the Friend of the Martyrs *is* adequate to be the Law, Liberty, Safety, Victory, of His tempted follower. Nothing else, nothing less, will ultimately do for our deliverance and our purity in the common day. But Christ is might as well as right. "Notwithstanding, the Lord."

48

Strangers and Pilgrims

Dearly beloved, I beseech you as strangers and pilgrims, abstain from fleshly lusts, which war against the soul—1 Pet. 2:11

We are fast approaching the close and death of another year. "A few more Sabbaths" now, a very few, "will cheer us on our way," and the way will have passed out of "the dear old year, the good old time," into another period. The thoughts stirred in the soul by such a recollection are familiar and old-fashioned. But the fashion is old because it concerns the most abiding facts of human life. The thoughts are familiar because they meet the heart not of some men only, but of all men who can think and feel. This mystery of time, these incessant reminders that we are always and inevitably on the move, towards a certain but unseen goal, that:

> All things are taken from us, and become
> Portions and parcels of the dreadful past;

that we are dying men in a dissolving world; all this is commonplace indeed. But it is everlastingly significant and impressive. Time, transition, death, "and then that vast Forever"—a million reiterations can never make these things trivial to the soul.

This is a fitting time to listen to Peter, as he comes to us with his First Epistle, his "Letter of Hope," and talks to us, in his own peculiarly gentle and brotherlike way, about time and our passage through it. Let us give him good heed. He is the Lord's own accredited messenger; he brings us a message whose every word is endorsed by his Master. He is also an old man, who has lived many years since he was the eager youth of John 21, "girding himself, and going whither he would" (see vv. 7, 18). He has long "kept watch o'er man's mortality." He speaks to us about time, with both the knowledge and the sympathy which only time can teach.

"Dearly beloved, I beseech you." The words are winning. The old Apostle might, I suppose, take another tone if he chose; he might say, "I am the bearer of Christ's commission of authority; I am inspired to speak Christ's words; I bid you listen, at your peril." But he does not choose to speak so. He, once the man of self-confident assertions, is now meek and lowly of heart, having found so much of his Lord's tenderness in his own case. So he prefers to say that he loves us, and has come to beseech us.

The thing which he has in mind as he thus beseeches is a great thing. "Abstain from fleshly lusts"; that is to say, from "desires," impulses, cravings, prompted by "the flesh"; that is to say, by that in us which is not subject to the Spirit of God. Such desires may be for things bad and gross. They may be, quite as possibly, for things pure and good, *but which will usurp God's place in our hearts*. In either case, if you see the danger, "abstain." Do not trifle, do not parley, but abstain. Keep your hands off, and your eyes, and your thoughts. These things are part of an enemy's strategy. They "war against the soul." There is nothing for it but to abstain. Peter "beseeches" us to abstain.

But now, he addresses us in a special character, to persuade us the better. "I beseech you *as strangers and pilgrims*"; as "outlanders and temporary residents," if we may give a more modern rendering. He assumes us to be Christians indeed, who have "believed through grace" [Acts 18:27], and who now belong to the Lord, and are "joined to Him." As such, we are this; strangers and pilgrims. That thought is to make us the more easily, the more naturally, and with the more resolve, abstain. It is to be a detaching thought; for the "fleshly lusts" belong to the scene around us only, and to that scene we do not really belong. It is to be an uplifting thought; for not only do we not belong to this scene—we do belong to another.

This last is the distinctive note of the words, "strangers and pilgrims." In exposure to "change and decay" the man of this world and the Christian are just on the same footing. The worldling is just as much a passer-on as the saint. He can count just as little upon the permanence of his home, his happiness, the objects of his affections. The tree on which *his* nest is built is "marked to come down," as much as any other. But to the Christian believer there is this immense difference. He is not merely a passer-on, uncertain of tomorrow. He belongs elsewhere. He is a passenger, to a definite point. "He seeks a country," (see Heb. 11:14) not in a blind, uncertain sense, but as the good ship "seeks" a distant shore, with chart and compass which can guide her straight to its unseen haven. He is an "outlander," because he belongs to a greater, an eternal, Empire. He is a temporary resident, it would not suit him to be permanent, because his "city-home is in the heavens" (Phil. 3:20).

> We've no abiding city here;
>   We seek a city out of sight;
> Zion its name; the Lord is there;
>   It shines with everlasting light.

Both for Peter's immediate purpose, that we may "abstain from fleshly lusts," and for the whole purpose of our Christian life, let us often clasp to our hearts those words, "as strangers and pilgrims." Interpreted correctly, they are a glorious inspiration to a life, here on earth, amidst the things present, which shall be one long faithful course of love, duty, service. Their *negative* message will detach us, in heart and sympathy, not from earth, but from earthliness. Their *positive* message will attach us, in a way which can lift and mold, here and now, our whole character, to the eternal home, the city of the saints, the city of the King.

"Strangers and pilgrims." Read in their true reference, the words are full to overflowing of the blessed prospect of resting and abiding forever. They point upward, to where those who go in "go no more out" (Rev. 3:12). Let us welcome them, at this solemn season, deep into our souls. So we shall be the fitter for today, because of tomorrow. We shall find ourselves the more fully ready for earth's working hours, because we belong elsewhere, because "our city-home is in the heavens."

49

The Restorer of Lost Years

I will restore to you the years that the locust hath eaten—Joel 2:25

Another Lord's Day of the closing year is upon us. Let us welcome as our visitor today, in this quiet hour, one of "the holy prophets," by whom the Spirit spoke of old, and still speaks even to the end.

Joel has had much to say about a vast incursion of locusts, the terror of the pastoral and agricultural East. We will not discuss here, what the expositors have debated at great length, whether Joel's locusts are literal or figurative; some have held them to be only a figure for locust-like "armies of aliens," invading the land of the Lord. That question does not affect our simple study today. Whatever the locusts were in the prophet's vision, whatever sort of mischief they had done, "eating up the years," the promise stands unaffected by that inquiry. The Lord undertakes that the mischief, whatever it was, shall be repaired. "I will restore unto you the years that the locust hath eaten." Whether the invaders were the insect devourers of grass, and leaf, and grain, or whether they were the human devourers of life, and hearth, and home, and state, the All-Sufficient Lord, in wrath remembering mercy, would "restore the years." There should be overflowing fertility in the fields, making the tiller's losses more than good. Or there should be a renewal of peace, order, and population, such as had never been before. He who had struck would heal, giving yet better health. He who had cast down would build the ruins again, into a nobler structure.

Without hesitation we may transfer this promise to the sphere of the heart and soul, and claim it for every member of "the Israel of God" (Gal. 6:16). The history of old Israel is, as was said long ago, a vast cartoon of the human heart and its story, above all, of the human heart as the subject of the grace of God, the field in which "the flesh lusteth against the Spirit, and the Spirit against the flesh" (Gal. 5:17).

So here, the locusts stand for all which, in the Christian's life, invades and wastes; the foes to peace and strength which, on the one hand, we have treacherously invited in, or which on the other hand the Lord has permitted or enjoined to afflict us in chastening pain. Is the Christian conscious of such incursions and distresses? Are they such as to make him sometimes think that he is rejected and forgotten? Nay; if he will but "turn to Him that smiteth" (see Is. 9:13) him, there shall be a blessed contrast yet. "I will restore to you the years."

What has the locust been in your case, dear friend and reader? If your "years" have lately seemed bare and fruitless for the Lord, what does conscience denote as the cause? If this past year, perhaps, has been such, a year which you cannot help contrasting with the green and prosperous landscape of some previous years of your converted life, how has it come about? Seldom, if we seriously take the question up, shall we fail of an answer. I remember a time in my own life when a year of rich and well-remembered blessing, deep and solid, was followed by a very "lean" year, sadly cold and barren. And I am perfectly conscious that the immediate cause was an undue, self-chosen, self-indulgent, devotion of time to a certain mental interest, perfectly pure and good in itself, but *out of keeping with God's work for me just at that season*. It so possessed the mind and interests that not only did prayer and Bible-study suffer, but the common duties of life received a less thorough attention than was right. And so, conscious love to Christ waned, and with it, inevitably, love to the souls of others. And many a secret advantage did the Tempter take, when he found that "the Prince Emmanuel" was not in full residence in "*the castle*" of "Mansoul." It was a year that the locusts settled upon; the locusts of sin, and then of chastening trouble.

But each heart must answer its own questions here. There are many species of the genus locust. There is greed of earthly gain, or of human applause. There is too keen an appetite for mere comfort, and for the avoidance of toil and pain, physical, moral, or mental. There is unfaithfulness in trusts, little or great. There is a fatal license to eyes, ears, imaginations, all too ready to trifle with sin. There is cowardice in confession of Christ. There is neglect of secret communion with God. There is slackness about His public worship, and His holy day. There is—let the reader, if need be, fill up the blank with just his own heart's answer.

What shall we do? Anything but despair. Humiliation is one thing; despondency, discouragement, is totally another thing. Humiliation let us covet, pray for, embrace. Despondency let us bid begone, in the Lord's name, so long as the Lord lives. With penitent but quite hopeful eyes, let us "look *again*" (Jon. 2:4) to Him who can "restore the years." When His Israel, when His Israelite, so turns and looks, "He delighteth in mercy" (Mic. 7:18). It shall be no grudging pardon, nor an abortive restoration. He will "restore the years."

True, there is a sense in which not even the Eternal can reverse a past fact, not because He is weak, but because He is one with His laws of being. What I did yesterday is forever done; a thought of untold solemnity. But the Eternal can so deal with us, in view of things done, as to transfigure our repentance into a perfect fountainhead of new blessings. It was so with Peter. Fearful was the locust-death of his religious life on the night of the denial. But the Lord, who brought him back to His feet for an absolute renewal, "restored the years," and that in such a sense that Peter rose to a height of loving humbleness and unwearied working love which he had never known before. Let us "look again." He will, for us also, "restore the years."

May we not lawfully apply the promise also to those sorrows of life which are less directly connected with sin? Have the locusts of time, change, decay, bereavement, "eaten the years" for you? Fear not. The future is all in the Restorer's hands, and it is full of His resources for restoration. Wait till "the things not seen" are unveiled. They will contain infinite surprises of recovery, renewal, reunion, as He, in heaven, "restores the years."

50

Abounding in Hope

Now the God of hope fill you with all joy and peace in believing, that ye may abound in hope, through the power of the Holy Ghost—Rom. 15:13

"Change and decay in all around I see." Such is the articulate sigh of many a heart, as life moves on and the years hasten to their end. Few readers of these lines can look back upon the now expiring year and see no special illustration of the mournful verse brought home by it to their own hearts. For my own part, as I review the months, they seem full of such messages, particularly in the death-roll of beloved friends. At least five dear lives which were much to my life have passed out of sight this year, and with them have gone many, less near to me, but known and honored, leaving blanks through which a little more of the cold outer air of "change and decay" blows in. Nor has death only been at work. Changes of many a sort, public, private, personal, social, have all contributed to the pathetic minor music of mortal life. And I am but a specimen of mankind in this.

How delightful it is to turn from such recollections to "the Book of Hope"! Amidst the many designations of the blessed Scriptures, I know none more beautiful, none more true, than this, "the Book of Hope." About the Bible there is everything that is grave, there is nothing that is melancholy. I mean, of course, nothing in its distinctive message. It speaks of the most melancholy of all things, sin, as no other voice of book has ever spoken. But it speaks of it not in despair or in bewilderment, but to unveil its infinitely glorious remedy in Christ. It speaks of death, but to "bring life and immortality to light" (see 2 Tim. 1:10). It speaks of vast ranges of the past, but to connect them with a golden future. It is full all through of "ever-lasting comfort, and good hope" (2 Thess. 2:16). And there is nothing on earth but the Bible of which that can be truly said.

Our chosen verse today is a first-magnitude star in the Scripture sky, in its constellation of Hope. Let us turn our prayerful thought upon it, and ask it, this December Sunday, for its message about an eternal Spring.

Notice first the precise rendering demanded by the Greek. "The God of *the* hope fill you with all joy, that ye may abound in *the* hope."

The Greek "*the*" here, without undue pressure on its significance, tends to define and concentrate the reference of the word hope. And I believe that here, as well as in many other familiar passages, far more passages than we often realize, the word "hope" is thus defined, and as it were fixed, in one glorious reference, namely, in a reference to the Second Coming of our Lord Jesus Christ, the blessed Advent of our ascended King, when, no longer in type or mystery, but in a wonderful actuality, "this same Jesus shall so come, in like manner, as He was seen going into heaven" (see Acts 1:11). It is to this, as I believe, that Paul here points the Romans. He prays for them that they may "abound" in *this* radiant expectation; that it may possess them with a delightful preoccupation in all parts of their thought and life; that it may flow through their active days and quiet nights, making a blissful difference in everything. That "bright to-morrow" is to "make a bright today" for them. In danger and persecution, if that should come, in the common toils and troubles which would always come, in the whole interchange and experience of life, he prays that they may "abound in the hope."

As with them, so with us. Nay, more and more so with us. "Now is our salvation nearer than when" *they* "believed" (Rom. 13:11), eighteen and a half centuries ago. It is a significant fact in the history of the Church that the "blessed hope" (Tit. 2:13), instead of fading with time, has come, in these latter days to be a vastly more prominent truth to countless Christians than for ages before. This last century has seen a remarkable development in the prayerful study of the great promise, and in the realization of its glory. Is this accidental? Is it not rather one of the deep, spiritual "signs of His Coming"? Does it not say to us, more than ever in our day, "abound in the hope"? And will not such "abounding" be a marvelous power in our lives to gladden, to animate, to expand, to liberate, and, in the most tender sense, to solemnize as well?

Then note some other points in this luminous verse.

See the Apostle's double reference to the divine power which alone can fully make this hope "abound" in us. "*The God* of the Hope*,*" "*in*" (so literally) "*the power of the Holy Ghost.*" Ultimately, it is a matter not for our mere research, reasoning, or computation, but for the Spirit's work in us. He must quicken, He must teach. He must so "take of the things of" the returning Lord, "and show them unto us" (John 16:14), that we shall, by a blessed necessity, "love His appearing" (2 Tim. 4:8), with a longing that is the very soul of expectation, and of the "peace and joy" of such a prospect.

Then on the other hand, note well the words, "*in believing.*" The Lord will do His part, in His own way. Let us, in His grace, do our part, which is, to believe, that is to say, to take His word, and rest upon it, and live in the spirit of men assured. It is not our dream, but His Word. Ponder it, repose upon it, and then from it look upward and look forward. What is hope, hope in the Scripture sense of the word, but faith looking forward, an expectation warranted by the trusted Promiser?

Such be our happy hope, and indeed it will make life happy all over.

> Earth is brighten'd, when that gleam
> Falls on flower, and rock, and stream;
> Life is brighten'd, when that ray
> Falls upon its darkest day.

51

God Incarnate

For unto us a child is born, unto us a son is given: and the government shall be upon his shoulder: and his name shall be called Wonderful, Counselor, The mighty God, The everlasting Father, The Prince of Peace—
Is. 9:6

We are close to Christmas Day. Our Sabbath meditation shall take its color from that fact. To be sure, no divine obligation whatever rests on the observance of the day. And many Christians (possibly the reader is one) have a scruple in conscience about such observance; a scruple which I would treat with all respect. But I am not now asking anyone to observe Christmas Day, though I believe its religious use is more and more frequent among Christians of most of our Churches. I am only taking the nearness of the ancient and widely-kept festival of our Lord's blessed Birth, as an occasion for throwing the glory of the fact of His Incarnation across the shadows of the closing year.

Very simple is the line I follow. I make no attempt to deal in any elaborate way with that mighty mystery, God manifest in the Flesh. That is rather for the theological book, or lecture, or for the careful pastoral teaching given in the Bible class or Bible circle. All I would do here in that connection is just to restate the essential faith of all the Christian ages, held by the saints, century after century, with the Bible open before them. The blessed and eternal Son, God the Son of God, "for us men and our salvation," "in the fullness of time," was pleased to become also Man the Son of Man. One Person, from eternity to eternity, He was pleased now, for the first time, and forever, to exercise His Personality in two Natures. The Christ, Babe at Bethlehem, Man at Nazareth, at Capernaum, at Calvary, at Olivet, was now always, and with equal truth, God and Man. Born a Child, He was yet the Mighty God. The Mighty God, He was yet born a Child. "By Him," personally, "all things were made" (John 1:3). He, personally, "was made in all things like unto His brethren" (Heb. 2:17). He grew, He learned, He hungered, was astonished, wept and died. Yet He was "Lord and God" (John 20:28), "over all, blessed forever" (Rom. 9:5).

Now what shall our thought be upon this mighty, surpassing, supreme Mystery? Shall we think at all? Shall we not rather say, with the Christian poet,

> Who is equal to these things?
> Who these mysteries can brook?
> Faith with eagle eyes and wings
> Scarcely there may soar and look;
> Thought must seek that height in vain,
> All her musings turn to pain,
> Whelm'd beneath the mighty load
> Of that word, INCARNATE GOD.

But after all we do not want to soar to the height where the eternal Sun shines. We only seek to kneel, and worship, and rejoice, where its blessed radiance falls around us on the earth. We only wish to clasp some of the treasures of the fact of the Incarnation, "for us men." For we remember that this wonderful Child is not only "born." He is "born *unto us.*"

In that simple view, let us reflect on the infinite store of cheer and peace which the divine Fact contains, in the midst of earth's shadows of sorrow, sin, and death. It has been well said that the festival of Christmas, to those who keep it with spiritual earnestness, carries a blessed message to sorrowing hearts, *standing just where it does.* It occurs, in our calendar, one week before the end of the year. Just as the year dies, if we may put it so, the Lord is born. Just when Nature is painting her great fresco of death, the Living One steps into the scene, and says, "I am your Life."

Believer, hail the message, and ask for grace to advance more and more into its blessed significance with advancing years. For the moment, only for the moment, I will put aside from immediate view

161

the grand revealed truth that the primary purpose of our blessed Lord's Incarnation was that He might die (Heb. 2:14):

> Taking flesh that Thou might'st die,
>   Suffering for sin,
> Thou dost bring the lost ones nigh,
>   Purified within.

That is a precious truth, unspeakably vital to our "peace and joy in believing." But, for a purpose, I do not dwell upon it now. For the moment, I go not to Calvary, but simply to Bethlehem. Standing there, kneeling there with the shepherds, what shall we say, as the utterance just now of our thankful souls?

God is made also Man. Therefore, how precious to God is man! "What is man, that Thou art mindful of him?" (Ps. 8:4). In himself, apart from Thee, he "is like to vanity" (Ps. 144:4). By himself, by his sin and fall, he is a thing of ruin, guilt, and woe. Yet to Thee he is precious, for he was "created in Thine image" (Gen. 1:27), and now, wonder of all wonders, Thou hast taken his image to Thee. O man, are you thus "His peculiar treasure" (Ps. 135:4)? Rejoice, believe, and love.

God is made also Man. Therefore, what purposes for Man must God have, hidden in Himself! Yes, let Man seem for the present like the withering grass, like the fading flower (Is. 40:7). The Incarnate God is the living and everlasting Token that it is not really so. In Him who has joined Manhood to Godhead in one Person, "it doth not yet appear what" Man "shall be" (1 John 3:2). But it *doth* appear that he shall, in Christ, "inherit all things" (Rev. 21:7). The Lord of all things has become one with Man.

52

The Old Christian's Best Friend

To your old age I am He—Is. 46:4

This is the last Sunday of the year. Let us address ourselves to the reflections it suggests to those who have lived far into life. Some of the readers of these short meditations may be actually aged, in the stricter sense; far past the threescore and ten of the Psalmist, and now living on into their "borrowed years." Very many more of us have not yet lived so long, yet long enough to have tasted deeply of the mysterious cup of time. We look back upon childhood, perhaps with that peculiar and pathetic clearness of vision which memory often possesses; and it seems to us like a journey to another planet. We walk again in the old world, amidst the old walls and trees; we hear again the beloved voices hushed so long, and see the very expression of the faces of the blessed ones. We feel the sensation of the old life, in its ancient joys and griefs. And then we awake broadly to the present. Can we be the same beings, in personal identity, as "the children sporting on the shore" of that time so remotely past? What is there that remains the same?

Such thought, or rather feeling, deep as consciousness, is what many a man and woman knows when the rush of life slackens, and "the dumb hour" calls us to remember. Disconnected from God, such thoughts can be unutterably sad. They can be not only sad, but dangerously enfeebling. Yet they spring from the inmost heart, and that heart God has made.

What shall we do with memory? We will take it and lay it quietly down upon the Word of God, "which liveth and abideth forever"

163

(1 Pet. 1:23). In particular, we will lay it today upon this sweet, tender, sympathetic, mighty oracle, in which the Lord of the Word bids it speak about Himself. Through His prophet, to His poor troubled people, He is speaking here about Himself. In His Eternity He is remembering their Time, and speaking about Himself in relation to it. Himself evermore the same, He enters into their existence of change, and applies to it the strong consolation of His sameness. "Hearken unto me, O house of Jacob, and all the remnant of the house of Israel, which are borne by me from the belly, which are carried from the womb: And even to your old age I am he; and even to hoar hairs will I carry you: I have made, and I will bear; even I will carry, and will deliver you" [Is. 46:3, 4]. Wonderful words from the "philanthropy" (see Titus 3:4) of the Eternal One! Wonderful sympathy of the I AM with the beings who decay and die!

The whole passage invites our loving and thankful thought. But today, and for briefest study, take just that one clause: "To your old age, I am He."

"To your old age," all the way along. Up from childhood onwards, through all the stages; through every change and evolution of circumstance; through all the history of our home, of our homes; through all the records of the soul, life unconverted and converted; through all the annals of the heart, joy and grief, company and loneliness, strength and weakness, culmination, decline, "the morning march that glitter'd in the sun," the journey carried on with toil under the sinking western light; all the way, up to old age, "I am He."

"I am He." That is to say, I am the same as ever. It is as if He said, "Go back to your very first days of dawning thought about Me. Do you remember what your father and your mother used to say about Me, and to say to Me? Do you recollect what I was to them? Is it present to you, in the holy stillness of reminiscence, how they loved Me, worshiped, followed Me? What my Word was to them, and my Worship, and my Day, and my Work, and my Cause? How I was known to them in my Son? How they found Me their all in all, living and dying? Do you not know that the beauty, the glory, of their remembered lives had their GOD for its secret and its heart, so that without Me they could not possibly have been what they were? Then, do you remember your own first real heart-knowledge of Me, the blessed 'Christian spring' of the first faith in Me, and the first love to Me? Well, *I am He.* In my divine Personal Identity, *I am He.* All that I was to your fathers, all that I have been to you, I am. Since those old days the world has changed, and the Church; and you have changed, more than you know, except at the heart of your nature and in the deepest of your needs. But I am the same, yesterday and today. I am your oldest Friend, and I am also the Friend most present to your newest moment and all its conditions. For I am eternal, and I am yours."

O blessed, heavenly, glorious, faithful Intimate of His people! To those who know Him, that "utmost solitude of age," of which the poet sadly sings, is impossible. They "walk with infinite companionship around them." For beside them, to the last, is their God in Christ, saying to them, "I am He."

BOOK TWO

From Sunday to Sunday

TO THE DEAR MEMORY
OF MY NIECE
ADELAIDE MARY MOULE,
MISSIONARY, BIBLE STUDENT,
FRIEND, EXAMPLE,
THIS BOOK IS INSCRIBED

SHE DIED NOVEMBER 4, 1901, AT HANG-CHOW,
IN THE HOUSE OF HER FATHER,
BISHOP IN MID-CHINA

What we trust
Unto the dust
Is but the earthly garb she wore;
What we love
Lives on above,
And will live on forevermore.

Preface

The following series of expository papers appeared first in the pages of the *Good Words*.

The plan and working out of the series is simple enough, and must serve, such as it is, for its own Introduction. The natural and Christian seasons have been kept in view in the arrangement of subjects, so far as seemed to be necessary or useful, BUT no elaborate adaptation has been attempted.

I shall be happy indeed if these brief expositions may contribute in some humble measure to a true spiritual use, in private moments, of that inestimable, that vitally needful treasure of the Church of Christ, the Lord's Day.

H. Dunelm
Auckland Castle,
Michaelmas, 1903

1

"All the Days": Part One

And, lo, I am with you always, even unto the end of the world—
Matt. 28:20

We could not ask for a better watchword than this at the threshold of a new year. Alike the Promiser and the promise are supreme. The words first fell, syllable by syllable, from the immortal lips of the Lord Jesus Christ, standing "in the power of an endless life" in the midst of His disciples, on that unnamed mountain in Galilee "where Jesus had appointed them." There He was, the Lord of death, which He had conquered, and of time, of which He took command, to hold it in His victorious grasp and use it all for the fulfillment of His purposes of grace and glory. Coming up from the grave, He now stood in a wonderful sovereignty above time; it was His absolute right to say what He would be, what He would do, in all its future course.

And then the words so spoken by Him were altogether full of Himself. He uttered no vague and general guarantee, but something as personal as possible. He undertook to be, *Himself,* the immediate Companion, Fellow-traveler, Fellow-worker with His people, to the very last of their travel and their work. To give His words in their precise order, as the Gospel in its Greek gives them, "I with you am." Person with persons, Heart with hearts, Savior with followers, Lord with servants, *"I, with you,"* this was the prospect. And the Promiser, true to His own eternity of being, casts the promise into a form perpetually present: "I with you" (not "will be" but) "AM." It is to be always *a present moment* of faithful fulfillment; up to the date of

172

every new stage of the way, they are to be sure that they have with them "Him that is."

And all this, "even unto the end of the world." We may render this more exactly, "even until the consummation of the age"; that is to say, in the sense of those words which is amply assured to us by Scripture usage, "Even until I, this same Jesus, in manifested glory, at the close of this great period of redemption, come again." The thought is not of a collapse of the universe, but of the gathering up of a process into its magnificent result; and that result is to be His Coming. So the presence now is but to be the path to the presence then. The unseen Divine Companion is to be but the Conductor of His saints up to the moment when, suddenly, He will dawn upon them as the unveiled Bridegroom, coming again, to take them to Himself.

Infinite treasures of peace, grace and glory thus lie hidden in those few words of the risen Christ. For they promise to His disciples the possession of Himself now, always now, as the avenue to Himself forever. They tell them that for their journey they shall have always, beside them, all that He is for them. And at the end of their journey they shall find an open heaven, in the fact of their being, after the manner of the life of glory, "forever with the Lord."

But we have not quite reached the last of the re-translations which the Greek of this wonderful verse invites. "Lo, I am with you always," says our Authorized Version. And the Revised Version retains the familiar rendering. But in its margin it gives us the literal and most significant equivalent of the original words: "Lo, I am with you *all the days.*"

Yes, this is what the Evangelist records precisely as the Master's promise; "all the days." We may even go a little further in exact translation, without straining the fine and delicate texture of the Greek grammar too far: "all the days, *and all day long.*"

Is this a mere phrase, meaning "always," only expressing the idea at more length? No rather, it expresses it in more depth, more detail, more intensity. It brings the Presence home to the very steps of the pathway, instead of leaving it to float vaguely over its general course.

"All the days"! Who does not know how day differs from day, even in a life of fairly even tenor? Who does not feel the difference of the days' surfaces, and see the varieties of their colors? From the golden sunlight of a day of joy to the blackness of a day of woe, through all gradations the scale runs as we travel on. From the grass of the meadow to the miry clay of the marsh, to the hot dust of the level road, to the flints of the steep ascent, to the waters of the cold river, varies the surface. And the great Companion knows it all. And He breaks up the great promise of the Presence to adjust it to every detail of our need. "I with you am, all the days, and all day long, even unto the end."

2

"All the Days": Part Two

And lo, I am with you always, even unto the end of the world—
Matt. 28:20

Come again with me to that mountain in Galilee "where Jesus had appointed them," and listen over again to the Promiser in His promise. He is always there, He is always speaking there, in this unalterable assurance, "I with you am."

Let us ask today, as we listen, a question left out of sight in our first meditation. What is the context of the words? How do they link themselves to the utterances just before? For manifestly they are somehow linked; the promise does not hover alone in the air. "*And* lo, I with you am." That small word *"and"* points us back; it is a cord which pulls at a weight of truth behind it.

The answer is obvious, and as momentous as it is obvious. The Lord had just uttered His great commission. His disciples were to spend themselves upon making Him known to "all the nations," gathering them into a believing and obedient host, sealed and signed with His baptismal blessing, brought "into the Name" of Triune love and life, into a living union with the God of grace and a living allegiance to His Will. They were to go out into the world to be witnesses to their Master, and willing laborers for Him and His kingdom. So, and with them as such, would He be present, even to the end. "*and* lo, I with you am."

The first and greatest reference of the promise falls then upon the Lord's disciples in their missionary capacity. Whether we think of the individual, or of the community, so it is. Behold the messenger of Christ in "the uttermost parts of the earth," perhaps in complete spiritual isolation, perhaps in bodily peril; in the African interior; amidst multitudinous masses of humanity in India or China; seeking the wanderers on the plains of North Western America, or even upon the ice of its eastern shores; penetrating the forests of the southern New World; landing on Pacific islands; attempting the iron gates of Arabia or of Tibet. Or behold the organized forces of Christendom on the larger scale, the enterprises of churches, of societies, in their councils at home and in their campaign among "the nations." For every faithful pioneer and pastor, for every organized advance, prayerful and believing, under the great commission of the risen Lord, this supreme promise has its first and special application. Let the missionary clasp it to his heart, above all when either the dangers or the monotony of his task lie heavy upon him. "I with thee am, I with you am, all the days, and all day long, even unto the consummation of the age." Yes, there He is close to you. His heart is laid upon your heart, His arm embraces your fatigue, His prescient eye is fixed upon the consummation of the age, which you cannot see, but which to Him is now and here.

Yet surely the missionary, in the particular and familiar meaning of the word, will not grudge an application of the promise to other disciples than himself and those who, like him, have, "Because that for his name's sake they went forth" (3 John 7). Not only by the evangelization of "the regions beyond" is that great commission carried out. "To make disciples of all the nations," to "teach them to observe all things commanded" by the beloved Master, is a work which is shared in true measure by all who truly live for Him, and who realize that they are all "saved in order to serve." The faithful pastor and evangelist in the Christian land, bringing into true discipleship the incredulous, the careless, the fallen, the "lapsed," teaching the nominal follower of Jesus really to "observe all things He had commanded" in a surrendered life, is carrying that commission out. So is every living and loving helper of the pastor's work. So is every disciple, of every kind and name, who, knowing and adoring the crucified and risen Christ, so lives on and in Him as to receive of His fullness, and to reflect His image, and to commend His blessed Name by that reflection, shining into the darkness of sorrow and sin around. Not only the devoted evangelist in the ends of the earth, but the mother manifesting her Lord in her home, the friend among his friends, found faithful to that Name in the tests of common life, in doing or in bearing—each and all have part in the commissioned work. And so by each and by all, and for all the days, and for all day long, the promise may be claimed, humbly, surely, joyfully; "Lo, I with you am."

3

The Message of the Long Psalm: Part One

How sweet are Thy words unto my taste! . . . Therefore I hate every false way—Ps. 119:103, 104

The hundred and nineteenth psalm is a singularly interesting study, and from many points of view. It has its considerable literary interest. It is the largest and most elaborate example of a device of Hebrew poetry intended evidently both to give a certain grace of form to the composition and to assist memory, namely, the alphabetical grouping of verses. The psalm is instantly seen by the reader to be symmetrically divided; it consists of twenty-two octaves of verses. In most English Bibles each octave is headed by the name of a letter of the Hebrew alphabet, which alphabet begins with *Aleph* and ends with *Tau.* A beginner in Hebrew soon discovers that each octave is so written that every verse in it opens with some word whose first letter is the letter which heads the octave.

This is interesting; an antique device of literary skill. Does it seem to us mechanical? Surely it is not more so than our systems of rhymes; a system elaborated even to extreme nicety in some of those hymns, modern and ancient alike, which live and move most vividly with poetic fire and heavenly grace.

Then, further, the long Psalm, on inspection, is alive with human interest.

Its writer half reveals himself to us by passing allusions. We gather that he is young, that he is solitary, that he is despised and persecuted. We see him on fire with love to God, and actually weeping over the rejection of God by man. We see him at private worship, "seven times a day." Above all, we see him with the holy Book before him. It is "the joy of his heart"; it is "a lamp to his feet"; "O how he loveth the law" of his Lord.

Who was he? Was he David? It is not likely, in view of some of the literary features of the Psalm; though this has been often assumed, notably in that rich treasury of spiritual gold, the commentary on the Psalm by the late Rev. C. Bridges, a saint the light of whose life I saw in my young days, and feel its radiance still. Was it Daniel? To me this has often seemed a probable conjecture. It may well have been he. But God knoweth.

Now, approaching the Psalm for some further study of its contents, we are met by one obvious and impressive element in them. The Psalm is full, from end to end, of the thought of the writer's love for the sacred Book of his Lord, of his assiduous study of it, of his mingled delight in its contents and awful reverence in presence of them. To quote in illustration would be to transcribe the much larger part of the Psalm. The Book bears many titles, but they all obviously attach to one subject. "The Word," "the Law," "the Statutes," "the Testimonies," "the Judgments," "the Commandments"; we need no commentary to give the terms their reference. The man has before the eyes of his heart the written Oracles of God, as they existed in his day. He was, perhaps unconsciously, himself contributing a new treasure to their store. But his own immediate thought was, that the store before him was unspeakably precious, sacred, sweet, wonderful, a field exceeding broad, a mine pregnant with thousands of gold and silver. To explore it, he was up before the dawn, and he got to his beloved task again before the night quite shut in the day. He found in it the guide of his inexperience, the strength of his heart, when tempted to give way to opposition, oppression, or scorn. The Scriptures were his "songs in the house of his pilgrimage"; his personal friends, the living and loving "counselors" to whom he turned, with whom he talked.

If we are right in our guess, the Psalm belongs to the age of the Exile, and so to a time when the old order of sacrificial worship was in long abeyance, to be revived again indeed, but only for a while. It is as if the Holy Spirit had seized the occasion of that valley of humiliation to open the eyes of the saints, as never before, to the immeasurable preciousness of the Written Word, that Word whose very details were to be so sacred at a later day to the Son of Man Himself.

There is a passage, attributed to St. Chrysostom, and certainly very ancient, in which it is foretold that in the end there will be great confusions in the Church, but that the Holy Scriptures will then prove to be, as never before, the rock and rallying-point of faith. Truly our confusions are many. May our Bibles become to us all the more what they were to the saint of the long psalm!

4

The Message of the Long Psalm:
Part Two

How sweet are Thy words unto my mouth! . . . Therefore I hate every
false way—Ps. 119:103, 104

We have watched the writer of the long psalm as he bends over
his beloved Book, and tastes the sweetness of its words, and praises
the Giver seven times a day for the gift of it, and rises very early and
saves time at night that he may know it better.

Let us steal up to him again, and catch some of the utterances of
his soul over his treasure. What, above all other things, gives to this
man his love, his passion, for his Bible? Does the long psalm tell us
in any intelligible way? Assuredly it does.

One thing is plain. The Book is dear to him for no merely anti-
quarian reasons, nor again as a mere exercise of his mind. Beyond
doubt its sacred prestige, from a glorious past, was much to him.
And no one can read his recorded thoughts without feeling that the
study of the Book, and his converse with it, had told powerfully upon
the elevation and firmness of his thinking power. But those things
are not before him, though they are in him. The thing which is to an
over-mastering degree both before and in him is the thought that
in the Bible he hears nothing less than his Lord and God speaking
to him, speaking with him, to let his servant know the glory of His
holy Will.

If the long psalm is on one side the glorification of the written
Word, it is on the other the glorification of the sacred Will. In octave after octave this strain sounds on. "Blessed are they who walk
in the law of the Lord"; "I thought upon my ways, and turned my

feet unto Thy testimonies"; "Order my footsteps in Thy Word, and let not any iniquity have dominion over me." Here again is an element of the long Psalm, so large, so deeply interwoven with its texture, that if we would illustrate it fully we should need to transcribe phrases from the whole length of the composition.

Yes, the sacred Book lies open here before a student who is supremely conscious that in those pages speaks the will of God. And to him that will is the very heart of Him whom he has found to be (v. 57) his "portion." Such has Jehovah become to the man that He is his wealth, his inheritance, his estate, his home, his all. By the Master's grace this has become the servant's experience. In the dialect of the Old Testament he expresses the choice and the joy which another of his race, long after, was to express in the dialect of the New; "I count them but dung, that I may win Christ" [Phil. 3:8].

And because that possessed yet ever-longed-for "knowledge" was of the spiritual sort, therefore its direct and profound result was a thirst and hunger after an ever-growing insight, for practical results of obedience, into the Will of God. Man may exercise his reason, aye, in the noblest sense of that great word, upon theistic study, and may reach in that line even sublime results, yet wholly fail to fall in love with the Will of God. But let man get some spiritual glimpse, some intuition, while not reason only but conscience and affection are touched and moved from above, into "the glory of the Blessed God," and then, by a law of the soul, he will love and long for the Will of God.

> Thou sweet, beloved will of God,
>   My anchor-hold, my fortress-hill,
> My spirit's silent, fair abode,
>   In thee I hide me and am still.

So sings Tersteegen. And his deep, sweet song is only the instinctive voice of the being which has "seen the God of Israel," the God and Father of our Lord Jesus Christ, as He *is* to be seen when He lifts the veil and shows us something of His fair glory.

So let us follow the saint of the long Psalm, as he beckons us in to read the Bible with him. By the grace of his God and ours the Book shall be to us what it was to him; with that wonderful and undeserved advantage for us, that what he had in part we have in

182

whole—evangelists and apostles crowning the work of prophets and of psalmists.

"Thou sweet, beloved Will!" And that Will is nothing other than the manifold expression of the eternal Love.

"Disce cor Dei in verbis Dei"; "Learn God's heart in God's words." So writes Gregory the Great to his lay friend Theodore, entreating him to read his Bible. We, too, will ponder the Word, that we may know the Heart, and do the Will.

5

Solitude in Company

And he went on his way rejoicing—Acts 8:39

This was "the man of Ethiopia, a eunuch of great authority under Candace, queen of the Ethiopians, who had charge of all her treasure." He had visited Jerusalem, we remember, as a religious pilgrim, and was now on his way back to the remote region which we know as Abyssinia. Somehow he had become a proselyte to the faith of Israel. To worship the Lord of Israel in His own temple he had got leave of absence from his sovereign, and had found his way, down the Nile, across the Isthmus, up from the Palestinian coastland, over the hill country, to Mount Moriah. Perhaps it was in Jerusalem that he had bought his copy of Isaiah. However, he possessed the great prophet's scroll, and was reading it aloud to himself as he drove slowly southward, when Philip came up, and with a tactfulness only the truer because he was filled with the Holy Ghost, got him into conversation about the Lord Jesus Christ.

Not by accident, but by the finest touches of the will of God the evangelist came up with the traveler precisely as the traveler was reading Isaiah 53. We need have little anxiety, in the light of that fact, about the prophetic import of that chapter. The finger of God has here written all over it the name of God's dear Son, the Lamb of Golgotha, the bearer of our sins, who sees in our salvation the fruit of the travail of His soul.

However, the two men read, and conversed, and opened their souls to one another driving mile after mile along the solitary road. Then they passed "a certain water," silent and clear amidst the waste.

And, behold, the new convert, beholding by faith the truth and glory of his Redeemer, and taught by his guide about that Redeemer's precept of baptism into the Holy Name, descends into the pool, and comes up a disciple indeed, accepted, dedicated, "joined unto the Lord" [1 Cor. 6:17].

How close, tender, profound, must have been the fellowship of hearts between Philip and the Ethiopian! Is there anything which so immediately and so fully opens the depth of one human being to the depth of another as the fellowship which has resulted in the one proving to the other the instrument of conversion? Everything would concur in the case of the Ethiopian to develop that experience to the uttermost. The mystery and beauty of the coincidence of their meeting, the unmistakable hand of God in the conditions under which they met, their isolation from the world of common fellowship, the glorious newness of it all to the traveler—everything would bring him and Philip together with an indescribable intimacy of thought and affection. Years of friendship would spring, as it were, instantaneously out of their converse, when that converse had led one of them, by the other's hand, to the cross, to the face, to the heart, of Jesus Christ.

What bliss now to journey on together! The treasurer will, of course, carry the evangelist with him to be his pastor, and the missionary-father of his native Ethiopia. Philip will be more than ever wanted now to develop the Ethiopian's knowledge and belief, to educate him, to encourage him, to equip him for his new life and its influences.

Not so, not at all. "The Spirit of the Lord caught away Philip, that the eunuch saw him no more." No, nevermore, till they met in the unseen bliss beyond the veil. No more talk together, nor worship together. As far as we can possibly tell, the new convert went on his vast journey homeward with nothing but his Isaiah and his baptism to help him: bereft of all we understand by Christian surroundings—no Christian public worship, no Christian communion, no Christian New Testament. But he had the supreme secret. He had found the Lord.

> For Philip indeed went, but Jesus stay'd,
> And travell'd with His friend.

185

And Jesus is the fellow-traveler still. In solitudes of place, in solitudes of feeling, in the last solitudes of life, time-worn and bereaved, the blessed "Great Companion" can work that miracle still, and show us how to travel to the end, "rejoicing."

6

The Consolation of Spiritual Fellowship

Knowing that the same afflictions are accomplished in your brethren that are in the world—1 Pet. 5:9

We may re-translate these words, with a very slight paraphrase in one or two details, the better to bring out the meaning of the Greek. "Knowing that the same types of our afflictions are being carried out for your brotherhood which is in the world."

Here the following points appear. First, "the same afflictions," as a phrase, gives way to another phrase which lends itself better to the thought that the "sameness" means not identity of detail, but identity of *sort;* a reflection which will spare us many a useless question in our hours of trial, whether precisely similar incidents can be conceived of as coming into another life. Then the word "accomplished," which might seem to mean "already over," and anyhow might seem only to imply the prospect merely of a termination, gives way to the words "being carried out." And these words put before us the thought of *a process* now going on, and moreover of a process which is tending not to a termination only, but to what is far different—an outcome, a result, an achievement, a something developed and attained as the purposed issue of it all. Here is a contribution real and precious to the full message of the sentence. We are reminded that these "types of our afflictions" are not merely so many dolorous experiences, made just tolerable by the thought that some day they will be over;

> For though the day be never so long
> At last it ringeth to evensong:

187

a view of things which may rise no higher than that of the malefactor on his way to the hideous execution of the "wheel" in old France: *"Le jour sera fort, messieurs, mais il finira";* "The day will be trying, but it will close!" No, Peter has a far different word for us than that. These things "are being carried out," "directed towards an end," as the skilled artificer directs all the blows of his hammer, all the wounds of his chisel, towards the shape and structure present from the first to his mind and reached at last by his manipulation. The Lord is superintending, adjusting, directing these "types of our afflictions"; let that truth be present to the spirit in each hour of suffering, and it will transfigure it. Lastly, our new translation brings to us, in its word "brotherhood," the delightful thought of the cohesion and solidarity of the family of grace. It is not only "brothers"; it is a "brotherhood." Alas! between brothers, taken as units, there may be contentions which are even "as the bars of a castle" (Prov. 18:19). But speak of a brotherhood, and we have before us the thought of brethren bound into heart-unity. The word implies a deep and sympathetic cohesion. It helps us to the thought of a magnetic intercourse, so to speak, alike in trial and in comfort;

> Our bodies may far off remove,
> We still are one in heart.

And now, in what connection does Peter place these facts of the spiritual sphere before his readers? His is writing under a great impending shadow of persecution; a time is at hand when the great enemy will have permission to "sift them as wheat"; "a fiery trial" (4:12) is to try them. And those Christians of Asia Minor in the first century were precisely as human as ourselves. Martyrdom was no easier to bear in the age of the martyrs than it is today. Lacerated hearts, not to speak of limbs, were then what they are now. Ruined homes, dislocated affections, not to speak of literal fire and sword, were terrific realities in the old world as truly as in this latest hour of time.

What were they to do? Supremely, they were to remember two secrets, which were divinely good for them then, and are equally good for us today, whether we are called to lay down life in the old style (as missionaries in China did in 1900), or to yield ourselves to the stress of trial in any other form whatever, stern or subtle. First, they were to "resist, made solid by their faith" (so literally); reliant on the Lord their Rock, and so drawing His Rock-strength into their weakness. And then, they were to remember in the dark hour that somewhere, somehow, a similar type of trial was being victoriously met by some fellow-believer, in that same strength; so met as to be not merely endured but taken as the means to a glorious end, "working out the exceeding weight of glory."

7

"The End of the Lord"

Ye have seen the end of the Lord—James 5:11

James here, as we remember, refers to Job. He briefly sums up the memorable book which bears that name under two headings, "the patience of Job," and "the end of the Lord." Terribly did the patriarch suffer. Not always did he suffer well; some sorrowful words, some even deplorable words, escaped him in his bewilderment of loss and misery, physical and mental. But upon the whole, in a very wonderful way, he had "patience"; he persisted in the conviction that the eternal Judge was on the side of right, not wrong, though the temptations to think the opposite seemed to crowd around His darkened eyes. Then at length the Lord interposed in direct remonstrance with His servant. He brought him to his knees in complete confession and surrender, by a path which we certainly should not have forecast, the manifestation of His inscrutable wisdom and power in the glories of creation. However, to his knees Job was brought, breathing out words which are now immortal forever as the voice of the awakened soul; "Mine eye seeth Thee, wherefore I abhor myself" [Job 42:5, 6]. Then comes "the end of the Lord." He turns towards His servant in a benign and wonderful reversal of his sorrows, yes, and a more than reversal. He gives him the splendid privilege of being the prevailing intercessor for his misguided friends, and then heaps upon him a rich abundance of temporal mercies, lighted up with the light of the smile and peace of God.

There is a message here which reaches far beyond the particular circumstances. Is not this view of the character of our gracious God, as it comes out in "the end of the Lord," a view to suggest encouragement to troubled faith under innumerable varieties of trouble? Does it not suggest to us the weight and truth of the often repeated appeals of Scripture, not least in the Psalms, to "wait for the Lord" [Ps. 130:5]? "Blessed are all they that wait for Him" [Is. 30:18]. "My soul, wait thou only upon God" [Ps. 62:5]. "Since the beginning of the world men have not heard, nor perceived by the ear, neither hath the eye seen, O God, beside Thee, what He hath prepared for him that waiteth for Him" [Is. 64:4]. "Said I not unto thee that, if thou wouldest believe, thou shouldest see the glory of God?" [John 11:40]; "What I do thou knowest not now, but thou shalt know hereafter" [John 13:7].

It is the very nature and function of faith, of reliance, to wait. "What a man seeth," says the great Apostle (Rom. 8:24), "why doth he yet hope for?" Similarly, what a man sees, what is before him this moment, why does he yet trust for? Faith, to take a practical definition, is reliance, *more or less in the dark,* upon the undisclosed action and purpose of a trustworthy person. It is a confiding expectation of "the end of" that person. And it will be more or less true to its nature, it will be more or less patient and willing to wait, other things being equal, as the person trusting more or less knows, is sure of, is satisfied with, the character and capacity of the person trusted.

In the case of Christian faith, the trusting person is the mortal man who has, by grace, got some sight of the trustworthiness of the God and Father of our Lord Jesus Christ. And in proportion to his insight into the divine character of the Person trusted will be the simplicity, the repose, the inextinguishable hope, of his reliance.

To aid us in this attitude of faith, an attitude distinctively and supremely Christian, let us remember often "the end of the Lord," the way in which His heart, repressing itself for a while, for good and disciplinary purposes, delights in the end to pour itself out in blessing. This is a characteristic of the action of our Lord and God, this breaking out of the sun after the discipline of cloud.

Let us remember this when our own life, in its personal experiences, has the shadows upon it. Those shadows are not "the end of the Lord." It is His character not to bring the clouds finally upon the sun, but the sun finally out of the clouds.

Let us remember it when we are sad about the Church. Poor Church Visible! Truly she is not her own savior. But the Lord has her in His care. And He has not exhausted His resources. Divine revival lies yet in His hand. Let us wait for the "end of the Lord."

Let us remember it for the weary, rebellious world. It has destroyed itself; it cannot possibly restore itself. But we have not yet seen, even for the world, "the end of the Lord."

8

"Ye Are of More Value"

Fear not therefore: ye are of more value than many sparrows—Luke 12:7

Our blessed Lord makes two allusions to the sale of sparrows, allusions singularly beautiful and significant from His lips, letting us understand a little how His sacred thought took in the smallest and the simplest things of earthly life. "Are not two sparrows sold for a farthing?" is His question in Matthew 10:29. "Are not five sparrows sold for two farthings?" is His question in Luke 12:7; showing that He condescended to notice how, when "a quantity was taken," one poor little bird was thrown into the bargain. And then, in connection with this pathetic cheapness of the tiny animal lives, comes in this assurance on the part of the eternal Son about the character of the eternal Father; "one of them shall not fall on the ground without your Father"; "not one of them is forgotten before God." Infinitely tender, infinitely humane assurances! Remember them well when the distressing problem, perhaps the distressing sight, of the sufferings of helpless, of affectionate, of beautiful animals (perhaps a pet) is upon your heart. Human mistreatment of animals is as painful a phenomenon of the world as can be named, next under the tremendous phenomenon of the cruelty of man upon man. And "the silence of God" seems, as a rule, to be unbroken over this sad scene. But here, through that silence, comes the Son of God, knowing all things that lie in the infinite heart of the Father, with whom He is one. And He says that no sufferings of the animal world are taken as nothing by the Eternal; "not one is forgotten before God." The poor tortured dog, the worn-out horse, the mistreated bird—eternal eyes are upon them all. The universe will surely hear further of it, for the supreme King remembers and takes note. Woe to the will that thinks scorn of the sufferings of the animal, whether the conditions of cruelty be savage or civilized, half-bestial, or cloaked with a scientific plea. "Not one of them is forgotten before God."

But our chief concern today is not with the animal, but with the man. The Lord Jesus spoke thus of the sparrows that He might with the more emphasis speak of His human followers, and of the thoughts of Himself and His Father about them; their personal work and value in those same divine eyes which took note of the birds and of their death. "Ye are of more value than many sparrows."

Here is a side of truth which is not always prominent in the Bible. The Law, the Prophets, the Master Himself and His Apostles, very often indeed present the exactly opposite side, the abasement of man, the utter and absolute unworthiness of man, the wonder that lies in God's taking account of him, above all the miracle of the mercy that God exercises in forgiving him, and allowing him to be his Lord's accepted disciple and servant at all. Yes, the message of man's total dependence on the Lord as His creature, and entire unworthiness of the least of His mercies as His sinning creature, is large in the Bible. It is not too much to say that without the fullest recognition of that message and the most sincere sympathy with it we shall find the Bible, the gospel, the Christ, either insoluble enigmas, taken as they stand, or voices which for us have only a faint attraction.

But then there is, thank God, this other side. There is a point of view from which man, and now particularly believing man, is of mighty "value" in the eyes of his Father and his Savior. True, he is a creature. But he is the creature made in the Creator's image. True, he is a sinner. But he is capable, in his Savior, of such a transfiguring restoration that he can be the temple of the Spirit here, and the exact reflection of the unveiled glory of Christ hereafter.

Yes, man is of "value" before God. He is no mere piece upon a chess-board. He is the precious masterwork of the eternal creating Love, and the dear object of that same Love redeeming. He is, let us dare to say it, sacred to his Lord. He is of "value" to Him, a value indefinitely greater than that of all the lovely tribes whose innocent life flits in the forest and sings beneath the vernal skies.

Then let him respond to the sublime regard of Him who made him, and who has saved him. Let him, let us, look up into those man-loving eyes, and yield ourselves unto God with joy.

9

"Against Thee, Thee Only"

Against Thee, Thee only, have I sinned, and done this evil in Thy sight—
Ps. 51:4

According to the very old tradition preserved in the headings of the Psalms, these words are part of a song of heart-stricken penitence, drawn from David's soul when "Nathan the prophet came unto him" (2 Sam. 12:1), and said to him, "Thou art the man." When the awful conviction once made its way into his inner being, it would thus appear that its prompt result was a cry of woe, shame, and repentance addressed directly to God. It was borne in upon him with an ineffable consciousness that, while he had sinned, and sinned tremendously, against Bathsheba, and against Uriah, and also against every soul (from Joab's onward) that could ever be stumbled by that great crime wrought by God's servant, he had first and in the deepest respect sinned against God. So deeply, so supremely, had he aggrieved Him, that the other aspects of the offense were swallowed up, in a sense, in this; "Against Thee, Thee only."

To be sure, we have no infallible certainty that David did write Psalm 51, and then send it "to the Chief Musician" for a setting. An important school of criticism denies totally that he did so; maintaining that at his date, and in his character as it is shown in the Bible histories, he could not have felt and spoken thus. I venture to think very differently from this view, as to the conditions of date and character. But this is not the place for such a discussion. I would only affirm that whether or not David was the author, the psalm breathes a spirit which, granting that David had any knowledge

196

worth naming of a holy, spiritual God and Lord, would exactly suit his case.

In any case, it is the utterance of an agonized human being, conscious of wrong. Some have indeed interpreted it as the confession not of a man but of a people, a cry from the heart of collective Israel. But the critic who pronounces thus, so I presume to say, may be versed to any degree in literary science, but cannot be equally learned in the science of the troubled human soul, the individual in his uttermost need. The soul has a cry all its own. And that cry is here.

But now, notice the precise direction of the cry. It refers to some great, definite, shameful sin. Every such sin has many aspects and relations. Nay, what sin has not? Take even the most suppressed and interior transgressions, sins of the silent thought. Do they terminate wholly within, even in regard of our fellowmen? No; the least indulgence in inward evil, let us be sure, impairs the moral state of the being which allows it. And thus it impairs that being for moral power and helpfulness around. No man can "regard iniquity in his heart" [see Ps. 66:18] and also be all he should be for his neighbor's good.

Yet, for all this, the psalmist feels every other aspect and relation of his sin absorbed in this one: "against Thee, Thee only." Its violation of God lays hold upon him, as its inmost and ultimate evil and horror. There is present to him, awfully present, a personal Being on whom his sin has impinged as a blow, whose infinitely sensitive perception has been outraged by its commission. He is there, present in the very soul of His servant. And His servant's soul has struck a hideous discord with His holy mind; not to speak of an act of high treason, punishable with spiritual death, against His holy law. It is "against Him, Him only" because He is in such immediate, such absolute contact with the being which He has made.

Has our own experience anything in its memories to correspond to this cry of the psalmist? Have we ever known what it was to be, in the old-fashioned sense, convinced of sin? If so, we know without a commentary what this sinner, this sinning disciple, meant by his groan, uttered so long ago but sounding still. Our sin had other aspects, no doubt. But the "inmost rudiment" of it was this, that it had aggrieved the holy Author and Sustainer of our being. Just because He was our God, it had *struck* Him as it could strike no other existence. It could strike others only, as it were, through Him.

We stood isolated, in an awful solitude, under that thought. Here am I, the sinner; here is He, the sinless Maker, Master, Judge; for the moment there was no room within us for any other fact than that. And did not that intuition force from the stricken spirit the cry (Luke 18:13) which no other, no subordinate sort of repentance can fully generate, "God, be merciful to me a sinner"?

These experiences are not too common in our day. Partly the hurry of life has bred a sad shallowness of self-knowledge. Partly false inferences from our observation of natural processes, false uses of such words as heredity and evolution, have enfeebled the sense of the awfulness of personality and of its responsibility to an eternal Person, holy and just. But for our very life let us resist that cold downward drift. Let us ask for just such conviction of sin as cannot but cry, "Against Thee, Thee only." For that is the cry of a soul on the one straight road to the Christ of God, the sinner's Peace, and Light, and Life.

10

Some Thoughts on the Bible

*God, who at sundry times and in divers manners spake in time past unto
the fathers by the prophets—Heb. 1:1*

I presume to take these words quite out of their context. To do
so needs an apology, for their context is full of matter of the highest possible importance. Here opens the great Epistle, with its first
great theme, the divine majesty of our Lord Jesus Christ; heavenly
prelude to all it has to say in sequel about His manhood, His sacrificial sufferings, His high-priesthood, His exaltation on the throne,
His covenant, His love.

Yet we may without offense, for this once, take this first sentence
of the Epistle to introduce and point some thoughts on another
line, which yet, we may hope, will prove a real contribution towards
our worshiping faith in Christ. I take it to make it the occasion for
a few words about the Bible; about one side and sort of the Bible's
witness to itself as the Book not of man only but of God.

To this end, look first at the Bible not as a Book, but as Books,
produced at "sundry times" and in very "divers manners" indeed.
Contemplate it for the time in its multiplicity, and from the point of
view of its human authorship. Reflect upon the remarkable phenomenon, that it is, in this aspect, as St. Jerome said long ago, not a
Book but a "Divine Library"; or now, for our purpose, simply
a Library, Divine or not. Like most Libraries, it is the result of grad-
ual and protracted collection. The first contributions to it were
made, on a moderate computation, a thousand years before the
last; old-fashioned people would say, more than fifteen hundred

years before. And the contributors all along were people who, from the human side, were curiously different from one another, and independent in many respects of one another. Some were compilers of histories. Others were poets, instinct with a glow of imagination, versed in the mysteries of their own hearts, and in the sorrows and struggles of other hearts around them. Others were friends of their country, called to the counsels of her kings. Another was an exile, constrained by circumstances to administer the finances of a pagan empire. Some were priests, others were peasants. Some flourished amidst the full sunshine of public prosperity; others lived in days of decline and apparently hopeless fall. Passing on to the latter section of the Volume, to the concluding classes of the Library, we have books contributed, some by a group of country men, one by a man of business, two by a physician, many by a trained scholar of genius; books, or rather pamphlets, produced under conditions "sundry" and "divers" to a high degree.

Reflect upon the further and important fact that these curiously miscellaneous works, brought into being in this somewhat promiscuous fashion, and collected we scarcely know how, are meantime the literature, or rather part of the literature, not of a race and civilization of the front rank, but of a minor people of Western Asia. Israel has had, as a fact, so vast a part in the world's making, through this Book, that it takes an effort to recollect that side of the matter. The people who, for some thirteen centuries or so, occupied, amidst frequent disturbance, and under frequent disturbance, and under frequent vassalage, the seaboard of Southern Syria and its not very extensive *Hinterland,* certainly would not, apart from this Book, have figured in history on any scale approaching to that of India, Greece, Rome, France, Italy, Germany, or Britain. They had, no doubt, remarkable characteristics. But they showed little sign, even in their palmy days, of being made for great predominance in the world, either by thought or by action.

Look again, then, at the Book before us. It is the product of "sundry times." It was brought to being in fragments often quite isolated from each other, and in very "divers manners." And it was part of the literature of a minor and provincial race of Western Asia.

Yet what is it on the other hand? It is, first, not a Library nearly so much as a Book. A mysterious coherence runs all through it. Take once more a reverent, while large, view of the Bible, and say if there is not *a personal character* about it from beginning to end. Test this along the lines of God, of man, of righteousness, of law, of sin, of pardon. Is not the Book, in its essence, one?

Take it in its moral power, its unvarying drift and bias towards all that is forever right. "The Bible," says a shrewd American, "is such that, dig in it where you will, you find at the bottom of the shaft, Do right." Yet it is the production, from the human side, of a miscellaneous company of Orientals, scattered over ages of time.

Then reflect on the fact that it, this Book of a subordinate eastern race, is now, nevertheless, the Book of the World. It is the holy Book of the foremost nations of European culture. It is also the holy Book of the most simple races touched by missionary enterprise. Of all "sacred Books" it is the only one which proves itself to have a universal mission.

Is there no mystery of heaven behind all this? Does not the Book bear witness to itself? Produced as, from the human side, it was, it can only be what it is because through it, "God spake."

11

Grace Sufficient

My grace is sufficient for thee—2 Cor. 12:9

This is a word spoken by the Lord Jesus, in and from His glory, to a disciple still wrestling along the path of the pilgrimage. As such it is one of a precious series preserved to us in the New Testament. We have words so spoken by that Speaker to Saul at his conversion (Acts 9:4–6), to Ananias at Damascus (9:10–16), and to Paul again at Corinth (18:17, 10), in the Temple (22:18–21), and in the Roman citadel at Jerusalem (23:11). But of them all surely none is more precious, more pregnant of "comfort and good hope through grace," more full of the unutterable heart of Jesus, than this.

It comes to us as part of a narrative of personal spiritual experience. We should know nothing of it had not Paul opened up this holy secret of his soul, and told the Corinthians, and told us through them, of that crisis (fourteen years earlier when he wrote) of awful need and of wonderful deliverance. Let us not take up this treasure lightly. It is a sacred thing, not only in itself, but because of our getting it through this personal disclosure and confession. It was with a great effort, probably, that the Apostle told the Corinthian converts about the "thorn in the flesh," "the angel of Satan," and of his three imploring appeals to the Lord to be set free from the intolerable trial. Deep souls (and Paul's was one) do not lightly open up their secrets. The more let us reverence and prize the gift when, as here, for our sakes and for the Lord's glory, the effort is made, the sacrifice of individual feeling is offered up.

Not one word need I say here on the question, what was "the thorn." A whole literature has been written on it. But for us just now it matters not what it was. Enough that it was, to a very strong man, a very tremendous trial; a something which for the time darkened his whole spiritual sky; a conflict which brought him face to face with the powers of hell.

He cried out for release. "I besought the Lord thrice that it might depart." He records the repeated entreaty without any regret, with no trace of a feeling that he ought to have endured in silence. "Learn to suffer without crying out," is a noble precept—as regards "cries" to man, which are often better forborne. But the maxim has no bearing upon cries to God, to the Christ of God. Too ready, too outspoken, too confiding, we cannot be in "telling Jesus all." Such "crying out" will not weaken us; it will only strengthen us. For it is the outgoing of our soul not only to infinite kindness, but at the same moment to infinite wisdom and strength. It is taking refuge in the Rock. It is "coming to the Living Stone." And that (1 Pet. 2:4, 5) is the way to become "living stones" ourselves, by contact, by contagion.

So he "besought the Lord thrice." He was answered. There was a divine attention and response. The Lord, once Himself driven to "strong crying and tears," Himself once a suppliant in a yet darker hour, asking, in the profound simplicity of pure human agony, for the "passing" of the "cup" of unknown sorrows, quite understood His servant. It must have been a help to the servant, heart-broken with the struggle, to reflect that he appealed to One who once said Himself (Ps. 69:20), "Reproach hath broken my heart." Paul could be sure then, as we may be sure now, of that Friend's supreme acquaintance with grief. Yet the answer was not, in form, an affirmative, a consent. The thorn was not willed away; the "evil angel" was not driven back into the deep. As in Gethsemane, so with the Apostle in his dark hour, there came not a consent to the request in detail, but the meeting of it with a transcendently higher blessing. "Thorn," and "angel of Satan," might, or might not, be ultimately withdrawn. But then and there in all His fullness, in His all-sufficient present Self (for "grace" is just the Lord of all love and power Himself, in action for us), Jesus Christ was given to His saint. In the power of that gift the saint found on a sudden that the dread adversity had changed its character and its position. It was not upon his head, overwhelming. It was beneath his feet, overcome. Nay, it was even better than overcome. It had been transformed into "an occasion," not "of falling," but of "mounting up with wings" [see Is. 40:31]. "Most gladly therefore will I rather glory in my infirmities, that the power of Christ may rest upon me" [2 Cor. 12:9].

"As then, so now." That ear is not heavy today, nor that arm shortened, nor that grace less sufficient. Nor is the assurance of its sufficiency couched less distinctly now than then *in the present tense.* The story has often been told (it is authentic; it is the experience of a great servant of God now living) of the agonized suppliant who, as he cried with tears, "Let Thy grace be sufficient for me," lifted his wet eyes and saw upon the wall, lately hung there, the words, "My grace is sufficient for thee." The *"is"* was painted bright and conspicuous, and it caught his eye and filled his heart; and he rose up, there and then, to a new life of peace and power. Yes, it is true today. It is an everlasting present tense. "It is sufficient," and "for thee."

12

Peace and Pains

On Thee we rest—2 Chr. 14:11
Giving all diligence—2 Pet. 1:5

Let us think awhile of two opposite aspects of the Christian life; contrasted, not discordant; two sides of one shield. Take first the aspect of rest, of faith, of the peace of an absolutely simple reliance. Take then the aspect of diligence, of pains, of watching and prayer, of the faithful use of appointed means.

(1) "On Thee we rest." This is the central secret of the Christian. It is the distinctive and characteristic thing in the gospel. "I believe," not "I will do," is the watchword the gospel gives us. "I rely, I confide, I trust, I entrust"; this is the very life of our religion, if it is the religion of the New Testament, the water from the fountainhead of the truth of Christ.

"By faith, and faith only, we are justified." This was the grand confession of the Reformation. It is to the full as true today. It means that we sinners, knowing something of the awfulness of sin, and of sin as guilt, go for the whole of our reason for "peace with God" to the Lamb that was slain, to Jesus Christ, who died and rose again, and is now our Advocate with the Father, being the Propitiation for our sins. It means that we go to Him "just as we are, and waiting not to rid the soul from one dark blot," as if we could so make ourselves worthier of Him. We came with empty hands to receive the gift of God. It is a profound (while salutary) humiliation. It "pours contempt on all our pride." But oh, how great a rest it is! It is Christ Himself for us.

"Purifying their hearts by faith" (Acts 15:9). Here is another living motto full of the soul's deep rest. For the conquest of evil within us, for emancipation from its tyranny as it lies around us, here, according to the gospel, is the heart, the center of our secret. "Through God we shall do valiantly; it is He that shall tread down our enemies" (Ps. 60:12). Yes, it must be even so. If evil is to be overcome indeed, not merely repressed but overcome, at and from the depths, there is only one adequate way. Expressed from one side it is—Jesus Christ, brought by the Holy Ghost to the very throne of the heart. Expressed from the other side it is—faith. That is to say, the true secret is a trusted Christ.

This fact of the spiritual life may be, of course, like every other, misstated, and misapplied. It may be put so that it seems to mean an absolute "quietism," in which the soul merely sits still and lets things be. It may be applied so as to seem to suggest a result in which the disciple shall come to claim an unsinning "perfection," getting beyond humiliation and the confession of sin. But the thing in itself stands sure. The one true victory over inward sin is a trusted Christ, in all the Divine simplicity of those words. Tempted man, defeated a thousand times after all your efforts, make this sacred experiment for yet one crisis more. Call in the Lord, the Stronger than the strong. Give yourself over to Him. He will hold you, and tread down the enemy. So, you, held up by Christ, shall in Christ tread him down; resting, yet victorious.

And is not our secret the same for sorrow, and at last for death? The trusted Christ is the one perfect Anodyne for a broken heart. And He is the one Friend who can cross with us the last river, and say, as we are passing, "Thou shalt not see death; thou shalt not taste death; thou shalt never die; thou who believest in Me. Rest, and in that rest go over."

(2) "Giving all diligence." Behold the other side of the shield. The rest of faith is anything but a way to contrive for us a safe "slackness" in the Christian course. Rather, the promise of it is the greatest possible stimulus to diligence. For it is an assurance that real diligence, applied at the right point, is immensely worth the while.

What is the highest and at the same time the simplest purpose of the means of grace—secret prayer, self-scrutiny before God, the

Holy Scriptures, the sacred Supper of the Lord, the Christian Sabbath, public worship, family devotion? Mainly, a twofold purpose, two aims converging into one; a growing knowledge of our need, and a deepening and ever-developing sight of our Lord Jesus Christ as "all our salvation and all our desire," so that we both love His will and rely upon His power. If we neglect "all diligence" in the spiritual life, then, let us be sure of it, we shall decline in the deep desire to be conformed to His image and to follow His steps. Further, we shall decline in the conscious activity and persistence of the faith which rests in Him for peace and for power.

So, for the sake of the "rest of faith," let us "give all diligence." Only let us be "diligent" all the while in the recollection that the life of our life, the soul of our secret, deep in the center, lying within, and above, and distinct from, all the means, is to the last, a trusted Christ.

13

The Cup and the Covenant

This cup is the new testament in My blood, which is shed for you—
Luke 22:20

One change in the translation is called for here. We will read the word "covenant" in the place of "testament"; "this cup is the new *covenant* in the blood" of the Lord. There can be no reasonable doubt that the Greek term is best rendered thus. The evidence lies not only in the term's ordinary usage, but also in the fact that our Master was here certainly making reference to the prophetic Scriptures, above all to the great passage of Jeremiah (31:31), where we have a "new covenant" announced. It is quite certain that the Hebrew word there *(b'rith)* is to be translated "covenant," not "testament." So the same word is appropriate in this sacred reference to the prophetic passage.

True, the word "testament," or "last will," would convey to us here thoughts full of beauty and power. It has been finely said that our Lord, in dying, bequeathed to us all His wealth, and then rose again to be His own Executor. And the story is told of a Scottish peasant girl, stopped by Claverhouse's troopers on her way to the secret worship place in "the moorlands of mist," and questioned where she was going. "Sir," she said, "my brother has died, and I am going to hear his will read, and to get my share."

It was an answer as full of true theology as it was full of wit too quick for the questioner, who let her go. The promises of Christ *are* a bequest, ordered, irrevocable, sure; the Will of the Elder Brother, in which "the whole family in heaven and earth" have share. So in deepest truth the gospel *is* a Testament. Still, as I have said, the word "covenant" is here the more accurate representation of our Elder Brother's utterance when He founded the covenanting Feast.

Taking the sentence so, let us look at some factors in it, the better to grasp and to use it.

(1) What *is* that "New Covenant" of which He spoke when He gave to them "the cup, after supper"? We find the answer primarily in Jeremiah 31. We find it twice again in the Hebrews, in the eighth chapter and in the tenth. And in 2 Corinthians 3 we have another passage, full of light on the matter, where Paul speaks of the gospel ministry as dealing with a "New Covenant," not of "letter" but of "Spirit"; that is to say, concerned not with the written tablets of Sinai, which condemn, but with the gift of Pentecost, which brings life.

Looking over these Scriptures, we read the undertakings of the New Covenant. They are two; each wonderful, each divine, and forming in their harmony the very "secret of the Lord." First, there is a grand *amnesty* for the guilty soul which accepts the covenant; "their sins and their iniquities I will remember no more." So it is undertaken, out of the sovereign mercy of the covenanting God. The subjects of the Covenant, infinitely unworthy, chargeable with rebellion, with countless wanderings from their Lord "everyone to his own way," shall be welcomed back as if all this had never happened. It is an "amnesty," indeed, an "act of oblivion," full and sincere as the heart of God.

Then, in living connection with this, comes in the grand second term: "I will put My laws in their hearts, and in their minds I will write them" [see Heb. 10:16, 17]. In Jeremiah and in Hebrews this term is mentioned first in the Covenant. But on reflection we find that, in the order of the thought, it comes in second. For it *rests upon* the other: "I will write My laws in their minds . . . for I will remember their sins no more." Even so; such is the divine way of peace. The forgiveness, absolute and (as to any cost of ours) unbought, precedes. Then, not till then, but then, comes the inward work wrought on the forgiven. The same Agent acts in both. The Giver of the amnesty is the Worker of the purity. And the same way to get each grant of heaven is prescribed to the subjects of the Covenant. Alike their pardon and their purity are to be *received* from Him. Their pardon of course, BUT their purity also. Let them bring "heart" and "mind," "just as they are," to His Spirit's operation. Then He, not they, will take the pen, and write: *"I will put* My laws in their hearts; *I will write* them in their minds."

Christian, remember the New Covenant—and use it. Welcome the legal force and tenacity of the very word Covenant. The Lord of mercy and life binds Himself with it, in the bond of His fidelity to Himself. Cast yourself at His feet—and then and there claim, in humble boldness, the peace and also the inward hallowing which He stands *covenanted* to give.

(2) This Covenant, says the Master of our souls, is "in My blood." Yes, it is as free to us as the summer air. But, that it might be so to us, it cost Him His agony and bloody sweat, His cross and passion; the *Lama Sabachthani;* all that was meant in the death of the Lamb of Golgotha. It is as sure as that unspeakably sacred preliminary can make it. No partial or precarious blessings are intended to be ours, when the Contract bears *that* Seal. And oh, what reverence, what consciousness of an inexhaustible obligation, what a bond (which yet is perfect freedom), will be upon the soul which takes, and uses, *all* the blessings of the New Covenant, when it contemplates that Seal upon that Deed!

(3) "This Cup is the New Covenant." Here is a message, straight from the heart of Jesus Christ, for our Communion hour. Take that Cup, O disciple; drink that Wine. As you drink it, recollect the Covenant. As you recollect, look again in the great Covenanter's face, by faith. As you look, and as you use His royal Ordinance, say to yourself, "As sure as this chalice is no dream at my lips, so sure His amnesty over me, and His sin-annulling power within me, are for my very soul no dream, but fact."

14

Contrasted Views of Self

My righteousness I hold fast, and will not let it go; my heart shall not
reproach me so long as I live—Job 27:6
Mine eye seeth Thee; wherefore I abhor myself—Job 42:5, 6

These two assertions come from one mouth, from one heart. They are pronouncements by the same speaker upon the same subject, himself. The contrast of the two is diametrical and absolute.

The wonder of this is to be explained not at all by the character of the speaker, as if he were a hasty, fitful, unstable person, who did not know his own mind from one hour to another, and were ready on slight inducements to recant his sayings. The explanation lies in the great difference of the light which fell upon the subject-matter at two different times; the light in which, at first and then at last, Job saw himself.

(1) The first assertion was made when Job had only human light to read his heart by. We remember the position; and certainly we shall be slow to judge Job severely as we do so. Nay, we shall be wise not to judge him at all, remembering, as someone has well said, that we, so ready to criticize our brethren, are not only not seated on the judicial bench, but not even summoned to the jury-box. We remember with sympathy and reverence, in Job's case, how terrific were his trials, how utterly inexplicable (except behind the veil which hid from him the action alike of God and of Satan) were his accumulated sufferings, and how exquisitely trying to his lacerated spirit was the line taken by his friends. Still, not as judges but as reverent observers, we have before us the fact that he took up an attitude of energetic

211

self-vindication, a tone of indignant self-assertion. In the light merely of man upon man he saw himself as a being pure of purpose, true of heart, just and kind. The baseless insinuations of his friends, who assumed that he had done some foul concealed sin, spurred him by reaction into the most extreme language of self-satisfaction. He was righteous; he was good; he had nothing to confess; his heart should "not reproach him as long as he lived."

There was a sense in which he was right. His friends did grossly mistake him. In respect of their opinion, he had reason in saying he was virtuous. Only in so doing he ran the tremendous risk of forgetting that there was another point of view, another kind of light; the light of a human standard was too dim to tell him *all* about himself.

(2) Then at last, as the wonderful story works itself out, another light is let in upon him. Not Zophar, or Eliphaz, or even Elihu, but JEHOVAH speaks to Job. Very remarkable is the way in which the book represents His action on His servant's conscience. He speaks very little, if at all, about Job's moral imperfection. He simply reveals to Job His own divine glory as the omnipotent Creator: Maker and Master of Creation, Cause of all existence in the world. He draws His disciple's eyes upward from self to attempt to gaze on Him in the inscrutable yet radiant majesty of His sovereign will. Then Job breaks down; he belies his misguided estimate of his own goodness, and "abhors himself."

We must not, indeed, think that Job was convinced of sin by the mere, solitary, isolated realization of the omnipotence of God. No; he knew God already, in a deep experience, so we gather, as just and holy. The convicting power lay in this, if we read the case aright; that the great Revealer so showed His absolute Creatorship to Job as to cast a new and awful consciousness upon him that God's justice and holiness were absolute and infinite, as the moral attributes of a Being absolute and infinite in the mysterious power to cause and to maintain the world.

However, it was the light of the Lord which showed Job himself, and brought him to his knees, and drew that word of self-abhorrence from his mouth, and then "stopped" that mouth in penitent silence at last.

Never did human hearts more need than now that illumination, that searchlight, upon themselves. At our day, conviction of sin is woefully uncommon. "What must I do to be saved?" is a question heard now, by man and by God, far, far more rarely than, let us say, sixty, or fifty, or forty years ago. Yet it is a question which concerns the very life of true religion. For "the glorious gospel of the blessed God" is calculated for convinced sinners, not for self-complacent virtuous men. The doctrine of the Cross is still "folly," except to the broken, contrite heart. Let such hearts cease to be, and the gospel will sound in vain; or rather it will be silent as airwaves are silent when there are no ears to know the wave as sound.

Where is the remedy? It lies in our being reawakened to a soul-sight of God, the infinitely Holy One. It is the promised work of the Spirit to reveal Him. Then "come, Holy Spirit, come"; show us God in Christ, as Fire, as Light. Then we shall see ourselves in our tremendous need. And then You can show us indeed that same God, in Christ, as Life, as Love.

15

The Emmaus Road: Part One

Behold, two of them went that same day to a village called Emmaus—
Luke 24:13

Let us join these two men on their walk. Perhaps we have done so often before. For surely there are few true Bible readers who do not love that perfect narrative, Luke 24:13–35, and have not often tried to realize the scene in some degree, feeling themselves there, thinking, talking, looking, listening, as if in companionship with Cleopas and his friend.

It is a scene inexhaustibly rich in help and comfort to the Christian. It carries with it, as great literary critics have pointed out, the deepest inward evidences of its own literal truthfulness. For it so narrates the communion of "a risen God" with commonplace men as to set natural and supernatural side by side *in perfect harmony*. And to do this has always been the difficulty, the despair, of imagination. The alternative has been put reasonably thus: Luke was either a greater poet, a more creative genius, than Shakespeare, or—he did not create but record. He had an advantage over Shakespeare. The ghost in *Hamlet* was an effort of laborious imagination. The risen Christ on the road was a fact supreme, and the Evangelist did but tell it as it was. And in that fact lies hid, safe and living, full of the power of an endless life and a blessed hope, the very salvation of our souls.

Well, if the narrative of that walk and talk is such, we need not fear weariness and monotony if we join once more the two pedestrians, however we may have done so before. This Sunday we will do so, and again, and yet again. Emmaus will yield us fruit each time.

Today, then, take the story from a side which is not often, I think, remembered by the reader. On what day of the week, and at what season of the year, did the incident happen? On the first day of the week, and at Passover-time. What do these notes tell us about the conditions and surroundings of that outdoor conversation, so deep in its topics, so wonderful and blissful in its results? They tell us that the surroundings were anything but sacred and retired. That road must have been a frequented one, not improbably a crowded one. Passengers were everywhere upon it, coming and going, passing and crossing. It was a scene full of the stir of publicity and the common day.

Most, if not all pictures, ancient and modern alike, which gave us the Emmaus Road, present to us a sort of Sabbatic scene. The two, the three, are seen pacing a lonely track over fields which look the very picture of repose. It is Sunday afternoon, in a hallowed region and in a devout age. All conduce to heavenly thoughts, exchanged in tranquil privacy, while the sun sets slowly upon the holy day.

But it was not actually so at all. To the Jew, let us remember, then as now, the first day of the week was the first weekday. As Saturday was his Sabbath, Sunday was as it were his Monday. With it, the stir of common life began again in force, and men went about their common ways of toil or pleasure. Nor only so. This "first weekday" was also one of the days of the Passover season at Jerusalem. And that season in that place meant a vast aggregation of pilgrims from all distances, the thronging of the neighborhood of the city with literally many hundreds of thousands of men and women besides the normal population. If we can combine in thought the crowds and stir of a modern English Bank-holiday with the conditions of an Oriental festival, religious in its essence, but assuredly also partaking in some measure of the nature of a fair-time, we place before our minds not inaccurately the state of things over the fields and roads of Judea on that particular day.

So the sacred Walk proves to have been a walk in public, in a crowd. It must have been carried on under difficulties, with many an interruption, as groups or individuals pushed past, or came in the way, while the three companions held onward.

Is there no message in this to us? Yes, there is indeed. He who found Magdalene alone (save for angels) in Joseph's garden, and spoke to her heart there in the sweet solitude, spoke with equal ease and power to Cleopas and that other troubled heart upon the open and often noisy road. He is the same today. Literally, perhaps, amidst the throng and the turmoil of the modern street, He is able to talk to his followers' hearts. "I have often found my Savior present with me on the foot-plate of the engine," said a Christian man a few years ago, a driver on the Metropolitan line. Yes, the most public, the most *blatant* surroundings can make room for the companionship of Jesus. And when we are not upon the literal highway, yet all too conscious in some other sort of the thronging noises of our modern life of publicity and haste, still let us remember Emmaus. Let us take it not as an idyllic picture, in contrast to our present lot, but far rather as a reminder that in our lot, just as it is, the Lord can meet us, and can talk with us, till our hearts also know what it is to burn with Him.

16

The Emmaus Road:
Part Two

Jesus Himself drew near, and went with them—Luke 24:15

Last Sunday we surveyed the probable scene on the Emmaus Road, as Cleopas and his friend set out upon it that never-to-be-forgotten day. We found it a busy scene, a highway alive with pedestrians coming and going, on a day which resembled our Monday more than our Sunday, and which bore some of the characteristics of a holiday as well.

This reminded us, by way of a lasting and general message, of the willingness and the power of our Lord Jesus to make His presence felt not only in secret places, or in sacred places, but "out in the open" of life, "before the sons of men" (Ps. 31:19).

Let us revisit that scene today. In thought let us steal up to that group of three, as they make their way along the road. Let us come near enough not only to look but to listen. Let us, above all, listen to Him who has just joined the two, and has somehow drawn them into a conversation, till by degrees He has raised it into a monologue, while they listen with eager ears and burning hearts.

Observe first that He is the kind *aggressor.* They do not accost Him, but He them. And His first words, if we interpret the Evangelist correctly, were not quite welcome to them. The Revised Version, taking a "reading" of the Greek which seems to be the best attested, renders the close of verse 17 thus: "And they *stood still, looking sad.*" Nay, we may even, with good support, translate the last word of the Greek not only by our word "sad" but almost by "sullen." It was the sadness of men too unhappy *to like* to be disturbed, particularly by one who

217

spoke cheerfully. And can we doubt that a sacred, radiant *cheerfulness* was on the Lord's face and in His voice that day?

Well, they met Him at best with small encouragement. But in a few moments He has got them to unbend their attitude of reserve. A kindly question unlocks the pent-up trouble. And point by point, burden by burden, doubts, and fears, and disappointments, and hopeless regrets, they have told Him all. He has let them speak on and on. Totally ignorant of His identity they are yet somehow put at ease by His bearing, His voice, His manifest goodness. Conceivably they might have feared He was an enemy in disguise, seeking to entrap the followers of the crucified Prophet to their own ruin. But that, they felt, was impossible. They trusted Him, and they told Him all.

Then, when they had quite done, He speaks. Their whole case is before Him. He can touch their wounds now with the fine precision of perfect sight as well as perfect skill. He can speak to men who *know* that He now knows.

"O fools and slow of heart!" [v. 25]. Was it a harsh beginning? In our English it is, BUT not in Luke's Greek. The *tone* of the Greek may be well represented by, "Dear slow-witted people!" or the like. And I dare to think it likely that the blessed Speaker not only spoke kindly, but smiled, nay, almost, (may I say it?) laughed a gentle laugh as He spoke. He had patiently heard them out as they stated their case, reckoning up on the side of despair one point after another, which yet was all on the side of "everlasting comfort and good hope through grace." Did He not feel, in His pure humanity—for the risen One is forever human—that there was matter here to move a smile, as He proceeded to sweep the whole bewildered tangle of mistakes away forever?

We know what followed; that wonderful Bible lesson, "beginning at Moses and all the Prophets." Till the sun was low He spoke and they listened. With faultless and tender power He pressed the anodyne of the holy Word upon their aching wounds. To Him in His Resurrection the Scriptures were, if possible more than ever, the Oracle of God, manifold yet one; and He was everywhere their true Theme. So He led them on, till, *before they knew it was He,* by the pure power of the Spirit upon the written Word, they were again at rest, about Him, and upon Him.

And now the walk ended, and now they, so lately almost sullen at His intrusion, would not let Him go. "Abide with us"; and He obeyed. Then they saw Him break the bread. Then they knew Him for Himself.

What does the walk say to us after this fresh review? It tells us that "this same Jesus," for He is today the same, understands the human heart. He knows how to approach it patiently, bearing with its shy and even sullen reserve. He knows how to "lay Himself alongside" the disturbed and restive spirit. He knows how to make the hearts He loves burn with faith and love towards Him. He knows how to make the sealed oracle stand open to the humbled soul, and how to tell the soul, through that oracle, about Himself. He knows how and when to let the veil drop, and to manifest Himself, "this same Jesus, the same yesterday, today, forever" [Acts 1:11; Heb. 13:8].

17

The Emmaus Road: Part Three

They rose up the same hour, and returned to Jerusalem, and found the eleven—Luke 24:33

Again, once again, we go out upon the Emmaus Road, and look for Cleopas and his friend. We have watched them to the end of their outward journey, with that unexpected and unknown Companion. Look, they have entered yonder house with Him, after a brief conversation at the door, as they press Him to join them for the night. Shall we see them again? Probably not; they will not stir out till morning. No, not so. Before very long the door opens, and our friends, Cleopas and the other, two now again, not three, step out and, at a pace far quicker than before, retrace their way and hurry through the shadows to where the far-off evening lamps glimmer from Jerusalem.

It is a walk now not to, but from, Emmaus. We shall find a message in this walk also. Why had the two friends left Jerusalem and walked away to the distant village? Can we doubt that the main motive was the desolateness, the repellent sadness, the hostile gloom of Jerusalem, now the Lord was gone? More than this, may we not think, for the heart was then what it is today, that they left Jerusalem not only because it was the abode of triumphant enemies, but because there they would meet woe-begone friends? They would only be the more deeply sad for companionship with those who had hoped so much with them, and then, with them, had met so awful a disappointment. Such, almost for certain, was the mood in which Thomas (John 20:24) absented himself from his brethren

220

that very evening. Such, in part at least, may well have been the feeling of these two.

There is a powerful *centrifugal* force in some forms of grief; not in all, but in some. Particularly, a bitter disappointment tends to disintegrate a circle. To use the expressive word common in Scripture, the disappointed man is "ashamed." He has been, he thinks, *fooled* by fortune. He would fain hide his face, and eat his troubled heart alone. To meet the partakers of his once cherished delusion is an unwelcome aggravation of his own mortified regret.

That force assuredly began to work when the Lord Jesus had died, and before His disciples knew that He was risen again. The circle began to break up here and there. Had He not risen, the centrifugal process would have gone on, for lack of a central magnet. And had the centrifugal process gone on, there would be no Christian Church today, and my reader and I would have been engaged with other themes than the person and influence of a half-forgotten Rabbi, who died in Judea very long ago.

Now let us think again of those two men hastening through the deep shadows towards the city. They are under the power of a *centripetal* force. They are bent upon rejoining their friends, for they have now good tidings of great joy to carry to them; and a great joy, particularly supposing it to be also a pure and noble joy, cannot rest without communication. So they make their way to the city, and to that upper chamber which had so lately been the disciples' rendezvous, that they may share their glorious secret. And they find their friends there with similar tidings so ready on their lips that the travelers have no time to speak first: "The Lord is risen indeed" [v. 34].

The Resurrection drew them all with one mighty embrace together; or rather, not the Resurrection, but the risen Lord.

Here is a weighty matter for the student of Christian evidence; one of the vast moral proofs which gather around the victory of our Master over "the dreadful tomb." It will bear close attention, and will reward it with a fresh conviction of the profound ultimate harmony of faith and reason at the door of Joseph's sepulcher.

But this is not all. The glad speed of the happy pilgrims of Emmaus back to Jerusalem tells us also some permanent spiritual truths. It says to us that nothing so draws human hearts together as a living and conscious contact with Jesus Christ. It bids us hope, amidst the countless confusions and disputes of thought, not in the world only but in the Church, that we shall yet find in a fresh Heaven-given realization of His life and love the great antidote to the earth-born spirit of division in our poor Christendom. And to the individual believer it says that he will surely find, in the experience of his soul, that two things will regularly rise and fall together—the personal contact of faith and love with the Lord Jesus Christ, and the longing impulse to tell others of His glory and His grace.

18

The First Easter Evening: Part One

Then . . . came Jesus and stood in the midst—John 20:19

It was the late evening of the Resurrection Day. In our last Sunday's study we traced that eventful day through the afternoon to some time after sunset, when the two pedestrians of the Emmaus Road hastened back to the city with their great discovery. Here we are admitted to a glimpse of the place where that return-walk ended, and of the event which presently occurred there.

We follow them to the city gate, which then probably, for it was Passover time, stood open all night. We trace them to the street where the house of the upper chamber stood; to the courtyard gate, fastened, "for fear of the Jews," but opened to the known voices outside; to the inner door, up a flight of stone steps, and opening directly into the great room. This also was unlocked, at the call of friends. And now the two streams of wonder and joy met together; the chamber was full of voices. "The Lord is risen indeed, and hath appeared unto Simon"; "We too have met Him on the road; He made Himself known to us in the breaking of bread."

What a scene of eager interchange of heart and speech! The spacious place, where light and shadow play from the evening lamps upon the company, is full of broken sound. Such a moment had never been on earth before. An event of infinite wonder was before them, as it were at their very feet. The dead was living, and in His own right and power. The seeming awful defeat of the Cross was only the antecedent to the supreme and irreversible victory in which the beloved Master, taking His life again, presented Himself as indeed the Life, "declared Himself to be the Son of God with power . . . by the resurrection from the dead" [see Rom. 1:4]; "the power of an endless life" [Heb. 7:16].

Behold, He made all things new [see 2 Cor. 5:17].

Let us often return in thought to that memorable hour. Again and yet again let us reaffirm to ourselves its immeasurable reality and radiant meaning. Vain, even to the understanding, even to common sense, are the efforts, whether crude or subtle, to explain it away. Sometimes the attempt is made with actually grotesque crudeness, as in a paper sent to me lately from India, gravely asserting that the Lord Jesus revived from half-death, lived to a good old age, and lies buried—in Cashmere. Sometimes the denial takes very different forms, graver, more thoughtful, more formidable. But all alike break and retreat at last, like waves from the shore, before the vast, immovable evidence of the fact of the Christian Church, and the historic certainty that but for a great and manifest victory of the Lord over the death of His sacred body the Church would soon have melted back into the world. Whereas, on the contrary, it promptly presented itself to the world as a force full of Him, an organism of transfigured lives, morally lifted to a height unknown before, totally different from their old selves, and spiritually capable of moving the whole human mass around them, "in the name of the Lord Jesus and by the Spirit of their God."

As we ponder the Resurrection, the two opposite aspects of it will appear equally important. On the one side is its literal verity, as an event of history, certain and trustworthy to the full along every line of inquiry and test proper to historical problems. On the other side is its supernatural mystery and significance; its process, defying, or rather transcending, imagination; its sequel, in which we see as it were eternity visibly inserted into time, a Being walking on earth, and taking meals at His friend's tables, and talking at great length to them, while yet the conditions of His bodily existence are inscrutable, miraculous, half celestial already.

The two aspects combine, for the thoughtful believer's mind, into one feeling of profound reliance upon the supreme and boundless trustworthiness of the risen Lord, as Fact, and as Power. Thinking ourselves back into that upper chamber we can repose ourselves be-

224

fore Him, while He tries our faith now by His silence, which leaves so much unexplained, and now by His words, as He speaks of things inconceivable to us as of simple certainties to Himself, and tells us, for example, that we, hereafter, having seen corruption, shall rise in glory. The Speaker is adequate to the promise. It is the Christ of God arisen.

But now a hush falls upon the groups in that spacious room. The doors, fastened again after the entrance of the two men from Emmaus, have not been again disturbed. Yet another person is suddenly with them, in bodily presence. He takes His place in the midst, and smiles, and speaks. It is the Lord.

19

The First Easter Evening:
Part Two

Then . . . came Jesus and stood in the midst—John 20:19

We placed ourselves last Sunday amidst the disciples, apostles and others, who saw the sudden, silent presence of the risen Lord in the midst of them while they were so preoccupied with talk about Him. The scene in itself is a means of grace. We may often say, each of us, with the Christian poet—

> 'Tis light at evening-time when Thou are present;
>> Thy coming to the eleven in that dim room
>> Brighten'd, O Christ, its gloom;
> So bless my lonely hour that memories pleasant
>> Around the time a heavenly gleam may cast
>> Which many days shall last!

But now let us turn to some of the spiritual messages of that hour.

It is full of such messages. It tells us, for example, how true the heavenly Master is to His promise, "Where two or three are gathered together in My name, there am I in the midst of them." He who is our Advocate above, in the celestial glory, on the divine throne, helped our faith to a firmer grasp on that great fact of the Unseen by offering, just once, here on earth, in audible speech, before His followers, that great example and specimen of His advocacy, the "High Priestly Prayer" of John 17. Even so He who invisibly, inscrutably, yet really, is always now present in each gathering of His dear disciples, helped their faith to hold that truth more fast and more fully by that visible entrance in among them after Resurrection.

226

Again, to take another example, the scene carries to us in living form that great message, that peace, joy, and power for His disciples are inseparably united to personal relations with Himself. How did the peace of God, passing understanding, come to them that night? By the manifested presence of Him who first said, "Peace be unto you," and then showed them His hands and His side. He came as His own supreme Evangelist, in His own utterance of "peace." He let them see Him as His own supreme Evangel, in His finished Sacrifice and that glorious sequel of it, His living Presence. So it is forever. There is no substitute, nor ever can be, for personal relations with Christ, crucified and risen. Would we taste a "peace" which is indeed "of God"? It must be "through our Lord Jesus Christ," as not a Principle only but a Person. Faith must see His wounds; faith must hear His benediction, nothing between; resting directly on Him. Only so will our life have banished out of it the bewilderment, the misgiving, which lie at the troubled heart of half-religion.

And when He poured into them "the oil of gladness," how was it? By His same wonderful yet divinely simple manifestation of Himself. "Then were the disciples glad when they saw the Lord" [v. 20]. He, the "Man of sorrows and acquainted with grief" [Is. 53:3] as indeed He was, and is—in the sense of that great saying, "To suffer passes, to have suffered, lasts forever"—is yet, to the believing soul, "my exceeding joy" (Ps. 43:4), by just being what He is, and being, in all that He is, present with His own. In His religion, while there is abundant room for holy griefs, there is no place for melancholy, which is the grief of perplexity and weakness. Christ is essentially not only peace but joy, just because in Him holiness, love, and power converge upon issues of victorious happiness for Him and for His. And our enjoyment of Him as our joy will be great in proportion to our faith's "sight" of Him as such. Look not for joy at a distance from Him, as a thing merely derived and secondary. *"In Thy presence* is the fullness of joy; *at Thy right hand* there are pleasures" (note the word) "forevermore" [see Ps. 16:11].

Then, when what they need is power, the secret is the same. Soon they were to leave "that dim room" for the outer world, with all its sins and all its enmity. They would need power indeed, not apart from peace and from joy, by no means, yet as a thing special and distinct. And it is the Lord Jesus Himself who gives it. "I send you"; "Receive ye the Holy Ghost" [John 20:22]. And the Holy Ghost is so inseparably connected with Jesus Christ that the symbol and warrant of the gift of Him came in the form of the very breath from the immortal lips of the Giver. And when that Gift is given, and *is received,* we know what the surest index of Its presence is; it is the growing greatness of Christ to the soul, and His growing power over it from within. "He shall glorify me"; "Strengthened by the Spirit, that Christ may dwell in your hearts by faith."

So the message of the upper room is, *Christ is All.* "Even so, come, Lord Jesus" [Rev. 22:20]; "come in, and sup with us, and we with Thee" [see Rev. 3:20].

20

The First Easter Evening:
Part Three

Even so send I you—John 20:21

We return to the upper chamber for one more study.

It is deeply instructive to observe the Lord's use of the occasion to remind His disciples at once of *their mission*. We might have thought it likely that this aspect of things would be reserved and postponed for a season. The very day of the Resurrection, we might imagine, would be given wholly to the consolation of the griefs of the disciples and to their profound enjoyment of the recovered, the more than recovered, Lord. On the walk to Emmaus, apparently, He had on the whole done so; giving no commands, simply chasing the mist of hopeless sorrow before the summer sun of His undying presence. But then again His very first appearance to Mary in the Garden, loveliest gem of all the narratives of Scripture, speaks another lesson. He had indeed addressed Himself first to her broken heart, and shown her how He understood her tears, and uttered her name in a tone which opened up all His heart to her. But then, He had at once sent her on an errand; instantly there was work for her to do for Him for others. "Go unto My brethren."

> She first, all-happy Magdalena, bore
> From Joseph's grot the bliss unheard before;

telling the apostles themselves that the Lord was risen, and on His way to the eternal throne. Yes, and the men of Emmaus, if they had no direct command to that effect, acted as if they had. As we saw a few Sundays since, their joy was *centripetal*. They were driven by holy instinct to communicate. They felt a mission to their brethren in the city, and hastened back to fulfill it.

So at the evening meeting. The Lord cannot let the happy company go with nothing upon their hearts but their own happiness, even though it was the purest happiness in Him. He lays *a mission* upon them, with a very definite commission, and He breathes divine power into them in view of it. "As my Father sent Me, even so send I you." "Receive ye the Holy Ghost." "Whose soever sins ye remit, they are remitted unto them; and whose soever sins ye retain, they are retained" [vv. 21–23].

Those last words I do not elaborately examine here. My conviction is that they were meant by the Lord in a sense as luminous, as perspicuous, as it was deep. Neither Scripture nor earliest Christian history witnesses, so far as I know, to His having meant a mysterious hierarchical commission, such that remission of sins must be conveyed normally through a clerical stewardship, or even through the stewardship of the whole Christian body; as if the soul's perfectly direct access to the Lord Himself, spirit to Spirit, were impeded. Rather, I take the words to be a commission to the Church to be the Master's messenger to souls, carrying to them His terms of pardon, and inviting them in His name to go with them to—Himself.

But there is no need for our purpose now to go further into this question. It is enough for us to remember the broad fact that the risen Lord Jesus did, then and there, give to His disciples first peace, then joy, but then also *mission*. He needed them for the purposes of His work in the world. He had truth to tell the world, and they must be His means of telling it. He had pardon, and holiness, and heaven, to impart to the world, and the impartation must be done through them as His agents, His very lips and tongue, as it were, charged with the proclamation of His covenant of life, and themselves instinct with that life; not His machinery, but His body, for His work.

It was a blissful thing to meet in the upper room; to sit there beneath the evening lamps, listening in quiet to "the pleasant voice of the Mighty One." But it was a bliss meant to issue in blessing for the unhappy world around. They must go forth to say, in His dear name, "Peace be unto you." They must point others to His hands and His side, till they too should be glad, seeing the Lord. Filled with the Holy Ghost, they must be living witnesses to others of the sacred pardon they had themselves received.

So that primeval congregation at last broke up, as commissioned messengers, and the room was dark and still again.

One of the most solemn of sights is a church left empty after divine worship and the preaching of the Word. Men and women have met before God—and dispersed to mix again with the world of common life. How have they gone? To be as if the holy hour had not been? Or to live amidst life's business and action as those who have seen the Lord, and tasted His joy, and received His Spirit, and who remember that as the Father sent Him, even so sends He them?

21

Lakeside Thoughts

Jesus showed Himself to His disciples by the sea of Galilee, which is the sea of Tiberias—John 21:1

Fair and beautiful is the narrative of John 21. Very few pictures, even in the long and luminous gallery of the Bible, surpass it in respect of either its landscape, or its figures, or their action. Have we not often shut the eyes, as it were, to the printed page that the scene may "flash upon the inner eye"?

But today I attempt no long "re-telling" of the inimitable, the inspired simplicity of the story as it came, touch by touch, to the pen of the aged John from his deep, clear memory. I ask my reader to reconsider it only that it may tell us some truths about our Lord Jesus Christ, so that we may afresh "believe that He is the Christ, the Son of God, and believing may have life through His name."

That is the aim and reason of the whole Bible. Assuredly it is the great purpose of every gospel narrative. Not to please the imagination, though nothing can so charm it as these holy scenes, but to make the Lord Jesus great and present to us—this is the purpose.

Looking then upon Him as presented to us in John 21 we note Him first as dealing with His beloved disciples through trial for blessing. Can we doubt that the long and quite fruitless "night of toil" was ordered by His will, or let us put it rather so, was allowed in order to the attainment of His end? If they had "caught nothing" all through those dark hours upon the flood there would have been far less preparation and fitness for the wonder and the joy of the morning. Yes, it was He assuredly, the Son of Man who rules all creation, "the fish of the sea, and whatsoever passeth through the paths of the seas" [Ps. 8:8], who willed them all away that night from the nets of His friends.

Jesus Christ sees far, and He plans on lines that "go off into mystery," though always, for His servants, into blessing. Let us learn a new lesson of personal confidence in Him by that midnight waterside. Wait for "the end of the Lord"; it will be seen tomorrow morning.

In a remote churchyard in Cambridgeshire I read a few years ago an epitaph, nearly a century old, on two aged sisters. The text included in it was, "When the morning was come, Jesus stood on the shore." It seemed to me to sum up lives in which the patience of faith had been the guiding principle. Those two forgotten disciples had trusted through the night and the toil. They were willing to wait. They knew it would be well tomorrow morning.

Then, the Lord appears in this scene before us in the solemnity, yet the blessed peace, of His absolute, autocratic masterhood. "If I will that he tarry, what is that to thee? Follow thou Me" [John 21:22]. It is the tone of one who, if not God, is speaking infinitely beyond His rights. Who is He, that He should treat these two profound human personalities, this great pair of heroic saints, as pieces on a chessboard, to be moved as He thinks fit as in some game He may be playing? He is Jesus Christ, over all, blessed forever. He is only acting upon His lawful footing. He has made, and He may dispose. But also "He has made, and He will bear" (Is. 46:4). His imperial tone is not that of the *mere* autocrat, vain of his authority, and enjoying it, cost what it may to the subject. It is that of the Divine Possessor, who holds indeed infinite rights over his possession, but who also cares for it with an individual and tenacious love. Those who know Him know that He is "altogether lovely," not as Savior only, but as Savior King.

Lastly, as we take from John 21 these specimens of its witness to Jesus, let us look at the Lord as He prepares the meal upon the beach, and gathers those seven men round Him, and gives them the food from the fire of coals. See here His character on that side of it so precious to us men, His holy love of our society, His kind, affectionate concern for our most common needs, His *philanthropy*, His "attachment to man"! Those seven men were indeed saints, by

His grace. But they were also mere men; they were peasants, men of the people, Galileans, provincials in a region which itself was provincial to the centers of the fastidious civilization of that time. And He was the Son of God, radiant and sublime in His immortality, mysteriously entered upon through the great Passion which redeemed a world. Yet He loved the people; all His saints were in His hand; they sat down at His feet (and at His side); "every one received of His words" (see Deut. 33:3).

He is the same Jesus still. His "philanthropy" is identical today. O man, mere man, sinful man, He does not love your sin. But He loves you. He loves your human nature, your human company. And He is able to make you, by being your Friend, fully capable of companionship with Him.

22

"Joined to the Lord, One Spirit"

He that is joined to the Lord is one spirit—1 Cor. 6:17

Here is a sentence deep as eternal truth can make it. Yet it stands in a context full of the harshest realities of tempted human life. A recent Corinthian convert is in view. Last year, perhaps last month, he was the slave of sensual vice. And he is in grave danger of returning to the mire, for he still has to live close to it. But he is now a Christian; not a great or advanced Christian, yet a Christian in truth. He has found His Savior, and surrendered himself to His life-giving hands. Therefore he has a vast resource of strength with which to resist the evil, or rather to rise above it, as a bird can spring on its long wings from beside the snare to the deep freedom of the skies. The man has spiritual wings, to escape upward to God. Has he come to the Lord? Then he is "joined to Him." There is vital continuity between Christ and the man. The forces of Christ are at his disposal, in immediate contact; a contact so deep and essential that it can only be expressed thus: Christ and the Christian are "one spirit."

Let him recollect that fact, and use it, meeting the enemy with the Friend who has knit up His glorious Self with His weak disciple. So he shall "more than conquer" [see Rom. 8:37]. He shall "mount up with wings" [Is. 40:31] and look down from above on the snares of hell.

So it was then; so it is today. The realities of life are still stern and urgent. Fierce are the temptations that still beset the weak will, at its weakest point. And still there is a way, present as it is divine, for victory, and more than victory, over the devil, the world, and the flesh.

"One spirit." The words lead us straight to the thought of the Holy Ghost. In view of Paul's general teaching, we may boldly take them as a short expression of the truth that when man comes in his need to Christ, for pardon, and for moral purity, then man is linked, by no mere impersonal influence, but by the living "Lord, the Life-Giver" (as the Greek of our Nicene Creed calls Him), in a vital bond, with his Redeemer. As the life-forces from the center of our own being articulate into oneness our head, and feet, and hands, so the Spirit of the eternal Life makes one the believer and the Lord.

It transcends all our analysis, but not our reasonable faith. More and more today we meet examples of the hidden force which one human spirit can, as it were, project into another, lawfully or not. Then why hesitate to think that the Divine Spirit can so occupy our spirit, not violating but indwelling, as to transform it within itself, and so articulate it to the life and will of Jesus Christ that it shall be no mere metaphor to say that we are spiritually His limbs?

"A member of Christ." Such we Christians are, as to God's gift. And what God gives, in Word and Sacrament, *we must take,* if we would have it real to us. The soul must welcome in its promised Lord, opening itself to His wonderful offered life, drinking in with its thirsty lips the stream of His Spirit. We must clasp the Christ offered us in His sacramental promise, yielding to Him, using Him. Then indeed we are "joined to the Lord," His living limbs, He and we one spirit.

> Within our veins His currents be,
>   His Spirit on our breath.

Such, in some measure, is the Pentecostal truth; such is this mysterious but most practical work of the Holy Ghost. He, according to Scripture, operates always for us with reference to the Son of God. He "glorifies" Christ. He brings us "to the obedience and the blood-sprinkling of Jesus Christ." By Him we are "strengthened, that Christ may dwell in our hearts," welcomed in by unfearing faith. He is the One Spirit of the one Body; animating, uniting; blessed be His sacred Name.

In closing, let us recollect some practical issues of the Christian's limb-relation, by the Spirit, to the Son of God.

(1) Here is a profound secret of liberty and power. My Redeemer is no mere distant Potentate, nor even merely a Friend at hand. He

is in contact with my inmost being, so that His will, His love, His power, are given to run, as it were, into me. Is this no dream, but His revelation? Then let me walk out in the path of His will habitually recollecting that it is so. Christ's limb bears Christ's life. It never need serve sin. It never needs to shun God's will.

(2) Here is a summons, clear and high, to a life of willing service to my Lord. Am I one spirit with Him, His living limb indeed? Then my true life is—to be the willing implement of His will. Our limbs exist, in the order of nature, not for themselves but for the imperial will above them. What is the function of my right hand? To do my will. And its health, its very life, depend on its articulation as my implement into me. Well, I am to Christ the hand, the foot, the lips. I exist, in union with Him, for use by Him. There is my wonderful function. There, too, is the law of my inmost health, power and joy. To serve Him is thus indeed to reign.

(3) Lastly, here is the living warrant for our great hope, the resurrection of the dead, the life of the world to come.

> Can the Head forsake the limb,
> And not draw it after Him?

No, thanks be to God, who giveth us the victory. "If the Spirit of Him that raised up Jesus from the dead dwell in you, He that raised up Christ from the dead shall also bring to life your mortal bodies, by His Spirit dwelling in you" (Rom. 8:11).

Nearly three centuries ago, good Bishop Hall set out this truth in his peculiar style of quaint beauty: "It is abundant comfort to us that our Head is in the fruition of that glory whereto we, the poor laboring part, strive to aspire. Our Head is above water, though we the limbs are yet wading through the stream."

23

The Holy Trinity

God is love—1 John 4:8, 16

Perhaps the reader, looking at this page, feels some surprise that such a title should go with such a text. The title directs our thoughts to a subject which is in any case a supreme mystery, and which to many minds presents itself as a theological riddle without a solution. The text, with its sublime simplicity, its three short words, each of them so luminous and so great, seems rather to direct us to thoughts level to the little child; to invite us away from every intellectual difficulty to a perfect rest, a quiet anchorage for soul and mind.

Yet the title and the text, if we approach them patiently and with prayer, will soon prove to be friends quite ready to embrace one another in a perfect harmony of meaning and message. Let us address ourselves to this thought, with our spirit's ear open to the voice of Him who on the one hand "dwells in the light unapproachable," and on the other hand is Love.

(1) The Holy Trinity. What does the Christian Church mean, in the essence of its meaning, when it affirms its faith in the Trinity in Unity, the Unity in Trinity? Very briefly, we may reply as follows.

The Holy Scriptures, from first to last, emphasize with awful earnestness the Oneness of God, the unique and solitary glory of the Eternal Being, in respect of that Being's sole possession of self-existence, of infinite power, wisdom, goodness, and of those supreme rights over all other beings which can attach to the sovereign Maker and Sustainer alone. "I am the Lord; My glory will I not give to another" [Is. 42:8]; "The Lord our God is One Lord" [Deut. 6:4]; that is the voice of Moses, Prophets, Apostles, Christ.

But then the same Holy Scriptures, in some degree from the first, and more and more to the last, give us another side of truth also. Pointing to the One Light of the One Godhead, they bid us listen to sounds from within that Light. Hearken; it is the voice of the Mighty One. Hearken again; the Voice can be heard also as Voices. In music, one glorious sound, as it peals from the organ through the minster, can be heard also by the instructed ear as three sounds in one—a *triad,* as the musician calls it; a chord, in which oneness has within it more-than-oneness, so that it is at once one and three. Hearken then again at the shrine of Light, and you will hear a Triune Voice. There is One within the Sanctuary saying, "This is my beloved son, in whom I am well pleased" [Matt. 3:17]. There is Another who answers, saying, "I delight to do Thy will; Thou lovedst Me before the foundation of the world" [Ps. 40:8; John 17:24]. There is yet another Voice, in which the Two wonderfully blend, yet bearing its own tone also; it speaks breathing from within that Light, and it says to us, "Come and know; come and see; come and live."

In other words, the Bible distinctly tells us that the Godhead is, *within the Oneness,* more than one. It presents to us Three Persons (we can use no weaker word), not fewer nor more, but Three; all within the sphere of the Supreme Being, for all have eternal and infinite power, wisdom, goodness; so related that never, from eternity to eternity, are They separate, but forever One in Their blessed Being; so distinguished that from One to Other flows, forever, in a fathomless and holy tide, the fullness of infinite Love.

(2) "God is Love" [1 John 4:16]. Is the text then, after all, out of tune with the title? "God is Love." The words are, as we have said, sublimely *simple;* yes, they are level to the heart of the little child. But then, they are *sublimely* simple. When we ponder them, there is a radiant depth in each, clear but unfathomable. Who can spell out all that is hidden in God? Who can analyze to all its depths what, in regard of Him, is meant by LOVE? Who can see all the splendor shining from that link of life between them, "God is Love"? For it tells us that the Eternal does not only know what love means, nor only feel it as an emotion coming over Him. He is Love; it is His Essence, it is

His Nature, it is His Life. Before all thoughts of loving action going out from Him stands here this radiant truth that Love lives and breathes forever *in* Him, as it were His very Self.

Now is not this almost a confession already of the glory of the Holy Trinity? For the faith of the Trinity is but the faith that the inner Life of the Godhead is no awful Solitude, but a blissful Society which yet is One. It says that there is a glorious sphere within the "One Eternal" for mutual Affection, infinite in measure, absolute in tenderness and joy. It tells us that at the heart and at the head of the universe of being there lives, and wills, and acts, not a remote Unit, but a gracious Unity, within whose bright Essence, "dark with excess of bright," Love is always meeting Love. And it bids therefore, not the little child only but the life-worn man, conscious of sin, of sorrow, of the grave, look upwards towards the Infinite with a certainty, deep as existence, that He can indeed be trusted and be loved, for He is Love.

> So God the Father, God the Son,
>   And God the Spirit we adore,
> A sea of life and love unknown,
>   Without a bottom or a shore.

24

"With Christ"

I am continually with Thee—Ps. 73:23
To depart, and to be with Christ—Phil. 1:23
We shall ever be with the Lord—1 Thess. 4:17

Here are three Scriptures with one message, three gems strung on one golden thread. The first refers to the life present, here and now, in the flesh, on the pilgrimage. The second takes us to the life after death, the state of souls, the home of the just made perfect. The third opens to us the prospect of the resurrection-glory, the final and eternal bliss. Each view, each region of time and being, has its own distinctive aspect and character. But for each and all these Scripture words give us one and the same secret for rest and hope; it is, the Companionship of the Lord. Alike for "life, death, and that vast Forever," the answer of peace is the same. The Christian quiets and strengthens himself for trial here and for the unseen things hereafter, reminding himself of an inalienable talisman which can charm all ill away and bring all blessing to him, alike "on the journey and in the fatherland," when he repeats to himself those words, "with Thee," "with Christ," "with the Lord."

"The great Companion"! It is indeed a recollection of peace. A gifted contemporary of mine at college, betrayed into mournful wanderings in the use of one of the finest of minds, till he reached at length what seemed a total unbelief, wrote in one of his books the words, full of an infinite sadness as I think of them, and of him, *"the great Companion is gone."* That would be the death-knell of all human joy, worth calling joy, if it were true. But it is not true, "blessed be the

241

God and Father of our Lord Jesus Christ." As we repeat that apostolic doxology does it not already calm us with a self-evidencing power? Let the bewildered reason, lost, in the forest labyrinths of the thought which has ceased to worship, turn again to contemplate, as if for the first time, that "Holiest of Holies, Jesus Christ our Lord." Let it ponder "the fact of Christ." It will assuredly, if it does so in simplicity, come to see that He, as we have Him in the Word, could not possibly be the invention, or even the evolution, of the human mind. That portrait, by those artists, could only be drawn, or rather photographed, from life. And it is the portrait of One who cannot but be—the great Companion.

Disciple of the great Companion, who died and rose again, and is alive forevermore, take then this watchword with you, and live for time and for eternity on its resources.

(1) "I am continually with Thee." This was Asaph's word, after the tremendous conflict with doubt which his psalm so candidly discloses to us. He emerged by the mercy of God, into a certainty, full of rest and hope, that he had the great Companion for his own. The air around him might be thick with mysteries, and his view of their solution in detail might be very dim at the best. But he had the great Companion; he was continually with Him; the hand of his eternal Friend was holding him, even in the dark. The Lord knew; and he knew the Lord; and the Lord and he were close together. That was enough. "Christ is alive today," wrote the late Dr. Dale, of Birmingham, beginning to prepare a sermon. And his own words flashed back upon his soul a new consciousness of Christ, transforming everything. Let us take the watchword up for our own life, and complete it; "Christ is alive today; and we are continually with Him."

(2) "To depart, and to be with Christ." Such was Paul's outlook into the state of souls. His immediately added words are, "which is far better." Better than what? Is it

> Far better, yes, than pain and care, than weariness and strife,
> Than fading hopes and gathering fears, and all the
> death of life?

Not at all. He has just been giving us his own estimate of what life—life in the body—is to him. It is a grand estimate. He has said that to him "to live is *Christ.*" And what can possibly be "far better" than that?

Nothing, except a very much larger measure of the same. So the state of souls is no state of abeyance, or of shadows; it is a life indeed; "far better" than the best hour on earth of an apostolic life of holy and rejoicing service. It is a nearness, conscious and ineffable, face to Face, spirit to Spirit, love to Love, with the great Companion.

(3) "So shall we ever be with the Lord." Here is the final prospect, the promise for the endless end. It is Paul again who speaks, writing to his bereaved Thessalonian brethren, and telling them of the eternal and ultimate joy, "the resurrection of the dead, and the life of the world to come." What does he say about that life? True to his Inspirer's example, he gives no detail, but goes straight to the essence, to the heart of heaven in its clearness. And that is just this companionship with the great Companion. "We shall ever be with the Lord."

And on the other hand, in the miracle of His grace and love, that Companion will delight Himself forever in our company! "Father, I will that they whom Thou hast given Me be with Me where I am" [John 17:24].

25

The Safety of Samuel

And Samuel grew, and the Lord was with him—1 Sam. 3:19

The story of Samuel shines out in the Biblical portrait gallery through a series of even unusually life-like pictures. From Hannah's silent prayer when Eli so greatly mistook her state and her spirit, to that mysterious and awful scene in the cavern at Endor when the departed saint returned to warn Saul of his end, the name of Samuel takes us over a course of narrative which has a power and solemn beauty of its own.

Let us linger a little this Sunday over that first stage of his life, his residence at Shiloh, prolonged till the little child, the child taken so pathetically early from home ("the child was young," as the moving words run in 1 Sam. 1:24) was grown up into the young prophet, whom all Israel knew.

Two impressive lessons, permanent for all human time, are read to us by those first experiences of Samuel. They are the opposites of each other. In the first place we have the dark phenomenon of Hophni and Phinehas. There, in the very sanctuary of Jehovah, in the priestly line, under the paternal presence of Eli (and Eli would not have "judged" Israel had he not been in some respects a noble man as well as a good one), dwelt two men who sinned with a high hand, habitually, grossly, and so as to poison the whole moral air around them.

It is one of numerous reminders in the Bible that official religion may be no barrier whatever to personal wickedness; a lesson taught us from the prophet Balaam down to the priest Caiaphas and the apostle Judas. It is an awful and far-reaching warning. Let us not judge Balaam, or Hophni, or Caiaphas, or Judas. Let us consider ourselves. "Many" will, "in that day," plead with the Redeemer Himself in their infinite alarm to spare them because they once had external communion with Him; "eating and drinking in His presence," and listening, perhaps with high *approval,* to His "teaching in the streets." In vain; "I never knew you; depart from Me, ye that work iniquity" [Matt. 7:22, 23]. May almighty mercy deliver us from the fatal snare of external without internal religion.

Then, in the second place, comes the message of the safety of Samuel in the place poisoned by Hophni and Phinehas. Did his pious mother know to what tremendous risks she was exposing him? She can scarcely have been quite unaware. But we may suppose that her faith, quickened by the manifest divine answer to her prayers in the fact that she was his mother, rose to the assurance that the Eternal Himself would watch over her darling when, keeping her vow, she "lent him to the Lord." If so, she is the prototype and the encouragement of many a mother of later days, who has been compelled, under some inevitable condition of life, to trust her Samuel to be kept pure amidst surroundings charged with strong temptation. If it is right that he should go, the Lord of the first Samuel can keep the latest Samuel safe, by the same secret which worked so powerfully so long ago.

Eli, to be sure, would shepherd the little Levite with affectionate anxiety. We can well believe that his weakness with his own rebel sons would only quicken his care over the young life which he held so much in his hands still. But who does not know how fatally strong can be a young man's bad influence over a boy, quite overmastering the weaker hold of an aged friend? If a power greater than Eli's had not been upon Samuel, he would have gravitated almost for certain to the attraction of the wicked priests, just because they were nearer to his own age. But a greater, a victorious Power was there, upon him, around him, within him. "He grew"; words that might have only led to the sequel, "and so he fell." But then comes the divinely saving clause, "and the Lord was with him." So he stood, and walked at liberty, and "served in humbleness and fear," and had ears for the very voice of the Holy One, and came forth at last the mighty messenger and minister of His will.

No place is safe which we enter against the will of God. No place can hurt us which we enter according to His will, and where we remember and respond to His presence.

The naturalist tells us of insects whose proper habitat is the air, but whose food is found below the water of, perhaps, a stagnant pool. They descend to find it, and in safety. For it is given them to collect about them a globe or envelope of air, and this protects them as they dive. Such was the Presence to Samuel at Shiloh; such it can be to us today.

A beloved kinsman of mine, long since departed to the Lord, was sent, a gentle lad fresh from home, to a military college. That college was then, below the surface, a scene of deplorable vice. No man of iron by nature, he was yet made strong in the Lord, just as he entered, by the discovery of his Savior in a full conversion. "He grew, and the Lord was with him." When, crowned with high distinction, after a three years' residence, he left the college, vice was out of fashion there.

Blessed be his dear memory. Blessed be his Lord's dear Presence.

26

At the Door of the Eternal Tents

That, when ye fail, they may receive you into everlasting habitations—
Luke 16:9

The best supported reading of the Greek here bids us make one material change. Instead of, "when ye fail" we should read, "when it shall fail"; that is to say when it, "the mammon of unrighteousness," shall drop away from you at death. This change leaves however unchanged the important point that the reference of the sentence is to death, to our hour of dissolution; not to the final prospect of the glorification of the disciple's whole being at resurrection, but to that mysterious time when our "flesh and heart faileth," and the external world of our mortal experience "faileth" from around us.

One word more upon translation. The Greek which is represented by "everlasting habitations" invites the more definite and vivid rendering, "the eternal tents." It is a clearly drawn picture. The Lord Jesus puts before our thought the unknown land beyond the veil of sense. The departing spirit enters it, to find, as it were, an encampment of the blessed ones who have already entered in. The "earthly house of this *tabernacle*" has, it would appear, its counterpart there. Perhaps to convey the truth that the conditions between death and resurrection are transitional, not final, the holy dwelling-places are imaged rather as tents than more solid structures; tents pitched in the Garden of Bliss, for the Israel of that happy Exodus in which "the souls of the faithful, after they are delivered from the burden of the flesh, are in joy and felicity."

So much for some details of the translation of this remarkable passage. But the main interest of it, for our purpose today, lies in those words which no examination of the Greek can alter, *"that they may receive you."*

I need only remind the reader in passing what is the context, the environment, of that phrase. The Lord, in this remarkable parable of the Steward, has told us how, by a financial stratagem, by using his discretion apparently in lowering the tenants' rate of rent in kind, the steward had secured himself a lasting welcome to the tenants' houses. From this the Divine Teacher draws the unexpected lesson that we too, if we will, may secure a loving *hospitality,* an affectionate *welcome in,* to abodes of bliss after death, on the part of those whom we may have helped heavenward by our use of the "mammon" of earthly means and faculties, too often perverted to "unrighteousness." We may, under God, smooth the upward path, and bring the pilgrim happily home, so to speak, by our use for others of what the Savior has entrusted to our stewardship. If so, and if the objects of our interest and aid have preceded us to Paradise, they, the denizens and, as it were, possessors of that blessed home will personally welcome us in when we come. They will, with thoughts of memory, gratitude and love, "receive us into the eternal tents." They will hail us as those to whom they owed so much in the dear days below.

The lesson of the passage, a ray of luminous truth and beauty shot from a deep and difficult context, has manifold aspects. But only one of these shall be set today before us; that which looks towards the question of mutual recognition in the unseen state.

Few, if any, passages of Scripture, if I am right, more definitely tell us that—

> Though changed and glorified each face,
> Not unremember'd we shall meet,
> To endless ages to embrace.

For what does the Lord manifestly imply? That the doors of the abode of the blessed will be, and are, the scene of personal and welcoming interviews. Whatever be the conditions and circumstances of the departed Christian soul, this is plain. The lips of Him who cannot lie, of Him who "has the keys of the Unseen and of death," assure us here of this. Just when everything of external resources "fails," then, out of sight, but in profound reality, a recognizing meeting takes place above in "the Paradise." The soul already at home sees and knows the soul just entering; remembers the incidents of the old life; recalls the benefit, the love, the obligation, and "receives" the new-comer not as some human being only, but as the particular human being who has proved so loving and so lovable.

> We bless His faithful word
>> Who once, in parable, withdrew the veil,
>> And told us that, when here His servants fail,
> The tidings there is heard;
>
> And friends with friendly feet
>> Make haste, delighted at the glad event,
>> And lift the white door of the eternal tent
> The arriving friend to greet.

Let us take this assurance, and use it, in simplicity and truth. Let it not take an undue place in our thought and hope; the supremely *first* element in all Christian hopes of heaven must be, as we lately saw, the fact that "we shall ever be *with the Lord.*" But this distinct prospect of a meeting, and more than meeting, full of memory and of love, vivid with mutual delight, is a glorious adjunct to that blessed prospect. Let us "comfort one another with these words."

Even so, Lord Jesus. Prepare us, by patient faith now, the faith which takes Thee at Thy Word, for that wonderful hour of sight, when *they* will hail us into *Thy* unveiled presence, blessed forever.

27

The Well of Sychar: Part One

Jesus saith unto her, I that speak unto thee am He—John 4:26

It was the Samaritan woman to whom thus the Master spoke, sitting at the well of Sychar, tired in limb, tireless in patience and in love.

A singular and beautiful interest attaches to that well. It is very nearly, if not quite, the only spot in the Holy Land where the pilgrim can say to himself, with reasonable certainty, that *here,* in a narrow and precise application of the word *here,* within the square of these few measured yards, once stood, once sat, the Lord. Of a score of localities we can be certain that He was *there,* in a sense less restricted. At Nazareth I have looked around the horizon of hills, and pondered the certainty that His eyes were familiar with the same contour. Upon the beautiful Lake, upon the top of Olivet, in the streets of Bethlehem, the similar thought lies with all its weight of wonder on the disciple's heart. But at Sychar we know that the well of today is the well of that immortal yesterday, so that there, just there, almost within the compass of a man's extended arms, Jesus our Lord was bodily present once.

The thought is not indeed all-important, however it may be impressive. Our certainties about Him who is our eternal Life and our "good hope through grace" [2 Thess. 2:16] transcend the curiosities of topography to an infinite degree. Yet the contemplation of the narrow, memorable spot has a spiritual use. It can aid the soul, however little, yet in reality, to concentrate, and to define, and to carry home to the imagination, so as to be made more concrete there for thought and faith, our spiritual certainty.

May it somehow thus serve us now, by His grace, and for His glory. Listening to the colloquy by the side of that old Syrian well, may we the better recollect and embrace the sameness, yesterday, and today, and even unto the long forever, of the heart, the will, the love, the Lord, who once said, beside it, "I that speak unto Thee am He."

That was a very wonderful utterance, in the clear depth of its simplicity, the monosyllabic simplicity which it wears in our English Bible. And it was the climax of a very wonderful conversation, wonderful in itself, wonderful in the parties to it. There, on *this* side, sat the Son of God, the Word made flesh, the blessed Christ. "Found in fashion as man," [Phil. 2:8], as true man, as tired man, as thirsty man, He sat there; only the more gracious and the more great because of the fact, which in Him and in Him alone was so marvelous, that He was Man. Holy, harmless, awesomely undefiled, infinitely separate from the sinfulness of us sinners, higher than the heavens, He was yet, quite as really, the fatigued wayfarer, fain to rest just as He was, (The Greek word used here *hóutos* seems to indicate the unstudied attitude of sheer fatigue.) on that rude seat, in a humiliation as mysterious and as sacred as His glory. There, on the other side, stood the poor Samaritan, setting down her heavy waterpot, to look Him cheerlessly and aimlessly in the face. Her lot, her character, her heart, what was it all? She was a damaged and broken instance of our fallen humanity; a provincial, a common woman, sinned against and sinning, discontented and embittered, vexed with circumstances, at discord with herself, and so far hardened, by the sad forces of a life lived away from God and tolerant of its own sin, that she would fain fence and parry with all her power when the thirsty Stranger turned from the request for water to speak about her God and about her soul.

Deep and moving is this contrast, Jesus and the Woman. And as we reflect upon it we remember that it is, in its essence, permanent, immortal. It is as enduring as is the Savior of man upon the one side, and as is the human heart, with which He comes to deal, upon the other. Let us seek our message of this Lord's day from that fact.

The Samaritan is not a person only, but a type. She is—may I not confidently say it?—the very picture of the soul aloof from God, in its debasement, its pollution, its unrest, its spiritual dullness and *ennui*. Do we see nothing of ourselves, in the days of our ignorance and alienation, in this poor peasant of Sychar? Indifferent, yet ill at ease, averse to true knowledge either of self or of God, soiled with many a stain—some of them external stains, some of them hidden deeper, too deep perhaps in the heart to look out on the surface of the life—is there nothing in all this to which conscience and consciousness respond from within? Does not our personality stand, in hers, confronting the Lord, and confronted by Him, in a contrast to Him which cannot be measured? Are not we, in her, searched, and rebuked, and shown something of our own inbred alienation and isolation from Him? "Depart from me, for I am a sinful man, O Lord [see Luke 5:8], and Thou knowest it too well. Do not look upon me so, do not look through me so. I must be repellent to Thee; for I know Thee who Thou art, the Holy One of God" [Mark 1:24; Luke 4:34].

28

The Well of Sychar: Part Two

Jesus saith unto her, I that speak unto thee am He—John 4:26

We listened and looked, at the well of Sychar, in our last Sunday's meditations. The interview spoke to us, perhaps in an unexpected way and measure, of ourselves. It placed before us a Jesus Christ whose juxtaposition with us cannot but force the soul to pause upon itself and ask what to Him it looks like, and whether He can be otherwise than repelled by what we are.

It is certainly thus, not seldom, with many hearts, and hearts which are by no means extreme examples, on human standards, of human sinning. Let *the average heart* be brought to any measure of real spiritual consciousness by the awesome beauty of the moral face of Christ; it will do nothing less than writhe under the tremendous difference; I use the word "tremendous" with deliberate intention. "Thou art of purer eyes than to behold iniquity" [Hab. 1:13]; "Mine eye seeth Thee; wherefore I abhor myself" [Job 42:5, 6]. There is nothing like that sight to engender that abhorrence, which, taken by itself, would be the beginning of the final despair.

But now turn again to the interview of Sychar. What is the Lord, the Christ, the Holy One, actually doing with this poor, weary, dreary, uninteresting, unhallowed human being? He is offering her, upon the spot, the life eternal. He is expounding and unfolding to her— HIMSELF. "If thou wouldst have asked of Me, I would have given thee living water" [John 4:10]. "I that speak unto thee am He" [John 4:26].

There are few scenes, even in the blessed Gospels, which throw into such supreme relief as this the willingness of our Lord Jesus

253

Christ to save a soul, to save it from itself, by Himself, and to do it then and there. I know not where else to go for a lovelier and more living illustration of that willingness, that promptitude, of a love which is its own eternal origin, to come and pour its inmost blessings out upon what we should call the most unpromising, the most unalluring of hearts. Poor Samaritan, who can care for her? No one—but the Son of God. And *how* will He care for her? Will it be by giving her a long preliminary discipline? Will it be by putting her to school on low levels of truth? Will it be by consigning her to His apostles till she is educated up to a capacity for Him? No; it will be by unveiling to her His own loving glory, "nothing between." It will be by the gift to her, without one shadow of intermediation, of His own eternal life. It will be by transforming her into a spiritual worshiper of Him who is a Spirit, in letting her see her Savior in the Christ of God.

Just as she is, poor, wretched, blind,

He lays His heart open to her unhappy heart. And, lo, the miracle is wrought upon the spot. She speeds away to the town, a messenger, a witness, an evangelist for Jesus.

The lesson, the type, the truth, is everlasting; it is up to this moment's date, and it is for us. What the soul needs, in precisely its low and broken estate, is nothing short of Jesus Christ Himself. *A Te principium, Tibi desinet:* "From Thee begins, to Thee shall end the strain." We shall indeed find, to the limitless ages, that to Him will forever gravitate and issue forth the highest and the utmost of our wonder and our worship, as we know the Father in Him, and Him in the Father, in the heavenly life. But oh, we must begin also with nothing less than Him at the very bottom of the process. Nothing can ever really save us but His personal gift of the eternal water, as the soul meets Him alone at the well, and even Apostles are not there to step between. Nothing can really show us either ourselves or our redemption but His own utterance to us, by His Spirit to our spirit, "I that speak unto Thee am He."

Long ago the Moravian saints, in their Greenland Mission in 1740, had besieged for years the half-bestial tribes (so they seemed) with the teaching of elementary moral principles; and they were scoffed at for their pains by the savages, who replied that they knew all that already! At last they told them of the crucified Lord, and kept back nothing from them of His love and glory. Then did Kainaek, the medicine-man, the ringleader of all the pagan devilry, step forward, saying, "Say that yet again, for I would also desire to be saved." And salvation came indeed to him and his fellows, and made a moral Eden in the wild.

> Thou, O Christ, art all I want,
> More than all in Thee I find.

His secondary blessings are precious indeed, with a glory shed from the hand which gives them. The society of the Christian Church; the hallowed and hallowing Sacraments, sealing all the promises of the blessed Book with the imperial seals of heaven— these things indeed are great. But their greatest function is to point onward, inward, upward, away even from themselves, to Him, the Personal Christ, the Lord, the Lamb, the King, the Priest, the everlasting Friend, who liveth, and was dead, and is alive forevermore, the same forever, everywhere accessible, face to face, spirit to spirit, heart to heart. Sinful soul, you may be a weariness to yourself, but you are nevertheless dear to Him. Here, wherever you are in need of Him, is the well, and He is seated by it, at leisure now, today, to bless thee with Himself. "I will give thee living water. I that speak unto thee am He."

29

A Limb of Christ:
Part One

We are members of His body—Eph. 5:30

For the word "members" here let us read "limbs." This rendering will bring us a gain in life and force, while equally true to the original. "Member" is indeed only a longer word for "limb"; the two are synonymous, one of Latin origin, the other of English; a limb means a member, and a member means a limb. Only there is this practical difference, that we have come in the course of time to use "member" in a large, vague, general sense, in which we do not use "limb." We speak of a "member" of Parliament, or of a committee, or of a club, but never of a "limb" of such companies of people. The word "limb" is much more restricted than is its parallel word to denote connections deep, organic, vital, between part and whole.

To describe the Christian, then, as a limb of the Lord Jesus Christ brings home to us in a special way the thought of a connection with Him mysteriously close and strong. It reminds us that the bond between follower and Master is far more than one of spiritual regard, however reverent and tender; far different from one which depends even upon His being the sublime Object of our worship and of our gratitude, as our Divine Savior from condemnation and our gracious Shepherd and Friend. It leads us deep into that wonderful secret of His love and power, our living union with Him. It points us to that gracious desire and purpose of His heart, that we, sinners of the dust, ruined and wrecked by the fall, "stained and dyed" by our own transgressions, should not only be mercifully rescued by His atoning work, but brought inconceivably close to Him in His holy and all-powerful life, and knit up with Him in it by living bonds, even as our hands and fingers are part and parcel with us, always close to us, always instinctively protected by us, as dear parts of our very being.

Can we dwell too much upon this side of the truth that "we are limbs of His body"? As I grow older, it seems always more wonderful and beautiful to me that the Lord should love us in precisely this way, with this deep desire for living union with us. His love might be conceived of as great and beautiful, while yet far short of this. We might well think it a great thing to be told that He cared so much for us as to plan and provide for our happiness somewhat as a great philanthropist might provide for objects of his beneficent efforts, whom he had found in the slums, and transplanted to some wholesome, cheerful training school, and there equipped them for prosperous life, and so transformed them into other beings. On these his *protégés* from time to time he would look in, and visit them, and talk to them, and greatly encourage them, and attach them to himself in personal affection. But the Lord's "philanthropy" is of an order infinitely above even that high level. He has, indeed, rescued us, and brought us under training for an eternal prosperity. But His heart is not satisfied with only that. He must have our very being joined to His. He must see us one with Him, and Himself with us. He must live, in His exalted life, so that He never lives apart from us. For He claims us to be "limbs of His body."

A few Sundays ago we briefly touched upon this aspect of truth, from another text; "joined unto the Lord, one spirit." But it will bear reconsideration, from many sides and from many texts. Deliberately I trace over again from this great word of the Apostle the lines of this inexhaustible treasure of truth, and press the happy, holy inferences upon my own and my reader's heart.

For the time, put other views of it away, and rest upon this, the insight which we get through this window of heavenly light into "the love of Christ, which passeth knowledge." For me, a sinner, the Prince of Glory thus cares. To Him, in all His majesty, "at the right hand of God, angels and authorities and powers being made subject unto Him," I am dear to this degree and in this sense. "He *hath a desire* to the work of His hands," though that work is my poor, broken, sin-spoiled self. And the desire is so tender, and so strong, that it cannot stop short of the will that I shall be His "limb." Ah, He does not merely condescend to touch my personality with His holy finger! That would be wonderful, far more wonderful than even His willingness to touch of old the corroded body of the leper. But it is not enough for Him to stretch out His finger and touch my fallen being. He must transfigure my being into a oneness with His which makes it, as it were, His finger; a "limb of His body."

Therefore I may indeed be sure that He greatly cares for me, if He thus so greatly provides for a ceaseless closeness to me and union with me. This is love indeed. Let us adore it by taking it at the word, and let us repose in the wonder of our being indeed, by His power and grace, "limbs of His body."

30

A Limb of Christ:
Part Two

We are members of His body—Eph. 5:30

Last Sunday we took up this sentence and weighed some of its
heavenly gold; remembering how the word "member," used by our
translators here, is only a longer equivalent for the word "limb." We
dwelt upon that word, with all its vivid, homely, powerful associations. We let it, above all, instill into our attentive and quiet hearts
just that thought, that He who claims us to be His limbs must indeed greatly love us; for our limbs are our companions, everywhere
and always; we and they are one thing, one interest, one life; their
condition is of untold importance to us; their very appearance is of
consequence. Union can no nearer go than it goes between limbs
and man.

Are we, we His unworthy disciples, limbs indeed of our all-glorious
Lord? Will the King take the peasant, nay, the mendicant, with damaged character, to be part and lot with Himself? Even so. "His desire
is to the work of His hands," for whose redemption He has given
Himself. He has come forth to be not only All-in-all to us, but One
with us. He has "joined us unto Himself, one spirit," even as we remembered a while ago. "We are very members incorporate," we are
limbs of His body." "Behold, what manner of love!"

Today let us take one step farther in thinking out this treasure of
the truth of God. Let us consider the light which it sheds upon *the
Lord's use* of His believing disciple.

Our bodily limbs, in the order of Nature, are dear to us. We take
a keen instinctive interest in them; we often consciously, more

often unconsciously, take care of them, "nourishing and cherishing." We clothe them, warm them, exercise them, heal them. Their well-being, even their well-looking, is a pleasure to us, at least so as to make their discomfort or defacement a pain.

But our thoughts of them do not terminate in this thought. The supreme interest to us of our lips, hands, feet, lies in our use of them. All day long we are, through them, carrying out our purposes, carrying on our business, getting our duties done, enjoying our pleasures.

It is indeed all-important to my hand that, for its own life and health, it should be in fullest living union with me. It is important to my comfort that it should, in such union, be alive and healthy, giving me no trouble by ill conditions. But it is above all things important to me that I should have always the freest and most instant use of it. Its own well-being is much. But my use of it in that well-being is more; it is the ultimate object of its existence as part of my system.

The moral is manifest. If we are indeed "limbs of His body," we are such, in the supreme and most noble respect of "membership," on purpose that our blessed Head may do with us, and through us, "the good pleasure of His will" [Eph. 1:5], everywhere and always; speaking His messages, accomplishing His works, traveling on His errands, by us His "limbs."

In the order of His actual plan and method, He has been delighted that it should be so. We may conceive of conditions under which His love might work by direct personal acts of volition only, dispensing with all intermediary channels. And never let us forget that He not only might but does so act in the inmost secrets of His relationshipwith human souls. Ultimately, whatever messengers He uses, it is He who touches, He who reaches, the soul of man.

But granting all this, none the less does the Lord actually, in the vast field of fellowship with our human lives, need and use us as His limbs. All through the story of Redemption it is so. In the Old Testament days He walked by Joseph, as His feet, to prepare deliverance in Egypt, and by Moses, as His feet, to lead up His people in triumph out of it. By Nathan, as His lips, He wakened David from his death-sleep, and by Isaiah, as His lips, He promised Himself to be the Lamb of God. In New Testament times He *"began* to do and to teach" (Acts 1:1) in His own person, BUT these words plainly imply that He went on to do, and went on to teach, through Peter, and John, and Paul, and Luke, and Aquila.

Even so to this hour. You, Christian disciple, are the Lord's limb not only for the sake of your life but for the sake of His work. By you He has action to do in this world of sin, and grief, and need. Through you He has to speak to human ears, or to succor human lives; through you to seek the lost, to support the weak, to visit the forgotten, to lead the blind.

Wherefore, you limb of Christ, who are also His loving and believing brother, "yield thyself unto Him, as one that is alive from the dead, and thy limbs as implements of righteousness unto God" (Rom. 6:13).

31

Two Aspects of Bethany

Lazarus, of Bethany—John 11:1
He led them out as far as to Bethany—Luke 24:50

Fair and dear to the Christian's heart is the name of Bethany. The associations of the life and love of Jesus have cast a beauty about the very sound: it breathes holiness and peace.

The village still exists. As the traveler leaves Jerusalem upon the Jericho road he arrives, after about half an hour's walk from the Damascus gate, which takes him into the Kedron valley, and then upward around the southern shoulder of Olivet, at the houses, gray, dilapidated, and not beautiful, of Bethany. Or he may take another line, and ascend Olivet to its summit, past the obtrusive structure of the huge Russian convent at the top of the road, and then find his way over fence and field to the minor hills of the eastward side of the mountain, where it looks down upon Bethany.

There is a charm about the surroundings, certainly when seen in spring, as there always is a charm over the rural landscape of that land of many-hued soil and of thronging flowers. But the villages of Palestine are seldom if ever in themselves pleasant to the eye, and certainly Bethany is not; actual or impending decay seems written upon its dwellings. Yes, but it still is Bethany. The immortal memories dignify and beautify it all.

For, indeed, there is that wonderful peculiarity about the memories of Palestine, that they are memories and so much more. In Rome, and in Athens, our thoughts are with "the great departed" in "the silent land." At Jerusalem they are with Him who was dead, but behold He is alive forevermore; His very name is life and hope; He is Lord of the future even more than of the past; He is, above all things, Lord of the present, "with us, all the days."

Pausing, and thinking of Him, at Bethany, we feel the power of two contrasted yet perfectly harmonious recollections of "this same Jesus."

(1) The first is the recollection of His almost home-life there. The Gospels, alike Luke (10:38–42) and John, tell us that Jesus was at home in Bethany. Just like the Gospel narratives, with their perfect blending of vivid picturing with grave reserve, they tell us little to gratify mere curiosity, but much to feed faith and love. At Bethany lived a family of three, two sisters and a brother, who drew to them the human love of the Lord, somewhat as John drew it. Jesus Christ took a gentle and gracious pleasure in them. He *liked* (may we reverently use the word?) their company, their house, their welcome of Him as their Guest. Long before the end of His blessed course, so Luke seems to indicate, He had become the well-known visitor, whom Martha served; to whom Mary listened wondering; who called Lazarus back to life, and a few days later supped with him at the same table. Yes, He delighted on His part, as Man with humankind, in their characters and conversation. True, He was the King of Glory. True also, He was the Man of Sorrows, passing on His mysterious way, spiritually *alone,* to the great Sacrifice. But He was also all the while *the Man.* "His delights were with the sons of men," and with the simple life of their human homes.

He could be just the Friend, the holy but none the less most pleasant Friend, perfectly used to every little household way in that dwelling at Bethany. It was almost His Nazareth again. He found two sisters and a brother there, not only three disciples. And in those last days of His, just at the close, in the very Passion Week, He *could bear* to be in quiet there, evening by evening—till He left the place on the Thursday afternoon to return no more as of old.

(2) Then came the Cross, and the Grave, and the Rising again "in the power of indissoluble life" (Heb. 7:16). How often in those Forty Days after resurrection He visited the beloved scene, we do not know. But at least once He was in the immediate neighborhood of Bethany. The crowning day had come. The Son, having glorified the Father

upon the earth, alike in death and resurrection, was to be "glorified by His side" above, "with the glory He had beside Him before the world was" (see John 17:5). Where shall He set His foot last, before He ascends to the Throne? "He led them out as far as to Bethany." Yes, once more the familiar village is to be visited. The scene of those home-hours shall be the point of departure for the eternal heavens. He takes the Eleven with Him; perhaps up that very path which I traversed, in 1897, to get, over Olivet, down towards Bethany, in order to see the spot which many thoughtful hearts hold to be the true scene of the Ascension. The Apostles and their Lord gather upon that ridged protuberance of the huge hill; for Olivet is indeed a mighty mass. Below is the village. There is the house of Martha—roof, window, door. Near it yonder is the face of rock where can be seen the empty grave of Lazarus. He who stands in the midst of the group sees it all, and takes it all with Him, as He ascends, blessing His followers, to the sky.

So the Lover of Bethany shows Himself to us there as the Jesus Christ alike of Home and of Heaven. Do our hearts love both those scenes? We do well. In Him they are akin. And in Him they shall coalesce at length into one bliss forever.

32

"No Root in Himself": Part One

Yet hath he no root in himself—Matt. 13:21

We find ourselves here in the midst of the parable of the Sower, and the phenomenon before us is that of "the stony ground." Or rather, and far preferably, for we are thus at once closer to the Greek and truer to the pictorial purpose of the Savior's words, let us call it "the rocky ground." So reads the Revised Version: "others fell upon the rocky places" (v. 5); "he that was sown upon the rocky places" (v. 20). The thought is not at all of a piece of ground encumbered with loose stones, needing to be picked out and thrown away. It is of a piece where under a thin layer of soil lies, broad and solid, a mass of rock, needing, if that were possible, to be upheaved, or to be crushed, that the fine roots of the sown grain might strike freely down and find the living moisture below.

The Lord Himself expounds this detail, as He expounds the rest of His great parable. The case indicated is that of the man who hears the gospel message, and "receives" it, takes it in some sense in; and does so "with joy." His emotions are stirred. He is charmed by the spiritual music, by the views and colors of the wonderful revelation of a mysterious happiness, exalted and exalting, here and hereafter. But unhappily the experience is not durable. The man comes to discover that the divine message involves pains as well as pleasures. He encounters "tribulation" in one form or another, in his Christian course. He is "persecuted" in one or another way, because he is an avowed disciple. And so "he is offended." He does not like it. His joy goes off. His reliance is shaken. His allegiance to

His Lord is too weak to bear a real strain. He has no "last"; a little while, and he has forsaken Christ for the world, and turned his back upon the celestial light.

A vivid illustration of the case is familiar to us in the early pages of the Pilgrim's Progress. There Pliable is seen setting out for heaven in company with Christian. They hasten together over the forlorn fields which border the City of Destruction; Christian impeded by the burden on his back, Pliable stepping out more lightly. They converse of the prospect which, so they are assured, awaits them if they reach the far end of the narrow way; the golden gate, the white robes, the angelic company, the face of the King. Then on a sudden, heedless of the ground, they both stumble into the Slough of Despond, and struggle miserably in the mire. Both at length climb out on to dry ground, BUT on opposite sides. Christian lands on the further bank, and plods on towards the wicket-gate. Pliable scrambles out, wet and wretched, with his back to heaven and his face to the City of Destruction, and leaves Christian, with an angry farewell, to "possess the brave country alone for him."

Pliable had "no root in himself." He "endured for a while." Christian had root. He was sad, and bewildered, and terribly defiled, BUT he went on.

The difference between the two wayfarers is plain to see, and it precisely points the moral of the parable of the Sower. Christian was convinced of sin. To the depths of his being he had come to know that sin was condemnable, and that he was himself indescribably "guilty before God." For him perseverance was a matter of life or death; he did not dare to return, for the thundercloud of judgment lay, for him, over the roofs and walls he had left. Pliable showed no sign, not the faintest, of real disturbance of the soul. He was pleasurably attracted by the prospect of a radiant future, and he liked, in respect of human sympathies, to be in company with one who was setting out in great earnest towards it. But he had no root *in himself.* His own conscience had never been awakened. Christian's convictions attracted and moved him, BUT they were not his own. He did not properly understand his own action. So when real troubles came across the track of it, he had no secret of resistance within him. He instinctively turned back—too probably forever.

Spiritual experiences differ very widely indeed. Not all pilgrimages present for our study the order of events which Bunyan gives us in his Christian's case. Not all pilgrims have in the same proportion the ingredients of alarm and of gladness dropped into their cup of life. But we may safely say that seldom will a Christian man be found, whose heavenward course is notably a persistent one, who has not, deep in his soul's inner history, the ineffaceable record of a "time of finding," a self-discovery never to be forgotten, when the Holy Spirit did His promised work, and "convinced of sin" that human heart, that it might be *driven* to believe on the Son of God, and live.

We will take the theme up again next Sunday.

33

"No Root in Himself":
Part Two

Yet hath he no root in himself—Matt. 13:21

The words "contrition," "contrite," are familiar in religious language. We well understand them to mean a state of moral regret, shame, and distress, produced by the thought of personal transgression. In Scripture we know the word "contrite" best, thank God, in a context full of the mercies of pardon, placed close beside the terrors of conviction; "a broken and a contrite heart, O God, Thou wilt not despise" (Ps. 51:17).

Dr. W. Kay, in his admirable commentary on the Psalms, a book of equal literary and spiritual value, renders the Hebrew word (*nidkeh*) not by the Latin "contrite," but by the Saxon "crushed." Let this remind us that exactly such *is* the meaning of contrite; it is just the Latin *contritus,* smoothed into an English form; and *contritus* means crushed, pulverized, broken into pieces.

Is not this a significant point, taken along with the picture of the "rocky" ground in the parable of Christ? What was the matter with that ground, from the sower's point of view? Precisely this, that immediately under the earth lay a hard floor of stone, cold and solid, upon which the feeble filaments of root would spread themselves in vain, only to die. It was a resisting mass which was not "contrite," and therefore impenetrable. Could some magic power have brought to it "contrition," could it have been *pulverized* where it lay beneath the upper earth, then through it the fibers could have found their way down, to reach at last the hidden moisture. Then the blade and ear above would have had the life of the deep ground in them, and have lasted, and have borne fruit "with patience." It was that uncontrite rock which frustrated all.

The moral is manifest. There is no bar to the living entrance of the message of Christ like that opposed by an unawakened conscience. For the gospel, while it carries in it, to be developed in time, and in eternity, a "power of God" capable of raising and glorifying our whole being as no other force in heaven or on earth can do, immovably insists on treating man first as a sinner, defiled and guilty before God. And where man refuses to see himself as such, there the necessary correspondence is absent; the key lacks its lock; the root lacks its soil. The crucified Lord, the Lamb of the Sacrifice—where is His beauty, that we should desire Him *as such*, till in some true sort we see *ourselves*?

But let that most merciful pain be granted to us to feel, and then it is otherwise. Let the sinner in some real measure see (and "abhor") himself, and let there then be presented to him the divine answer to his awful need—Christ for him, Christ in him—and then it is otherwise. Then the root strikes down, and finds the eternal watersprings. The convert then discovers *"in* himself," though indeed not *of* himself, a root of certainty, of possession. He "knows whom he has believed," in a way which makes him able to last, because he dares not live apart from the secret of continuance.

He may be attacked and fatigued by "tribulation," or even by "persecution"; and his frail humanity may feel them as keenly as any other man's. Yet how can he leave the Lord, whom he so immeasurably needs? He may be even more formidably beset by mental or moral doubts, seeming to touch the very base of things. Yet at his darkest hour he feels that there is such a correspondence between his central needs and the Christ of the gospel that a deep internal evidence of Christianity lives in him, and moves about with him; "he hath the witness in himself" (1 John 5:10). It is no mere wish to believe, conjured into a phantom of certainty by his personal preferences. It lies deep in the moral nature of things. It springs up through his personality, but from a depth beneath it. He knows that his conviction of sin is the voice of an infinite and everlasting Righteousness. And he knows that the Jesus Christ of the Cross and the Resurrection meets it as key meets lock—a purposed adaptation.

"Come, Holy Spirit, come";

> Convince us of our sin,
>> Then lead to Jesu's blood,
> And to our wondering view reveal
>> The secret love of God.

"He will reprove—He will convince—the world of sin because they believe not on Me" (see John 16:8, 9). If I interpret that great word correctly, it is just to our point today. The Lord Jesus finds a world that does not believe on Him, and He wants it to believe, that it may be saved. Therefore He promises that the Comforter shall convince it of sin. For then, and only then, it will be shut up into faith in Jesus Christ as its life and hope. When the rock is contrite, the root will strike indeed.

34

The Conviction of Sin

He will reprove (better translated, "convince") the world of sin—John 16:8

Yet once more let us linger around that grave theme—conviction of sin. For two Sundays now we have been in face of it, pondering the parable of the rock and of the root. But the theme is not only permanently momentous. It is peculiarly a matter for our time, when a thousand influences, mental and moral, obscure and stifle in the common mind the sense of sin. Yet, as we have remembered before, some genuine sense of sin is vital to a full perception of not only the glory but the profound reason of the gospel. For Jesus Christ came into the world not merely to cultivate and develop humanity, but "to save sinners" [1 Tim. 1:15] to "save His people from their sins" [Matt. 1:21].

As we saw last Sunday accordingly, there is a connection, deep as spiritual facts can make it, between conviction of sin and that sort of faith in Jesus Christ which means reliance and surrender.

I do not intend to offer any deep discussion. Rather, our study today shall take a simple narrative form. Three incidents lie in my memory, for the truth of each of which I can vouch; one of them came almost within my personal observation.

The first is a narrative of warning. There is such a thing as an abortive, or fictitious, conviction, the cold result of a sheer dread of personal consequences, where the will all the while remains in itself centered upon evil. Not that all alarm in view of judgment means this sort of conviction. In our complex being there is a subtle possible connection between the deeper sorts of fear and the genuine

271

awaking of the conscience, so that the alarmed being not only dreads the sword of divine justice, but sees its worst terror to lie in the cutting the man off from the holy and gracious Judge who made him. Such fears are true steps in the path to supreme blessing. But there is a baser sort of fear, where the criminal dreads the sword, but wishes as much as ever still to do the crime.

A friend told me the tale, a few years ago, as we paced together the deck of a steamship on the Mediterranean, and talked of the things unseen. The chaplain of a prison, intimate with the narrator, had to deal with a man condemned to death. He found the man anxious, as he well might be; nay, he seemed more than anxious; convicted, spiritually alarmed. The chaplain's instructions all bore upon the power of the Redeemer to save to the uttermost; and it seemed as if the message were received, and the man were a believer. Meanwhile, behind the scenes, the chaplain had come to think that there was ground for appeal from the death sentence; he placed the matter before the proper authorities; and with success. On his next visit, very cautiously and by way of mere suggestions and surmises, he led the apparently resigned criminal towards the possibility of a lesser sentence. What would he say, how would his repentance stand, if his life were granted him? The answer soon came. When the prisoner discovered that the death sentence had been dropped he asked a few decisive questions; then *threw his Bible across the cell*, and, civilly thanking the chaplain for his attentions, told him that he had no further need of him nor of his Book.

The next incident is so far within my own knowledge that I remember seeing, in my early childhood, the dear and beautiful subject of it, the aged widow of a farmer in my father's parish. My mother took me to visit Mrs. E. one day in her farm-kitchen. It was, I think, in 1849. I still *see* the brightness, the sweet radiance, of that venerable face; it shone, as I now know, with Jesus Christ.

At the age of about eighty-one, after a life of blameless kindness, so that to say she had "never done harm to any one" was from her no meaningless utterance, she was, through the Holy Scriptures, convinced of sin. "I have lived eighty years in the world," was her cry, "and never done anything for God." Deep went the divine work in the still active nature, and long was the spiritual darkness. Then, "the word of the Cross" found its own way in her soul, and "believing, she rejoiced with joy unspeakable." Three or four years of life were yet given her. They were illuminated by faith, hope, and love in a wonderful degree. To every visitor she bore witness of her Lord. Nights, wakeful with pain, were spent in living over the beloved scenes of His earthly ministry; "I was at the well of Samaria last night"; "Ah, I was all last night upon Mount Calvary." In extreme suffering an opiate was offered, and she declined it; for "when I lose the pain I lose the thought of my Savior too." At last she slept in the Lord, gently murmuring, almost singing, *Rock of Ages,* with her latest breath.

Wonderful is the phenomenon of the conviction of the virtuous. But it is a phenomenon corresponding to the deepest facts of the soul. My last incident is another of the same type. Eighty years ago or so, one of the scholarly and estimable Valpys, of Reading, a blameless man of letters, was in his last days convinced of sin. He left a record of it, in four lines, which I have often read, printed on a card, on cottage walls:

> In peace let me resign my breath
>   And Thy salvation see;
> My sins deserve eternal death,
>   But Jesus died for me.

35

Christ's Grave and the Christian's

There laid they Jesus—John 19:42

Much emphasis is laid in Scripture, and also in the great Creeds of the Church, upon the Burial of the Lord. Each gospel of the Four gives us a careful account, down to the details, of His funeral. Paul expressly refers to it among the other great facts of the crisis of Redemption, when he sums up his "Gospel" to the Corinthians (1 Cor. 15:4). The Apostles' Creed, and again the Nicene Creed (I use the common names of those two precious confessions of the Church's faith), both expressly recite that He was buried.

Undoubtedly the main reason of this lies in the fact that the Burial put an authoritative seal, so to speak, upon the Death, and thus accentuated the supreme event of the resurrection. The grave of Joseph did not indeed logically prove that the Lamb, on the "green hill" just above it, had veritably died; for the living have been buried by misadventure. But at least it threw the otherwise provable death into a solemn public prominence; it announced it as absolutely complete. So when, on the next day but one, then and there, that grave was found empty; when friends and adversaries alike, watching each other, looked in vain for the linen-wound Body; the Resurrection was fully evidenced to be no mere fancy, raised by an impression of uncertain causes on excitable emotions; nor again any mere putting forth, however wonderfully, of a spiritual but disembodied force. It was the triumph of the Lord's whole Being over death. His Body had been placed within the clasp of the grave. And His Body no more than His Soul was left within it.

274

But also in a way most precious, while subsidiary, the Burial of the Lord claims its place in the Bible and the Creeds as a fact of most tender application to the suffering heart. Do you know what it is to stand, or sit, or kneel, heart-stricken, beside some mounded spot of green earth, unutterably dear? More mournful still, is it yours to be far away from it, perhaps separated from it by lands and seas, while you carry ever within you the consciousness that there it is— the grave, the silent holder of all that remains below of that beloved presence?

Ah, let us speak reverently of such griefs. But let us meet them always, persistently, with the Lord Jesus, and His burial. He died for us; there is our peace with God. He rose from death, and is alive forevermore; there is our eternal certainty that we live, and shall live, with Him, "in the power of an endless life." But also, between the two, He was buried. So that dread thing, the grave, is itself transfigured. Not only will it be grand, one wonderful day, to have done with it forever, and to inhabit that great City which needs no cemetery, the heavenly Jerusalem, BUT even now, while the grave lasts, it is altered, it is transfigured, because in it the silent Lord, in the reality of His human death, lay before us. I love to think of every Christian churchyard, every Christian grave, as linked spiritually to Joseph's garden; a sort of extension of it, so that as it were the Lord's sepulcher—now open to the eternal day—is always one among the sepulchers of His people. I have tried to put it thus in simple verse:

> There is one resting place, and only one,
> For those who fall asleep in God's dear Son.
> To our weak thought indeed and sense's eye
> Far distant each from each may seem to lie;
> By Thames, by Nile, or on the silent breast
> Of ancient China softly laid to rest.
> But faith and spirit see them, each and all,
> Carried to one green spot for burial,
> Where erst, unconscious of its glorious doom,
> Arimathean Joseph carved his tomb,
> And fenced the ground with marble in, and bade
> Cypress and olive weave a glimmering shade.
> There soon he bore his Savior, newly slain,
> And there the sleeping Christ arose again,
> And trode the paths in victory serene,

And turn'd to heaven the grief of Magdalene.
He now, from every land and every deep,
Brings His beloved there, and gives them sleep,
Still gather'd up in peace, while ages run;
A countless host, and yet in Him but one.
There, seal'd awhile, now open, the holy cell,
Where folded grave clothes lie, where angels dwell,
Assures the mourner of His life and power
Who for His saints prepares their rising-hour.
And He meantime, in glory and in grace,
Immortal Gardener of the flowery place,
Walks 'midst His people's tombs, and all the while
His eyes, so wet of old, foreseeing, smile.

36

Steadfast and Abounding

Wherefore, my beloved brethren, be ye steadfast, unmoveable, always abounding in the work of the Lord—1 Cor. 15:58

The context here is all important and of the noblest significance. That golden link-word, "wherefore," takes us back to the whole contents of the chapter which closes here—that great chapter, that oracle of "everlasting consolation and good hope through grace" [2 Thess. 2:16], which tells us of the destruction of death and of the prospect, sure and certain, of the final glory, the perfect consummation and bliss both in body and soul, which awaits the children of God. Blessed be the Inspirer of 1 Corinthians 15, and forever dear to us be the Apostle through whom the Inspirer caused it to be written down. Many a reader of these lines knows what a genuine voice from heaven that chapter can be as it is read in the quiet church where the mortal part of our beloved lies waiting to be laid beneath "the clods of the valley" [Job 21:23]. Then, just then, comes the Church of Christ, and tells us, through the unerring Word, that not we shall die at last, but death, and that a glory beyond our holiest dream awaits our whole being at the coming of the King.

Well, just after that promise comes this precept. The gaze into eternity is not granted for the sake of reverie, but with a view to work. True to its genius, here as everywhere, the gospel opens heaven to us precisely so as to glorify duty. Behold the coming bliss, O saved sinner, O serving disciple. Therefore, now, labor on. Get back to "the work of the Lord." Let the sight of that world, and the resurrection of the dead, make the next thing sacred and beautiful to you. You have had a foresight of the harvest under the sky of the eternal summer. Let its light fall bright and warm on the furrow, and the plowshare, and the team, as you work on under the November clouds of time.

It is just in the same spirit that, one line below, the Apostle writes, "now concerning the collection" [16:1]. The vision of glory is to affect the practical duty of subscriptions and donations. You are heirs of heaven. Therefore be cheerful, and also diligent and methodical, *givers* here on earth.

But we will not follow the resplendent context further. Enough now to take the text in itself. Here is a precept with two noble sides to it, bearing upon the spirit and quality of the believer's work for God. Look at it, and take the two sides of it in turn.

(1) Be ye steadfast, unmoveable." This is to be the first characteristic of our "labor in the Lord." It is to be persistent, and consistent. As little as possible is it to admit the element of fitful and uncertain fluctuations; energy today, languor tomorrow; sounding programs, lean and half-hearted performance; retreat in face of discouragements before they have been steadily met and firmly dealt with. If the expression may be allowed, the true Christian is to display a holy *obstinacy* in the work of the Lord. Having the goal of his service clear and bright in view he is to labor on towards it with a resolve unshaken. To him it is to be *the* work of life. He is to turn aside to no secondary ambitions and treat them as if first. "This one thing" [Phil. 3:13] he does, till his working day is done; steadfast, unmoveable; "the same yesterday, today, and" tomorrow [Heb. 13:8]—in this respect, that he lives as one who exists to do the will of God.

Even when strength fails him, in the sense of mortal strength, he will still go on. "We must go on," said John Newton, "even when we find we are going off"; doing still, steadfastly, what we can. My beloved friend, now in the heavenly rest, the Rev. C. A. Fox, true saint, true preacher, true worker, and wonderfully true sufferer, and also true poet of purest genius, wrote at the end of a short note to me (I found it lately after a long loss) these four deep lines:

> Two glad services are ours;
>   Both the Master deigns to bless;
> First we serve with all our powers,
>   Then with all our feebleness.

(2) "Always abounding." Here is the other side. We have looked a little on the "unmoveable" aspect of the disciples' life. Now Paul reminds us that by such "immobility" he means anything but a mechanical persistence, a labor which has become a mere habitual monotony to the worker, and perhaps, too, to those for whom he works. Alas, such "immobility" there sometimes is. The man, the good man, while he toils on, has somehow come to see little in his work but its exterior outline, and very faintly indeed to see his Lord. But that is not the ideal, nor need that, "in the Lord," be the actual. The steadfast servant is so to keep in touch with the inexhaustible resources of his Master that over his persistency shall evermore be shed the living dew of a divine abundance. In Christ, his sympathies shall be forever young. In Christ, his heart-resources shall be forever fresh. No drought shall wither his "leaf," for his root is in the very river of life that issues from the throne.

Do we not know exactly such two-sided lives for God? And cannot He make even ours resemble them?

37

Personal Evidences of Christianity

Knowing of whom thou hast learned them—2 Tim. 3:14

We have Paul here, writing to his dear "son" Timothy. It is a dying letter, a last solemn deposition made on the borderland of eternity. Every paragraph of this short Scripture carries with it the tender awe which attaches to last words; the writer is "now ready to be offered; the time of his departure is at hand."

I know no book in the whole range of the Bible which seems, if I may put it so, more alive and pulsing with the deepest emotions of the human heart than this. Those who question the authenticity of the Epistle, as some have done, must assuredly have left this feature of it out of their estimate of evidences. It is little in the manner of fabricators, such as we know them from other sources to have been in the early generations of Christianity, to personate profound emotion in a way which still, to the sympathetic reader, can literally make the eyes wet. No; the man who thus wrote of his own affections, his own tears, his dearest memories, his loneliness, his coming death, his faithful Lord, was no personator of someone else. He was wholly himself; therefore he was Paul.

Among other of these heart-evidences of the truth and authenticity of the letter stands this reference to Timothy's early teachers; those "from whom he had learned" the Word of life, at whose knees, in his long-past childhood, he had come to know "the holy Scriptures" [v. 15], which now, in his maturer years, were to be his anchor while everything else drifted around him. We cannot help connecting this allusion with that other passage, earlier in the Epistle

(1:5), where the Apostle speaks of Lois, Timothy's grandmother, and Eunice, his mother, and of "the unfeigned faith which dwelt in" them. It was their dear memories that the now grown-up and anxious pastor, amidst many perplexities, was to recall, and to be calmed, reassured, strengthened, by the recollection. He was to remember what they were, and so to be made quite sure again that he had "not followed cunningly devised fables" [2 Pet. 1:16], but stood with his feet upon the rock.

Let us ponder a little the thought here suggested, the help to faith drawn from the character, the personality, of the teacher.

To be sure, such evidential help is not meant to be taken wholly by itself, as a thing which can stand quite alone. The most beautiful life does not secure the being who lives it against mistakes, whether these be mistakes as to fact, or as to judgment upon facts. Some of the fairest Christian characters, for example, in past days, have been developed in men or women who were infected by current superstition, people (in that respect) of their time; and their moral excellence does not guarantee to us the superstition. But that sort of guarantee is not what is in Paul's mind here. He takes for granted the gospel's *moral* grandeur. And he is prepared, if need be, to restate the *historical* basis of its position, as he does in the opening verses of 1 Corinthians 15. But then he appeals *besides* to a phenomenon which had brought that gospel, in its direct and legitimate effects, close to the conscience as well as the heart of Timothy. He reminds him that his teachers, in those beloved old days, were no mere mechanical transmitters of a formula, but beings personally transformed by their faith, by the faith which had become their message. And he asks Timothy if that is not a mighty contribution to the certainty that the gospel not only looks beautiful morally, and has vastly much to say for itself historically, but is also, what it ought to be if its story is true, a spiritual power, all alive, formative, able to transfigure. Well, if it be so, let him welcome that thought deep into his heart, and feel in it the whole weight of the reality of the gospel put into living and immediate contact with his soul.

Has my reader learned Christ from a Lois, a Eunice? If so, let him thank God and take courage, and use with a glad mind as well as heart the deep, the pregnant evidence enshrined in their memory, or, if that is granted to him still, in their living presence.

O my Mother, permitted to bless me here below till I stood "in the midway of this our mortal life," and now resting these six and twenty years with your Lord in bliss, I remember you, I embrace your memory, and as I do so I go on again, amidst the infinite confusions of our time, the surer of that gospel which did so wonderfully make you what you were. *That* was no cunningly devised fable. The Lord Christ, whose atoning Cross was your repose, whose living Presence was your strength, whose very Name was your joy, in that life of yours so nobly natural, so sweetly supernatural, He is power and fact indeed. Your son, by His mercy, will "continue in Him," remembering you, and looking to rejoin you in that place of light to whose reality your being was a witness all along.

38

Accepted yet Chastened

The Lord also hath put away thy sin; thou shalt not die. Howbeit . . . the
child that is born unto thee shall surely die—2 Sam. 12:13, 14

I do not intend to tell over again the infinitely sad story in which
these words find place, or to moralize in detail upon it. This is assuredly one of the very darkest pages in that truth-telling Bible
which shows us the sins as well as the virtues of the saints—this history of David's great and complex sin. And the sequel is as full of
sorrow as the initial incidents are full of sin; as the narrative takes us
on to Amnon, to Absalom, to Amasa, to Abiathar, to Joab, to Shimei,
in steps stained with wrong and blood; and David himself all the
while, almost to his very end, is the mournfully altered man; under
the shadow, under the rod.

A recent renewed study of those latter days of David's reign has
left on my own soul an impression of peculiar sadness. There is
nothing quite like it in the Bible. Look at this man who, from one
point of view, was "after God's own heart," yet from another was so
awful an example of the deceitfulness of sin, and so woefully chastened for it. There is no other Bible portrait with quite this tremendous *chiaroscuro*, this dread contrast of light and night.

But I take today this point in the story to read us a general lesson
as to the spiritual life. Put aside the special features of the case;
think only of a servant of God, truly a servant of God, but who has
sinned; what will his Master do with him?

The answer comes to us, surely, in the double burden of Nathan's
message. The prophet is sent to tell David two facts about his sin;

first, that it is "put away," as regards a sentence of death on David; then, that it will be chastened with rigorous faithfulness, for "the sword shall not depart from his house" [see 2 Sam. 12:10] and the child, the beloved, shall surely die.

Am I wrong in tracing here a lesson for all believers? In the light of Scripture at large, I think, the case of David is typical. Here first is a man who, by the plain testimony of the holy history, *was* a sincere servant of God, having really entered into the covenant of love and loyalty with Jehovah, "giving" really his "heart," and his life, in a true purpose, to His will. In New Testament language, he was a veritable "child of God," to be known by plain marks from "the children of the devil." He was so truly, in the gospel phrase, "born of the Spirit" (John 3:8) that men "heard the sound thereof." But then, this man was taken off his guard by temptation, and fell such a fall as indeed in itself merited a hundred times over the soul's final loss.

Yet, "thou shalt not die." No matter for us now what precisely Nathan understood by those words; it is plain that they indicate to us that David was held fast by the divine mercy, and was still owned by the Lord as His. Now this, I venture to affirm, is typical. In the whole range of Scripture I find no clear case of the final loss of the real servant of God. I read of no man, nor woman, once unquestionably "right in the sight of God," and then unquestionably cut off from Him forever. I somewhat deprecate the phrase, "the perseverance of the saints"; I would rather say, "the perseverance of the Savior." And I am amply aware how greatly, how grossly, the thing meant may be misrepresented, by advocates or by opponents. But I do think that the Bible on the whole encourages the faith that where once the grace of God has knit indeed the bond of actual part and lot in divine life and love, there the fidelity of the Shepherd's hand is never relaxed, to let the soul perish forever.

There are Scriptures in which we find relations towards God, connections with Him, true and sacred in their order, which yet can be and are broken off. But I do not find in any Scripture an example of the ultimate killing of the true "life hid with Christ in God."

But then, "the sword shall not depart"; "the child shall die." Here, too, are typical words. Understand the "putting away of sin" to mean, as it surely does, the acceptance of the person as the Father's true child, the instatement into the real family and home of grace; and I venture to hold that in that sense the "putting away" is persistent, faithful to itself, faithful to the end; in that sense pardon is, for Christ's sake, perpetual. But the family, the home, has its discipline. The Father has His rod. The child has to meet his domestic sentence, his domestic punishment. He is a child still. He is not banished "to the tormentors"; he is not even turned into the street. But he has to taste the awful bitterness of a frown upon the brow of Love, and a scourge in its hand.

May we, in our manifold needs of spiritual experience, be mercifully kept sure of both truths; the acceptance in our all-sufficient Lord, the chastisement, sternly gracious, prepared for the offending child.

39

Our Angelic Friends

Fear not ye—Matt. 28:5

The doctrine of the Angels is no small treasure among the Revelation of the Bible. Let the reader take the Book up with this one aim for once, to collect from it, literally from Genesis to Revelation, the materials given us for forming our belief about the angels, and he will find he has a large store of golden truth in his hands. He will probably put on one side those many passages of the early books of the Old Testament, where, we can hardly doubt it, an "Angel of the Lord" is spoken of who is angel and more than angel; who speaks at once as Messenger and Master; who must be the pre-incarnate Christ Himself. But when he has done this, and, if he keeps himself to the most unquestionable and explicit passages only, he will surely seem, like Jacob at Mahanaim, and like Elisha at Dothan, to see the air about him almost visibly alight and alive with these glorious beings, pure, strong, loving, wholly given up to God, not identical with man indeed, yet mysteriously near to him in thought, in sympathy, in action.

Never for a moment does the Bible authorize angel-worship. Even a personal appeal from man to angels to help him does not appear; a solemn note of caution, as if the Book would discourage any, even in themselves blameless, dealings with the Unseen, which would tend to deaden the fine touch of direct fellowship with God. But the Bible does put before us the being and presence of the holy angels as a fact unquestionable, in our Lord's opinion, and therefore in ours.

One feature, and only one, in the Scriptural view of the angels, would I point out to my reader today. It is their "philanthropy," their love of us men, their friendship and fellowship with us mortal disciples of their Lord.

Here again let the reader take up his Bible. Everywhere this lovely phenomenon appears. The first mention of an angel at all, under that name, is where poor Hagar, flying from the unhappy tent, is accosted by an angel, cheered, guided, more than lifted up [Gen. 21:17]. Again, in that black scene at Sodom, how friend-like are the angels, ministers of doom as they are, in their dealings with unhappy Lot in his alarm [Gen. 19]. It is an angel who soothes and feeds Elijah, in gentlest sympathy with his human weakness [1 Kgs. 19:5]. And when we come to the Gospels and the Acts, our "elder brethren of the sky" come out upon the scene in a frequency altogether new, and with a fellowship of spirit towards us most beautiful and precious. Let us deliberately read over the "words of the angels," from book to book of the New Testament; we shall find noble illustrations everywhere. The angel of Bethlehem—listen to him as he brings the "good tidings of great joy" [Luke 2:10] to those poor shepherds on the hillside. He is no mere official of the court of Heaven, delivering a message in proper form. His very phrase shows that his own immortal heart is in the message; it is joy to him to communicate the greatest of all joys to mortal men in their low estate. Turn again to the angels who appear at the Resurrection [Matt. 28], and these two among them who accost Magdalene in the Garden. Or listen to the "shining pair" who met the Apostles the moment after the Ascension [Acts 1]. It is still the same. Their love, their all-generous *friendship*, goes with their words. The weeping woman, the group of frightened women, the eleven wonder-stricken men—all are important, all are dear, to these glorious *friends* from heaven. Every detail of the position is present to the angelic thought; everything is known and noticed; the fear, the perplexity, the promises, the mistakes, the hopes.

One beautiful utterance above others seems to rise unbidden to the angels' lips when they accost men or women of the family of God. *"Fear not ye"*; how often they say it, at Bethlehem, and in the garden of Joseph! Man instinctively *fears* the sudden manifestation of the Unseen; he trembles with unutterable awe when he knows he is in the open presence of a personal spiritual Power. But these Powers of the upper world, "excelling in strength," "the heavenly *army,*" as Luke calls them in the Bethlehem history, are gentleness itself with a troubled human being who loves God. Whatever their unseen sphere contains, it contains nothing for such to fear. It is a scene of fraternal kindness for us mortals. It is thronged with "an innumerable company of angels"; and they are all the kind friends of the believer in Jesus, their Lord and ours.

40

Redemption, Endowment, Service

He brought forth His people with joy, and His chosen with gladness, and gave them the lands of the heathen, and they inherited the labor of the people; that they might observe His statutes, and keep His laws—
Ps. 105:43–45

It is a remark of Dr. Arnold's, I believe, that in the history of Israel we have, on a large scale, the history of the redeemed human soul. Assuredly it is true, for the believing reader of the Bible, that the history of the dealings of God with Israel gives us at every turn teachings and suggestions as to His will and way with the soul.

I do not hesitate to take the three verses at the head of this chapter in that light. They are the final cadence of that noble Psalm which casts into a form of choral beauty the history of the Exodus, ushering Israel into Canaan in the full tide of heaven-given victory. They lend themselves (so I hope we shall find) with perfect fitness, under the illumination of other Scriptures, to set out the purposes of God in Christ towards the man whom He redeems and saves. Consider each main point in turn.

(1) Redemption and its joy. Behold the captives of Pharaoh led out into liberty by their Lord. It is His victory altogether: It is a deliverance as magnificent as an almighty Friend can make it. The joy is as radiant as the wonder is divine. The dance and song on that memorable shore, where Israel comes up from the waters while Egypt lies whelmed beneath them, are as if we could watch and listen still.

The "bringing forth" of the soul into the liberty of Christ is only the Exodus repeated in a greater glory, worthy of a deeper and brighter jubilation. Whether we ponder the Finished Work of the Lord Jesus in itself, or whether we think of the sinful man's acceptance of it, so that it enters, by faith, into the personal history of his soul, which then humbly claims, if I may dare to put it so, a Bethlehem, and a Calvary, and an Olivet of its own—it is an Exodus of more than mercy; it is a liberation into a *"joy* unspeakable and full of glory" [1 Pet. 1:8]. Do we think the phrase too strong? If so, it is the fault of our faith, not of its object, not of its reason. Let us pray, with a resolute desire, for such a sight of our Egypt, our Exodus, our Canaan, as shall clear our eyes to see our joy more truly as it is.

(2) Endowment, and its fullness. "He gave them the lands of the heathen," "the labors of the people." Here is a feature of Israel's entrance upon Canaan often emphasized in history and psalm. They were not only emancipated; they were endowed. It was no wilderness of field or forest into which the liberated tribes were led. There, ready for their fruition, lay the old wealth of a land which more and more, as modern exploration discloses to us what it was, appears to have been indeed a vast treasury of rich and cultivated abundance. Cities, roads, wells, vineyards, cornfields, all were there, ready and in order, transferred by the supreme Possessor from the Amorite to His own Israel.

Here also, imperfect indeed yet abundantly suggestive and impressive, is a parable for the soul. Pardoned, justified, liberated out of the slavery of the Fall into the Canaan of filial peace with God in Christ, we see here our call not to freedom only but to wealth. The Lord suffered for us not that we might have a mere wilderness liberty, but that we might be "in everything enriched in Him"; that "in Him," who is our true Promised Land, we might find ready for us, in perfect order for our use, in fairest beauty for our pleasure, "the unsearchable riches." In our holy inheritance we are to look around and say, with humble but doubtless confidence, *"we have."* We have the promises; we have the Spirit, the "Unction from the Holy One" [1 John 2:20]; we have the Great High Priest; we "have access into the holiest" [see Eph. 2:18]. We have; and so we are called upon not to acquire but to employ. Arise, and let us live upon our wealth.

(3) Obedience to the Giver. "That they might observe His statutes, and keep His laws." Again we read, in Israel, the intended story

290

of the saved soul. By a profound law of spiritual life and order, "we are saved *to serve.*" To all eternity, the creature will never find its true ideal satisfied, and so its true bliss secured, except in the inner harmony of a loving and adoring loyalty to the Creator. So the heavenly resources of the life of faith, its holy wealth, will be never rightly spent, and therefore never entirely enjoyed, except in the line of His blessed statutes and His dear laws; in the surrender to Him, now and forever, of the whole being which He has first redeemed and then so wonderfully enriched.

Come, let us reaffirm to ourselves, undoubtingly, our full redemption, and our vast endowment in the Lord. Then evermore let us "yield ourselves unto God . . . as instruments of righteousness unto Him" [see Rom. 6:13].

41

The Word Hidden in the Heart: Part One

Thy word have I hid in mine heart, that I might not sin against Thee—
Ps. 119:11

Far back in the year, within its first weeks, we turned to the hundred and nineteenth Psalm for our theme of thought. Under autumn skies we open it again. It is a Scripture always timely. For not only is it a part of that "Word of God which liveth and abideth forever" (1 Pet. 1:23), and which alone opens to us the secret for ourselves of a part and lot in the ever-abiding life. Its own great topic, from the first to the last of its long and holy strain, is that same Word of God, and its revelation of divine love, and divine hope, and the divine will. That topic is never out of date. Least of all is it out of date today, when the believing Church seems as if it were called to travel over Bunyan's "Enchanted Ground," upon paths thick with shadows of discouragement and decay, and where the air is drowsy with the malaria of materialistic thinking, "heavy as frost, and deep almost as life."

Amidst the many urgent calls upon the Christian traveler at such a stage of the pilgrimage is a better and better acquaintance with the Holy Bible. Nothing can be a substitute for that, at a time of mingled mental and spiritual trial. On the other hand, nothing is more likely to be silently pushed aside at just such a time than this personal acquaintance with the Bible. The temptation to neglect it may come from many different quarters. One mind is diverted from assiduous Bible-study by a mere consciousness, however vague, that the peculiar character and authority of Scripture is at present widely doubted

292

and freely denied. A subtle sympathy with the current thought of our time lies latent in us, almost all; even where we least like the type of thought we feel it; it stirs to some extent within us; we sympathize with it, not in the sense of approbation but in that of sensibility to influence. Another mind, more active and resisting, is impelled by the unbelief around to a diligent study of "apologetics," and works hard over books which undertake to defend the Bible; a perfectly legitimate and often necessary task, but one which can never take the place of personal acquaintance with the Book.

There are times, and they come very often, when we need to go back to the Bible deliberately, and on purpose, and avowing it to ourselves, *in a spirit of old-fashioned expectation*. We need to open it with the "working hypothesis" (for the sake of argument I may use the phrase and not be misunderstood) that it is just the Book of God, given by Him as His Word to man. We need to invite it to be its own best vindicator by proving its power, when so listened to, to bless the inmost heart, awing it, cheering it, uplifting it, humbling it, sanctifying it through and through with a fresh sense of the horror of sin and of the glory of the love and of the will of God.

"Do not read the Bible; learn it." Such was the appeal with which a young Christian man, upon his dying bed, addressed his "young men friends." He had come, happily for him, to a firm faith in the divine truth and authority of the Bible. He had carried that faith into "works," by laboriously studying it, and coveting a close familiarity with its words in detail, learning large quantities of the Bible by heart, so as to have the Word constantly with him as the companion of his thoughts. And now, just about to step beyond books into eternity, he passed on his experience to those he was leaving, to the young minds of his own generation, as a watchword for their own future; "Learn the Bible."

That is, quite obviously, what the Psalmist meant here when he wrote that he had "hidden the Word in his heart." He had stored it there, not for concealment, but for readiness for use. It was hidden, not as the talent was hidden in the napkin, but as the golden grain is hidden in the furrow. He got it "by heart," in the double sense of memory and of meditation. And indeed it fructified; it brought forth the fruit of holiness; he did "not sin against" his God.

A venerable godfather of mine, who died not long ago, full of faith and hope, within twenty months of a hundred years old, was a great lover and learner of the Bible. In his own best loved copy of the Book he had written—so his son told me when he was gone—the pregnant words: "This Book will keep you from sin, and sin will keep you from this Book."

Yes, "this Book will keep us from sin." Not mechanically, not perfunctorily, but so that the man who converses spiritually with the stored-up Word shall find that it tends divinely to assimilate his thinking to its own. *"Studia abeunt in mores,"* writes Erasmus: "study passes into character," if the "study" is the work of heart and mind alike. The temptation to impurity, to untruth, to injustice, to worldliness, to irritability and causeless anger, to shame of the blessed Name, will fall dead, not living, upon the heart which it finds stored with that Word, and in sympathy with that Word, which at once unveils the face of God, and expresses, as with "the pleasant voice of the Mighty One," His "good, and acceptable and perfect will" [see Rom. 12:2].

42

The Word Hidden in the Heart:
Part Two

Thy word have I hid in mine heart, that I might not sin against Thee—
Ps. 119:11

We reflected last week upon the need of a close personal acquaintance with the Bible, not least in our own time, and upon the spiritual power of it. It is a truth worth reiterating, and infinitely well worth putting to the proof. The committal to memory of words, sacred or secular, is not so large a feature as it used to be in early education. There was perhaps a time when "repetition" in our great schools was practiced to an extreme, BUT I do not think that time is now. There was perhaps a time when in Christian homes the learning by heart of chapters of Scripture, or even of whole Epistles, was made too large a part of teaching, BUT that is by no means the present risk; if one may judge by the rarity of accurate quotation of the Bible, even in the pulpit. We need to return now from the other and much worse extreme, and to resolve afresh to "hide the Word in the heart," till the hiding place is redolent of the fragrance of its treasures.

Happy the Christian to whom his Bible is so familiar that it goes not only with him, but within him, wherever he goes. It comes out from its recess in the memory, and talks to him in that dialect of grace and truth which is all its own. It converses with him on his solitary walk, or finds him out, quite as easily, in the deeper and dreary solitude of the world's crowd. It springs up close to the pulses of thought and will when the tempter whispers to him. It meets the foul suggestion, which can defile the whole imagination in a moment, with the reminder that "every man that hath this hope in

295

Him purifieth himself, even as He is pure" [1 John 3:3]. It calms the awful struggle of the spirit under some dead weight of loss or pain by the recollected assurance that "what I do thou knowest not now but thou shalt know hereafter" [John 13:7]. It brings heavenly companionship all around the solitary pilgrim, till the famished eyes of the bereaved almost see the reunion that is coming; "we also that are alive and remain shall be caught up together with them in the clouds to meet the Lord." It speaks to the believer in the worst straits of life in a voice clear and decided; "He hath said, I will never leave thee" [Heb. 13:5]. As the man draws upon the wealth "hidden in his heart," he knows how to turn the wakeful hour at midnight, or that often more trying hour of the cold, white, silent, earliest morning, when sleep flies too soon, into a time of peace and reassurance and "that blessed hope" He then gathers and arranges the hidden possessions of his "heart." [Titus 2:13]. And not the isolated text only, but the wonderful symmetry and correspondence of the vast structure of the Scripture message, bids him tranquilly recollect that his "confidence," even when it is embraced with tears, "hath great recompense of reward." And as he recollects, he realizes. As he muses, the fire burns. The sin of a misgiving of his God is exorcised by the heart-hidden Word.

Kindred to the experience of such an hour is that indefinable but profoundly real impression which is sometimes made upon the mind by what I may call the self-evidential power of even a single great typical utterance of that wonderful Book of books. Lately, in the ordinary course of daily devotional study of the New Testament, I arrived at that ever-marvelous passage, the eighth chapter of Romans. How often had I read it before! Twice, I am almost ashamed to say, have I commented in print upon the Epistle throughout. Yet the chapter seemed to challenge an attention as particular and exploring as if I had never read it; almost as if it were a new treasure unearthed from some convent library of the East. I reached that noble verse, the thirty-seventh, where the Apostle affirms, for himself and for his fellow believers, that "in all these things we are more than conquerors through Him that loved us." That sentence made on me an impression sudden and peculiar. It was not merely that it was eloquent to the highest degree. It was not merely that there was a tenderness as well as courage in it which was beyond analysis, yet none the less potent on the emotions. I did not contemplate it only as the expression of the heroic certainties of a great soul amidst great trials. I felt in it a solid angle of the vast rock of absolute reality, and my own faith, not by emotion but by the touch of truth, was strong again.

Truth, of the highest order, is apprehended not by the logical faculty only but by the whole spiritual being. To such apprehension, I humbly but boldly assert, that sentence, in that context, in that writing, in that volume, presents itself as irrefragable truth. This more than victory, at once meek and sublime, over the whole range of human ills; this Personage, described without a name, this wonderful "He that loved us" [see 1 John 4:10]; such things, so spoken of, with all that lies behind them in this Book so multifold yet one, cannot, in the nature of things, be waves on an ocean of illusion. They are of the structure of the Living Stone.

43

Boldness with God

O Lord, how long shall I cry, and Thou wilt not hear?—Hab. 1:2

These are strong words to be spoken by messenger to Sender, by servant to Master, by saint to God. They are part of a whole context of similar strong words. Habakkuk returns to his passionate outcry again and again. "How long shall I cry out unto Thee of violence, and Thou wilt not save? Why dost Thou show me iniquity, and cause me to behold grievance? Therefore the law is slacked, and judgment doth never go forth."

So strange is the phenomenon of such an address to God that it has presented to many pious readers an even distressing problem. Our great Elizabethan divine, Richard Hooker, has devoted two sermons to the question, taking for his text those words, "Therefore the law is slacked." He thought it worth his labor elaborately to vindicate Habakkuk from the charge of having committed the great *sin of despair.*

Certainly the words, as we ponder them, are a shock to one side of Christian feeling. They do, in terms, read almost like a reproach upon the action of the Lord, or rather upon His inaction. In our own time, in a powerful book by Sir R. Anderson, voice has been given to the thoughts of innumerable hearts upon the mysterious *"Silence of God,"* His silence kept in face of humanity's sin and sorrow. Habakkuk shows us that the pain of that mystery is no modern thing. It was the silence of the Lord Jehovah which wrung his soul and made him open his prophecy with a cry like this, an almost discord amidst the song before the throne.

And Habakkuk is not alone in the Bible with this startling appeal, I had almost said this displeased protest. Asaph, in Psalm 73, confesses to us how the silence of God had nearly made an infidel of him. Jeremiah (12:1) reasons with his heavenly Master about the inexplicable success of the wicked. Job's whole being is tossed in a long tempest over the same problem. Finally, we have the sixth chapter of the Revelation, where the veil is lifted from eternity, and we hear the voices of saints who have suffered and are at rest pleading with their Lord, asking how long He will be silent and delay: "How long, O Lord, holy and true, dost Thou not avenge our blood?" [v. 10].

This last example must not be pressed too far, for the scene is largely, perhaps it is altogether, symbolical. But the other cases of expostulation (we can scarcely use another word) with a silent and apparently passive God are not figurative at all. They show us hearts like our own, burdened with mystery and speaking out their trouble, sometimes in terms almost or altogether impatient, into their Master's ear.

What shall we say? The first remark that arises, and the most obvious, and surely the most consoling and encouraging, is that indeed the God of the saints and prophets is a patient and generous God. He comes into our view here, in His own Word, in scenes and colloquies which He has Himself caused to be "written for our learning" [Rom. 15:4], as a Friend indeed, so friendly that He lets a Job, and an Asaph, and a Habakkuk pour out to Him all the embitterment of their souls, and yet only loves them, bears with them, listens to them, and waits to bless them. It is a glorious side-light which is thus thrown upon the Personal Character of our ever-blessed God. How can we describe it better than by that familiar word *generous?* What is it but a long-suffering sympathy? The infinitely Great is great enough to look out through the aching eyes of His sincere while unworthy servants, and to feel with the feelings of their bewildered hearts, and to bear with them, as man bears with his fellow, when he knows more than his fellow knows, but loves him well enough to understand and to respect his inability to see the whole meaning of a complex case, and to forecast its end. Such, sublimely greater in measure, yet akin in its personal nature, is the generosity of God.

Then, and therefore, we have here, "written for our learning," a noble and moving encouragement, straight from the heart of this same Friend of friends, to speak to Him all that is in the burdened soul, just as it is. The New Testament repeatedly speaks of the "boldness," the "access with confidence" [Eph. 3:12], to which we are invited as we draw near the Holy One. In the Greek, in many of these places, a notable word is used by the Apostles: *parrhêsia,* that is to say, literally, the freedom which can *"say anything,"* telling out the very thought, unrelieved, exactly as it is.

It was *parrhêsia* indeed when Habakkuk said, "Why do I pray to Thee, and it seems to result in nothing?" His awful trial told hard on him. He felt as perhaps he should not have felt. But he was perfectly right in telling out his feelings, right *or wrong,* to his Lord. For he was free to "say anything" to Him. And we, we in the light of our revealed nearness to Him in Christ, we indeed are meant to "say anything" to Him, feeling the bewilderment, "but knowing Whom we have believed" [see 2 Tim. 1:12].

44

A Child of God

The creation itself shall be delivered from the bondage of corruption into the liberty of the glory of the children of God—Rom. 8:21 (literally rendered)

From a paragraph of supreme interest and significance comes this great promise. In the midst of what is, on the whole, the deepest and largest chapter of spiritual teaching and promise in the whole range of his writings, the Apostle here, suddenly, lifts the veil from the future of universal creation, of what we commonly mean by Nature. About that creation he tells us two main truths; the first, that it is now in a state and stage of unrest and suffering; the second, that this stage is related to a condition into which the creation is yet to pass as travail is related to birth; a time is coming when the groan shall be stilled, and the tossing quieted, and the constraint exchanged for liberty. It is now an iron age. But the age of gold is not, as to the pagan poets, lost in the vanished past. It lies in the yet curtained future. The year of bliss is in front. The creation is yet to be delivered into a liberty supreme and final, towards which already in mysterious yearnings it may be said to look and to move.

What that liberty shall be, in its details and also in its essence, "it doth not yet appear" [1 John 3:2]. But we may reverently conjecture that it shall be the experience of a state in which the Lord of finite Existence, whose will alone is its ultimate law, shall decree the removal out of His handiwork forever of all friction and all decay, commanding Nature at last to enter, in a profound transfiguration, upon a state over which all that we mean by death and by dying shall no more have dominion. He who alone knows the

301

inmost truth alike of mind, of force, of matter, as they rest for their being upon Him, shall so readjust them to Himself and Himself to them that the civil wars of creation shall be forever over, and finite being, in all its regions, shall be at peace within itself; in the kingdom of matter, as in that of spirit, "God shall be all in all."

> O eternal Life,
> After storm and strife,
> When, when shall come Thy peaceful glories in?
> All things yearn and sigh
> Till that hour draws nigh,
> Till God's great days of endless calm begin.

He who is "Head over all things to the church" (Eph. 1:22) is also identically He who is the Cornerstone of Creation, "by Him all things are held together" (Col. 1:17). He is the very Life of both worlds; and both worlds at last shall come out into that bright fulfillment of which His Headship is the pledge.

But our highest purpose today is not to discuss the future of the Universe. It is to direct one simple but illuminating thought upon "the glorious liberty of the children of God," and so upon the glory of being a child of God indeed. In a wonderful way the Apostle makes the emancipation of Creation to hinge upon "the manifestation of the sons of God" (Rom. 8:19); its "liberty" is bound up with "the glory of the children of God" (see v. 21). The supreme freedom for the weary Universe will not come *anyhow;* it will come when they, the children of its Maker, enter on the full and eternal fruition of their "adoption, to wit, the redemption of their body" (see v. 23) in the resurrection-bliss.

Think of the testimony of such a truth to the grandeur of the privilege of such a sonship, such a childhood! "Behold, what manner of love the Father hath bestowed upon us, that we should be called the sons of God"! (1 John 3:1). By the vastness and splendor of the attendant "deliverance" of Nature, we may estimate in some small measure the transcendent wonder of that gift of grace, the new birth of sinful men into the very family of the Eternal. And shall we not covet a full and everlasting part and lot in that "adoption," in that "regeneration"? And shall we not aim, in our study of its nature, its conditions, its evidences, as high as possible? If I read the Scriptures correctly, I trace in them what I may call concentric circles of divine sonship. There is indicated, though dimly and with reserve, a divine sonship in man's nature and man's race as a whole, such that the creature "made in the image of God" is, as such, His "offspring" (Acts 17:28). There is further revealed a sonship of gracious connection with Him in His redeeming plan, such that Israel of old was "His son" (see Ex. 4:22), and all now who are baptized into the name of Christ are "His sons." But, shining out with a solemn light as the central circle of all, and seen in passages of weight and number large indeed, appears a supreme sonship—the sonship of the human souls which actually believe, and love, and overcome the world, while "the world knows them not" [see 1 Cor. 1:21]. Read for illustration and evidence that one short but unfathomable book, the First Epistle of John, and ask if the thought there is not altogether of this inmost and ultimate reality, the regenerate sonship of the living saints?

Well, the living saints, be their outward lot what it may be here below, have before them an amazing future. "It doth not yet appear what they shall be" [1 John 3:2]. But it does appear that for the bursting of the bud of what they are into the flower of what they shall be, the whole universe is waiting, yearning, groaning.

> With them number'd may we be,
> Here and in eternity.

45

The Generous Master

They have kept Thy word—John 17:6

We owe to the Germans, I believe, that beautiful title for the seventeenth chapter of John, "the High-Priestly Prayer." Wherever it originated, it is a perfect designation of this sacred passage, "the Holy of Holies of the Bible," as it has been also called. For He who spoke this exalted Intercession, with eyes uplifted to heaven, while His disciples listened around Him, was indeed the supreme "High Priest of our profession" [Heb. 3:1], almost in the act of offering up Himself as the Propitiation for our sins [1 John 2:2; 4:10]. And in this utterance He was doing His High-priestly work as truly as in His act of sacrifice. For the high-priests of Aaron's line, His types and forerunners, were at once sacrifices and intercessors. Every autumn, on the great Atonement Day, when under the open heaven they had done their altar-work outside the sanctuary, they entered, alone, into its curtained recesses, and appeared as intercessors in the Holiest, before the Ark, the Cherubim, and the Glory, pleading Israel with the plea of the victim's blood.

Our blessed Aaron, the Lord Jesus, had not indeed as yet offered up Himself, actually, on His dread altar upon Golgotha. But that work was all complete in the eternal purpose before the world began to be. And so nearly was it over now in historical accomplishment, so close to Him now were the Garden and the Cross, that He speaks to His Father as of a deed already done; "I have glorified Thee on the earth; *I have finished* the work which Thou gavest Me to do" [John 17:4].

So His prayer is founded on His work. It rests upon His offering. It is an intercession altogether sacerdotal, priestly, high-priestly, in its kind and its power. Surely it was spoken, just then and there, within the very sight and hearing of His followers, that they might the better realize what was to be the tone and burden of that wonderful "advocacy" which He should carry on for them in the heaven of heavens itself, "seated at the right hand of the Majesty on high."

Let us draw near in humblest reverence, and in the very simplest faith, and listen for ourselves to the blessed Intercessor, as if we also stood beside Him in the upper room, or in the Temple court under the Paschal full moon, or just at the water's edge before He crossed the Kidron; wherever it was that He spoke to His Father for His Apostles and (17:20) for us.

As we listen, one element in the Prayer shall today leave itself particularly upon our hearts. I mean its element of a tender and wonderful generosity, if the word may be used without presumption. In the course of praying for the disciples, the Lord incidentally speaks about them, by way of description and character. They are "the men whom Thou gavest Me out of the world" [John 17:6]; the men who are "Thine," and therefore "Mine," in a profound connection. "They have kept Thy word. They have known surely that I came out from Thee; they have believed that Thou didst send Me. . . . I am glorified in them. The world hath hated them, because they are not of the world" [John 17:6–14].

Such is the great Intercessor's view of His followers, and His description of them, in that deep colloquy with the eternal Father's heart. How grand and noble a picture it is! What a group of heroic saints must this be, gathered around their Leader, filled with His Spirit, entering into His purposes, open-eyed to His glory, responsive to His will, true to all the finest touches of His truth and love!

As a fact, how was it? Reverent be all our thoughts of the holy "Apostles of the Lamb." Who are we that we should discuss them lightly, or name without a certain solemn shrinking any even the slightest weakness in men forever now bound up with their Lord's glory? But it is no irreverence to take and remember their own description of themselves. It is they who with noblest fidelity to truth tell us how dim their insight was, all along, up to and beyond that hour, into the splendor of their Redeemer's being, into the holy awesomeness of His atoning work, into the coming triumph of His resurrection. It is they who depict to us Peter, and Thomas, and James, and John, and Philip, in their mistakes of word and conduct; their own protests against His coming sufferings; their flight from beside Him in the Garden; the terrible oaths of denial of Him in the house of Caiaphas; the total failure to expect His victory over the grave.

Such were the men who heard themselves thus spoken of by the Son to the Father when, in their presence, yet as if alone, He lifted up His eyes and prayed.

How shall we explain the beautiful but surprising paradox? I do not think we are to say that the great Advocate, in that act of prayer, viewed them as involved in His merits, clothed in His righteousness, hidden, and so in some sort transfigured, in Himself. No doubt, for glorious purposes, they were, and we ("who believe through their word") are, in mysterious reality, involved, and clothed, and hidden, and transfigured so. But that is in respect of our need of finding, as guilty beings, a sinless welcome to the home of the present love and peace of a reconciled God. It is not in respect of our personal characters, and actual thoughts, and actual exercises of will and affection. And it is of these that Jesus is speaking here.

Two suggestions in elucidation may be made, both drawn from the heart of Christ, both running up in reality into one.

The first is that He, absolutely clear-sighted, saw into those troubled and imperfect hearts to a depth where, by His grace, latent but genuine, lay the seeds, so to speak, of that Pentecostal life which was so soon to be fully theirs, and in which so largely, so luminously, in a true transfiguration, He *was* to be "glorified in them" [v. 10]. He saw the seed, and in the seed the flower, as if it bloomed before His eyes.

But then, secondly, He who thus saw, saw with eyes not only absolutely clear but also generous, with a love before which the objects of its regard were beautified and glorified by its own light. It belongs to the supreme personal character of the Son of God to delight to welcome and to praise, to seize the least occasion for it, and to hold up the thing so honored in a radiance of kindness which makes it already, to His heart, what He would have it be.

For such a Master who, that gets one glimpse of Him, would not live and die?

46

The Theism of the Lord Jesus

Father, the hour is come. . . . Holy Father. . . . O righteous Father—
John 17:1, 11, 25

We listened last week to our great High Priest, our Intercessor and Advocate, as He prayed for His Apostles, and for us "who have believed through their word." We observed then that gracious aspect of His prayer, the generous love with which the Master thought and spoke of His servants, looking at their imperfect graces in the light of His own sublimely tender affection, till those graces shone transfigured by that radiancy into something nearer His own bright image.

Today let us approach and listen again. And our attention now shall be given to an altogether different element of the High Priestly Prayer. We will follow it, so far as we may, not downward towards its human objects, but upwards towards the Hearer of it above, the Father thus invoked by the Son. So listening, so pondering, we shall learn a little of the Theism of Jesus Christ.

"I believe in GOD." It is the very first article of the Christian creed. It is the first article of creeds not Christian, the Jewish, and Islamic. It is a confession to which witness is borne, deep and manifold, from every various quarter, first and most weightily by the conscious self of man, then by the whole universe mental and material around it. Conscience and science alike, heard in quiet, affirm the existence, the will, the presence, at once above and within the world, of a personal Majesty, ultimate and supreme.

Yet few are the thoughtful hearts that do not sometimes feel the mystery of their confession more intensely than its certainty. Reason itself sometimes, and imagination often, falter, or seem to falter, questioning in the silence and the dark whether indeed the Personal can be also the Infinite; whether a supreme Free Will can indeed be trusted to be at work under the seemingly absolute uniformity of the world-process; whether the course of experience, alike in the universe or in the individual, accords with the assertion that over everything, always, everywhere, a holy and kind purpose presides. There are hours when even the established disciple passes under the cold shadow of such questions. Perhaps it is in illness, when the body weighs down the spirit. Perhaps there has just happened one of those great public calamities which make even the modern world shrink and pause; a ghastly wreck at sea, or on the railway, or, on the larger scale of things, an eruption of Krakatoa, or of Mont Pelée. (It is said that a perceptible wave of atheist feeling in Europe followed upon the great earthquake at Lisbon, a century and a half ago.) Or the wheels of ruin come over our own hearts; our home is shattered by bereavement; we have often spoken sympathy to others; perhaps a little too easily and glibly, "but now it is come upon *thee*, and thou faintest; it toucheth *thee*, and thou art troubled" (Job 4:5); and the stricken soul asks, is there indeed a Father who "pitieth His children" [Ps. 103:13]? Why does He let things happen, then, which no earthly father would permit, if he could help it, to fall upon his child? Why does He let them happen, *and keep silence all the while?* Such thoughts, if not brought to a halt somehow, may go on till they slide downwards to that dread abyss of Jean Paul Richter's "Vision," where the soul seemed to see, at the center of the universe, *a socket without an eye.*

Many are the reflections, simple and profound, by which the "mind" whose "loins are girded" (see 1 Pet. 1:13) *can* bring such thoughts to a halt on the dreadful incline, there to wait for light and power from on high. But I know none of them at once more simple and more deep than that which remembers Jesus Christ, and listens again to His Theism. Behold this Personage. To His moral glory, unique and supreme, universal conscience witnesses, far beyond the pale of His Church. His transcendence over the law of death is assured by His resurrection from the grave, without which the worldwide worship of His name at this day cannot be explained. His contact with an eternal plan is evidenced by His appearance then and there in the world, at the end an issue of a vast avenue of prophecy and preparation. Contemplate His person, His character, His work, His infinite influence. Is He not to be trusted as one who stood in true relations with the unseen and everlasting?

With such thoughts, look upon Him and listen to Him again as He "lifts up His eyes to heaven," and speaks into the other world. What does He see there? Whom does He address? To Jesus Christ, behind all veils, above all mysteries, "eternity" is "inhabited" by One who lives, who loves, who hearkens, who is holy, who is righteous, who is on the throne of things, who is His own sacred Father. "Thou lovedst Me before the foundation of the world. O righteous Father, the world hath not known Thee, but I have known Thee. This is life eternal, to know Thee, and Me whom Thou hast sent. I have finished Thy work. Now come I to Thee" [see John 17:3, 4, 24, 25].

Come, let us look up through our Master's eyes. Let us ascend upon His words. So we shall go at length where He is gone. And we shall rest meantime, with thoughts like these, in the unalterable certainty that GOD IS LOVE.

47

Personal Confidence and Its Power

I know whom I have believed—2 Tim. 1:12

Here we have two personalities in immediate contact, "nothing between." On the one side is the man believing, this human Ego who asserts this individual knowledge about the Object of an individual reliance. On the other side is that glorious Object, also personal; not "it" but "He," not "which" but "Who." Unnamed, He is however, in the context, unmistakable. He is the Lord and Savior Jesus Christ, whom to know is life eternal, whom to trust, in spirit and in truth, is "pardon, and holiness, and heaven."

The man believing, the person who relies, and who affirms his personal knowledge and personal faith, is Paul. His course is very nearly at an end, after all its eventful experiences. "He is ready to be offered" [2 Tim. 4:6]; he is writing his wistful, wonderful farewell to the living man he loves best, with the practically certain prospect, within a few months at latest, of a martyr's death. He is left almost entirely alone as to old companionships. He is shunned by ordinary society, as he never was before, for it is a reign of terror now, and he is its leading designated victim. He is called to the singular sorrow of going down to death amidst the apparent ruin of his whole life's work; for truly to every eye but that of the firmest faith the enterprise of Christianity must have seemed to be on the verge of extinction at the date of the death of Paul.

Yet his tone is calm, and his hope is unshaken. Not that he does not feel, and has no tears. As we reflected in an earlier chapter, no writing in the New Testament is so full of deep and strong human emotion as this Second Epistle to Timothy. The critics who would make it out that the "Pastoral Epistles" are a fabrication, falsely signed with the Pauline name, can never duly have weighed this great element of the evidence in their favor, this accent of the suffering heart in the Second Epistle, an accent which religious fabricators of that age were quite incapable of personating. No, this is the writing of a real man in real pain, tenderly conscious of the "tears" (1:4) of his friend, dwelling with yearning love on the names and memories of other days (1:5), and alluding, though only alluding, to heartbreaking sorrows and solitudes of his own (2:9; 4:10, 11, 16). The tone, the dialect, is pathetically authentic; the inventor's miserable art could not approach it.

But then, the assurance and repose of this man's spirit, beneath his sorrows, is unbroken. He has no misgivings about his cause; "the foundation of God standeth sure" (2:19). And as to himself, far from a sense of collapse and failure, he has an even exulting consciousness of a task accomplished, a victory won, and "a crown of righteousness" ready for him in the hand of a triumphant King (4:7, 9); for him, and for an uncounted multitude besides, who share with him the brightest of all hopes; "not to me only, but unto all them also that love His appearing" [2 Tim. 4:8].

What is the secret? Stated as briefly as possible, and in its essence only, it is faith. "He believes, therefore he thus speaks." "This is the victory that overcometh the world, even our faith." And what is faith? In the sense at once of common language and of divine truth, of the marketplace and of the Bible, faith is trust, it is personal reliance.

This man, awaiting the death-warrant and the executioner, is sure of ultimate success and of eternal life not because he is a philosopher, nor even because he is an inspired prophet of the future, but because he personally relies upon Jesus Christ, who has promised him peace and glory, and who is such that His cause cannot possibly do other than prevail. It matters little whether Paul can so foresee as to be able to say, however vaguely, by what methods the triumph will be won. It is enough that he knows his "glorious Leader"; to know Him is to be sure of himself, for he is joined to Him, and it is to be sure of the outcome of the long campaign, for the Commander is almighty and infallible. The man who belongs to Jesus Christ and who relies on Him may well be at peace. He is lifted above perplexity and disappointment in the arms, and at the heart, of his redeeming King.

Such is always the victory of the saints, over sorrow, over mystery, over everything that threatens. It was Peter's victory when confronted (John 6:68, 69) with the unfathomable mysteries of Christ's teaching: "To whom shall we go? Thou hast the words of eternal life. We believe and are sure that Thou art the Christ, the Son of the living God." It was Martha's victory when wounded to the heart (John 11:27) by not only her brother's death but the seeming indifference of her Master about it; "Yes, Lord, I believe that Thou art the Christ."

It is a truth of deepest reason as well as of purest revelation, that "we are saved by faith." For the meaning of those words in Holy Scripture is that we are saved by *a trusted Christ*. Here is no mere formula of dogmatic thought. It is the watchword of the living soul which has seen in any measure its "own exceeding need," and has been shut up to that "confidence of self despair," which finds in Christ *alone* the infinitely adequate basis of its reliance.

"I know whom I have trusted; I am persuaded that He is able."

48

Christ Our All

Who of God is made unto us wisdom, and righteousness, and sanctification, and redemption—1 Cor. 1:30

In the margin of the Revised Version a rendering of Paul's Greek here is given, which interprets it, as I believe, better than any other rendering. Quoting the passage consecutively, to include the margin, it runs thus: "Christ Jesus, who was made unto us wisdom from God, both righteousness, and sanctification, and redemption." The Apostle's meaning is thus represented to be that the Lord is given to us, by His Father's supreme bounty, to be our "wisdom," our secret and solution for all our perplexities and needs; and that this "wisdom," when applied in detail, takes a threefold aspect, in relation to a threefold primary necessity of the soul of man, man the sinner and the mortal. As regards the problem of guilt and condemnation, Christ Jesus is our "wisdom" in the form of *"righteousness."* As regards the problem of the power and tyranny of besetting sin within us, He is our "wisdom" in the form of *"sanctification."* And as to the last great problem, death and the grave, "this same Jesus" is our "wisdom" in the form of *"redemption,"* "to wit (Rom. 8:23), the redemption of our body."

Even if we retain the "Authorized" rendering, or that given in the text of the Revision, the explanation of the passage will work out much as I have here given it, if we illustrate the great words "righteousness" and "redemption" by Paul's own use of them elsewhere, and remember that the *"and"* which connects "wisdom" with them is a very elastic link-word, and readily lends itself to the meaning *"even,"* where the context favors. But I repeat my belief that the margin of the Revised Version is the truest counterpart of the actual wording of the apostolic Greek; and it most certainly gives us this for its message, that Christ Jesus, as our wisdom, is such in this *three-fold* aspect of grace and blessing.

Placing the verse before us for our study, let us first very briefly recite afresh to our hearts what these three sides of mercy are.

(1) "Righteousness." For commentary, we turn to the Roman Epistle, written very nearly at the same time. In it we open that golden chapter, the third, at the 25th and 26th verses. Take them with their context, and carry on your study over the fourth and fifth chapters, and can you doubt what is meant there by "righteousness," "the righteousness of God"? It is nothing less than His own secret of peace, the acceptance of sinful man, in Christ, as if he were not sinful; His "justification" of "the ungodly" (4:5); His welcome of the offender as satisfactory to the very law he has broken—not for no reason, but because the blessed Christ of God, one with the Lawgiver, has become the propitiation for our sins. If words have meaning, that is the message there. And it is the message also here, by the same great messenger. Christ Jesus is our "wisdom," "our thought profound," in face of the problem of our acceptance. For He is "the Lord our Righteousness."

(2) "Sanctification." That is to say, an inward hallowing, a willing, self-surrendering, dedication to the holy Lord. Truly the problem here involved is sacred and deep. It is well to be pardoned. It is wonderful to be accepted, justified; which is more than to be pardoned; for pardon need say no more than, "You may go," while acceptance can say no less than, "You may come, even to the heart and home of God." But it is impossible for the living conscience to be ultimately content even with that amazing blessing *isolated from its intended sequel,* the purity of the heart of the accepted man. And what shall inwardly cleanse that polluted recess? Can toils and tears of ours do it? Can laceration and mortification of the body do it? Not at the center, not in the depth. There is only one effectual "wisdom" *there.* It is Christ Jesus, our "sanctification," the personal secret of our inward separation from sin to God. "I have learned the secret at last," said a naturally passionate man, asked how he had come to be all that was

kind and patient. "I used to try to keep my own temper; I now trust it to my Lord to keep for me." He had found Christ Jesus his "wisdom," in the aspect of sanctifying presence, peace, and power.

(3) "Redemption." This, as I have indicated, is to be taken here, following thus *last* upon those other words, as the final redemption, "the redemption of our body" [Rom. 8:23], foretold of old by the prophet (Hos. 13:14): "I will ransom them from the power of the grave; I will redeem them from death." How shall it be? Nothing that we can watch seems more final than death, more hopeless than the grave. Our "wisdom" breaks down there, in dust and ashes. But not so "the wisdom of God," which is His Son, Christ Jesus. In Him we behold death actually conquered, and the human body actually transfigured into immortality. He has given practical proof that "He can subdue all things unto Himself" [Phil. 3:21]. And He has given His word that they who are joined to Him shall share *the whole* of His victory, in body, soul and spirit.

In closing, let us stand back from this wonderful verse and look at it once more, not in its threefoldness but in its unity. Three sublime blessings have passed before us, covering (when we think them out) our whole need as sinners who must die. But they all run up into one thing. Nay, into one Person. They are not abstract propositions about Christ; they are Christ Himself. No distant effects, ejected afar from Him the Cause, are here in view. He, living, loving, suffering, triumphing, indwelling—HE IS ALL!

Therefore the "all" on our side is to accept Him, in all the fullness of what He is, with the open hand of the very simplest personal reliance, taking Him at His word.

49

"This Same Jesus in Like Manner"

This same Jesus, which is taken up from you into heaven, shall so come in like manner as ye have seen Him go into heaven—Acts 1:11

As the year of our common calendar runs out to its close, the ancient seasons of the Christian year begin their course. Advent, the Season of the Coming, is upon us with December. The sunset of time is annually preluded by the commemoration of the rising of the eternal day.

We cannot claim any conscious original purpose for the arrangement. It has come to pass we hardly know how. But it is a recurring fact, however caused, full of solemn and of heart-uplifting significance.

The Coming of Our Lord! The words, to be sure, have a double reference, and may lead us, according to connection, to ponder either His "coming in great humility" as the Infant of Bethlehem, or His promised glorious Return. Today however we will think only of this latter. Later, with the Christmas glory before our eyes, we will speak of the former.

There is no need to recall at any length the occasion of the words at the head of this chapter. It was the moment after the Ascension. The "eleven disciples" were following their Lord upward with longing eyes, from that eastward spur of Olivet of which we thought in an earlier chapter, when suddenly beside them stood two "men," in bright, luminous clothing, and spoke the words before us.

Stier, at the close of his *Words of the Lord Jesus,* makes some beautiful comments on this utterance of the angels, dwelling on the fraternal

317

sympathy it displays, and even on the *local* sympathy, if we may phrase it so, which comes out in the address, "Ye men of *Galilee.*" But we will not linger over this; it is just one of those many examples of angelic brotherhood with man which we dealt with some weeks ago. All that we will particularly remember now is that this most definite of predictions about the glorious Return *is* angelic; it is a report upon the purposes of Heaven brought to us from within the veil by the heavenly ones themselves.

What does it say to us?

First and most conspicuously, perhaps with more perfect distinctness than any other prediction of the Second Coming, it assures us of its absolute "literality." The language of that Oriental book, the Bible, is rich in the figurative element. Take for example Psalm 18, where David sums up the divine instances of deliverance he had experienced, and observe how he throws his thought into the shapes of the earthquake, the thunderstorm, and a manifestation of Jehovah as miraculous as that at Sinai. Yet in all David's recorded history nothing of that kind, we may say emphatically nothing, appears. The Lord's "advent" for David's deliverance was in reality a succession of providential interpositions in which miracle was at most a very subordinate element; and the Psalm sums it all up in a magnificent figure. We are tempted to ask, May not the final fulfillment of the purpose of God take the same form? May not the "coming of the Son of Man" prove to be, in reality, no more than a grand series of events, providential to be sure, but not "miraculous":

> No living Lord, when man once saw,
>> Nought but some vast event,
> Some gradual, self-working law
>> In large embodiment?

Not so, say the angels of the Ascension. In one supreme respect at least, "that blessed hope, the glorious appearing of our great God and Savior" [see Titus 2:13], will be full of a sublime "literalism." For not only shall the central Figure be supremely personal, "this same Jesus." He shall "so come, *in like manner as*" He was seen going into heaven.

Yes, in the unknown future to which we move incessantly forward, this thing is known, this point is fixed. There shall be an hour, as distinct and single as the hour of His retreat from earth, when to earth He shall return. From the deep Unseen *He* shall, "in like manner," come again within the range of human senses, of human vision. Be the attendant mysteries what they may, this shall be true; "every eye shall see HIM."

Can anything be more penetrating, more fit to touch the conscience, than that simple prospect, when we reflect that no veil, no film of interposition, shall in that day float between our very eyes and the personal presence of "Jesus Christ the Righteous," that we shall give account then not through any intermediary courts of investigation but face to face with Personal, Eternal, Incarnate, Truth and Holiness? Think it through sometime. Realize, if it is possible, what it would be to be called, tomorrow, to some specified spot upon this earth, to have an interview of account with Jesus Christ, immediate and direct.

On the other hand, for the servant who is at once "found in Him" and true to Him, what can measure the bliss of that prospect of sight? A beloved friend of mine, years ago, in a solemn dream, saw the Return. Three glorious figures were beheld, through her chamber window, advancing in the sky. One she knew not; one was the archangel; the Other was—the LORD. And at *that* sight all the unknown springs of love and joy within the soul rose in blissful power *to fill* the being; and she woke.

> Thou art coming, Thou art coming;
> We shall meet Thee on the way:
>   We shall see Thee, we shall know Thee,
>   We shall bless Thee, we shall show Thee
> All our hearts could never say:
> What an anthem that will be,
>   Music exquisitely sweet,
>   Pouring out our love to Thee
> At Thine own all-glorious feet!

50

The Last Command

Ye shall receive power, after that the Holy Ghost is come upon you: and ye shall be witnesses unto Me . . . unto the uttermost part of the earth—
Acts 1:8

The Revised Version gives us one change of rendering here which is to be observed. Instead of "witnesses unto Me," it reads, "My witnesses"; and this is a closer rendering of the Greek of Luke, or at least a rendering more likely to be quite close. Yet the difference, while we notice it, is not such as to negate, but rather to include, the meaning of the Authorized Version. The thought which it accentuates is that the "witnesses" *belong to* Christ as their Master, and exist, as witnesses, for His ends. The other rendering rather puts to the front the thought that Christ is to be the matter of their witness; they are to be "witnesses *unto Him.*" But in either view *they are to be witnesses.* They are to be, not inquirers, thinkers, philosophers; they are not to set out upon a mission of mental or moral research and discovery; they are not even to be, primarily, prophets of righteousness and judgment. They are to bear witness, to offer a personal testimony to the world; to inform it of a revealed certainty, of something which they know and which it needs. And the whole record of the Gospels, and of the Acts as the sequel to that record, tells us beyond mistake what that revealed certainty is; it is nothing less and nothing other than our Lord Jesus Christ Himself.

The two Versions together thus contribute to assure us this, about the Apostles first, but then also, to the end, about the believing Church which was to carry on their work; they were, and we are, to be witnesses to the world of Jesus Christ, as those who belong to Him, purchased by His blood, and appropriated by His grace, on purpose that we may be such.

This is the very last command of the Lord. He stands, as He utters it, with His feet upon the steps of the heavenly throne. As all through His earthly ministry, so now, almost from the place of bliss itself, "He commends Himself." He sends His followers out into the world on purpose, as their work of works, to bear a testimony. And that testimony is to be borne, first and last, to Himself. Man's immeasurable need is to be met by telling man, as only those who personally know can tell, about the Son of God and Man, the one Name of Life, Christ Jesus the Lord.

As we approach the year's close, and while we think (as we thought last Sunday) upon the Second Coming, it will be well once more definitely, solemnly, and with great simplicity, to recollect this final edict and charge of Him whom we love, and whom we look forward to see face to face, "this same Jesus."

The world has many religions, some of them older than Christianity, as Brahmanism and Buddhism, some later, as Islam; not to speak of Judaism (whose relation to Christianity sets it apart), and the countless minor phases of belief. Through the disturbing, often woefully distorting, medium of the non-Christian creeds, some great original truths unquestionably shine. At the very least and lowest, the persuasion of the existence of unseen personal power is maintained by them. And behind them all the human conscience, the candle of the Lord, however dim, however its lantern blots its light, says something to man everywhere of temperance, righteousness, and judgment to come. The Christian missionary, wise and sympathetic, never willingly forgets this in dealing with pagan or with Moslem. Nay, he finds in this recollection his best foothold for advance in the name of Christ upon the non-Christian soul. But all the more, nonetheless, he knows that what that soul unspeakably needs, in order that it may find out accurately both itself and its God, is precisely what not the most exalted non-Christian creed can give it, namely, Jesus Christ. So he addresses himself with his whole being, (keeping that being, by a watchful faith, filled with Jesus Christ,) to be His witness, a witness unto Him.

"Our sacred books in the Far East have many noble moral precepts. But your sacred Book alone shows how such things may be done." So said a young Oriental to me, a nominal Buddhist, a Japanese student at Cambridge. It was twenty-one years ago, in Moody's inquiry-room. The youth was just then trembling on the verge of the discovery of his Lord, of whom that great "witness" had spoken as only they speak who have heard Him speak to them. Within a few weeks from that day I baptized Nathaniel Kenzo, a convinced and rejoicing believer. He had found the heavenly secret which comes to us not by investigation from below but by revelation from above, from the very heart of God. "Eye had not seen, nor ear heard, but God revealed it to him by His Spirit" [see 1 Cor. 2:9, 10].

"Occupy till I come" [Luke 19:13]. He who gave us that last command, to witness unto Him, expects the obedience of His Church, and is coming, when "the times and seasons in the Father's power" have run out, to inquire into the results. He knows HIMSELF to be the world's supreme and vital need, and He has equipped us to convey Him to the world.

As a fact, one half of the human race have not yet heard His sacred name. And eighteen ages and two-thirds are gone. His Return may well be drawing very near. Shall we, shall believing Christendom, awake at length, at length, to the conviction that we exist as His witnesses, to witness unto Him?

51

The Birthday of the Lord

God sent forth His Son, made of a woman—Gal. 4:4

The time draws near the Birth of Christ. The old year is sighing to its end, under the shadows of December. But the sigh is lost, for the believing Christian, in the song of Bethlehem. Time says, "we die, we perish, we all perish." But the Lord of Eternity comes into time, and takes up the existence of the children of time into His own, and says, "Behold, I make all things new" [Rev. 21:5] because I live, ye shall live also" [John 14:19].

"Thou didst not abhor the Virgin's womb." So says that old and glorious song of our Faith, *Te Deum laudamus,* sung now for some fifteen centuries upon this poor earth, just as we sing it now. Sacred, unfathomable, is the mystery of that Virgin Birth. We can scarcely wonder that it has been doubted, discredited, even denied, within the Church itself; pronounced even by devout minds to be not altogether an article of faith; to be separable from the truth of the Incarnation, God's becoming also Man; so that we may hold fast this latter and yet think the story of Matthew 1 and Luke 1 and 2 to be a poem, a myth, a dream. For my part, with profound conviction, I dare to say that so it cannot be. Not to dwell on the fullness of Luke's story, and its primeval date (for such is its date to all but an artificial critique), and the countless fine touches of internal evidence to its solid structure of sober fact, consider a point of thought about it which lies near to the essence of our belief. If the Son of Mary were indeed the Son of Joseph too, He would assuredly have come into human being, as we come, *a human person,* separate and individual.

He would not have come as God made Man, one blessed Person forever, so that it was the identically same Christ who, "for us men and our salvation, came down from heaven," lived, suffered, rose again, ascended, and shall return. He would have come as *a man,* who might indeed have been then "possessed" by the divine Son, but could never, to all eternity, be personally identical with Him. He would be such that we could never say, looking up to the Throne, and to Him who sits there by the Father's side, as He sat there before the world was (John 17:5), *"Thou* wast made flesh for us" [see John 1:14]; *"Thou* didst die for us" [see Rom. 5:8]; *"Thou* art able to be touched with our infirmities, for *Thou* wast tempted like as we are, yet without sin" [see Heb. 4:15]. All that wealth of "everlasting comfort and good hope" which comes with the thought that "the Son of God loved me and gave HIMSELF for me" (Gal. 2:20) would disappear, as to any power of ours to grasp it as a fact, if we must think of our dear Lord (were it possible) as two persons, one "possessed" by the other; *a man* taken up and used by the eternal Son of God; and not, as our sure faith affirms Him to be, our One Lord, One Life, One everlasting Hope and Friend.

Let us hold fast the Birth of Jesus, of the holy Virgin, by the Holy Ghost. It is no mere abstract tenet of correct belief. It is an element, infinitely sacred and tender, of the very life of our spiritual peace and strength.

That granted, that secured, then let us give ourselves in thankful simplicity of thought to the wonder, joy, and gratitude which only the full truth of the Annunciation and the Nativity can ensure.

> Dear are the names of classic story
>   That thro' the bosom strike a living thrill;
> Olympian snows reflect unfading glory
>   And Heliconian springs run music still;
> And Troy and Athens yet retain
> Their spell for pleasure and for pain;
> But there is that which passes them—
> 'Tis Thy blest history, Bethlehem!

"His Son, born of a woman." Supreme wonder, most tender consolation, spring of a hope which cannot possibly make ashamed! Here is solved, in a fact, in a Person, forever, that old riddle of the mind of man, how the Infinite and the Finite can really, absolutely, meet. Behold the CAUSE of all things, "the Mighty God," without whom were not made "Arcturus and his sons, and the sweet influences of Pleiades, and the bands of Orion," and the angelic orders, the principalities and powers of heaven. Behold Him, wrapped in swaddling clothes, laid in a manger! He has entered human life *by our door;* for He is a Mother's own Son. He is one with us indeed, in the profound bond of a common nature. And He, no other, even He, is one with the eternal Father too.

Blessed Birthday, dear to eternity and to time! Let us hasten with our Birthday Gift and lay it at His feet—ourselves, our hearts, our all!

> From the Father's glory,
>   From the Virgin's womb,
> Infant and Eternal,
>   Savior, Thou art come.
>
> Older than Creation,
>   Cause of things that are;
> Younger than the Mother-Maid,
>   Tender Morning Star.
>
> Goal and rest forever
>   Of the life-worn mind;
> To the little children
>   Infinitely kind.

NOTE: I am indebted for some valuable suggestions, used in this chapter, to an essay in the *Churchman,* June, 1903, by the Rev. J. Foxley.

52

His Face: Their Foreheads

They shall see His face, and His name shall be in their foreheads—
Rev. 22:4

We have come to the last Sunday of the year. Does it not seem as if it was but a week or two ago that we thought over, on its first Sunday, the promise of the Presence "all the days"? Today, as in the Psalmist's time, "we spend our years as a tale that is told" [Ps. 90:9], and seem to hear already the hush that will succeed the tale, as the night falls upon the listening circle by the fire, and they separate for sleep.

But the Word of God, which so fully recognizes the deep pathos of Time, is rich in antidotes to it. One such antidote we sought to use last Sunday, the supreme remedy, the Coming into time of the eternal Son of God, made one with man. Another, virtually related to this, yet also to be contemplated apart, is before us here in this great promise of the eternal future. True always to itself, the Bible, "the Book of Hope," closes its oracles with the revelation of a be-ginning which has no end. It lifts us beyond "the shadow of our night" to the prospect of a life out of which the pathos of time is ex-orcised forever. Resting that prospect not upon emotions, however tender, but upon the Person and Word of the risen and glorified Redeemer, who is the Morning Star (22:16) of the final day, it bids us be sure that there shall come in at length for the life-worn soul of believing man a state as full as divine love can make it of sorrow-less as well as sinless perfection, in which "He that sitteth on the throne" [Rev. 7:15] will "make all things *new*" [Rev. 21:5].

No tremulous joy, no tear-besprinkled happiness, bearing a relic of sorrow in its heart, is promised us in the Scripture doctrine of the future. Ours is a "hope full," to its brim, "of immortality." We look for a world where, as the Rabbis have somewhere wonderfully said, the blessed grow not older but younger as they live on in heaven.

Out of this last outburst of the Oracle of Hope let us take this short sentence, and think upon its double glory.

(1) "They shall see His face." Here is the supreme promise of the Gospel. "Blessed are the pure in heart, for they shall see God" (Matt. 5:8). "Now we see by a mirror, in a riddle, BUT then, face to face" (1 Cor. 13:12, literal rendering). "Thine eyes shall see the King in His beauty" (Is. 33:17). Throughout the long Christian ages, this hope of "the beatific Vision," of that Sight of the Lord which makes absolutely blessed, has shone before the eyes of the Church on her pilgrimage, as the ultimate rest and glory. So it must be. Heaven is to be the scene of an endless life. That prospect, apart from the sight of God, would be even terrible; it would more than realize the sorrowful Tithonus-legend of the Greeks, the woe of the being who, asking for immortality, forgot to ask also for immortal youth. Nothing but the Vision can keep the finite creature new and young forever. But that can; each for himself, all for one another, and for the Lord, the blessed shall be forever crowned with an unfading, yea, a blossoming life, seeing Him.

"His face." And whose, exactly, is that fair and vivifying Countenance? It is not the presence of a "God in the abstract," a benignant but nameless Deity. Look at the verse preceding, and know that it is the face of God in Christ. What else is meant when the seer of the Revelation, using to the last the peculiar imagery of his great prophecy, looking into the Holy City and discerning there its everlasting center of order and of love, writes that "the throne of God *and of the Lamb* shall be in it and His (not Their but His) servants shall serve Him" [Rev. 22:3]? Forever they shall, on the mount of the Vision, "worship the Son in the Father, and love the Father in the Son."

(2) "His name shall be in their foreheads." His Name, the transcript of His Character, the celestial family-likeness of His children,

shall shine unmistakable upon those white tablets—the foreheads of the glorified. "They shall be like Him, seeing Him as He is." Observe that significant touch in the picture, "in *their foreheads.*" No vague and (so to speak) inarticulate radiance circles the throne of God and the Lamb. It is a multitude which cannot be numbered. But it is no mere mass, no mere aggregated unit. It is a host of faces. Look, the very foreheads are to be seen; each forehead there, as it is here, the seat and the expression of personal character, of individual thought, and will, and affection; no two precisely alike there, anymore than here, while all are suffused with the inner oneness of the family of God. Each happy personality, while one with Him, and in Him one with all, is *itself* for all eternity, sustained by Him unwearied in its blissful identity, and so contributing *itself,* that individual radiating point of life and love, to the joy of all.

"'Tis heaven at last." So sings Horatius Bonar, in a poem full of his own characteristic mingled joy and pathos, imagining what it will be to look around at length, and behold, beyond all the traveling, it is veritably the eternal Home!

So shall it be for us, "when rolling years have ceased to move," through the great mercy of our God in Christ. As I think that thought, I seem to see it embodied in a certain inscription, on a marble slab, outside the southern wall of a village church, the church of Hilterfingen, which looks from its gentle eminence across the waters of the Lake of Thun. The stone bears the name of an English woman, long departed. It seems, by what its English legend implies, to tell us that she had in her time tasted deep of the cup of loneliness and sorrow. But now, so its words of triumphant faith, grandly adapted from Isaiah (60:20), assure us, all this is over, and the Vision has satisfied the solitary pilgrim's eyes: THE LORD IS MY EVERLASTING LIGHT, AND THE DAYS OF MY MOURNING ARE ENDED.

BOOK THREE

The Sacred Seasons

To

M. E. E. M.

FOREVER WITH THE LORD

AND

IN THE LORD

WITH US

1

The First Sunday in Advent: The "I Come" of Christ's Return

"Behold I come quickly"—Rev. 3:11; 22:7, 12

Four times over in the Book of the Revelation the glorified Savior speaks explicitly the "I come" of His sure and speedy return. "Behold, I come quickly: hold that fast which thou hast" (Rev. 3:11); "Behold, I come quickly; blessed is he that keepeth the sayings of the prophecy of this book" (22:7); "Behold, I come quickly, and my reward is with me" (22:12); and "He which testifieth these things saith, Surely I come quickly. Amen" (22:20). Great is the emphasis, mighty and holy indeed the import, of such a personal promise. Let us comment a little on this "I come," so as to meet equally (as I think we may do) the hearts of *all* Christians who look forward to a literal and glorious Coming, as the great Church of God has looked from the first. The mysterious bliss of the Thousand Years, and the questions gathered around the word "premillennial," may *practically* be laid out of view sometimes in this matter, and believing students may sometimes meet, as it were, behind them. It is somehow possible for *all* who love and submit to the written Word, and hold heartily that definite prediction is a divine reality in that Word, to look up *together* into heaven, "waiting for the coming of our Lord Jesus Christ" [1 Cor. 1:7], "loving His appearing" [2 Tim. 4:8], "looking for the Savior, who shall change our body of humiliation," and who shall welcome us to "meet Him in the air" [1 Thess. 4:17]. It is possible somehow for us *all* to be thus standing with our loins girded and our lamps aflame, as men waiting for their Lord, and not knowing in what watch of the night He will suddenly come and knock.

"Behold, I come quickly; surely I come quickly; this same Jesus." What common ground for loving, solemn meditation may we find here? In the *"quickly"* of the promise we are all to read that the disciple's attitude, as it was with the Israelite of the Exodus, is to be that of the man whose shoes are on his feet, and his staff in his hand, *ready*. It is an old story, but never out of date, certainly not in this age of enormous worldliness, this "hour when they think not" [see Luke 12:40]. "Let not this world our rest appear," no, not even when it looks at us through well-loved and fruitful work, or through the joys of a pure and happy home: all these things are dissolving. In the very midst of them, In His own time, He who comes as the thief in the night, but who is also (blessed be His name) the midnight Friend, will be here—and a very different order of things will begin with that Arrival. Is the prospect being recollected and cherished? Are we maintaining it in the souls' sanctuary as a dear and joyful one, so far as our own personality is concerned? We may, we must, cultivate such a view of Him as shall naturally spring up into an instant and enraptured welcome, "My Savior, O my Savior," come when He may, come in upon what He will—"the King in His beauty."

And let us think quite simply of that part of the promise (which is indeed the heart of it) which tells us that it will be personally HE, and that with Him, in direct personal contact, we, each one, I and you, will have to do. The Return will be a time, a moment, a crisis, never to be forgotten; a point of interview between the disciple and the Master, the servant of the Lord, at the solemn close of this working day. Laborer for Him, speaker in His name, "fetch that day to thee, and make it thy company keeper." We are all, we are each, on our way to "give account of the things done in the body" [see 2 Cor. 5:10], of what we have "gained by trading" [Luke 19:15], of how we have lived for Him. We are on our way to an interview with our Master in which, even for the saved ones who shall be with Him forever, *an enquiry* will take place as complete as Christ can make it. And the report upon it will be made as only He can make it. "He will manifest the counsels of the hearts, and then shall every man have praise of God" [1 Cor. 4:5].

"How shall I meet His eyes?" As regards acceptance—only by looking from them to His hands and His side, and hiding there.

As regards all other aspects of the matter—by "walking in the light' with Him now, on the way to see Him face to face in that examination then.

2

The Second Sunday in Advent: The Holy Scriptures

However this Book, the Old Testament, came to be, in detail, there it is before us, a thing august, mysterious, unique. There is nothing really like it upon the earth.

There are other books, old Sacred Books of Gentile religions, and those books have in them many a passage which indicates that law which God, in conscience, gives to man. They are not to be thrown aside, neglected or despised, by the Christian reader; from every one of them may be gathered precious things of precept and of fact. Yet they are not therefore Bibles; they are not even secondary Bibles. The Koran of Mohammed, the Zend-Avesta of ancient Persia, the "classics" of Confucius in China, these writings are not Bibles. And why? Because they have no *imprimatur* put upon them by One who had proved Himself to be the Lord of the unseen. There is nothing in the world of literature upon which God has set His seal as He has set it, in the Person of Christ, upon this Book. There it stands, in that respect—not in all respects, but in that respect—unique of its kind. It is the solitary specimen of a book given through men but counter-signed by God—as a Literature which He built, as a System which He designed, a Work which He superintended. It is, as the One Author who stood behind the many authors designed it to be—the Oracle of God.

For all the things forewritten, written in the Scriptures of the elder time, in the age that both preceded the gospel and prepared for it, *for our instruction were written* (with an emphasis upon *"our"*), *that through the patience and through the encouragement of the Scriptures we might hold fast our hope,* the hope "sure and steadfast," of glorification in the glory of our conquering Lord. That is to say, the true "Author behind the authors" of that mysterious Book watched, guided, effected its construction, from end to end, with the purpose full in His view of instructing for all time the developed Church of Christ. And in particular, He adjusted thus the *Old Testament* records and precepts of "patience"—the patience which "suffers and is strong," suffers and goes forward—and of "encouragement," the word which means more than "consolation," while it includes it; for it means the voice of positive and enlivening appeal. Rich indeed are Pentateuch, and Prophets, and Hagiographa, alike in commands to persevere and be of good courage, and in examples of men who were made brave and patient by the power of God in them, as they took Him at His word. And all this, says the Apostle, was on purpose, on God's purpose. That multifarious Book is indeed in this sense one. Not only is it, in its Author's intention, full of Christ; in the same intention it is full of Him *for us.* Immortal indeed is its preciousness if this was His design. Confidently may we explore its pages, looking in them first for Christ, then for ourselves, in our need of peace, and strength, and hope. The use of the Holy Book—of those "Divine Scriptures" as the Christian fathers love to call them—in the spirit of this verse, the persistent searching of it for the preceptive mind of God in it, with the belief that it was written for our instruction, will be the surest and deepest means to give us "perseverance" and "encouragement" about the Book itself. The more we really *know* the Bible, at first hand, before God, with the knowledge both of acquaintance and reverent sympathy, the more shall we make it our divine daily manual for a life of patient and cheerful sympathies, holy fidelity, and "that blessed Hope" [Titus 2:13]—which draws "nearer now than when we believed" [Rom. 13:11].

It is in special connection with the life of Christian Holiness, the life of new Obedience, that I speak of Scripture study; and especially in view of the fact that Scripture is the one *articulate* account, by the Lord Himself, of His "will in Jesus Christ concerning us." For you, believing friend, who long to know and to do His will, as at once your rest and your goal, let the Bible bear *this* aspect of sacredness very specially, that it is the one definite and articulate utterance of that Will by our Master Himself. From this point of view how singular is the value of Psalm 119! It has been beautifully said that the essence of the thought of that psalm is, the sacredness and sweetness of God's Will, to be known and done by His bond-servant; so that we may reverently read, as it were, the word "will" into it, as a synonym for "law," "statutes," "judgments," "precepts," and the rest. Try this holy gloss, and see how the verses shine with the glory of a loving surrender to the will of God. But then, on the other hand, beyond all question, the psalm in its direct purpose is one long strain of prayer, and praise, and self-consecration, *over the Bible*. The saintly soul's thirst after the Will of God leads it not to the mirage, but to the waterspring of the Word. With every access of love and longing, with every step in conscience and obedience, he feels new need of the Book, he bends over it, he bows to it. So be it with you and with me.

3

The Third Sunday in Advent: Christ Knocking at the Door

Behold, I stand at the door, and knock: if any man hear my voice, and open the door, I will come in to him, and will sup with him, and he with me—
Rev. 3:20

"I will come in to him." The context is solemnly familiar. All know the Laodicean Epistle; all have felt the awful penetration of its reproofs, convictions, and threatenings. Not least have we done so who are the ordained ministers of Christ and His flock; we remember that the words were immediately addressed to a chief pastor. We have heard the heavenly Master speaking through these verses; finding us out in some miserable moment, it may be, of spiritual self-complacency, of satisfaction with our own words or works; telling us that at such moments we are the "poor, and wretched, and miserable, and blind, and naked" [see v. 17]. The very name of Laodicea has derived thus in our minds an association with shame and alarm. Most rightly, from one side. But then let the convinced clergyman, the convinced Christian, remember on the other side that, if there are Laodicean threatenings, there is also this most glorious, this most tender, endearing, Laodicean promise, "I will come in to him."

Let us look at the promise itself.

Full of holy pathos as well as divine instruction is the imagery in which it lies. A dwelling-place is before us, and its door is fastened from within. The shadows gather, for it is the hour of the evening meal. "Behold a Stranger's at the door"; yet not a stranger too, for He has once been within. Now, somehow, the King stands outside, and the door is barred, while all within is dark, and cold, and out of gear, and the man sits in the gloom, moody and miserable, or sleeps heavily on the restless bed. The King knocks, and speaks. He will not apply force of hand. Not that He has no gentle omnipotence, no prevalence and secret drawing, or that He will not use it. But He *does not enforce* His will; His will shall take effect in and through His servant's repentant willingness. Once let the servant listen, and walk to the dark chamber's door, and move the bar, and lift the latch; lo, without a moment's more ado, without one prefatory condition, without one grudge because of the treasonable past, the King will enter. And His entrance shall be the signal for light and warmth within, for love, and friendship, and plenty, and a wonderful mutual hospitality. He will at once sit down to the table, and let His servant be His host. And He will then Himself make His servant His guest, and be Himself the bountiful Host, within the man's lately famished and gloomy dwelling.

Such shall be the secret spiritual Advent of the Lord Jesus Christ in this soul which lets him in at His knock, at His request. It shall be a definite and personal Advent, an In-coming, to a presence and abode such as *was not* just before. Jesus Christ shall be *in* that man's inner chamber of the soul, in a sense and manner positive and special. He shall be there not to find, but to make, light and order within; to be the fire on the hearth, the Lamp on the table. He shall be there as Guest, to feast upon the one provision the man can set before Him, the one provision which the King cares to accept, and which He loves to taste—the presented and surrendered will and life of the servant. And He shall be there as Host. He shall crown the poor table with the living bread and the new wine of the eternal Kingdom. He shall transfigure the narrow chamber into His own "banqueting house" [Song 2:4], feeding and filling the self-starved being with Himself, with all He does *for* His happy followers, and with all He is *in* them. And the imagery of the table suggests not only food but converse.

The woeful estrangement, the dull, rebellious silence on the one side, the solemn, censuring reserve on the other, are over. Host and guest, guest and Host, they look into each other's face, they hear the utterance of each other's heart: "I am thine, thou art mine; nothing between."

"I will love him, and will manifest myself to him" [John 14:21]; "That Christ may dwell in your hearts by faith" [Eph. 3:17]; "Eat, O friend, drink, yea, drink abundantly, O beloved" [Song 5:1].

4

The Fourth Sunday in Advent: Moderation or "Yieldingness"

Let your moderation be known unto all men; the Lord is near—Phil. 4:5

The word "moderation" in this verse is not quite self-explanatory. Neither moderation in the sense of self-government, nor its counterfeit, moderation in the sense of *point de zéle* is in view in this verse; most surely not the latter. Not that the gospel here or elsewhere means therefore to inculcate a hot, untempered, inconsiderate enthusiasm. Indeed, enthusiasm is not a New Testament word; and no wonder, when we remember that its old connection was with the frenzied excitements of the Greek worship of Bacchus. Enthusiasm is not, indeed, a word to be discarded; yet it is a word which too often suggests hasty and ill-considered resolutions, a flow of animal excitement very likely to ebb, a heat that outruns light. And all these are things of nature, not of grace; of fallen, not of regenerate humanity. The zeal and love of the gospel spring from deeper and purer wells, have a more serene flow, and are altogether nobler things than what commonly passes under the name of enthusiasm.

But the Apostle here is looking in quite another direction. The word here rendered moderation in our Bible is connected by derivation and usage with ideas not of control but of yielding. It is rendered *Lindigkeit,* "yieldingness, giving way," in Luther's German Bible; and I fully believe the interpretation to be right. "Forbearance," and "gentleness," are the alternative renderings of our Revised Version, and both suggest the thought of giving way. "Let your yieldingness be known unto all men; the Lord is near." Paul is dealing throughout this passage with certain holy conditions necessary to our experience of "the peace of God, keeping the hearts and thoughts, in Christ Jesus" [Phil. 4:7]. Standing fast in the Lord, harmony and mutual helpfulness in the Lord, rejoicing in the Lord, and prayerful and thankful communion with the Lord, are among these conditions. And with them, in the midst of them, appears this also: "Let your yieldingness be known unto all men; the Lord is near." This connection with the deep peace of God throws a glory over the word and the precept. The yieldingness which is here enjoined is nothing akin to weakness, indolence, or indifference. It is a positive grace of the Spirit; it flows from the fullness of Jesus Christ.

What is it? We shall find the answer partly by remembering how, from another point of view, the gospel enjoins, and knows how to impart, the most resolute *un*yieldingness. If anything can work the great miracle of making a weak character strong, it is the gospel. The gospel can make the regenerate will say "no" to self on a hundred points where never anything but "yes" was heard before. Nothing in the moral world is so immovable as the will of a living Christian, sustained by the power of God the Holy Spirit, on some clear case of principle. Yieldingness in our passage, is, in fact, *selflessness*. It is meekness, not weakness; the attitude of a man out of whom the Lord has cast the evil spirit of self. It is the discovery and practice of the blessed secret how to put Jesus Christ upon the throne of life, and to let that divine fact within work upon the life without. It is the grace which manifests itself in a calm, bright, willing superiority of thought and purpose to considerations of self's comfort, credit, influence. It is the noble, the holy readiness to rejoice, for instance, in the success of others in the field of Christian work, as simply and naturally as in our own. It is the aim not to get a reputation, but to walk and please God; not to secure the applause of others, but to compass their good and blessing; not to vindicate our opinion, but only and purely our Lord's word and truth; not to be first, but where He would put us; not to get our rights, for our sake, but to be loyal to His claims, and attentive, for His sake, with a scrupulous and kindly attention, to the rights and wants of others. Nothing does the world's microscope discover more keenly than "self-fullness" in a Christian man or woman. Nothing at once baffles its experience and explanation, and attracts its notice and respect, like the genuine selflessness, the yieldingness, of the grace of God. Let ours, then, "be known unto all men"—not paraded and thrown into an attitude, but kept in practice and use in real life, where it can be put to real tests. And would we read something, in this same verse, of its heavenly secret? It lies before us: "the Lord is near." He is near, not here in the sense of coming soon, but in that of standing by; in the sense of His presence, and "the secret" of it, around His servant. The thought is of the calm and overshadowing of His recollected and realized Presence; that divine atmosphere in which bitter things, and things narrow with the contractions and distortions of self, must die, and in which all that is sweet and loving lives.

5

Christmas Day

Then said He, Lo, I have come to do Thy will, O God—Heb. 10:9
Then said, I, Lo, I have come: I delight to do Thy will—Ps. 40:7, 8

I invite you this Christmas Day to lift up your hearts. Let us look up from beside the sacred Cradle to the Heaven of heavens, and ponder a little while that great antecedent to Bethlehem, the self-consecration of the Eternal Son to His incarnate life and work.

This lies here before us in the Scripture of the text, in the New Testament and in the Old.

The Scripture, with both its hands, the prophetic and the apostolic, lifts for us here the veil, and discloses to us "the mind that was in Christ Jesus," when, in the eternity which is above our time, He, the Son, "beloved before the foundation of the universe," willed to come down, and to become flesh. It utters to us the thought with which He, being true God, elected to be also true Man. It lets us hear His resolve to come, and to do the Father's will in saving us.

❦

As we stand listening to the voice which thus, even from the divine glory, speaks of surrender and of service, let us, with the Scriptures in our memory, recall in shortest summary some of the truths told us through this utterance, "Lo, I come to do Thy will" [Heb. 10:7].

Why does He come, as to the immediate and urgent element of His purpose? What is the aim set *in the foreground* of the eternal thought, indicated in the Psalm and developed in the epistle? Is it,

345

immediately, to knit up mankind together into one? Is it, immediately, to redeem the race—by Incarnation? It is, immediately, to be "Sacrifice and Offering." It is to do at last the work which the altar, under the old law, could never do. It is that the Incarnate, being such, might "put away sin by the sacrifice of Himself" [Heb 9:26]. Such was the first, ruling purpose of the self-consecration of the Son. The Self-Consecrator had in view, above all things, His Death, His Sacrifice, His Expiation, His Propitiation. Psalm, and Hebrews, and Philippians, all, in this matter, gravitate upon the Crucifixion. "A body hast Thou prepared me" [10:5]. He took share and share, with His brethren, in flesh and blood, "that through death he might destroy him that had the power of death" [2:14]. "Being the brightness of the Father's glory . . . by Himself He *purged our sins*" [Heb. 1:3]. "He . . . became obedient unto death, even the death of the cross" [Phil. 2:8].

The Scriptures are eloquent of the pain and yet joy of the untold Humiliation of the Lord. They tell us of His willingness to be made like us, with a likeness that should be no trope or figure, but a reality to its depths. They reveal His divinely free consent, in the full light of God, to enter personally within the essential and sinless limitations of Humanity. He willed, as Man, to experience what is meant by growth and development, what it is to weep and to wonder, what it should be to say, "Thy will be done," not only in heaven, as the Son Eternal, but as the Son of Man, under the olives of Gethsemane. He willed to cry, when the last darkness gathered around the Cross, to Him whose will He was wholly content to do, "Why hast Thou forsaken me?" [Matt. 27:46; Mark 15:34]. He willed to commit the out-going Human Spirit into His hands, in the awfulness of human death.

Let us end where we set out, in faith and in adoration, before the Self-Consecrating Savior.

We are keeping the festival of joy. The splendor of God, once poured upon the field of the shepherds, shines forever upon this day. The great carol of the warrior-angels, the melodious "heavenly army," sounds on forever in our winter sky. For us men God is made Man.

But the roots of our Christian joy are watered with the sorrows and the Sacrifice of our Redeemer. They cost Him dear. They involved His infinite Humiliation. As we rejoice, let it be with that thought in our souls. Let us bless Him with the love of penitents; let us follow Him with the love of witnessing disciples. "Lo, I have come." So said the Son of God, in view of His Cradle and of His Cross, as He saw them from above all the heavens. "Lo, I have come to do Thy will." And we are His. We are, through His grace, in Him. Then let it be ours, this day, this Birthday, to say the like, in our little measure, as if we had never said it before, for His sake and in His name. For trial, for humiliation, for the death of self-will, for whatever may be for us "the cross," let us, His members, draw from Him the power to say, "I have come," and to delight "to do the will of Him that sent us" [see John 4:34], and to finish His work.

6

St. Stephen

When the blood of Thy martyr Stephen was shed—Acts 22:20

This, you remember, is the reminiscence of Paul—he looked back and recalled the day when he kept the raiment of them who hurled the stones against the dying Stephen. Then he had looked on him as a man blasphemous toward God and a traitor to the hopes of Israel. Now he recalls him, in the light of his own knowledge of Jesus, as "Thy martyr Stephen." Let us think a little today, with St. Paul, about holy Stephen and about the martyr spirit, and the claim of the religion of Jesus that the martyr spirit should be present in His followers.

Stephen was chosen at first to be a server of tables; even for that work, let us note it well, the apostolic Church thought it needful that the server should be "full of the Holy Ghost and of faith" [Acts 11:24]. And doubtless in that divine power Stephen did his daily duty with wisdom and diligence. But he could not help overflowing into other work. He wrought great miracles, and he bore powerful witness, till opposition came, and then arrest, and then trial by the Sanhedrin, and then he was cast out of the city and stoned, yielding up his spirit to the Lord, having first seen in a wonder vision where that spirit was going—"I see the heavens opened, and the son of Man"—not now sitting, but, in that great hour, to succor and to meet him—*"standing,* at the right hand of God" [7:56]. So fell the first man who yielded up his soul in violent death as a martyr, that is to say, a witness, to his glorified Redeemer. From that day literally to this the martyr line has been continuous. To refer only to modern times, there have been martyrs by the hundreds in Armenia, Madagascar, and Uganda, and by many thousands in China, in the great persecution of 1900. The anguish and the glory of these our martyred brethren make us also, as disciples of Christ, ask what is there in His gospel that can claim such sacrifices.

What is the essence of the martyr spirit? Circumstances may differ infinitely, and to the vast majority of Christians in all ages the actual experience of violent death has not occurred. But *the essence* is for all places and for all times. For it is just this—the willingness, in the name and in the power of Christ, to suffer anything rather than deny Him, and violate His will. Such a spirit is present when a Stephen dies by the stones, a Paul by the sword, a Polycarp by the fire, an Ignatius by the beasts. But it is present also when a John is ready for the like fate, but is called to confess his Master in a long life. It is present when the Christian of today, in any degree in which God asks for it, is ready to suffer for his Lord in mind, in feeling, in money, in reputation. Wherever in any way suffering and loss is preferred to unfaithfulness to the will and name of Jesus, there, just so far, is the spirit of the martyrs.

7

St. John the Evangelist

And when I saw Him I fell at His feet as dead. And He laid His right hand upon me, saying unto me, Fear not; I am the first and the last; I am He that liveth and was dead; and behold I am alive forevermore, Amen; and have the keys of hell and of death—Rev. 1:17, 18

I ask you today to watch John, far along his course, towards the close of his following of his Lord; not now by the shore of the peaceful Lake, but in the late evening of a life so long, laborious, and burdened, waiting till he should meet Jesus again. The "beloved disciple" was in the Isle of Patmos, probably in the act of suffering for the gospel's sake; for he appears to have been in exile, and was perhaps condemned to penal toil. Then, on a certain day, "the Lord's Day," he "was in the Spirit" [v. 10], and saw things we cannot see, and heard things that ears untrained cannot hear, and met his Master once again. Perhaps sixty years had passed away since that scene by the Lake of Tiberias when he had "followed" along the beach. Friends had gone, times had changed, and the Church was undergoing "fiery trials" [see 1 Pet. 4:12]. And John had been laboring on, and suffering on, growing in grace, growing in the Spirit's power, till now, in that wonderful and ripened sanctity of his old age, there came to him this supernatural manifestation of his Lord. What was the effect upon him of the sight of the glorified Jesus? It caused the collapse of his whole being; it was, if I may use the word, an unspeakable physical shock. Think of the wonder of this. Here is no unconverted sinner, but the most advanced and spiritual of saints. And he sees, presented to his consciousness, the full glory, the full and awesome holiness, of Jesus Christ. And he falls at His feet as dead. Let this remind us that the sight of Christ, which is the secret of all joy, is also, and first, the most abasing thing that can ever be. Are we not yet low enough before God? If so, it is not only because we have not yet seen enough of ourselves; it is because we have not yet seen enough of our Savior and our King.

But now, how does our Lord meet John's abasement? Does He spurn him? Does He leave him there, and turn away? No, in His majestic tenderness He takes His prostrate servant literally by the hand. He puts His own infinite dignity and holiness into direct contact with the nothingness of His mortal follower, and says, "Fear not." When the soul is at His feet, silent and convinced, and when His hand is laid upon it so, tender indeed and all-effectual is the utterance, "Fear not."

But let us listen again. "*I* am alive forevermore." These are the supreme reasons not to be afraid, and they lie wholly in HIMSELF. Great is the joy of our first real grasp of the fact that we are dealing with "the *living* One," with the Lord who liveth and loveth, the same in His personality today as yesterday, and not only so, but tomorrow and forever. And then, "I *was dead*"; or, more literally, "I became dead." The Lord of life will not let the believing soul forget His death. He seems to say, "Behold me; on me was laid that sin of yours, the consciousness of which now lays you at my feet." And then, "I *am alive* forevermore." Thanks be to the Savior who became dead, but now lives—lives to be every moment the personal Friend of His saved ones, and also, as the living One who was dead, to apply and shower down on the believer the innumerable benefits of His Passion.

8

The First Sunday after Christmas: "Hitherto, Henceforth"

Hitherto hath the LORD helped us—1 Sam. 7:12

It is easy to explain away the interest of the Old Year's night, to say that the crossing the threshold of the New Year is nothing more than the perpetual step forward which we are always taking with every heartbeat. But let us pause for a moment (though we never really do pause) at this milestone, and in the light of God's Word let us look both backward and forward over our way. In 1 Samuel 7:12 we are told that Samuel set up a stone, and called the name of it Ebenezer, the Stone of Help, saying, "Hitherto hath the Lord helped us." There was a long future before Israel, and even to Samuel that future was in a large measure unknown, and wholly untried. But to him the help of the "hitherto" was a guarantee for the "Henceforth," whatever it might bring. He put up the Stone of Help, a solid, tangible witness of what God had been in the past, even to that hour. And because He had brought His Israel safe "up to date," they would trust Him to carry them into the dateless future before them. So now, in the name of every deliverance given us in the past, let us put up our stone of help, and remember that every "Hitherto" of the past year is the prelude to a "Henceforth" in the unfailing plan of the love of God.

In John 5:17 our Lord says, "My Father worketh *hitherto* and I work." Jesus Christ is a living, a *working* Savior. As to His atoning Sacrifice, His work is finished; as to the results of His Sacrifice, His work is never finished to all eternity. Have you looked to Him to work in you what is acceptable to God? And have you found Him true? Then give Him thanks for that "Hitherto," and let it fill you with bright expectancy for the "Henceforth" that is to be. Wonderful is the perseverance of our indwelling and *working* Lord, who still goes on despite our frequent failure to cooperate with Him. Shall we not "henceforth," yes, from this day forward, aim at being indeed and in truth "fellow-workers" with God?

And now let us turn to some of the "Henceforths," written on the other side of the milestone as we pass on into the New Year; let us take their messengers of light, and sun our hearts in their warmth. In Micah 4:7 we read, "The Lord shall reign over them in Mount Zion *from henceforth* even forever." If we look at the context we see the picture of a soul that has been compromising, halting, feeble. Well, let the thus "afflicted" soul turn with a fresh and whole-hearted allegiance to Him, and then what a promise is here of weakness made strong under the sovereignty and mastership of the Lord! If the context of 1 Samuel 7:12 describes our "Hitherto," let this promise picture our long "Henceforth, even forever." For we may group it with the assurance of Psalms 125:2: "As the mountains are round about Jerusalem, so the Lord is round about His people—from henceforth even forever." Here is the keeping Presence and Power of Him with whom there is no 'before" or "after"—who never wearies of His watch, or needs to be relieved of the weight of His weak ones, as they lean helpless upon His strength.

Again we turn to a word from our Lord's own lips, John 15:15: "*Henceforth* I have called you friends." Let us cultivate the "Henceforth" of developed intimacy with Him in this New Year. "That I may know Him" [Phil. 3:10]; here is a study which needs always to be beginning over again.

Yet one more of our motto words remains, Hebrews 10:13: "From *henceforth* expecting till His enemies be made His footstool." The unknown future holds many uncertainties before us; it will bring many a surprise of sorrow and of joy. But one thing within it is certain—all things, whatever they may be, are to be put "under His feet," the feet of Him to whom we belong. He is another year nearer the satisfaction of His heart, nearer the triumph of His people as well as of Himself. Sin now seems often much stronger than righteousness, wrong than right, death than life, the grave than the "blessed hope." But

Christ is at the right hand of God, and there He is only waiting, "expecting," till the last enemy, death, shall be made His footstool, and He shall put His foot on death, and sit so in the eternal calm of life.

He will not be disappointed, and *we* shall not be, as we cast our every care and need on Him, and go on in Him from our "Hitherto" to our "Henceforth," from the past of His faithfulness to all its future steps, even to His welcome to the endless joy.

9

The Second Sunday after Christmas: God's Timing

If I will that he tarry till I come, what is that to thee?—John 21:22

In these words note two points. First, *"If I will."* Here the Lord Jesus speaks as the sovereign Possessor of His servants. Are you His servants? Then remember what this implies. Count the cost—a cost which enfolds a boundless gain. Christ is the Master of your soul, your lips, your time, your thoughts, your ambition; to be His servant means, on His side, and absolute ownership.

Think of those two men, Peter and John; think of them simply as individuals, personalities, made in God's image, made new by God's dear Son. Well, Jesus Christ claims to rule them absolutely, as their Possessor; "I am about to deal with you, Peter and with you, John, concerning the date and the manner of your lives and of your deaths, exactly as I please."

Come to Him, and you will find, as Magdalene did, the most tender of friends; you will find a kind Companion on the road, as the travelers to Emmaus did; you will find strength and power for every day, in your life and labor for Him; for He is your very life. But all this must be bound together and made strong by that one word, 'Master"; by the fact that *He possesses* you, always and in everything.

Then secondly, the Lord here witnesses to Himself as the *coming* Savior; "If I will that He tarry *till I come.*" Here is His own implied promise that He is coming again. Does He seem to linger long? To Him a thousand years are as one day; and when we see what was rightly apportioned, and ah, how short it then will prove to be compared with the eternal Sequel! I am no prophet, BUT it seems to me

355

to grow ever more probable that He is indeed coming very soon. What a prospect for those who have met Him here—on the road, and in the garden, and by the shore! The Risen One made no careless, unconsidered promise when He undertook to come again. So let us cherish that undertaking of His; let us live in the light of that hope. "Yet a little while, and He that shall come will come, and will not tarry" [Heb. 10:37]—"this same Jesus," whom we have seen by faith, to whom we have surrendered, whom we have found true, and who comes at length that we may "enjoy Him fully forever."

10

The Epiphany

The Gentiles, once far off, now made nigh—see Eph. 2:11, 13

Let us first reflect a little upon the splendid close of this paragraph (Eph. 2:11–22), and then note some of the steps which have led up to it. This order of thought will have its message for us in the end.

What a climax is reached in verse 22! Here is the eternal destiny of the true Church of God. It is not only that it is to be "saved in Christ forever," ineffable as is the wonder of that fact. It is not only that it is "to enjoy God fully forever," though that amazing prospect is so amply and definitely revealed. It is—to be a "holy Sanctuary," a Shrine, a divine Presence-chamber; "a permanent Habitation of God." In measure, the wonderful fact has already begun to be; already He "dwells in" His people, "and walks in them" (see 1 Cor. 6:16); already the eternal Son resides in the very heart of the true member of the Church, by faith. But a yet greater time is coming, when the everlasting Father will perfectly reveal Himself to all the watchers of all the regions of the eternal world, not anyhow but *thus*—in His glorified Church, in the Race, the Nature, once wrecked and ruined, but rebuilt into this splendor by His grace. In the Church of the Firstborn, in the Bride, the Lamb's Wife, the blessed Universe shall see forever God present, God resident. A transfigured Creation shall be His temple-courts; a beatified human Church shall be His sanctuary. That sanctuary shall reflect without a flaw its Indweller's glory; our union and communion with Him shall be, in other words, perfect, absolute, ideal. And the crowning thought, for the soul which loves God, is this, that we shall be His Abode, He shall somehow find His Home, His Shrine, His Throne, in our happy congregated being.

"It doth not yet appear" [1 John 3:2], no, not yet. It is coming. Every evangelization, every conversion, every spiritual union and combination now, is a contribution to that result. It is coming. But what will it be when it is come? Then at length the desire of God will be fulfilled, and His eternal joy will be felt through all the once "groaning and travailing creation."

Now let us recall what the paragraph presents to us as some of the steps of truth leading up to this climax of blessing.

First, we reverently remark the uncompromising remembrance, over again, of the *mercy* of salvation. The Apostle cannot let the Ephesians forget the past, lest they mistake the blissful present. He is indeed in the act of reminding them that they have been brought not only into a place of mercy but into all the wealth of covenanted privilege. They are incorporated, out and out, into the true Israel of all the promises; not mere resident aliens, lodged in the suburbs of the holy Zion, but full citizens of the place—members of the royal family of its King. They are "one body" with patriarchs, and prophets, and high-priests, and psalmists, and with the apostles of the Lamb; they cannot be nearer to God, for they are in His Christ. But then, all this is emphatically, and in their case even eminently, a gift of mere original mercy. They were outsiders once. They had not the slightest claim upon salvation. Not only as they were men, fallen and sinful, but also as they were "Gentiles," they stood upon ground where redemption found them outcast and outlawed. Sovereign mercy (it was such, of course) had given Israel long ago a standing in a place of light, hope, and promise, BUT *they* were not there. And who should dare to say that the Eternal would have been unrighteous had He left them where they were, "dead" as they were "in trespasses and sins" [Eph. 2:1], at "enmity" with infinite Holiness? It was mercy from first to last; they must remember this, step by step, as they ascend, in their new life, from strength to strength, from grace to glory. It must be reiterated to them, now in this form of thought, now in that, "lest they forget" [see Prov. 31:5]; lest their Christian life fatally degenerate by an oblivion of what went before.

11

The First Sunday after the Epiphany

I beseech you, therefore, brethren, by the mercies of God, that ye present your bodies a living sacrifice, holy, acceptable unto God, which is your reasonable service—Rom. 12:1

The Epistle for the day lies here before us, full all along of that deep characteristic of gospel life, surrender for service. The call is to a profoundly passive inward attitude, with an express view to a richly active outward usefulness. Possessed, and knowing it, of the compassion of God, the man is asked to give himself over to Eternal Love for purposes of unworldly and unambitious employment in the path chosen for him, whatever it may be. In this respect above all others he is to be *"not conformed to this world"* [v. 2]—that is, he is to make not himself, but His Lord, his pleasure and ambition. *"By the renewal of his mind"* he is to view the Will of God from a point inaccessible to the unregenerate, to the unjustified, to the man not emancipated in Christ from the tyranny of sin. He is to see in it his inexhaustible interest, his line of quest and hope, his ultimate and satisfying aim because of the practical identity of that Will and the infinitely good and blessed Bearer of it. And this more than surrender of his faculties, this happy and reposeful consecration of them, is to show its reality in one way above all others first; in a humble estimate of self as compared with brother Christians, and a watchful willingness to do—not another's work, but the duty that lies next for the man himself.

This relative aspect of the life of self-surrender is the burden of this great paragraph of duty. The man rich in Christ is reverently to remember others, and God's will in them, and for them. He is to avoid the subtle temptation to intrude beyond the Master's allotted work *for him*. He is to be slow to think, "I am richly qualified, and could do this thing, and that, and the other, better than the man who does it now." He works as one who has not to contrive a life as full of success and influence as he can imagine, but to accept a life assigned by the Lord who has first given to him Himself.

The passage itself amply implies that he is to use actively and honestly his renewed *intelligence*. He is to look circumstances and conditions in the face, remembering that in one way or another the will of God is expressed in them. He is to seek to understand not his duties only but His personal equipment for them, natural as well as spiritual. But he is to do this as one whose "mind" is "renewed" by his living contact and union with his redeeming King, and who has really laid his faculties at the feet of an absolute Master, who is the Lord of order as well as of power.

What peace, energy, and dignity comes into a life which is consciously and deliberately thus surrendered! The highest range of duties, as man counts highest, is thus disburdened both of its heavy anxieties and of its temptations to a ruinous self-importance. And the lowest range, as man counts lowest, is filled with the quiet greatness born of the presence and the will of God.

12

The Miracle at Cana

Jesus . . . manifested forth His glory—John 2:11

The miracle at Cana forms the gospel for this Sunday. You will see without difficulty *why* it has been chosen. This is the season of the Epiphany—that is, as the word signifies, of the Manifestation, the making plain, of the Lord Jesus the Savior. And John tells us that this miracle at Cana was, in a very special way, an occasion on which Jesus manifested, epiphanized, made plain, His glory.

"His glory." What a rich and magnificent word that is—Glory? Vision of light and majesty break on us as we use it. We think of Him who dwells in the light no man can approach unto. We remember Him, even Christ Jesus Himself, who appeared in Patmos in glory; "His eyes like fire, His face like the sun in his strength" [see Rev. 2:18]. WE recall how Stephen looked through the heavens, and saw glory there—the glory of God, and Jesus at the right hand of God. We hear the Savior saying, in His own high-priestly prayer, "Glorify thou me with thine own self with the glory which I had with thee before the world was" [John 17:5]. We read in the Epistle to the Hebrews that this same mighty Son of God is "the brightness of His Father's glory, and the express image of His Person" [Heb. 1:3]. We remember His own promise that He will come again in glory—the glory of His Father, and of the angels, and His own. Views, and memories, and hopes, of power, and splendor, and royal and divine dignity, gather round the word glory.

But there was little of all this at Cana. We read of no blaze of light around the Lord's body. He sat there on no throne. His voice

361

there was not as the sound of many waters. His enemies were not made His footstool there, as they shall be hereafter. None of the marriage guests fell at His feet, entranced with His overwhelming greatness. No; He was there as Man with men, a Guest with guests, a Friend with friends. He put forth His power gently, and in silence. And He used it to supply a family need, and to help a household difficulty.

Thus did He "manifest His glory" in that mighty but gentle act of care and love.

Glory indeed it was—the glory of the Son of God, the only begotten Son, the loving and beloved Son made man; the glory of Him who was so mighty, so divine, that He had time and range *at once* for the Creator's power and the Creator's tenderness; for the greatest and for the least. It was the glory of the eternal Shepherd's tireless care for the least and most feeble of His flock.

My brethren, let us fix it in our very souls that "this same Jesus" [Acts 1:11] is the same in His glory now; the same yesterday and today.

He is a living Person now. We see Him not; we cannot hear His blessed voice, BUT oh, He lives! Surely as He died and rose, He lives; He lives in the power of an endless life, an endless love, an unwearied grace and care. He is the same in His nature and character as God; "God over all, blessed forever." He is the same in His nature and character as Man; able to save to the uttermost, able forever to be touched with the feeling of our infirmities.

Then, if He is such, let us use Him. Let us pray that not only may His precious blood be not in vain for us, not only that, through a simple and adoring faith, we may be safe forever from wrath through Him—but that His present life may not be in vain for us; that having such a living Lord Jesus we may deal with Him, commune with Him, cast our care on Him, allay our griefs in Him, commit our way to Him. Let us be very sure that to Him, this Lord of Cana, we may confide our humblest, our smallest needs. Nothing is too common, too little, to tell to Him, just because he is both true Man and Eternal God.

Tears in secret—sighs over precious memories known only to ourselves—thoughts of love and longing, wakened by some simplest thing, yet stirring and shaking our inmost being—fears and anxieties over which the world's movement passes as with iron force and a leaden weight—these things are not trivial to the Lord of Glory. He, mightier than the world, cares and loves. He who bore the sins of sinners—yes, He too bore our griefs, and carried our sorrows [see Is. 53:4]!

Come, then, to this wonderful Consoler. Come, to see for yourselves the manifestation of His glory as the Shepherd, as the Friend. Find Him as the Savior, and you will find Him *also* as the Consolation. Accept Him because you are a sinner, and you will soon bless Him also in regard of your being a sufferer too.

And at last you will see Him as He is [1 John 3:2]; you will behold His glory, at His own table, at the marriage supper of the Lamb.

It will be the glory of the manifested presence, the unclouded face, the everlasting consolations, of the Friend who loved you and give Himself for you [see Eph. 5:25].

13

Resisting Evil

Be not overcome of evil, but overcome evil with good—Rom. 12:21

"Be thou not conquered by the evil, but conquer, in the good, the evil." Such is the closer rendering of the Greek.

"In the good"; as if surrounded by it, moving invulnerable, in its magic circle, through "the contradiction of sinners," "the provoking of all men." The thought is just that of Psalms 31:19, 20:

> How great is Thy goodness, which Thou has laid up for them that fear Thee, which Thou has wrought for them that trust in Thee before the sons of men! Thou shalt hide them in the secret of Thy presence from the pride of men; Thou shalt keep them secretly in a pavilion from the strife of tongues.

"The good" of this sentence of Paul's is no vague and abstract thing; it is "the gift of God" (Rom. 6:28); it is the life eternal found and possessed in union with Christ, our Righteousness, our Sanctification, our Redemption. Practically, it is "not It, but *He."* The Roman convert who should find it more than possible to meet his enemy with love, to do him positive good in his need, with a conquering simplicity of intention, was to do so not so much by an internal conflict between his "better self" and his worse, as by the living Power of Christ received in his whole being; by "abiding in Him."

It is so now, and forever. The open secret of divine peace and love is what it was; as necessary, as versatile, as victorious. And its path of victory is as straight and as sure as of old. And the precept to tread that path, daily and hourly, if occasion calls, is still as divinely binding as it ever was for the Christian, if indeed he has embraced

364

"the mercies of God" [Rom. 12:7], and is looking to his Lord to be evermore conformed, by the renewing of his mind [see 12:2].

As we review this rich field of the flowers, and of the gold, of holiness, this paragraph (vv. 8–21) of epigrammatic precepts, some leading and pervading principles emerge. We see first that the sanctity of the gospel is no hushed and cloistered "indifferentism." It is a thing intended for the open field of human life; to be lived out "before the sons of men." A strong positive element is in it. The saint is to *"abominate* the evil"; not only to deprecate it, and deplore. He is to be energetically "in earnest." He is to "glow" with the Spirit, and to "rejoice" in the hope of glory. He is to take practical, provident means to live not only aright, but manifestly aright, in ways which "all men" can recognize. Again, his life is to be essentially social. He is contemplated as one who meets other lives at every turn, and he is never to forget nor neglect his relation to them. Particularly in the Christian Society, he is to cherish the "family affection of the gospel"; to defer to fellow-Christians in a generous humility; to share his means with the poor among them; to welcome the strangers of them to his house. He is to think it a sacred duty to enter into the joys and sorrows around him. He is to keep his sympathies open for despised people, and for little matters. Then again, and most prominently after all, he is to be ready to suffer, and to meet suffering with a spirit far greater than that of only resignation. He is to bless his persecutor; he is to serve his enemy in ways most practical and active; he is to conquer him for Christ, in the power of a divine communion.

Then, meanwhile, the life, so positive, so active in its effects, is to be essentially all the while a passive, bearing, enduring life. Its strength is to spring not from the energies of nature, which may or may not be vigorous in the man, but form an internal surrender to the claim and government of his Lord. He has "presented himself to God" (6:13); he has "presented his body, a living sacrifice" (see 12:1). He has recognized, with a penitent wonder and joy, that he is but the limb of a Body, and that his Head is the Lord. His thought is now not for his personal rights, his individual exaltation, but for the glory of his Head, for the fulfillment of the thought of his Head, and for the health and wealth of the Body, as the great vehicle in the world of the gracious will of the Head.

Everywhere the gospel bids the Christian take sides against himself. He is to stand ready to forego even his surest rights, if only *he* is hurt by so doing; while on the other hand he is to be watchful to respect even the least obvious rights of others, yea, to consider their weaknesses and their prejudices to the furthest just limit. He is "not to resist evil"; in the sense of never fighting for self as self. He is rather to "suffer himself to be defrauded" (1 Cor. 6:7) than to bring discredit on his Lord in however due a course of law. The straits and humiliations of his earthly lot, if such things are the will of God for him, are not to be materials for his discontent, or occasions for his envy, or for his secular ambition. They are to be his opportunities for inward triumph; the theme of a "song of the Lord" [2 Chr. 29:27], in which he is to sing of strength perfected in weakness, of a power not his own "overshadowing' him (see 2 Cor. 12:9, 10).

Such is the passivity of the saints, deep beneath their serviceable activity. The two are in vital connection. The root is not the accident but the proper antecedent of the product. For the secret and unostentatious surrender of the will, in its Christian sense, is no mere evacuation, leaving the house swept but empty; it is the reception of the Lord of life into the open castle of the City of Mansoul. It is the placing in His hands of all that the walls contain. And placed in His hands, the castle and the city will show at once, and continually more and more, that not only order but life has taken possession. The surrender of the Moslem is, in its theory, a *mere* submission. The surrender of the gospel is a reception also; and thus its nature is to come out in "the fruit of the Spirit" [Gal. 5:22; Eph. 5:9].

14

The Covenant Promise

This is the covenant which I will make with them . . . saith the Lord; I will put my laws into their hearts, and in their minds I will write them; and their sins and iniquities will I remember no more—Heb. 10:16, 17

A covenant; the word has a certain strictness and fixity about it. It indicates a clear understanding or legal settlement. It is not an "emotional" word. But for its particular purposes it is far better than the expression of the warmest emotions. A deed of gift, in the driest terms of law, is far more effect as an assurance of possession than the most affectionate private letter could be.

Now, God has deigned to put Himself, in this matter, into the position of man. He has entered with us into a covenant. He has (Heb. 6:18) confirmed His word by an oath. What? Is His promise not enough? No, not for the assurance of our fears. He who infinitely understands the hearts of men condescends to come down to our level. He does not demand of you, barely and sternly, that you should believe because of His *Word* only; He gives oath and a *Covenant;* He bids you read His will to bless through the fixity and formality of a Covenant; He asks you to lie down, with all the weight of your misgivings, upon the immovable rock of His Covenant. "For the mountains shall depart, but the covenant of my peace shall not be removed" [see Is. 54:10].

Let us prize the word Covenant, then. Let us love its very legality and formality. For all this says that our God has taken care of the fact of our doubts and fears, and has therefore cast into the strongest possible terms of compact His offers of peace, and holiness, and heaven.

This great Covenant of grace was first explicitly revealed through Jeremiah (31:31), the passage quoted in our text above. And the Lord Jesus, at the Last Supper, took up those words, and linked them with the sacred Cup, of which He said, as He gave it, "This cup is the new covenant, in my blood" [Luke 22:20 NIV]. There, sealed with the blessed blood of the Lamb, represented to faith by the holy wine, we see the covenant, in its two great articles.

The first article, in the order of thought, is *Forgiveness,* free and full, for His name's sake: "Your sins and iniquities I will remember no more."

The other article is *Holiness.* It is the writing by the Lord's own hand, of His law in the heart, and the putting it into the mind. It is not I who am asked, with my trembling hand, to write this new inscription, to reform my will, my mind, my soul. God takes the pen: "*I* will write," not upon the rocks of Sinai, but "on the fleshy tablets of the heart." Yes, it is God the Spirit's work. And how? By applying Christ in His grace and glory to the soul; by making our union with the Lord a living, bright communion every hour; by "bringing every thought" into delightful "captivity," deep but willing, to Christ.

The Lord Himself *undertakes* to do it; and He puts Himself under covenant to fulfill the word. It is no matter of peradventure. Remember, O man, who has entered into Jesus Christ, that among your possessions there lies this divine certainty—He will write His laws in your heart and lodge them in your mind [see Heb. 8:10; 10:16]. In other words, He will touch you and tune you into a harmony of will with Him. Leave Him to do *the writing;* you do *the reading* of the Will of God, transcribed from His Word upon your own regenerate soul.

The renewed will, the power *through* Christ to walk *with* Christ— these things are pledged to us under covenant. We are to act as knowing that it is so. We are to step out upon our daily walk looking to Him to fulfill His word of covenant, inscribing His will on ours.

I have already spoken of the double nature of the Covenant promise. There remains the singleness of the Person of the Surety. Its security is lodged in Him, not in you or me. Its certainty is in Him. The Covenant of works, the compact of Creator with creature in the mysterious Garden, was lodged with a Covenant Head who could fail, and who did fail. The twin promises of remission and of purity are

368

lodged both in one Covenant Head likewise, who has overcome for us forever. Yes, both are in His hands; not remission in His gift and purity in our winning. Both are in Him. He is the perfect sacrifice for sin. He also is the perfect treasury of holiness. In Him is stored up, as it were, the new nature of regenerate man; and regenerate man enjoys the Covenant benefits in Christ, as if he had done the whole law himself. From that treasury man may draw unceasingly, grace for grace, the needed gift for every hour. To Him, then, let us go. Rather, in Him let us dwell, from Him drawing—not as from a distance, but as from the well in the courtyard of our own dwelling place—alike the peace of perpetual remission and the spring of unfailing power.

"Consider Him," believing man. Take up, weigh, count over, your treasures in Him. Get acquainted with the depth and height of what is meant by Him, by Christ Jesus, our Head, our Brother, our Bridegroom, our Surety forevermore.

It is the season of the Epiphany, of the Manifestation of Christ. Shall it be true to its name to us? Follow the star of the Word to the blessed Bethlehem of a deeper manifestation of the Lord; trace the path thither, fenced and guarded by the Covenant ordered in all things and sure; and rest, and worship, and live, and serve, in the peace and strength of covenanted grace.

15

"Putting Off" and "Putting On"

Put off all these: anger, wrath, malice, blasphemy, filthy communication out of your mouth. . . . Put on therefore, as the elect of God, holy and beloved, bowels of mercies, kindness, humbleness of mind, meekness, longsuffering—
Col. 3:8,12

Shall we, my reader and myself, deliberately remember that *imperative* of the Apostle, *"put off,"* and the things which it includes? We have here before us, not sins of the scandalous order, as it is supposed especially to be. We are concerned only with the facile transgressions of the temper, and of the tongue; anger, wrath, malice, railing, and talk that is not quite clean, and that is not quite true. Take this to heart, Christian man or woman, professing to "live godly" in common life in the modern world. The precepts given here lay hands on a great many things tolerated all too easily at the dinner tables, and in the living rooms, and at the holiday resorts, of such as we are supposed to be. Our offenses may not perhaps look great in point of scale. We may not be violently passionate, or positively abusive and indecorous in speech, nor may we be of those who deliberately "love and make a lie." But do we not too easily let ourselves sin on a moderate scale in things which are just the same in kind? We are irritable; we carry about a cherished grudge; we speak harsh words of the absent, when no good purpose whatever underlies the speaking; we needlessly allude to sin; we trifle with truth and manipulate it, when to do so will save us a little trouble. And all these things are identical in kind with the worst bursts of anger, or the most cruel forms of rebuke, or the openly unclean word, or the gravest false-

370

hoods. They lie on the same inclined plane, away from the love of God, and towards the outer darkness. Then we will take no half measures with them. We will "put them away," just as we would put away a filthy garment which it would be misery to wear for another quarter of an hour. And what will be our motive and our power for doing so with such pollution? Behold, in our own name and strength the effort will be vain. To the repressive exertions of self, the sins of self are like the shirt of Nessus upon the tortured and helpless Hercules. The very struggle, when conscience goads the unregenerate will, may even develop the *virus* of the habit. But the Apostle knows a better way. He gives the Colossians a command, but he supports it and makes it possible by a divine fact. He reminds them that *as a fact* they have passed from death unto life, and have exchanged condemnation and bondage in Adam for the pardon and the power which are in Christ. Whether they are subjectively "feeling it" or not, *this is* the objective fact and law of their position and of their condition; they are in Christ, and Christ is in them. And their brother Christians are in Christ, and Christ is in every one of them. Let them recollect their own life in Him, and His in them, and they will bring in an invincible force against their sins. And let them recollect the life of their brethren in Him, and His in them, and they will need little else to teach them the lesson of unselfish love.

But now he passes into further details in the same line. And his tone is now positive. We have thought thus far mainly of "putting off." It is well, it is vital, to do so. But it is not enough; it is to be done only in order to "putting on."

Put on therefore, clothing yourselves anew, *as God's chosen ones,* "chosen in Christ before the foundation of the world" [see Eph. 1:4], on purpose to be like Him, *holy,* dedicated by that sovereign choice to Him, *and having His love set upon you,* in that sublime original exercise of it; put on, I say, as your "beautiful garments," *a heart of compassion,* sympathies ready and open, *sweetness* of temper and bearing, *humble-mindedness,* the attitude of a soul "which has lost its pride in discovering the mercy of its salvation," *meekness* in submission under pain and trial, *longsuffering,* the spirit which will not be tired of pardoning, hoping, loving; *bearing with one another, and forgiving one another, if* (the "if" puts, as it were reluctantly, a case just supposable)

371

anyone has a grievance against anyone—for you are all erring sinners still, and *may* give each other occasion for such victories of good over evil. *Just as the Lord* (so read, probably; not "God"), the eternal Savior and Master, with His infinite rights, *did forgive you,* as you rejoice to know He did, *so do you too;* using your assurance of pardon, your doubtless certainty that your sins are forgiven you for His Name's sake," not for indolence and slumber, but for the glad activities of a self-forgetting kindness. But over all these things, as it were the girdle upon and around all these graces, bracing them into one, *put on love, which is the bond of perfect unity* [see Col. 3:14]; for it makes and it maintains, as no other power can do, the "perfectness," the wholeness, the sweet ripeness, of the Christian character, whether in the man or in the company. "Seeking its joy in the felicity of others," it must be so, it will be so. *And let the peace of Christ arbitrate in your hearts;* let every inward debate between self and God, between self and others, be ruled and guided by the deep consciousness that in Christ you are indeed at rest; let the plea for self-assertion be ever met and negated by the decision of that *umpire* in favor of love. For that "peace of Christ" is given you, not for yourselves only as individuals, but for the community; *into it you were in fact called,* at your conversion, *in one body;* you were brought one by one under its gentle power, as those who were now to be one with one another in a society whose inmost law should thus be holy peace. *And be ye, become ye, more and more,* thankful; prompt to see your mercies, and to praise the Giver—sure and blessed secret for a tone of loving and generous sympathy towards all.

16

Thoughts on the "New Heaven"

And I saw a new heaven and a new earth . . . and there was no more sea—
Rev. 21:1

With this verse begins the closing passage of the Book of God; the revelation of the things beyond the end. The long history of sin, and trial, and of the strivings of grace with evil, is over at last; and the last partition has taken place. The light has cast out the darkness forever. The tares are forever gathered out from among the wheat; the impenitent are severed from among the just; the judgment has been set, and the judgment is done, forever. Now the veil lifts for the last time; and behold, the New Universe. He who in the beginning created the heaven and the earth now reveals, to the gaze of faith, His second and final world. Behold, He makes all things new; new heavens, new earth, a new Jerusalem, the nations of the new birth dwelling there, the new song going up forever before the everlasting Presence.

The whole language refers to a state of which we are absolutely without experience. It tries to break up, and to bring down within our reach, in words that picture to us things that we can understand, some fragments of the eternal future, BUT, as we read, we see proof upon proof that the main use of the words is to suggest things spiritual and divine. The "City" is called, in the same breath, the "Lamb's wife." Its very shape is mystical, not literal; for it is represented as fifteen hundred miles broad, and long, and *high*. And the sunlight over the whole is no material splendor; "the Lord God giveth them light [22:5]; the glory of God doth lighten it, and the

Lamb is the light thereof" [see 21:23]. So with our text; "And there was no more sea." It is plain that the main purpose of the phrase is spiritual. We are to put before us, as we read, a state not so much in which we shall never look out on a waste of tossing waters, in which "no galley with oars nor gallant ship shall pass," in which no drowning victims shall plunge into the black depth, no whirlpool suck down its prey, no rocks tear the wreck to pieces; as a state in which the *sea of the soul* shall be forever gone; in which none of those evils of which the great waters are the parable *to the soul* shall be heard of or remembered anymore.

There shall be a *new Heaven* there; a new and eternal sky, with its radiance and its breathing airs—even the presence and the vision of the King. There forever, in that infinitely invigorating atmosphere, the soul of each glorified saint and the whole vast host of souls together shall live, and move, and feel, and exercise a force, an energy, of power and interest, to which the most intense moments of mortal will and power are but as living death. And there shall be *a new Earth* there. Man, in his full and final reality, man in his individual life, man in the countless interest and exercises of his congregated life, shall be there beneath that sky of the Eternal Presence, and breathing that air of the Eternal Love.

But "there shall be no more sea." No *local* parting is there; "where they are gone, adieux and farewells are a sound unknown." No grave is dug there; no deathbed is wept over there; no waving farewells over the dividing waters are seen there. And no *moral* parting is there; no misunderstanding, no jealousy, no pride, no wrath, no self-seeking, can there for one moment part the sympathies of the children of immortality. There, heart with heart will make as it were one bright, beautiful, continuous continent of sympathy and mutual joy. *"Together—forever—with the Lord."*

The new Universe will come. All these things shall be dissolved. He who created can uncreate the material things around us that seem so lasting. One word, one act of will of His all-wise omnipotence, and the present frame of things would not so much break up as cease to be. It exists only because it rests upon His will.

We know from this Scripture what will follow that awful crisis in creation. He who can uncreate will yet create. There shall be a real world, final and eternal, and blessed, for His redeemed. They that have fled to His refuge here shall dwell in His city there. They that have come to the Lamb's blood of sprinkling now, that have hung their whole hope on the Cross of the Lord Christ Jesus, shall dwell, in real energy and infinite joy, before the Lamb's Throne then. And there, on that new earth, and beneath that new Heaven, there shall be no more sea of agitation, no more sea of separation through the long fair eternity.

17

Studies in Genesis

Gen. 1—3

These first chapters of Scripture must certainly, if I read them correctly, be received by the Christian as records of fact. They are not merely parables, or of the nature of mere imaginative poems, embodying general principles. A parable, like Jotham's, for example, need not be a matter of fact at all. An imaginative poem like *Paradise Lost* makes no pretension to authority on matters of fact. But our Lord Himself appealed to Genesis 1 on the law of marriage, and the Apostle appeals to Genesis 3 for the fact of the fall of man. On the other hand these chapters, by the nature of their contents, invite us to interpret their language with a certain reserve as to literalism. They go back to a period antecedent to all human experience; when they do come to the creation of man they depict what is almost equally beyond our understanding, the beginnings of the being of the very first members of our race, or, to vary the metaphor, not of its members at all but of its head. So viewed, as dealing with facts which are all mysteries, the chapters suggest an element of mystery in their language which would be quite out of place in, for instance, the history of Joseph, or that of the shipwreck of Paul. They find an analogy in the two closing chapters of Scripture, with their picture of the new heavens and earth, and of the holy city. There we have indeed facts put before us; a future state of glory, the abode of the saints of God in a blessed eternity of joy and worship. But we do not regard the language of the description as necessarily literal. The streets of gold, the gates of pearl, the bright river, the tree of life—we are willing to read these rather as hieroglyphics than as pictures or photographs of scenery. Is not the like the case with Genesis 1—3? We are not bound to believe that the Creator literally spoke the syllables, "Let there be light," or "Let us make man" [1:3, 26]. We are not bound to literalism in the mysterious details of the creation of woman. We are not bound, as to an article of faith, to a literal rendering of the details of the temptation. These things are not a parable, for Scripture itself treats them as matters of fact, BUT they are facts conveyed in hieroglyphic signs. The facts are that man was so made as to be the personal reflection of the divine Personality; that he was brought into being under conditions which made him purely responsive to the will and voice of God; that an evil power led him, through his senses, to rebel against that will; and that so human nature was defiled. We thus have Scripture beginning and ending with facts so mysterious that they need a mysterious representation. Between those two points we have the history of Redemption, actually worked out on the field of human experience, and therefore capable of a literal narrative. To speak of one important detail—the verses which describe the action of the serpent seem to me a possible case of hieroglyphic. Should I come to know that what actually happened did not involve the use of human words by an animal, I should feel no shock to my faith in the Scriptures, anymore than I do when in the Revelation I read of the Church as of a woman pursued by a dragon which pours a river from its mouth. That is a prophecy of fact, conveyed through hieroglyphic symbols; and Genesis 3, as I take it, is of the same class.

Let us approach these mysteries in the spirit of that wise saying, "Never let what you know be disturbed by what you do not know." In this case we know the Christ of the Bible, Son of God and Son of man. We know that to Him the Bible was authoritative and divine. Let us hold fast those known facts, and let not our repose upon them be disturbed by things unknown, which attend upon the process of the delivery of the message of God in His Word.

18

The Fruit of the Spirit

The fruit of the Spirit is love—Gal. 5:22
And now abideth faith, hope, charity, these three, BUT *the greatest of these*
is charity—1 Cor. 13:13

We come to Paul's delineation of this pure and sweet Fruit of the Spirit. Let us take it up for a few very practical inquiries and remarks.

The first point for observation, an obvious one, but none the less to be definitely considered, is that the Fruit of the Spirit consists in its essence not of doing but of being. There is nothing in this description which directly speaks of energetic enterprise, multiplied labors, severe sufferings, great material sacrifices. The activities of life are in fact almost absent from the immediate view, and the passive, the patient, aspect of the spiritual man's contact with life and men is alone very visibly present.

What do we read in this? That the spiritual man is called, as his highest calling, to cut himself off from active, willing, practical service of others? That the celestial fruit will grow, and ripen, and be ready for the festival of God, most favorably in a "life of contemplation," in a desert, or a cloister, or a jealously isolated study? The whole New Testament negates such a thought. In it, the ideal Christian life is the life in which the Lord is glorified and manifested amidst the manifold relative duties and labors of the life of home, of citizenship, of public ministry, of active evangelization. It is a life in which the cross is daily carried—the cross not of our willful and ambitious choosing, but of the Lord's humbling and searching allotment in the daily path. If the life of a monastery were contemplated in the New Testament at all, as it is not, surely it would be presented there as a "counsel" not "of perfection" but of imperfection; a lower path of surrender and of service, while the higher path was that of the mother, the child, the servant, who, in the midst of common life, "did the will of God from the heart" (see Eph. 6:6).

But then, the impartial gospel does not say that work is therefore life. It points to the eternal necessity of right being in order to right doing. It bids the Christian live to serve, but live *behind his service* in and with his Lord and Life. It asks, ultimately, not whether you give your goods to the poor, or your body to the fire, but whether you love.

So "the Fruit of the Spirit" is a divinely given and developed *character,* drawn out of the fullness of Christ; a character which must express itself in service, but whose essence "is hid with Christ in God" [Col. 3:3]. This is the "fruit" which, according to the Lord Jesus Christ's own words, we shall surely bear if by the Spirit "we abide in Him." Of this fruit, says the same Teacher, we are able to bear "much," to the glory of His Father. We may or may not, in His providence, have much to do for Him in enterprise, in effort, in public testimony, in memorable suffering. Perhaps His will for us, as we submit ourselves wholly to it, humbly ready to toil "and not faint" [Is. 40:31] in His name, may be to do the most silent of domestic duties, or to bear the most exhausting weakness or pain in a neglected sickroom. But these questions touch the accidents of the matter, not the essence. The "fruit" is the character derived for us by the Holy Spirit from Jesus Christ our Head. The "much fruit" is that character, not stunted and dwarfed by the frosts of unbelief, but expanding in sweet and strong development in the sunny open air of the simplest faith.

And now we will look at the particulars of the description, at the elements which this inspired analysis shows us in the texture of this fruit of Paradise grown on earth.

Those elements are nine: "Love, joy, peace, longsuffering, gentleness, goodness, faithfulness, meekness, self-control." And we may, without over-refinement, trace a threefold grouping in the nine. "Love, joy, peace," if I read their reference aright, describe the character in its immediate relation to the Lord, who is its spring of "love," its cause of "joy," its living law of internal "peace." "Long-suffering, gentleness, goodness," describe it in its relations with men, as the Christian comes evermore from the "secret of the Presence" to live his "hidden" life, unharmed and bearing blessing with it, amidst "the plotting of men" and "the strife of tongues" [Ps. 31:20]. "Faithfulness, meekness, self-control," denote the Christian's characteristics not so much under the trials of opposition or provocation as in the common calls and duties of the day. And so the "fruit" appears in its fair roundness and ripeness. So the man, born of the Spirit, led of the Spirit, taking step by step by the Spirit, filled with this same blessed Spirit, lives, moves, and has his being, with and for God and man. He is one personality, and so his regenerate and Spirit-developed character is one, from the "love" to the "self-control"; from his inmost fellowship with his Lord to his act of most watchful and practical self-discipline in open human life. What he is as indeed a Christian, *in general,* that is the Spirit's fruit.

19

The Temptation of Christ

Tempted of the devil—Matt. 4:1

The narrative of the Temptation of our Savior must have come in the first instance from Himself alone. We will accept it then with worshiping faith as a record of facts, and then will study the message of the facts to us. We have, then, first the solemn, searching mystery of the allotment of temptation to the Son of God. Even He is not to be exempt. The test of the Father, the allurement of the enemy, must be applied even to Him. The King must needs be tempted; therefore let not His followers complain. But then, blessed be the name of our King, "He is able" now "to be touched with the feeling of our infirmities, *for* He was tempted in all points like as we are, yet without sin" [see Heb. 4:15]; our experience is His; His sympathy, *all the stronger for His sinlessness,* is ours. Then further, we have the fact that the holy Tempted One is assailed by the Tempter, with consummate skill, on the side of His holiness. He is tempted to satisfy His great hunger, not anyhow, but by an exercise of wonder-power *as an evidence that He is the Son of God.* The enemy's inner aim is to beguile Him out of the attitude of waiting on His Father into the attitude of self-chosen and self-hastened action. But this is veiled, and it is veiled under the invitation to Him to give a miracle-proof of His Sonship. Then again, taking Luke's order, He is tempted to leap into universal empire by an act of vassalage to one who assures Him that he is God's delegate in these matters— *"it is delivered* unto me." This was an allurement addressed to the noblest possible aims and hopes; would it not be an infinite blessing to the kingdoms of the world that He should be their Sovereign, *and at once?* Then, on the "turret" of the Temple, He is invited again to evidence His Sonship, and to do so in connection with one of the holiest of truths—namely, the willing ministry of angels, guaranteed by a Scripture promise. Were not these attacks skillfully delivered? Did not the Tempter, in a certain sense and within certain limits, know his Object of assault? Enticement from beneath can come to us through things given to us from above. It was so with the divine Sonship and the divine Royalty of the Lord Jesus Christ. Noble natures have vulnerable points in their very nobleness. There is no ultimate safety even in the nobleness; there is none outside the Lord and His Word. And He, *by experience,* understands the danger and the need. Then we have the fact of the Lord's *way to victory.* This is a very wonderful study. The one solitary weapon which He uses, what is it? It is the Written Word. I do not think we can ponder this fact too carefully, especially in our day, when even excellent people are telling us that we have to learn that there are untrustworthy as well as trustworthy parts of Scripture, and that we must somehow distinguish them. It is refreshing and reassuring to turn from such suggestions and listen to the Lord Jesus Christ while He quotes the words of Deuteronomy three solemn times as the sufficient reason for His replies, and does so with the simple formula, "It is written." The Lord met the Tempter with the Scripture as His only sword.

But how was He prepared for the true use of His weapon? By the fullness of the Spirit, and by that great Fast in the desert. "Full of the Holy Ghost, He was led by the Spirit into the wilderness" [4:1]. The message of this to us—what is it? That for us too, if our Bible is to be assuredly our victory over the Evil Power, it is urgently needful that we so open our spirits to the Eternal Spirit that God shall be in us of a truth, and that this blessed Presence shall be cherished and developed in a life of which the Lord's Fast is the perpetual type, the life of holy watching, and holy self-control.

20

God's Testing of Abraham

And it came to pass . . . that God did tempt Abraham—Gen. 22:1

Let us take the Temptation of Abraham, given us in the twenty-second chapter of Genesis. "God did tempt Abraham." He "proved" him. We know *how* He proved him. He put a tremendous strain at once on his affections and on his spiritual hopes. Isaac was the tenderly beloved son of his old age. What parent cannot picture the deep fondness of the father's yearning over him? Isaac was rising now into the strength and responsiveness of young manhood; he was beginning to be his father's friend; he was evidently partaker of his father's faith. And, then, Isaac was also the child of the Promise. It was "in Isaac" that Abraham's seed was to be "called." As Isaac's descendants they were to live and prosper as the chosen people. And now Isaac was to be put to death—by his father's hand!

This narrative has been an awful difficulty to many. It is said by some that the whole incident must be explained by ideas in Abraham's mind suggested by the practice of human sacrifices around him. It is held that Abraham thought on these, and brooded over them, till the feeling arose that *His* God also must demand nothing short of the life of his best-beloved treasure; and then this feeling mastered him, as a passionate resolve, till he *all but* slew his son.

Such a view I am unable to accept. I am quite sure that it is not the view meant to be given by the narrative, and I am quite sure that the narrative had the approval of that supreme Reader of the Bible, our Lord Jesus Christ, as a true account of His Father's will and work. So I am sure that somehow, divinely, the Lord conveyed to Abraham His command as the absolute Owner of the life of His creatures; that Abraham obeyed not his own feelings, but that command; that he was divinely prevented from doing the final act, when his willingness to do even it at his Lord's word had been shown; and that his whole conduct received a glorious crown of approval then and there from heaven. All this I steadfastly believe, BUT I do not wonder at the difficulties which many hearts have felt over this story.

Now, here note some of the messages carried to us by Abraham's temptation.

First, it was obviously a case where "test" and "allurement" might, and no doubt did, beset Abraham at the same time. His heavenly Friend was testing him. His dark enemy is not mentioned: Genesis has no clear reference to the Evil One at all after the third chapter. But we may be sure he was watching his occasion, and would whisper deep into Abraham's soul the thought that, if this call was from God, the Lord was an awfully "austere" Master; would not some other deity, after all, be more kind and tolerant? Should not Abraham turn and serve another god?

Then, further, we see where the essence of the awful test lay. Tempted Abraham was asked, in effect, two questions. He was asked whether he absolutely resigned himself to the Lord's ownership. He was asked also whether he absolutely trusted his Owner's truth and love. The two questions were not identical, but they were twined close together. And the response of Abraham to both questions, by the grace of God in his heart, was a glorious "Yes," an "Amen" which sounds on forever through all the generations of the followers of the faith of Abraham. He so acted as to say, in effect: "I am Thine, and all mine is Thine, utterly and forever." And this he did, not as merely submitting in stern silence to the inevitable, but "in faith." He was quite sure that "He was faithful who had promised" (see Heb. 11:17–19). He was sure of this be because he was sure of His character because he knew God, and, knowing Him, loved Him. So he overcame; so he received the crown; so he was blessed himself, and became a blessing to the world.

Are we ever "proved" in ways which in the least degree remind us of Abraham upon Moriah? Has something come upon us which seems very strange, very dreadful, very arbitrary, to our poor aching eyes? Let us remember whose we are, and whom, because we know Him, we trust. We belong to Him by purchase, by conquest, by surrender of ourselves. Therefore all our "belongings" belong to Him, in the sense that He has a perfect right to detach them from us if He thinks it well. And we rely on Him to whom we belong. *We know* that not only are His rights absolute, but so also is His love, which abides, which is indeed *Himself.* And He has promised. And He is "faithful; He cannot deny Himself" [see 2 Tim. 2:13]. So we will, by His grace within us, say "Yes." And so we will stand the test, and so reject the allurement. And, ah, we have not yet "seen the end of the Lord" [James 5:11]. No, nor shall we ever see it, in all its loving glory, till "we see Him as He is" [1 John 3:2].

21

Self Surrender:
"Take Up Your Cross"

And He said to them all, If any man will come after me, let him deny himself, and take up his cross daily, and follow me—Luke 9:23

Let us study these familiar words a little in detail.

(1) Observe the Universality of reference. "If *any man* wills to come after me; whoever desires to follow my lead; then let this man, be he who he may, do thus: Let him deny himself, and daily take up his cross and follow me. Let any man who wills to follow me, and does not do thus, by no means marvel if his following, such as it is, proves to be a disappointing, a disheartening thing. Let such a one prepare to find my yoke uneasy, and my burden heavy, and my commandments grievous."

(2) Then, "Let him deny *himself.*" Always let us emphasize, in thought, and in tone, that last word, "let him deny *himself.*" And what is *Self*-denial? The word is often and much mistaken in common use, as if it meant much the same as self-control—the control of lower elements of our being by higher. If a man postpones the present to the future, resolving on present loss for the sake of future gain, this is often called Self-denial. If a man, for some high object of his own, abjures inferior pleasures, "scorns delights, and lives laborious days," this is often called Self-denial. If, in the highest sphere, for the sake of rest hereafter, he inflicts on himself great unrest now, this too is often called Self-denial.

Now the doing of such things may be wrong or may be right in itself, BUT it is not self-denial, as the phrase is used here assuredly by our Lord.

In effect, the Lord's precept comes to this—the real displacement of self from the throne of life in its purposes and hopes, and the real enthronement of Another. It comes to—unqualified self-surrender. We all practically understand what we mean when we speak about self and its surrender, and the enthronement of Jesus Christ. We mean that whereas yesterday our aims, many of them, some of them, one of them, terminated in ourself, today, so far as we know, they all terminate in our Lord. Yesterday, perhaps in some highly refined mode, perhaps in some mode not refined, we lived at least a part of our life to self; now, in full purpose, we live the whole of it to Him who died for us and rose again.

(3) "And let him take up his cross daily, and follow me." Every word is pregnant here, the "taking up"—the acceptance by the regenerate will, with a true surrender, of whatever may be meant by the cross. And then, "the cross"! Observe, it is not the yoke, the burden, but the *cross*—a word of very definite imagery; a thing to be carried indeed, as any burden is to be carried—but whither, and why? To a Calvary, and because of a crucifixion to be done there. The "self" just "denied," just ignored, rejected, is to be also bound and nailed as to a Roman cross, and this with the consenting act of the regenerate will, which has taken up that cross for that end.

But *"daily"*; without intermission, without holiday; now, today, this hour; and then, tomorrow! And the daily *"cross"*; a something which is to be the instrument of disgrace and execution to something else! And what will that something be? Just whatever gives occasion of ever deeper test to the Self-surrender of which we have spoken; just whatever exposes to shame and death the old aims, and purposes, and plans, the old spirit of Self and its life.

(4) 'And let him follow me." This may refer especially to the last previous words, the cross-bearing; it may indicate a following of Him who "went out bearing His Cross" [John 19:17]. But it may better be referred to the whole previous verse, to that mysterious Self-denial of the Son, whereby, throughout His blessed course, "His meat was to do, not His own will, but the will of Him that sent Him" [John 4:34], and to glorify Him upon the earth.

I leave upon the heart, with little attempt at system, just this utterance of the Christian's Master calling His bondservant out to the path of holiness. Listen, weigh, and apply to the inmost self. Let the cost be counted before the results are claimed. Would you know what it is, in the strong but gentle realities of a happy experience, to be "he that overcometh" [Rev. 3:5], to have "heart and thoughts kept by the peace of God" [see Phil. 4:7]? Then more is needed than even the holiest aspirations. There needs certain definite demands on the regenerate will. You must draw for every victory upon divine resources. But you must do it as one who is, in full heart-purpose, self-surrendered, denying the life of self, and daily taking up the cross.

22

The Temptation of Joseph

How can I do this great wickedness and sin against God?—Gen. 39:9

So said Joseph, alone with Potiphar's wife. The unhappy woman had been enticing Joseph, then about twenty-seven years old, to gross and grievous sin. Sin had first mastered *her;* she was the insane slave of its power. Now she in turn craved, by a sort of dreadful "law of sin," to drag down another soul with her into the pit.

Joseph was not a glorified spirit. He was a young mortal man, subject to "like passions" to our own. The fiery arrows of the words, actions, looks, of the temptress were aimed upon no statue, no automaton, but upon a being full of the perils of our nature in its glowing prime. Not only so: this young man, this young Oriental man, was placed in circumstances exquisitely difficult for virtue and terribly easy for moral relaxation. Outwardly, there was no call upon him such as the words *noble obligation* imply; he was but a purchased slave. And he was in a country—namely, Egypt—which was infected to an extreme degree by moral pollution; he had breathed for some time the air of its opinion and practice everywhere around him. His home in Canaan had been no perfect home, yet the breath of the Lord and the Promise had been in it. But now here he was, a young man, away from home, awfully far away, helplessly separated from all its helps, including the moral influences of a father who had "seen God face to face" [Gen. 32:30], imperfect as his use of that blessing had often been. Moreover, Joseph had been carried off from home by an act of atrocious injustice and cruelty, enough to embitter his spirit for all time. And has my reader ever felt bitterness of spirit? If so, he

389

knows well what a "place" it can "give to the devil" [see Eph. 4:27]. Awesome is the tempter's power when he comes with some seduction, and finds that at that moment the spirit is in rebellion under some real injury, angry with man the wrong-doer, and fretting against Him who has permitted the wrong to be done.

We can hardly imagine a position more terribly difficult than that of Joseph, as regarded the open avenues for the temptation. And now, in all its force, the temptation came.

In this case, unlike Abraham's, the temptation is put before us as an allurement from the powers of darkness. But we saw in Abraham's case how the Enemy must have used *the test as a lure*. So here, in a converse way, we may be confident that Joseph's eternal Master and Friend used *the lure as a test*, in His divine faithfulness and love. He took the occasion to give Joseph just that victory which is won by tested faith alone. The young man put the sin away at once, in the name and in the power of God, sure that He was real, holy, and at hand. He was instantly conscious of two things—that sin was sin, and that God was near. His moral standard was true. Egypt might condone what it pleased; as for him, this act was a "great wickedness." And the essence of it was that it was "against God." He said nothing of Potiphar's wrath. The all-possessing thought was God. Jacob was far away, BUT God was there. And how *could* he "sin against God"?

Through Joseph's temptation and his victory over it comes this message, that the Word of God knows all about these fierce assaults. And in that one simple reflection lies a help and hope very precious to tempted hearts.

The Book which calls all the Lord's disciples, in sacred earnest, not only to virtue but to holiness, does not underrate the fact and the power of the fiercest and crudest temptations to sin. The Bible "knows all about it." It therefore speaks advisedly when it speaks of a "more than conquest" [see Rom. 8:37] as possible all the while.

Joseph's secret of victory was "the practice of the presence of God." We read nothing, all through Joseph's life, about his inner spiritual experience. But this one sentence, spoken in the hour of temptation, is eloquent to tell us what it must have been. He must have walked with God in very close and watchful fellowship indeed. Perhaps that awful hour in the dry pit at Dothan was his great crisis, in which he discovered the supreme reality of God for his soul. But however, God *was* in all his thoughts—in the Egyptian house, in the daily servile tasks, and therefore in the fierce temptation. The Enemy assailed him with desperate force. But it was in vain. The chamber was "swept and garnished" [Matt. 12:44; Luke 11:25], but *not empty*. God was at home within.

23

Christian Training

Take heed unto thyself—1 Tim. 4:16

What is the chief and highest end of man?" This is the first question in the Scottish Catechism. And no Christian will dispute the truth and grandeur of the answer; "The chief and highest end of man is to glorify God, and to enjoy Him fully forever." And what, we may go on to ask, is the final requisite to that end? It is a character in harmony with God, and capable therefore of the heaven of His presence. And what, so far as we are concerned, is the ultimate aim of the divine gospel? It is to make that character.

The Cross, trustfully accepted, is indeed the penitent's title, his one title, to eternal life. But the title is not the whole process of salvation. There must be training too. And the grant of the title is thus but a step, though immeasurably important, in the whole process. It lifts away the millstone of condemnation, on purpose, above all things, that the pardoned may be made effectually willing, with a will disengaged from the fears and the repulsions of the unpardoned state, to be trained into a character in harmony with God, and capable of His heavenly presence.

It is deplorable, because it is so entirely unlike the Bible, to forget the immovable truth that the penitent is accepted, not only that he may be spared the sorrows of a lost eternity, but that he may be brought decisively under training into a character at harmony with God, and capable of the eternity of His heaven. "Being made free from sin," that is to say, from its claim, "and become servants to God, ye have your fruit unto holiness, and the end everlasting life" [Rom. 6:22].

It must be then a study of supreme importance to trace in Scripture some of the principles of that process which tends thus to educate the soul that has fled into that refuge which becomes also, instantly, its school.

There is a real risk now, if ever there was, of the cancer-growth of self-indulgence. Too often, amidst this atmosphere, the soul that has grasped personal justification (and thrice happy the soul that has done it) yet forgets to grasp what should be its direct result; no negligent repose in sacred privileges, but the real and glorious work of the will in the strength of the peace of God. The assured and gladdened disciple very often needs to be reminded that his liberty is a liberty to observe, and love, and do every detail of his Redeemer's will; that in his happy faith he is to find the nerves of an unwearied virtue; that from his whole plan of life down to its *minutiae* of daily personal habits—public, private, and solitary—down to his sleep, his table, and his dress, he must habituate himself to the moral and spiritual consciousness of being under discipline. For he is being trained, under his Lord's grace and guidance, into *the character* of the gospel.

Self-discipline is not holiness. You may be profoundly devout, and not know God. You may wear your body to a shadow, and not know God. But the soul that does know God, or rather is known of Him, will seek and will practice reverence most deep and self-discipline most attentive; for they are part of the training, under the grace of God, of that character in which the justified will stand out, at last, the glorified.

The justified Christian who is self-indulgent, who takes not heed to himself, is an anomaly on gospel principles. I need not explain that I do not mean that the justified are to mask themselves in an artificial sanctimony. They are not to treat human life as an idle dream, for it is their very training-ground. They are not to be morose and unsympathetic among their neighbors. They are not to suppress all that is warm and radiant in their own circumstances of endowments. No, BUT they are *to control* themselves in these things, in the light of the will of God. They are expected by the whole gospel to take heed unto themselves. If, claiming to stand among the justified, they find themselves remiss in common things, lax in personal conduct, uncaring of the claims of others, discourteous, thankless, dutiless, let them take heed unto themselves. Precisely because they are justified, they are under training, and strict training. And eternity will bear the imprint of what that training has been for them.

24

Palm Sunday

And that every tongue should confess that Jesus Christ is Lord, to the glory
of God the Father—Phil. 2:11

So closes one of the most conspicuous and magnificent of the
dogmatic utterances of the New Testament. Let us consider it for a
few moments from that point of view alone. We have here a chain of
assertions about our Lord Jesus Christ, made within some thirty
years of His death at Jerusalem; made in the open day of public
Christian rapport, and made (every reader must feel this) not in the
least in the manner of controversy, of assertion against difficulties
and denials, but in the tone of a settled, common, and most living
certainty.

These assertions give us on the one hand the fullest possible assurance that He is Man, Man in nature, in circumstances and experience, and particularly in the sphere of relation to God the Father.

But they also assure us, in precisely the same tone, and in a way
which is equally vital to the argument in hand, that He is as genuinely Divine as He is genuinely Human. Did He come to be in
Bondservant's Form [see v. 7]? And does the word "Form" there,
unless the glowing argument is to run as cold as ice, mean, as it
ought to mean, reality in manifestation, fact in sight, a Manhood
perfectly real, carrying with it a veritable creaturely obligation to
God? But He was also, antecedently, "in God's Form" [see 2:6]. And
there too, therefore, we are to understand, unless the wonderful
words are to be robbed of all their living power, that He who came
to be Man, and to seem Man, in an antecedent state of His blessed

395

Being was God, and seemed God. And His becoming to be one with us in that mysterious but genuine Bondservice was the free and conscious choice of His eternal Will, His eternal Love, in the glory of the Throne. When He came on earth abased, He was no victim of a secret and irresistible destiny, such as that which in the Stoic's theology swept the Gods of Olympus to their hour of change and extinction as surely as it swept men to ultimate annihilation. *"He made Himself* void" [see v. 7], with all the foresight and with all the freewill which can be exercised upon the Throne where the Son is in the Form of the Eternal Nature. Such is the Christology of the passage in its aspect towards Deity.

Then in regard of our beloved Lord's Manhood, its implications assure us that the perfect genuineness of that Manhood, which could not be expressed in a term more profound and complete than this same "Form of a servant," leaves us yet perfectly sure that He who chose to be Bondservant is to us only all the more, even in His Manhood, Lord. Was it not His own prescient choice to be true Man? And was it not His choice with a prescient and infallible regard to "the things of others" [v. 4], to us men and our salvation? Then we may be sure that, whatever is meant by the "made Himself void," which here describes His Incarnation, one thing it could never possibly mean— a *Kenôsis* [vainness] which could hurt or distort His absolute fitness to guide and bless us whom He came to save. That awful and benignant "Exinanition" placed Him indeed on the creaturely level in regard of the reality of human experience of growth, and human capacity for suffering. But never for one moment did it, could it, make Him other than the absolute and infallible Master and Guide of His redeemed.

Now, in closing, let us remember for our blessing how this passage of didactic splendor comes in. It is no lecture in the abstract, it is not in the least a controversial assertion. It is simply part of an argument to the heart. Paul is not here, as elsewhere in his Epistles, combating an error of faith; he is pleading for a life of love.

The passage before us is charged to the brim with the doctrine of the Person and the Natures of Christ. And why? It is in order that the Christian, tempted to a self-asserting life, may "look upon the things of others," for the reason that this supreme Fact, his Savior, is in fact thus and thus, and did in fact think and act thus and thus for His people.

O reason of reasons, argument of arguments—the Lord Jesus Christ!

Nothing in Christianity lies really outside Him. His Person and His Work embody all its doctrinal teaching. His example, "His Love which passeth knowledge" [see Eph. 3:19], is the sum and life of all its morality.

Be ever more and more to us, Lord Jesus Christ, in all Thy answer to our boundless needs. Let us "sink to no second cause." Let us come to Thee. Let us yield to Thee. Let us follow Thee. Present Thyself evermore to us as literally our all in all. And so through a blessed fellowship in Thy wonderful humiliation we shall partake forever hereafter in the exaltations of Thy glory, which is the glory of immortal love.

25

Good Friday

The Church of God, which He hath purchased with His own blood—
Acts 20:28
He that spared not His own Son, but delivered Him up for us all, how shall
He not with Him also freely give us all things?—Rom. 8:32

We meet around the Cross of Jesus, where the work is finished, the Lamb slain. Now, to faith and memory, the holy body is laid in Joseph's tomb. We gather around the empty Cross, and by the grave henceforth glorified by the presence of Jesus; there to think of the treasures and glories won for us by the Crucifixion. The Lord transfigured the grave by lying in it. All thoughts of the grave are now to be penetrated with light, and joy, and hope, for Jesus lay there, and is "the first-fruits" out of it.

Two aspects of the atoning Sacrifice are given to us in the text. First, *the purchase by blood,* then, *the free gift of all things with Christ.*

(1) Paul says to the elders at Miletus (Acts 20:28) that Jesus died that He might *"purchase."* Yes, there is in the death of Christ a transaction of purchase, a sublime *commerce.* Remember, O Christian, that the act which has rescued you has also bought you. Good Friday is the day of your purchase, the anniversary of that great transaction by which actually you have been made the property of Another; the day for fresh recollections of the sale and purchase through which they who "belong" have gone. Let Christians who recognize what has been done for them in pardon turn around the document of acquittal and see on the other side the deed of purchase. Let them gather around the Cross, to spell in the light of the death of Jesus

(for His death is a Shechinah-cloud, full of light) the watchword, *"I belong."*

Is it strange that such Value should have been given for you and for me? But the case demanded it. Nothing less could avail if the captives were to be lawfully delivered; and therefore the vast price was paid. So, not because of your emotions, but because of the blood of Christ, you are His "peculiar people," He has bought you, soul and body, means, time, temper, tongue.

And oh, *what safety* to be owned by Him! What certainty of guidance is here given, what guarantee of sure keeping! The Hand which has thus appropriated you will make no mistakes with you, will not leave hold of you when the foe assails. There is nothing so strong, or so gentle, in heaven or earth as the possessing hand of Jesus Christ, who has bought you so dear and holds you so fast. So do not fear that sovereign ownership. It makes altogether for peace and order. The Lord does not dislocate human life by possessing it. He does not put "secular" interests, as such, under a ban, when He claims mastery over them; rather, He hallows them. He puts all in order, by centering all upon Himself.

(2) The same Apostle, not at Miletus but in his room at Corinth, writing to Rome, asks the question, "How shall He not *with Him* also freely give us all things?" (Rom. 8:32). He does not mean that the "all" things are to be given beside Christ, and apart from Him, but that they are involved in the gift of Him. They are to be enjoyed because the Father has given the Son. In proportion to the depth of the death He suffered, and the vastness of the price He paid, is meant to be the height to which He raises us, the liberty and relief to which He calls us. Do we seek to show our thanks to Him for His atoning grief? Let us enter on the blessings He died to win us, those innumerable benefits which, by His precious blood-shedding, He hath obtained to us. If we do not enter upon them, is it not to withhold the thanks which will best please Him? When David's three mighty men burst their way to the well of Bethlehem, and came back victorious to their king, he poured out the precious water as a libation to the Lord. It was a sacred act, BUT surely, in a human way, the heroes must have grieved that their lord missed the draught which they had won at their lives' risk for him. The Lord Jesus

Christ, bursting through the powers of darkness, has drawn the water of life for us, winning for us, from a deep well, rest of soul, strength in weakness, joy in sorrow, power for service. How can we requite His act? By drinking heartily the water He has won; by entering into the possession He has purchased; by letting Him thus "see of the travail of His soul." Our great Savior has "offered rest"—rest not after toil, but in it. It is put into our hands by Him who went down into the depths to purchase it, by the sacrifice of Himself. Then—let us take it, and be glad.

The Father loves to give great gifts with His Son. Open that divine Casket, His Name, and see the treasure within. "All things"; "all grace" [2 Cor. 9:8]; readiness for "all the will of God" [Col. 4:12]; the working of "all things" for your good [see Rom. 8:28]; "all the fullness of God," to take possession of your weak heart, and make it what your Redeemer died that it might be.

26

Easter Sunday

The first day of the week cometh Mary Magdalene early, when it was yet dark, unto the sepulchre, and seeth the stone taken away from the sepulchre—John 20:1

We observe the connecting "now." It points to previous details, and reminds us that the Resurrection is indissolubly linked, in significance as in fact, to what precedes it—the Cross. It is these two which make the one glory of the work of Christ. It is "the Living One who became dead" (see Rev. 1:18) who is our Peace, and who can lay His hand on us and say, "Fear not."

As we review the interval between the two, I would touch on one point only in the picture of the disciples drawn for us in the gospel narrative; I mean the collocation and the contrast, so startling yet so deeply truth-like, of the total failure of their faith and the survival of their love.

When the Lord rose, perhaps no living person, excepting surely His mother, consciously and intelligently believed on His Name. No living person except her, trusted His promise to rise again, and understood His death in the light of it, resting the soul upon His sacrifice. So this very passage tells us in regard of no less personages than John and Peter. But such a statement would have been the very last thing which a fabricator would have concocted, and the very last which would have arisen unconsciously in minds (such as many historical critics assume all the minds of the primeval Church to have been) pregnant with legend, or facile vehicles for the growth of myths. Who in that simple age, with its literary "helplessness," would

401

have thought of constructing an utter collapse of faith in the central circle of the disciples, just when Jesus was accomplishing His alleged victory—a collapse just because of the Cross, which so soon became somehow the hope and glory of His followers?

But knowledge and reflection now show us how true to history, to time and conditions, and to the human soul, all this picture is. All the prepossessions of those men and women, and their cherished wishes, lay in the direction of a triumph not through death at all. The attention they ought to have given to their Master's words about His death had been all the while distracted and neutralized by these intense expectations and preferences. When the stern fact of the Crucifixion came, their confidence was not only surprised, but crushed; and so it would have remained, if Jesus had not risen again.

And yet—they loved Him. They must have been tortured with worse than doubts about His Messianic character, if, indeed, in those distressing hours they had mental leisure to *doubt* amidst their absorbing *grief*. But *some* formidable questioning, not only about Him, but about all they had known or hoped about God, must have mingled with their tears. And yet—they loved Him. Women, Apostles, all, in one degree or another, they loved Him still. And in this, too, there is a deep and verifiable truth of the human heart. Mere grief and alarm may easily be imagined over the unlooked-for death of any strong leader. But the leader these persons had lost was Jesus—the Man Jesus, such as the Gospels draw Him. Such a Chief, even had He misled them in the end, must still (it is true in the logic of the heart, which alone is in question here) be loved, for the time, with an intensity only the greater for His fall.

May I draw a somewhat evident lesson? Let us give continual thanks for the broad, strong foundations of fact and reason, of cogent and manifold proof, which lie beneath the assertion of the Creed, that He who died for our sins rose again the third day. History has nothing else in it so firm and solid, in the historical sense, as that position. But the human mind is a strange and subtle thing, and it is possible that we may, in certain states of it, find ourselves doubting, as it were, against our reason; seeing the steps and links, but so as to fail to combine them at the moment into a result of conscious and invigorating certainty. Then let us be thankful indeed if we bear about in us another part of the vast evidence of Christianity, that is, of Jesus Christ; the thing which kept the adherence of those disciples tenacious when, for a dark season, their full faith was gone. This Jesus Christ has, somehow, touched and changed, and set free, my soul, my being. The more I have seen, trusted, loved Him, the more always I have stood clear of sin, of self. I cannot but love Him still. And as for these haunting doubts, I will at least drag them into the light of His love, and look at them there. If I feel for a sad moment, "They have taken away my Lord" [v. 13], I will at that very moment remember why, among other reasons, I can call Him "my Lord" at all; He, or if not He, then nothing, has freed me from many more than seven sins. Is not doubt about such a Power a self-detected fallacy already?

But on the other side, we must not press too far the resemblance between Mary's case and our own. What was, after all, this passionate love of the disciples when their faith was gone? In a great measure, it was only passionate. Warm as it was, it could not well have persisted. As time went on it must have been infected with the bitterness of an ever-growing pain at the loss, the blank, the *mistake*. It was the love more of nature than of grace—let us not fear to say it—which brought Mary to the tomb. The heavenly love—the joyful, holy, undecaying love—was yet to come: love stirred from its depths by light and power divine. But in order to this she had yet to know Jesus as the Risen One, who was dead, but is alive forevermore.

As such we know Him, and have felt His power.

Let us stand by the side of Mary Magdalene, with that knowledge and consciousness in our grateful hearts. Let us look into that tomb, and see it full of light—the seat of angels, the gate of heaven. Let us turn around with her, and see the reason of it all—the Lord Jesus risen indeed: Jesus calling us by our name, while we answer, "Rabboni, my Master, O my Master!" [see v. 16].

27

The Emmaus Exposition

And beginning at Moses and all the prophets, He expounded unto them in all the scriptures the things concerning Himself—Luke 24:27

What a delightful contrast between the end and the beginning of this story! The two disciples set out at noon with heavy hearts and weary steps; they hasten back in the dark to meet joy with joy, and to find the Lord again.

It is delightful to feel that all the difference was made by Jesus Christ. And it is so now with those who seek to follow Him through the pilgrimage of this world. The great and glorious difference between depression and discouragement, and hope, and sympathy, and joy, will ever be made by the realized presence of Jesus Christ.

The Savior spent that afternoon exclusively with the Bible. He was determined to be known of them *first* through the Bible, even before He was known in the breaking of bread. Such was the Bible to Jesus Christ that He knew it to be better to reveal Himself, not through a vision of glory from His risen form, but through the written Word. Now for ages and ages He has been out of sight, but the very means which He used that afternoon to make them realize their salvation we have in our hands today.

Let us open our Old Testament always with the light of the Walk to Emmaus shed upon it.

We gather that the passages He chose were all connected with His sufferings. Observe that the very first word which we can interpret of the Savior (Gen. 3:15) was of His *sufferings*. That first prophecy meant mercy to us and defeat to Satan, but defeat through the sufferings of the Conqueror. Again, we may be sure that the fifty-third chapter of Isaiah, and the twenty-second Psalm, the psalm of glory through exceeding pain, were parts of the Emmaus exposition. It had all been fulfilled within about thirty to forty hours just past; in His eyes, as He came back from eternity, what must the reality have been!

But now they drew near to Emmaus. The sun was not quite set; it was *"towards* evening" [v. 29]; "and He made as though He would have gone further" [v. 28]; and so indeed He would have done if they had not detained Him. He knew what was about to happen, as eternally He knows, BUT none the less He left them to ask. It was doubtless an effort to ask, for there was surely an awe upon them, BUT they made it, and they were rewarded. Let us too remember that He delights to be invited in. He "stands at the door and knocks" [Rev. 3:20], BUT He rejoices also when His people speak to Him, without the knock, and say, "Abide with us" [v. 29]. So they "constrained" Him, reverently but really. And it was for a very simple reason; they could not do without Him.

With what a *homely* argument they plead with Him to give them His presence still! "Stay with us, You who have charmed our sadness away; give us Thy company, and if Thou wilt, take ours, *for it is getting dark."* So He went in, this great Conqueror, "declared to be the Son of God with power" [Rom. 1:4]. He went in, at the cottage door, to sit down with those two troubled men, those slow hearted disciples. He was none the less ready for their humble company because he was the almighty Victor over sin and death, just come from the battle to the triumph.

So it is with the Savior still. Speaking from His glory (Rev. 3:20), He still says, "I will come in and sup with him." In asking Him so to come, let us rest upon the fact that He is indeed willing to do so; *He delights* to give us His time, His presence, Himself.

It seems unlikely, to be sure, that the supper at Emmaus was a Communion. But we can well adapt the record here to what Christians find at the Table of their Lord, as they recognize that the holy Feast is the Lord's own pledge of all His blessings; His own autograph, as it were, under all His promises. If so, and when we take the Emmaus meal as a suggestion of the Lord's Supper, let us recall the

Bible lesson which led up to it, and let us prepare ourselves for the Holy Communion by study of the Holy Word.

Perhaps it was not physically good for them that the deep, wonderful joy of that recognition should continue long. Perhaps to train them at once to walk by faith, not by sight, He made this interview short, and vanished from their eyes.

And now, they turn and speak to one another. "Did not our hearts burn within us?" [v. 32]. Probably they had not said so at the time, BUT the confession was irrepressible now. And observe in the next place, that the personal joy they had attained set them instantly upon work for others. At midday, when they left Jerusalem, they thought only of themselves. Now they are sure of the Lord Jesus for themselves; and they immediately think of others who need to find Him too. There is nothing so unselfish in its tendency as a thorough grasp of Christ for ourselves. So "they rose up the same hour and returned to Jerusalem" [v. 33]. It was a dark walk back, but darkness or light would be alike to them in that hour of unspeakable joy, and on the way to carry it to other hearts.

28

What if There Were No Resurrection?

And if Christ be not raised, your faith is vain; ye are yet in your sins: then they also which are fallen asleep in Christ are perished. If in this life only we have hope in Christ, we are of all men most miserable. But now is Christ risen from the dead, and become the first-fruits of them that slept—
1 Cor. 15:17–20

We gather here what would be *the state of the case if Christ had not risen*. Go back in thought to the garden-sepulcher. Imagine the third morning come, and gone, and no motion of that corpse within its linen folds; no stirring of that sealed stone! Imagine the day wearing through, and still no sign of life. The Roman guards at last would have gone, and the place would have resumed its quiet. What would have been the sequel? Assuredly, for one thing, we should not now keep a day in memory of Jesus Christ. We should never have heard of Him. For there would have been no Church, no faith, no gospel. The disciples would have soon scattered, to mourn, to forget, to die. What course the world would have run into other things, we know not. But of this we may be sure: no Resurrection—no gospel; no resurrection—no faith in Jesus as the Lord of Life.

No risen Jesus—no salvation, no pardon, no heaven for sinners! Not only would no temples of worship have ever risen to Christ's dear Name; not only would no Christian world have ever grown up, BUT no sinful soul of man would have escaped its doom. Observe St. Paul's reasoning here. He writes to *the believers* at Corinth; to Christians, true Christians; men who had repented of sin and were living a new life; men who were walking in the narrow path, and suffering in it too. Nevertheless, these, even these, these altered, purified, saintly believers, would have been, says Paul, still in their sins, if Christ were still in His grave.

Mark well that truth. For what does it tell us? It lays it down, clear as the day, that in order to a sinner's peace with God the all-important thing is the completed, successful Work of Christ; the slain Lord risen; the sacrificed Savior accepted in our place.

But from Joseph's grave into Joseph's garden the Risen One stepped forth in the power of an endless life; rejoicing in that deep morning calm over His atonement finished and accepted for us. Therefore is the believing sinner accepted in Him. Your faith is *not* vain. Ye are *not* still in your sins. For He is risen.

"Then they which fell asleep in Christ are perished. If in this life only we have hope in Christ, we are of all men most miserable."

Paul is still carrying on the question, "What if He had not risen?" He has just said that believers *in life* would have nothing to believe; faith would have had no resting-ground, sin no pardon, no atonement; for if the Lord had not risen, His death would have been there-by proved a failure, His sacrifice a vain attempt. And now, with stern consistency, Paul follows the thought *beyond the grave*. Think, he says, of your brethren gone before. Think of their happy deaths, their dying testimony of peace and hope. Think how you speak of them as "forever with the Lord"; as resting from all toil, pain, and care, in Him. Ah, if Christ be not risen—it is all an awful delusion. If He did not rise, those seemingly happy ones woke in the other world to a lost eternity! They too, if He had not risen, would have been still in their sins. Yes, he continues, if in this life only we have hoped in Christ; if, that is, our hopes in Christ are confined to this life, if they are a delusion; if He is not real (and He would be so, if not risen); if, when we pass the river, we find on the other shore no risen Savior there, no Christ for us in eternity; then, be sure of it, no past thoughts, or resolves, or reformations of ours will save us. We shall go down to the darkness "most miserable of all men," for to our then present woe will be added the nameless weight and agony of the surprise, the difference, the disappointment, of those who had looked for heaven, on what seemed good grounds—and behold it was shut forever!

"But now is Christ risen from the dead." Here, thanks be to God, is the fact. We have viewed the awful alternative—which *we* should have been helpless to prevent. But the Lord prevented it. The Father accepted the sacrifice of His Son. The Atonement was sealed by the Resurrection. Christ rose, to die no more. And the Resurrection tells us that it is so!

"The First-fruits of them that slept."

So closes the text, linking, with the adamantine chain of God's purpose, the rising of the Savior to the rising of His buried saints. Jesus rose from Joseph's tomb; therefore, as sure as an eternal Will can make it, yonder graves of saints around us shall give up their treasures. Earth and sky may roll their round in silence. Tomorrow may *look* just like today. But it will not *be* just like today; for it will be one step nearer to the morning of our resurrection. For Jesus rose again.

Oh, blessed Easter truth! Oh, double light! Look backward; yonder is the light of the Cross; the finished Atonement; the soul pardoned for His sake. Look forward; yonder is the dawn of the coming glory; the eternal city; the soul's home forever with the Lord. Yet a few steps further; a little longer strife with sin, and care, and woe; and behold, the last great Easter—the endless farewell to evil—the great rejoicing around our Lord Jesus Christ, as we rise form our graves to meet Him. For if Christ rose, the first-fruits, then they which are Christ's must also rise at His coming.

29

The Resurrection of Lazarus

Said I not unto thee, that, if thou wouldest believe, thou shouldest see the glory of God?—John 11:40

The Savior is here speaking to a disciple who was under a great strain. Martha and her sister had just had their faith put to a tremendous test. Lazarus had been ill; they had sent, and in time, to the Lord to come and heal him, and He abode two whole days without stirring, and only arrived when Lazarus had been some days buried. Under these circumstances, with her brother in the grave close by, and in the grave *because* the Lord had come too late, Martha met Him.

Very wonderful is the strength and simplicity of faith seen in Martha here. The Lord had asked the way to the grave; on the way He "wept" [v. 35], and again, He "groaned" [v. 33]. This looked little like one who was about to put forth almighty power; rather it looked like one who had failed, and was at a loss. Yes, it was a great trial to faith that "Jesus wept," and "Jesus groaned in the spirit, and was troubled."

They come to the grave, with its heavy stone door; He bids them take away the stone. Remember, we know what was about to happen, but Martha did not know; to her the moving of the stone seemed only an exposure of the reality of her brother's death. All this was a tremendous strain, a strain upon the inmost heart, lacerated with grief.

Already Martha had been put through one sore test. Jesus had said to her (v. 25), "He that liveth and believeth in Me shall never die." But Lazarus had lived, and Lazarus had believed, and Lazarus was *dead.* Yet her Lord turns to her and says, "Believest thou this?" Let us put ourselves in her place. How should we have answered? How *have* we answered, in times of agony, when the shadow of death has come down upon us, and into us?

Remember again that it was *Martha* to whom this question was addressed. If we had been contriving the story, surely we should have made Him ask it of Mary—Mary, the spiritual disciple. But it was Martha who won the victory; she could not explain the mystery, but she knew the Lord. "Yes, Lord, I believe that Thou art the Christ" (v. 27). "I cannot explain the Resurrection, but I *know Thee.* I have found Thee in the light, and now I trust Thee in the dark. I have seen Thy face, and though now I scarcely feel Thy hand, I trust Thee still."

How was her faith rewarded? Behold the brother restored to life; Jesus Christ and His Trust magnificently re-established, glorified with tenfold brightness, "after she had suffered for a while."

Let us take this as a message for ourselves. Our Savior makes demands upon us sometimes for great self-denial, or for very difficult duty, or again for reliance quite in the dark. Many of us know what it is, under the long strain of sorrow, or under its sharp and sudden pangs, to find it very difficult indeed to say with Martha, "Yes, Lord, I believe."

But "said I not unto thee, that if thou wouldest *believe* thou shouldest *see* the glory of God?" (v. 40). So He said that day; so He says now. "If thou wouldest meekly consent not to know all at once, but to trust me whatever I do; if thou wouldest lie still in my hand, while I carry thee through the waters or the fires—then, what? Then, one day, thou shalt see." "We walk by faith, not by sight" [2 Cor. 5:7]; that is the rule at present. But to walk by sight, not by faith, shall be the rule hereafter. We shall one day be where everything is cleared up, and there we shall see that what our Savior led us through in the darkness was used with supreme skill by Him to train us for that perfect light which pours from His unveiled smile.

30

Christ's Post-Resurrection Interviews

He showed Himself alive after His passion by many infallible proofs—
Acts 1:3

My object in taking these words is a simple one. Let us watch the Risen Savior as He appears to His followers and deals with them in His Resurrection life and power, on some representative occasions. And let us thus remind ourselves that He offers Himself to be the Friend, Companion, Guide, and King of His disciples under all the circumstances of human life.

I take first the interview with Mary in the garden, recorded by John (20:11–18). In this, His first interview after the Resurrection, He deals in the solitude of private intimacy with a soul apart; He meets it, not in a consecrated temple, but in a quiet garden.

I gather from this short history that Christ offers Himself to each of us as the individual Friend. In times when perhaps you are literally alone, or alone as to heart-sympathy, your Lord offers to be the Friend who comes closer than any other individual spirit can come to yours. He comes to call you by name, to hear what you have to say in the deepest confidence to Him, to bless you with the friendship of Himself. Wonderful thought! He rises in majesty from the dead, and what does He first do with His victory? He comforts the solitude of a woman's broken heart, by showing Himself to her as her Shepherd, Healer, Friend.

The risen Jesus offers likewise to be your individual Comforter, your understanding Pastor. And He has all the gracious leisure of an endless life in which to attend to you.

We note that this conversation of friends took place in a garden— as if to remind us that not only when we are worshiping in the house of prayer, but out under the sky of the common day, "Jesus is there," the unseen, inseparable Companion.

And now, another interview occurs (Luke 24:13–32). It is the afternoon of Easter Day. Observe again the Lord; it is the hour of His triumph; He has conquered the powers of death. How does He spend the triumph-time! Walking as Man with men along a country road; keeping company with two Galileans, slow of heart, disappointing in spiritual condition. Gently he introduces Himself, and then talks to them about the Bible. Their hearts burn as they go. At last they sit down to a meal with Him, as with a friend. He breaks the bread; they know Him; it is the Lord.

Here the Risen One offers, in the majesty of His eternal life, to enter into human fellowship, to make Himself harmoniously "the third with the two." Blessed is the friendship that is ruled by the Walk to Emmaus. Blessed are those, in any way associated with each other, who have the Lord in their company, to sweeten it, to hallow it, to fill it with His peace. Till grace teaches us better, we are all shy of Him. We may willingly pay adoration to His name, BUT when He says, 'Shall I sit by you in your home, and go with you when you walk, and be everywhere your Friend, and overhear your hourly talk?"—then it is grace, not nature, which welcomes Jesus in. But shall we be afraid of "the Son of the Blessed" [Mark 14:61]? Shall He not be loved, as the unseen Listener to all we say to one another, the intimate Associate of all our life? Shall we not make the experiment? We shall find that, far from spoiling any friendship worth the keeping, He will elevate and sweeten it unspeakably. And where will He do so? Emmaus answers that He will do it "out in the open"; where people were passing up and down; in the business of everyday life. It was just thus (for that day was not the Sabbath, but the day after) that He gave Himself to those two friends, and so that the walk to the village was for them a walk to the gate of Heaven.

Another interview; and now it is the evening (John 20:19–23). The doors are shut on the disciples; the meal has been eaten; the food is still on the table. And again, it is no sacred place, in the sense of temple or of church; it is a "living-room." "Then came Jesus, and stood in the midst." Here I see Him offering Himself as the Friend of our social hours—when we are gathered, not at His Table, but at our own. He cares to be the companion of our common life; not to throw a chill over it, not to rebuke one single thing worth the attention of the heart and mind of man; only to be the ruling Presence, the willing Associate, who is also Lord and King.

Looking at this scene, I plead for such a heart-welcome of Him that it shall never be unnatural if the name of Christ comes out in the common conversation, or if the work of Christ enters into it. Does this sound paradoxical? It ought not to be so. Approach this social enjoyment of your Lord by the path of a personal intimacy with Him. Approach it by the secrecy of Mary's interview, and by the privacy of that at Emmaus, and you will find that there is nothing strained in the recognition of His nearness at your home table, or by your home fireside.

It was (and I believe that it still is) the custom of the Jews at the Passover to leave *an empty chair*—for the expected Messiah to find ready if He should come. I do not say that we should literally so set a seat for Christ, BUT let us do so in spirit. I have heard it said that the subject of religion is not suitable for a living room. No, the Lord of the Upper Chamber claims all our chambers, if we ourselves belong to Him.

Lastly we have the interview (John 21) by the lakeside in Galilee. The Lord has watched His people through their night of toil. As the morning dawns He stands on the shore; He grants them a great haul of fishes; He makes Himself known to them in an act of power and love. They see and know Him; then they sit down with Him and break their fast on the beach, in His company, and as His guests. What do we learn here! Again we are out in the common places of life. The garden, the walk, and now the shore—it was there that Jesus "showed Himself after His passion." And here again we behold the willingness of our Master to be with us in whatsoever the common day may bring. The disciples are in the midst of their earthly occupations, busy with boat and oar, fully occupied with the interests of their common work; and He thinks this no unsuitable opportunity for manifesting Himself to them. I learn thus that He claims our hours of labor and of business—not to put the daily duty out of order, but rather to glorify it and speed it, by the thought that He is there.

Thus the Risen Savior, in His mysterious human life, claims for Himself, not parts and fragments, not nooks and corners, of your heart and life, but the whole space, the whole time, that He may bless it all. Is this thought welcome to us and dear? To many, as I well know, it is the very joy of their hearts to know that they cannot ever be out of the reach of their unseen Lord. Well, let us *cultivate* this joy. Spiritual joy, what is it? It is the Lord Jesus Christ realized. Cultivate this joy, then, by getting better and ever better acquainted with Him.

So let the Risen One come to you, and manifest Himself to you, and open to you His heart, and His arms.

Blessed are they who have so seen His face that they shall not be afraid of being held forever in His hands who is their Master and their Friend.

31

Love for Christ

So when they had dined, Jesus saith to Simon Peter, Simon, son of Jonas, lovest thou me more than these?—John 21:15

The silent meal was over, and Jesus speaks. He speaks so as indeed to answer fully the unspoken question, if they had felt it stir within them, *Who art Thou?* He who now speaks is indeed THE LORD.

Peter is addressed; he is singled out to be for a while the one figure, with Jesus, in our view. And this is done (the Lord often does so still in His grace and providence) so as to leave the disciple at once humble and happy.

We may suppose that Peter needed both humiliation and happiness especially just then. His struggle to reach the shore may have had in it some slight trace of a personal display of devotion. And on the other hand there was a deep wound in his soul, left by the denials of that remembered and recent night of terror. Self-assertion and inmost sadness sometimes lie near together. And to both maladies the blessed Lord knows how to apply His searching, healing hand.

The Lord deliberately and solemnly restored Peter, with His own lips, and before six apostolic witnesses. The mighty wound needed a proportionate remedy. And the remedy was to be such as also to remind him forever of his snares and his weaknesses, that he might watch and stand.

"Simon, son of Jonas, lovest thou me more than these? does your heart, with a strong, full choice of love and gladness, choose me? Does it rest in me, as all its salvation and also all its desire?" Wonderful question! Wonderful in that it shows such a care on the Lord's part for the love of such poor hearts as ours! "Give me *thine heart"* [Prov. 23:26] is the most searching, as it is the most characteristic, of the demands of the God of Revelation, of the God of Christ, of Christ the Son of God.

Let me quote the words of one of the greatest of modern preachers, Adolphe Monod; words in his sermon entitled, *Dieu démandant le coeur á l'Homme:*

> No other religion presents anything which resembles this invitation to give God the heart. Give me thy observances, says the god of Pharisaism. Give me thy personality, says the god of Hegel. Give me thy reason, says the god of Kant. . . . It remains for the God of Jesus Christ to say, Give me thy heart. . . . He makes it the essence and the glory of His doctrine. With Him, to give the heart to God is not merely an obligation of piety; it is its root, its beginning, its middle, and its end.

"Lovest thou me more than these?" Such was the question put by Jesus to Peter, on the shore, by the fire, in the presence of Peter's six listening friends—a question altogether of the heart, the inner heart, not of the outer act. Let us sit reverently down beside the Apostle, and humbly put ourselves also in the line of that question. Do not ask others whether they think you love Christ. Let Christ ask you. Friends will be very kind; and so will the Lord Jesus be. Only, He will be omniscient also, and will not for a moment mistake act for motive, hand for heart. When He puts the question, we shall have to reply with Peter, *"Lord, Thou knowest all things, Thou knowest*—what shall it be?—*that I love Thee"* [v. 17]? Why should it not be so? If you love, not worthily (that is impossible) but really, you may surely *know* it. And why not love really? Nothing can prevent it but blindness to what Jesus Christ is, oblivion of what Jesus Christ is and does for you.

Oh, sweet it is to know, most simply, that the soul loves Him; not indeed as it should love Him, and not "more than these," with a glance of self-consciousness around, BUT that indeed it does love Him.

417

32

The Ascension

And He led them out as far as to Bethany, and He lifted up His hands and blessed them. And it came to pass, while He blessed them, He was parted from them, and carried up into heaven—Luke 24:50, 51

"Out as far as Bethany," there "He blessed them," and there "He was parted from them." What a beautiful collocation—the home of Martha and Mary, and the Lord's Ascension into Heaven! Truly He was true to the kindred points of Heaven and Home. Bethany was a dear place to Him, because of the sanctified human affections which gathered round and settled in it; and now He makes it His last stage on the way upward. However distant they may be in region, a sanctified home and a glorious Heaven are close together in the plan of God.

The Lord's last ministerial deed was one of blessing; and His blessings are not mere formulas but actual impartations of spiritual gifts. In the very act of going away He displays Himself as the Giver of all the blessings which we have "in heavenly places in Him" [see Eph. 1:20].

"They worshiped Him." As Thomas a few short weeks before had fallen down before Him, and cried, "My Lord and my God" [John 20:28]; and as the answer of the Lord then was in words implying only that he should have uttered that confession sooner; so now they give, so now He accepts, this solemn token of divine honor. And what the disciples did as they looked up after the ascending Savior was done by all the heavenly host as they gazed on the Savior ascended; so the Seer tells us, in Revelation 5. The apostles were but reflecting the heavenly worship on the hill of Bethany.

Observe the results of this wonderful scene on their own souls. What a farewell it was for them! Everything, surely, would look blank and dark to them after the departure of Jesus. For it *was* a departure; "I depart," He had said; and though the Holy Spirit was promised to come to them, as "another comforter," the blessed visible Body of their King at that moment left the earth, for them, forever. The absence of Jesus from sight had already begun to be the law of experience for His people; from that moment the Apostles had to forego the presence of which they had enjoyed the ineffable reality as they walked in Galilee; and they might well have felt bewildered at first and oppressed by the void and the change. But no; they waited only for the radiant word of promise from angel lips, recorded in Acts 1, and then "returned to Jerusalem with great joy," and there were "continually praising and blessing God" [vv. 52, 53].

What a lesson for us is this "great joy" at the Lord's farewell! If it was possible for them to look on His withdrawal out of sight as linked with joy, not sorrow, so with us, here and now, it may be even the same. What were the elements of their joy? First, surely, a loving gladness at the certainty of their Master's triumph; a worshiping, unselfish happiness in His exaltation. The Savior of sinners had done with the sorrows of His pilgrimage. There would be no more agony and tears for Him, no more Cross and grave. He was gone to sit on His Father's throne; "in all things" He was now, and forever, to "have the preeminence" [Col. 1:18].

Let us seek, not artificially to force such feelings into our minds, for we cannot do it, but spiritually to drink in what will beget them. Let us draw close to the Lord Jesus Christ in heart and mind. We only need to know Him better to enter into that apostolic experience, of returning to Jerusalem with great joy.

But in their joy was a view also towards their own spiritual gain. All existence was gloriously altered now to them by the triumph of their King. To be sure, they would soon have trial, difficulty, persecution, to encounter, BUT all would be met now in the power of their Lord, who was exalted forever for them. A transfiguration of everything around had taken place because their Jesus, though out of sight, was eternally Conqueror, and was all in all for them.

What did it matter that for a few short years they had to do with-out the physical sight of His face? Soul-sight is a better thing than eyesight. They had seen, once for all, what Christ Jesus is; faith car-ried on that sight, inwardly, through all their days. And we too may see Him thus, and as truly. We may have just that soul-sight of the glory of God which shall make us, with a profound reality, *glad* in Him; stepping out of ourselves into the region where great joy dwells, and where we therefore may dwell with great joy.

His Kingdom had already begun on that Ascension Day; all His future triumphs would only bring out the fact.

So the disciples, gazing upward, were ready for the angels' mes-sage that "this same Jesus, in like manner, should come again" [see Acts 1:11]. Their happiness was lodged altogether out of themselves; it was "hidden with Christ in God" [see Col. 3:3]. And Christ is in God today, and our life today is with Him there, and therefore our joy also, today, may be a "great joy" in Him.

33

The Doctrine of the Trinity

And he showed me a pure river of water of life, clear as crystal, proceeding out of the throne of God and of the Lamb—Rev. 22:1

This passage shows forth the doctrine of the Holy Trinity in glorious life and action. We see in picture before us a Throne, and two Persons upon it, and a River of Water of Life proceeding out of it. "This spake He of the Spirit" [John 7:39]. Here, in this last glowing book of the Bible, where the very scenery of Heaven opens before our eyes, here we have the Father and the Son, and the Holy Spirit proceeding forth from Them.

The doctrine of the Trinity, with all its mystery, is after all only the putting together, the outcome, of some of the great facts of the Word of God.

The uncaused, self-existent External is indeed One, One God. But within the bright shrine and sanctuary of the Godhead there is *more than Oneness*. Deity is no bright solitude, but the Scene of mutual affection. Deity contains forever the mighty flow and movement of an infinite Life of responding, interacting Love.

The words "God is Love" get a bright illumination from this doctrine; for how divine is the light that falls upon every *stream* which has its source in such an *ocean-fountain* as the love of God for God!

The teaching of our text, though its context refers to heaven and immortality, is not confined to it. For grace is but the shadow and the germ of glory; there is no blessedness of the heavenly world but has its counterpart on earth. Later in this chapter the longing and thirsty soul, "whosoever will," is invited even here and now to drink of the "water of life, freely" [Rev. 22:14].

So whatever be this eternal River which flows from the Throne of God, it has its rills and offshoots here below, from which we may drink. So we not only slake our thirst, but we do so by partaking of the very life of Heaven.

The Throne is "the Throne of God and of *the Lamb*" [Rev. 22:1, 3]; yes, of the Lamb of Calvary, the Lamb that was slain. It is a fact never forgotten in Heaven that He has been *slain*. Then let His redeemed on earth never forget it. Let your allegiance to your master be marked with the blood of the Cross, always and everywhere. And this once slain and now exalted Lord, whose favored subjects we are, and who from another point of view is our great Elder Brother, He, with the Eternal Father, the First and Second Persons of the Holy Trinity, He is *on the Throne*. The Third Person, the Holy Spirit, figured out in this passage in His glorious capacity as Life-Giver, "proceedeth out of" it. From the depths of the Throne, from the inner secrets of the life of God, from which only God can come, He comes, the Stream of Living Water.

So His eternal origin, His union with the Father and the Son, and also His work, which is to glorify the Father and the Son, are all pictured here. We will not with our finite thought attempt to trace further the infinite mystery of the Triune Godhead. But let us walk down the river that proceeds out of the Throne; let us see the trees of healing on either side of it; and whosoever is athirst, let him take of the water of life freely—that is to say, to render the Greek exactly, "let him take it *gratis,*" or "for nothing."

What does this mean? It means the work of obedient faith; it means the taking the Giver at His word. To believe is not merely the path to reception; it *is* reception. The Lord of love offers to each one of us to be partaker of the Holy Ghost; yes, to the soul that is most weary with failure, to the existence that seems to have least to look back upon, and nothing to look forward to. The Holy Ghost is the power which can meet the need of the weak and weary spirit, the tempted and fallen will; which can take and make all things new, and can prove indeed the Life-Giver by uniting man to Jesus Christ—for salvation, for service, for life, and for death.

The River leads to the Throne. What a restful, immovable "dwelling place" for those who have made their God their refuge and their Home!

Heaven is a place with *a Throne* in it. The very essence of its life will be an everlasting surrender and loyalty to its King. There will be no self-seeking, no self-dependence, in Heaven. There will be no rivalries there; for "His servants shall" all "serve Him." From one point of view it will be a life of eternal manhood and maturity; from another, a life of eternal youth and childhood.

But for those whose hope is set on such a future there must be a present germ of it here and now; a life on earth in which the Throne of God is set up in the heart, and the life of the Spirit flowing from the Throne into all the inner world.

34

"All Things"—Through Christ

I can do all things through Christ which strengtheneth me—Phil. 4:13

Compare with this text the last chapter of Joshua. There the Israelites were undertaking, with a light heart, to "serve the Lord." Joshua, who had been on Sinai with Moses, understood more of the holiness of God, and—looking from their own point of view—he warned them, not that they should not but that they *could* not do it! It is a dangerous fallacy to say absolutely that what we cannot do we are not bound to do. But it is a valuable lesson in the process of discovering the abilities of grace to learn, low in the dust, something of our own disabilities. "You *cannot,*" said Joshua to those who were taking easy views of God's requirements. And it was the warning fitted to their need.

But here in our text is the voice not of Joshua to the careless, but of Paul to the believing. He is writing of what we may do in union with the Lord. And what does he say? "I can do all things," I can walk and please God, I can be more than a conqueror [see Rom. 8:37], I can quench *all* the fiery darts of the wicked one, "in Him that stengtheneth me."

"I can do all things." What does this mean? Certainly not that I am omnipotent. Paul was as little able to open the door of his Roman prison as if he had been a heathen criminal. He was just as little able, by any supposed drawing on divine strength, to do anything *outside the path of duty,* as he was before he knew Christ.

What then do the words mean? Consult this same Epistle to the Philippians; it shows us some noteworthy specimens of the "all things" which, in his Lord, Paul could do. We find there, first, that he had a sufficiency of strength to enable him cheerfully to suffer the disappointments and privations which darkened his path. His soul, an eagle-winged soul, was shut up in the cage of a Roman prison. And there he was tried severely in patience and in temper (and Paul was "a man of like passions" [James 5:17] with ourselves) by hearing of the unkindly doings of those who perversely sought to "add to his afflictions" even in their preaching of Christ, BUT his "all sufficiency" [2 Cor. 9:8] expressed itself in the meek acceptance of their adverse action as a part of the will of God. Again, his life or death hung on a caprice of the imperial despot who for long months, apparently, did not take the trouble to arrive at a judgment; and it was not easy, under such conditions, to enjoy perfect peace. But Paul enjoyed it. Throughout the whole Epistle we find a spirit of deep calm, though it was written by a man who did not know but that within a week he might be led out to a violent and unjust death.

When Paul speaks thus about his own resources for life, and labor, and victory over sin, he would say to us today, "What is for me, is for you. Come with me to the Fountain, and, whether you bring to it a vessel great or small, that vessel will be filled." And why? Because the Lord in whom Paul lived, and from whom he drew his ability to do and to bear, is the same Lord here, and for us; able and willing still to be the peace and power of the humblest of His people. He can be the secret of spiritual success for the domestic servant, for the Sunday School teacher, for the man of business, for the man of toil, for the victim of pain; the same in a life of large publicity, the same in the deep privacy of home; in any and in every sphere to which He may have called us.

In the gospel of Christ we find, in perfect harmony, the principles of Heaven working themselves out in the practice of earth. It is the gospel of eternal grace which heals the plague of the tongue, which takes out of home life its friction, and brightens its hearth, and trims its lamp. Yes, all goes well when Jesus Christ who *strengthens* is allowed to be Jesus Christ who *rules*. Paul's secret in the Roman prison eighteen centuries ago is the secret of English men and women in our common life today, in the busiest life, and in what looks the earthliest.

To do it we must be "in Him." Make sure of your spiritual connection with Jesus Christ; keep in living contact with Him; take pains over it; watch over it. Then you need not fear. Then will the words of the hymn be translated into a happy and brightening experience; you will have peace, perfect peace, by thronging duties pressed: sufficiency for all things of God's will, in Him who gives you power.

35

Gideon

The Lord looked upon him and said, Go in this thy might—Judg. 6:14

The history of Gideon is one of the most striking pictures in the whole Old Testament. As a study of natural character, Gideon is deeply interesting; one of those many personalities shown in Scripture full of individual and minute consistency, and marked by traits of weakness as well as strength, which proclaim themselves to be—not composed pictures but photographs from life.

Gideon is everywhere the same character. It is not too much to say that this man, called to so mighty a work, and enabled it, was not naturally strong; an unlikely instrument, as we should say, for the terribly difficult work that had to be done for Israel. Gideon was no man of iron. If I am not mistaken, he was the man of all others to look back in a melancholy way and contrast a dreadful present with a glorious past. He would feel that it was too late; things had sunk too low; circumstances were too much for him; he must drift with the tide. Had he not a strong temptation to such thoughts? Would not you and I have had them had we lived there and then? Think of only one fact of the time. It was a capital crime at Ophrah, we find, to cut down the altar and the idol! But it was a capital crime by the law of the God of Israel to have anything to do with such an altar and such an idol! So awfully far had the Lord's people gone on the downward path, so deep had they sunk into spiritual death; turning His statutes thus literally upside down. And meantime, in flowed the wild deluge of their savage pagan enemies like the sea through a broken dyke—"the Midianites, the Amalekites, and the children of the East" [v. 3]. At such a moment the Lord took up and fashioned as an instrument for His use just this man, and turned him who was by nature the victim of his surroundings into an instance of glorious strength perfected in weakness.

Is there anything in all this that comes quite home to my friend the reader? Are you at all "discouraged because of the way," or because "the days are evil"? Disheartened friend, Gideon has a special message to you. Listen, and let him speak it out.

(1) He tells you that God can "say to the weak *be strong.*" He can make you strong just at your weakest points. That indolent habit, that rough or peevish temper, that imagination so prone to wander in doubtful or forbidden regions, that entangling love of the world, so different from an unselfish interest in all around you—the Lord can take away all these things, and can somehow say to you as He said to Gideon, "Go in this thy might."

(2) He tells you that, as with character, so with circumstances, God can deal. We have each our Midianites. We have fightings without and fears within. We have difficulties today, due perhaps to our mistakes and follies of yesterday. We have, it may be, very real sorrows, very real cares, for others. Anywise, we have the threefold host of the world, the flesh, and the devil, to deal with as we go. But *in spite of circumstances* the Lord said to Gideon, "Go in this thy might" [v. 14]. And He says it now to you.

Now, what has it which made this weak man strong? God answers the question, and answers it for you, discouraged friend, in the story of the Oak of Ophrah. It was the Look of God. There stooped Gideon, threshing the wheat in the winepress; and there sat under the oak One watching him in his weakness and his gloom. His Master's mighty, loving eyes are upon him, though he know it not. Even so now, Christ is present before yet Christ is seen.

"The Angel" speaks again, and not only speaks but *looks* upon the man. It was transfiguration for the soul of the disheartened Gideon. There was that in the look which conveyed to him even more than the outward message in the words.

What made Gideon strong? It was only this, that he was drawn in his weakness to forget himself in the strength of God. Hitherto he had, in a sense and in a measure, been faithful, but he had not yet come into a magnetic contact, if I may use the word, with Jehovah's life and power. Now the look and the word drew him into this, and Gideon was so gifted now with a power not his own that he became, weak as he was, the vehicle of the Almighty. Note the literal Hebrew given us in the margin, just below (v. 34): "The Spirit of the Lord *clothes Itself with Gideon.*" Amazing phrase! But such things happen still in the sphere of spiritual strength and victory. It was so with Paul in later days: "When I am weak, then am I strong" (2 Cor. 12:10). It can be so with you, with me. Just where you are, and as just what you are, the Lord looks on you, and bids you look on Him. He will lift you out of the sore entanglement by the magic power of His presence, of His look.

36

"Resist the Devil!"

Whom resist, steadfast in the faith, knowing that the same afflictions are accomplished in your brethren that are in the world—1 Pet. 5:9

If you examine this passage of Peter you will find that the connection is most important. It has to do with the great living enemy of man, "your adversary the devil" [v. 8]. It tells us that for the Lord Jesus and His Apostles man's great enemy was indeed a person. Many would persuade us otherwise now, as if "the Devil" were but a figure of speech, a personification of evil. But if so, Scripture is mistaken; and in this, as in other things of the soul, to agree with the Holy Book is the deepest wisdom in the end.

To remember that the enemy is personal is a powerful means of compelling the soul to fly to nothing less than the personal almighty Friend.

Peter tells his converts of abundant danger from themselves and from the world, BUT he does not let them forget the third member of the unholy alliance, our enemy the Devil. He reminds them that they are not only surrounded by an army, but that this army has a general, who knows how to throw his forces on to the weak point, how to make the evil do its work. And for them, as for us, the only perfect victory was to be won by casting themselves on Him who is "stronger than the strong."

"Whom *resist.*" Such is his bold appeal. In one sense they were to be utterly afraid, afraid of themselves, afraid of their own weakness. But they were not to be afraid when that weakness was hidden in their almighty Friend. "In God we shall do great acts."

But how could they resist? *"Steadfast in your faith";* so, rightly, reads the Revised Version. And the word rendered "steadfast" means, precisely, "solid." The thought is of a resistance in which there shall lurk *nothing hollow;* which shall be genuine through and through, a phalanx of rock breaking the waves of all attack. And this was to be thus "in your faith," that is to say, your believing; "in" or "by" the secret of a true reliance on your Lord. In other words, the victory lies in Jesus Christ, and is to be made yours by Him; calling Him in, committing your soul to Him, telling Him all—so shall you overcome. The foothold for resistance is a trusted Christ; the weapon for resistance is a trusted Christ; not by self against self, but by Christ used and trusted, is the victory to be won.

> "In thy weakness, in thy peril,
> Raise to heaven a trustful call;
> Strength and calm for every crisis
> Come in telling Jesus all."

But now look at the latter part of the verse. Here the Apostle turns to another aspect of the matter; to the encouraging fact that in this conflict, with Christ for our weapon, we are not alone. All over the world where He is loved and followed we have "brethren," exposed to the same trials and dangers, and they are winning victories of precisely the kind which we long to win. See the words as they stand: "Knowing that the same afflictions are accomplished in your brethren that are in the world." And the margin of the Revised Version, reads they "are *being accomplished,"* that is, are on the way to completion. Observe, further, that the word rendered "accomplished" is not a mere expression for "are taking place," or "are being experienced." It means that these afflictions are being *carried to their purposed end, directed upon their goal.* Yes, remember, O Christian soul, whatever "affliction" may lie just now upon you, someone else, somewhere else, is bearing the like, and Christ the Lord is "carrying it out" in that person to a glorious "end."

What a brotherhood is here suggested to our thought! It was large in Peter's day. It is vastly larger now. From every region now we hear of "the brethren that are in the world." "Afflictions" are "being accomplished," and God is being glorified, in every race and tongue of man, from the Fuegian, once thought by the scientific visitor to be only half human, to the noblest specimens of the most cultured races of Europe and of Asia. From every quarter come voices testifying that the enemy is indeed around us, but that the Lord is within us; our "afflictions are being carried out" to their perfect end; they are occasions for knowing Him better now; they are preparations for enjoying Him forever more perfectly hereafter.

So let us resist. If we are not merely drifting with the tide, let us be encouraged by this message of God's Word; let us use this mighty secret against a mighty, but not almighty, foe. From sorrow, from temptation, from failure, it bids us look up and look around; up to Jesus Christ, to call Him ever in; around, on the thousands and thousands of "the brethren that are in the world," men who are being by Him made strong out of weakness, and who with us one day shall gather around the great Elder Brother, to bless Him for what He, in us, here below, did in treading down the enemy.

37

Reflections of Heaven

Rev. 22:1–5

This passage is a revelation of the life of the blessed ones in the glory above. And a counterpart of it is to be always found in the life of grace below.

There is no truth revealed to us about Heaven that has not its germ and counterpart here, its reflection from heaven upon earth, in the Christian's present course.

Our text here tells us of provision for that heavenly life—the river for thirst, the fruit for food; and it tells us of that life's condition too. It is a life with a Throne in the midst, "the Throne of God and of the Lamb"; a life in which "His servants serve Him" [v. 1]; a life in which we shall "see His face" [v. 4]; a life in which "His name is on our foreheads" [v. 5]: a "life without night," and all that night signifies; a life in which we shall "reign forever and ever"—yes, with a royalty all the more real and triumphant because the kings are bondservants, first and always, to their God.

Now note the counterpart; what are the characteristics of a true Christian, on his pilgrimage?

(1) His is a life with a Throne over it. Above, there is one eternal Monarchy in the community of the Blessed; they live, and move, and have their being in the shadow and the light of the absolute Throne. Even so here, the Christian life is lived, day and night, hour and minute, under the shadow and the light of the Throne of a royal Christ. Now as then, here as there, His bondservant serves Him; purchased, conquered, and also yielded up of his own will, he

433

serves forever. The Greek rendered here, "shall serve Him," implies the service of adoration. And as in heaven, so on earth, the life of the servant of God is a life of "reverence and godly fear" [Heb. 12:28].

(2) The heavenly life is a life of sight; "they shall see His face" Yes, and this also has its answering experience below. "If we walk in the light" (1 John 1:7), if there is no cloud between, it is our present privilege to "behold the glory of the Lord" [Ezek. 3:23; 43:5; 44:4], to stand in peace and simplicity before Him, and in some merciful measure to see into His love and will.

(3) Then further, "His name on their foreheads" there. Yes, and on the Christian's life, here in this mortal tabernacle, is to be written, "Holiness to the Lord." All our ambitions and our aims are to be according to His mind. Our life is to be clear as day in purity of aspiration and endeavor. The *family likeness* is to begin to be developed here.

(4) Again, there is no secondary illumination, no sun nor moon; God is their Sun, and the Lamb is their Light. So now, in the spiritual sphere, there *"Need be no night"* in the Christian's life below. For him there shines even now an inner sun, making always an inner light, the light of the peace of God.

(5) Yet further, the heavenly life is a life of royalty and reigning. We do not know what this will mean in detail in the world to come, but we can know what its counterpart should mean today:

> "Tis His grace His people raises
> Over self to reign as kings."

A "reigning" life, in the Christian's experience, is one in which the man has dominion over temptation instead of being its slave, and "walks at liberty, keeping His commandments."

Such, in the grace of God, is meant to be the experience of day by day under the practical conditions of our "life in the flesh." How can this life be lived? It is a beautiful picture, BUT is it not disheartening too? Shall I, who so often fail, who seem to myself the very proverb of weakness, ever hope to be thus a conqueror? But our chapter opens with the description of what is to be the provision and sustenance for the heavenly life; and the counterpart holds good here also.

Behold, the River of Life! That is to say, the Holy Ghost, poured forever through the being of the glorified. In some way utterly unimaginable, the Third Person of the Holy Trinity will have infinitely much to do, forever, with the fullness of the life of Heaven. But even so, in gracious and real measure, it is to be on earth. Let not the truth of the Holy Ghost be a "forgotten truth" to you, Christian man, ambitious of a true life in God. "He that believeth on me," saith the Lord (John 7:37), "out of him shall flow rivers of living water." There is intended to be such a flowing fullness of divine grace in our lives that it must needs overflow to others; and this, not from great saints only, but from all "them that believe on His name."

As with the water of Heaven, so with its food. The Tree of Life there blooms and bears, perennial in the sustenance it provides, yielding its twelvefold fruits through the year of eternity. But again, that fruit is brought forth also for the pilgrim's strength in his mortality. Christ is the food of His people, here and now; not only our sacrifice of peace, but also our very life, "the food that weary pilgrims love," on their way to the eternal country.

Above, they find always that fruit in its season; the holy trees "yield their fruit" every month. There is no winter and starvation in that year, no decline or going off in that blessed life. Even so here also. We never need fail of our supply. Our spiritual continuance is to be perpetual, because it is sustained not by itself, not by our zeal or love, but by the fullness of the life of God, given us in His Son.

We are just about to partake of the Holy Communion. In it we shall not only commemorate our Lord, but shall eat and shall drink of Him. The Lord Himself, through His minister, will give us, as He gave the apostles at that first Supper, the precious bread and wine which "is," to faith, His Body and His Blood. And so He will say to us upon the journey, as He will say hereafter and forever in the country above, "Because I live ye shall live also" [John 14:19].

38

Paul: Nearing the End

For I am already being poured out like a drink offering, and the time has come for my departure. I have fought the good fight, I have finished the race, I have kept the faith—2 Tim. 4:6, 7 (NIV)

Let us think of these words about Christian death spoken by this great Christian, Paul, close to his end. They have much to say, not for an apostolic martyr only, but for us also, the rank and file of what is yet, down to its least notable genuine member, "one army of the living God."

(1) "I am being poured out as a drink offering." Such to Paul was his impending death. For him, to be sure, the phrase had a dread particular fitness; when his death came it would come by the sword; the red torrent would flow, like the wine of the altar bowl, drenching the holocaust, enriching the sacrificial fume. But we need not bind the whole truth of the phrase to such a solemn literalism. Every devoted life, if it is really devoted—a word which means so much more than only devout—is a sacrifice offered on the altar of love to the God of our salvation, "a living sacrifice," as Paul long before (Rom. 12:1) had called it. And when that life, devoted to the last, reaches its climax in a death full of surrender to the will of God, the blood may not literally be shed, yet spiritually the death is none the less a libation which enriches all the antecedent toil and pain. John, sinking to sleep on his bed at Ephesus, truly "poured himself out" as Paul did when he knelt to die at the Three Fountains outside the gate of Rome. Bede, lying down after his life's long work in the cloister-school at Jarrow, "poured himself out" as truly, though in a

436

far different way, as Huss did in the fire at Constance. To all these saints life was "a living sacrifice," *even unto death*. So their death, their last outpouring of the vital power, yielded up to their God, was the libation upon the sacrifice.

May it be ours, through our Master's grace, so to be faithful *even unto the libation*. May we, in Him, "yield to the Lord, with simple heart," not only our full energies but also "ourselves, our souls and bodies," when they are weak and worn with mortal exercise. We adore His will; and that will *may* ordain that they should be "yielded" to Him rather as passive under pain or paralysis than as working on still, in some measure, in their decline. But however, by His grace, the spirit shall be willing to maintain its happy surrender even to the last—even till we "are being poured out."

(2) Then we have here another aspect of the death of the servant of the Lord: "the time has come for my departure." The word rendered "departure," *analusis*, is the Greek original of our "analysis." An analysis means a setting free, a detachment, a separation of things or thoughts from one another. The original noun here, like the kindred verb in Philippians 1:23, denotes the undoing of a connection, as it were the untying of a cord, the weighing of an anchor, so as to set the voyager free to seek the further shore. To the Philippians, in that earlier day, Paul had owned that his "desire" was "to unmoor, and to be with Christ" (Phil. 1:23). And here the desire is about to become fact; "the season of his unmooring is upon him."

It was no light thing, we may be sure, when this realization of that desire actually "came" on. It is nature, not sin, to shrink from death *as death*. The greatest saints, in their Lord's own words (John 21:18), when they come to die, are carried *"whither they would not"*; they are living men, *embodied* spirits; they would rather "not be unclothed, but clothed upon" (2 Cor. 5:4). But then there is the glorious other side, which filled Paul when he wrote Philippians 1:23, and which surely rose in conquering greatness before him now. The death which in one aspect was a last sacrifice was, in another, that delightful moment when the friendly flood heaves beneath the freed keel, and the prow is set straight and finally towards the shore of *Home*, and the Pilot stands on board, at length "seen face to face." And lo, as He takes

437

the helm, "immediately the ship was at the land whither they went" (John 6:21).

⁂

Two metaphors, under which Paul pictures his life's end, have just passed before us—the libation shed upon the altar; the boat unmoored from our mortal shore, set free to cross the narrow strait of death to the better land. Here he is metaphorical again, and the metaphors cover now not the end but the course, not martyrdom in prospect but life in retrospect. And here again, as in the previous verse, the old saint's mind goes back upon mental pictures dear in earlier days, and he sees again the struggling limbs and the swift feet of the Greek athletes. Life had long ago seemed to him to be vividly parabled by those scenes. In one great passage (1 Cor. 9:24–27) he had developed the illustration in minute and powerful detail; the stern discipline of training, the strict rules, the rejection which must follow an infraction, the straight eager course of the runners, the terribly purposeful blows of the boxers, the wreath of leaves, "corruptible" shadow of the amaranthine crown of the victorious Christian. Again and again, in other less conspicuous passages, he had used those familiar and eloquent associations to animate himself and his disciples to live true to the Lord, true to present grace and to coming glory. Once more here, yet once more, the *athlete of Christ* speaks the old dialect, but now with the accent of achievement and repose. He is so very near the end, so very much of the peculiar trial of his lot is forever over, the "journeyings often," "the care of all the Churches" (2 Cor. 11:26, 28), and so certain is his Master to love him and to uphold him over those few difficult paces before the end, that he speaks as if already off the field. Christ Jesus had enabled him so long for such a life that it was a relatively minor thing (may we not dare to say it?) to be sure that He would enable him, with a glorious adequacy, for the one last step of death.

39

"Pleasures Forevermore"

They shall be abundantly satisfied with the fatness of Thy house, and Thou shalt make them drink of the river of Thy pleasures—Ps. 36:8

The prayer for this Sunday is a prayer which seems to breathe and move with the thought of the heavenly love and the hope of the eternal joy. Its prayer that we may supremely love God is uttered as if by those who see heaven opened, and to whom the coming bliss is half revealed already. Let us think together, then, today of the offer and promise of joy, of gladness, of eternal pleasures, which God makes to the soul of man.

"Blessed are they that are called to the marriage supper of the Lamb." Yes, by that word, the marriage supper, the bridal feast—a thing meant to be so full of both actual and hoped-for happiness—the Lord sets forth the light of heaven. Heaven will be a scene of spotless holiness and eternal worship; a "city of solemnities," but also, and all the while, it will be an existence of vivid and innumerable pleasures, even "pleasures forevermore" [Ps. 16:9]—pleasures in which deep enjoyment and ardent expectation will form, as has been said, "one eternal feeling."

Let us quicken our remembrance that such is God's promise, by a few brief thoughts upon this passage of the Psalm. And may "the Lord God of the holy prophets" [Rev. 22:6] reveal to us indeed, in His own way some of the realities of these things to come.

What says the text? We may be very sure that it says what it says, ultimately, of heaven. Its words carry in them a precious truth for earth, I know. But we may be quite sure that not the psalmist, but the Holy

Ghost, has scattered words like these over the Old Testament to be read by us in the light of Christ Jesus. The full meaning given them in Him is their final, truest meaning. And in Him "life and immortality are brought to light" [see 2 Tim. 2:10]. The veil is rent, the gate opened, the way into eternity made plain. So now indeed to us, who have heard the word of Christ, such oracles of God as these glorious promises of the Psalms point to the eternal Home of joy.

What says, then, this heaven-revealing text?

(1) *"They* shall be abundantly *satisfied."*

Forget not who are meant by "they." You see this from the seventh verse. It is, "the children of men who put their trust under the shadow" of the eternal wings [Ps. 36:7]. It is those who find out the excellence, the preciousness, of God's lovingkindness. *They* shall be satisfied. They come to His shadow here; therefore shall they see His light hereafter. They come to taste His lovingkindness now; therefore shall they drink eternally of the river of His pleasures then.

But not all the children of men—would God it were so! Would God that all the souls which He has made would put their trust beneath His shadow. But do they? Do they obey Him when they hear of Him? Is it a law of nature that man sees beauty in God, to desire Him, and embrace Him, and love Him with adoring love? No, it is not. That is, it is not a law of our nature in its fall. Its law, its course, lies the other way. "The thought," the bent, "of the flesh"; "the carnal mind"; what is it, according to the Bible? It is "enmity against God."

The Bible has no absolute universal promise for all mankind. It has a universal invitation. It has a capacity to bless all that will come. But it has no promise, none, save its most faithful and merciful forewarnings, for those who will not come to Him to have life.

But they who do come, the weary, the sinful, the desponding but awakened souls that come to God in Jesus Christ—what of them?

They find, first, the lovingkindness and the reposeful peace promised in verse 7. They find here below that the Lord is gracious; they "taste" it, to use Peter's forcible word—so perfectly expressive of what is soberly meant by "Christian experience." They "sit down under His shadow." Amidst sins, and doubts, and fears, they yet *have found* a refuge and a rest which the world knows not of—till it comes to try. And. . . .

Then, secondly beyond the veil—God says it, the God who cannot lie—they are abundantly, overflowingly "satisfied" with the richness of His everlasting House. They drink of the river of His pleasures. They are filled from His well of life. They see light in His light.

(2) "Thou shalt make them drink of *the river* of Thy pleasures.

In this powerful and beautiful expression the Bible evermore sets out the life of heaven. It tells of "the streams of water" by which the Redeemer leads His people; "the living fountains of waters" [Rev. 7:17] to which the Lamb conducts the great multitude before the Throne; "the river of the water of life, clear as crystal, which flows from the Throne of God and of the Lamb" [Rev. 22:1]. Perhaps the thought has descended from Eden; from the river which flowed from Eden into the garden of God to water it for Adam's delight. But in any case the picture of unwearying joy thus given is marvelously bright and clear.

Such is the unimaginable blessedness of heaven. Such it is in its everlasting freshness; in its undeparting brightness; in its perpetual succession, while yet it is the same. Nothing, still nothing, but joy; pleasures—not pleasure only, but "pleasures—forevermore"; an inexhaustible fountain, still pouring out what will make each sensation of the eternal life a thrill of exceeding joy.

Ah, it is easy to speak of; it is not so easy to grasp it as a living hope. Sorrow, trial, care; losses, changes, fears; the anguish of sin in the saints themselves; these things are so interwoven with our inmost life that the heart seems often unable to believe that they are not inseparable from it; that the time will really come when the children of men who have come to the Lord's shadow, who have really fled to the Lord's refuge here, will really hereafter, and forever, experience nothing but the eternal feeling of intense and unmingled joy. Yet so it is. "They shall obtain joy and gladness, and sorrow and sighing shall flee away" [Is. 35:10]. The sufferings of the present time are not to be compared with the "eternal and exceeding weight of glory" [see 2 Cor. 4:7]. The servant enters not into his Mater's mercy only, but into his Master's "joy." He is "presented before the presence of His glory with exceeding joy" [Jude 1:24].

But all the joys will yet be one. All will be filled with the presence of the Lord. To all the living fountains the Lamb will lead them. To be with Him will rule and qualify the whole. *"Thou* shalt make them drink of the river of *Thy* pleasures."

Such is some faint outshadowing of the gift of God—eternal life. He indeed giveth liberally, and upbraideth not [see James 1:5]. Not one soul by that riverside but once deserved eternal death. But Jesus died, and the Spirit led to Jesus; and, to the praise of the Lamb who was slain, the sinner shall dwell securely in that eternity of joy.

And therefore it is an eternity open to "whosoever will" amongst us here this day. Each, in ourselves, we can claim only the merited exclusion. But each, through our Lord Jesus Christ, may really come and humbly claim the promised joy. Oh come, then, whosoever thirsteth, come ye to the waters—to the river that flows from the Throne of the Lamb. Whosoever will, let him take freely, for nothing, without money and without price, of the river of the water of the eternal life [see Is. 55:1].

40

Is Life Worth Living?

Being then made free from sin, ye became the servants of righteousness—
Rom. 6:18

The Apostle's aim in this whole passage is to awaken his readers, with the strong, tender touch of his holy reasoning, to articulate their position to themselves. They have trusted Christ, and are in Him. Then, they have entrusted themselves altogether to Him. Then, they have, in effect, surrendered. They have consented to be His property. They are the bondservants, they are the slaves, of His Truth—that is, of Him robed and revealed in His truth, and shining through it on them in the glory at once of His grace and of His claim. Nothing less than such an obligation is the fact for them. Let them fell, let them weigh, and then let them embrace, the chain which after all will only prove their pledge of rest and freedom.

What Paul thus did for our elder brethren at Rome, let him do for us of this later time.

He has appealed to the moral reason of the regenerate soul. Now he speaks straight to the will. You are, with infinite rightfulness, the bondmen of your God. You see your deed of purchase; it is the other side of your warrant of emancipation. Take it, and write your own unworthy names with joy upon it, consenting and assenting to your Owner's perfect rights. And then live out your life, keeping the autograph of your own surrender before your eyes. Live, suffer, conquer, labor, serve, as men who have themselves walked to their Master's door (Ex. 21:5, 6), and presented the ear to the awl which pins it to the doorway, each in his turn saying, "I will not go out free."

To such an act of the soul the Apostle calls these saints, whether they had done the like before or not. They were to sum up the perpetual fact, then and there, into a definite and critical act of thankful will. And he calls us to do the same today. By the grace of God, it shall be done. With eyes open, and fixed upon the face of the Master who claims us, and with hands placed helpless and willing within His hands, we will, we do, present ourselves bondservants to Him; for discipline, for servitude, for all His will.

"Is life worth living?" Yes, infinitely well worth, for the living man who has surrendered to "the Lord that bought him." Outside that ennobling captivity, that invigorating while most genuine bondservice, the life of man is at best complicated and tired with a bewildered guest, and gives results at best abortive, matched with the ideal purposes of such a being. We present ourselves to God, for His ends, as implements, vassals, willing bondmen; and lo, our own end is attained. Our life has settled, after its long friction, into gear. Our root, after hopeless explorations in the dust, has struck at last the stratum where the immortal water makes all things live, and grow, and put forth fruit for heaven. The heart, once dissipated between itself, and the world, is now "united" to the will, to the love, of God; and understands itself, and the world, as never before; and is able to deny self and to serve others in a new and surprising freedom. The man, made willing to be nothing but the tool and bondman of God, *"has his fruit"* at last; bears the true product of his now re-created being, pleasant to the Master's eye, and fostered by His air and sun. And this *"fruit"* issues, as acts issue in habit, in the glad experience of a life really sanctified, really separated in ever deeper inward reality, to a holy will. And the "end" of the whole glad possession is "life eternal."

Those great words here signify, surely, the coming bliss of the sons of the resurrection, when at last in their whole perfected being they will "live" all through, with a joy and energy as inexhaustible as its Fountain, and unencumbered at last and forever by the conditions of our mortality. To that vast future, vast in its scope, yet all concentrated around the fact that "we shall be like Him, for we shall see Him as He is" [1 John 3:2], the Apostle here looks onward. He will say more of it, and more largely, later, in the eighth chapter. But as with other themes, so with this, he preludes with a few glorious chords the great strain soon to come. He takes the Lord's slave by the hand, amidst his present tasks and burdens (dear tasks and burdens, because the Master's but still full of the conditions of earth), and he points upward—not to a coming emancipation in glory; the man would be dismayed to foresee that; he wants to "serve forever"—but to a scene of service in which the last remainders of hindrance to its action will be gone, and a perfected being will forever, perfectly, be not its own, and so will perfectly live in God. And this, so he says to his fellow servant, to you and to me, is *"the gift of God"* [Rom. 6:23]; a grant as free, as generous, as ever King gave vassal here below. And it is to be enjoyed as such, by a being which, living wholly for Him, will freely and purely exult to live wholly on Him, "in the heavenly places" [Eph. 1:20].

41

Walk in the Spirit

As ye have received Christ Jesus the Lord, so walk ye in Him—Col. 2:6
If we live in the Spirit, let us also walk in the Spirit: (or, more literally), "if
we live by the Spirit, by the Spirit let us also order our steps"—Gal. 5:25

These two texts I take in the closest connection, and the second I take in order to throw light on the message of the first. Three points we notice in it, and then pass back with them to the first passage.

(1) "By the Spirit we *order our steps.*" The word rendered "walk" here, in the Authorized Version, differs from that rendered "walk" in most passages; it means walking as to its detail—the particular steps, not merely the general course. We are reminded that in the Christian life nothing is unimportant, and that in nothing can we really afford to go alone. In detail as well as in general we need our Lord's holding and guiding power.

(2) "Let us order our steps *by the Spirit.*" The blessed Comforter has given us life. But He has not given His gift and gone away; He stays always beside us, to assist us in its use. We are to work out the gift—by the Giver's teaching and in the Giver's strength.

(3) Our first text speaks of the Lord Jesus, our second of the Holy Spirit. But these Two, in their divine being, and in their saving work, are One. Particularly the Holy Spirit, so it is revealed, delights to work in us by revealing and applying to us the Lord Christ Jesus. If we may say it with reverence, He "preaches not Himself but Christ Jesus the Lord"; He manifests Him, He guides us to Him, He makes us one spirit with Him. So the "walk" which from one point is a walk by the Spirit, from another point is a walk in Christ. We speak

446

then of Jesus Christ, and of walking in Him, but with the recollection that this walk is only possible for us through the working of the Holy Spirit.

And now we turn directly to Collossians 2:6.

(a) "*As ye have received* Christ Jesus the Lord." He refers here to their definite reception of "the truth once delivered to the saints" [see Jude 1:3]. They had heard the revelation made once for all; they had received and believed the truth as it is in Jesus Christ, who was in the eternal glory, who came as Man upon earth, who died, who rose, and "in whom is no variableness nor shadow of turning" [James 1:17], "the same yesterday and today and forever" [Heb. 13:8]. It was the one Lord Jesus Christ, God the Son of God, Light from the Eternal Light, who for us men and for our salvation came down from heaven, and was made Man, and was crucified for us, and rose again the third day, and is at the right hand of the father, and shall come again. Here is no shadowy Somewhat, shifting from age to age; it is "this same Jesus" [Acts 1:11].

Thus had they "received" Him, as their creed, their truth. But then also they had received Him in their heart, to be their life. He had come to them in spiritual reality and power, loving, changing, saving, ruling, in the inner man. So they were to fall back, not only on their first hearing, but on their first life in Jesus; the days of their remembered conversion "to newness of life" [Rom. 6:4].

My friends, let us also do this. When sore beset by the thousand currents of conflicting thought around us, let us fall back, each for himself, on our first experience of a dying and living Savior. Many a tempting voice will die away before that remembrance.

(b) "As they had received Him, *so let them now walk in Him*" [see Col. 2:6] "in" this unalterable Lord of glory, and of death, and of eternal life, they were to walk. What does he mean? The phrase sounds like folly, or like nothing, to the world. But to those who have got even a glimpse of Christ's fullness it speaks the very wisdom and the power of God. It is mystery, but it is fact, fact as present as it is definite. Do not banish it, as it were, to heaven. There indeed it will be developed into an eternal completeness, but the glory of it is begun below; the weakest believer is today in Christ, and is called to walk in Him. They were *"in Christ* before me," says Paul (Rom. 16:7),

447

speaking of friends in Rome who, like him, were then in the very midst of a world of sorrow, sin, and death. "In Christ"; not only near Him, but "in Him." The man who has come to His feet, and touched His garment—behold, he is joined to his Lord's living Body! The branch is in the Vine; the limb is articulated to the Head; the bride with the Bridegroom is forever one. Say it to yourself as a fact; "I, a sinner, have come through grace to my Redeemer; I am now in living reality His member, animated by His life, operated in by His will, instrument of His purposes; in Christ."

Well, then, *"so walk ye* in Him." What does this mean? It means *divine life applied.* You know the difference in science between the "pure" and the "applied"; the "pure mathematics" of figure and number in themselves, the "applied mathematics," where principles result in the practical triumphs of the engineer. Our test calls us to a union with Christ "applied"; to spiritual fact developed into action. *"Walk* ye in Him," do not sit still and muse, but walk. Take this wonderful union down into practice; bring this secret of the heaven of heavens to touch the earth of earth. In Virgil's great poem he represents his hero Aeneas traversing the streets of Carthage veiled in a magic invisibility. He walks in the place, but not of it, observing, but untouched. Imperfect as the parable is, it has something to say to us upon our holy theme. Walking in Christ, the Christian may tread this life's streets, spiritually screened, as it were, from "this present evil world" [Gal. 1:4]. "Thou shalt hide them in the secret of Thy presence" [Ps. 41:20], even "before the sons of men" [Ps. 31:19].

"Walk in Christ"; "order the steps by the Spirit." You shall find it possible then to tread over the hot ashes of the temptation to anger, and be at peace. You shall step with clean feet where otherwise you would plunge into the moral mire. The briers and the thorns of care and worry shall mysteriously be beaten down before you reach them. You shall "tread upon serpents, and scorpions, and over all the power of the enemy, and"—wonderful promise—"nothing shall by any means *hurt* you" [Luke 10:19].

42

The Net

Mine eyes are ever toward the Lord, for He shall pluck my feet out of the net—Ps. 25:15

Let us think awhile together of a certain Scripture parable of the spiritual life. Let us look at and handle the texture of the word "net" and then ask how to escape and how to avoid the thing it signifies. The word "net" is a word of definite imagery, and carries its own special lesson. One great requisite in a net is that it should be more or less concealed; it must be imperceptible to the victim as it lies hidden, in the grass, or among the bushes. And even when seen by eyes ignorant of its purpose, it is little to look at. It is slight, and, taken in detail, it is even weak. But it is so woven mesh into mesh that really it is formidably strong while perfectly elastic, as tenacious as it is in appearance frail.

The net is thus an apt parable of such spiritual risks and temptations as lie in the familiar path of every day, temptations which may come in the form of the commonest of our common incidents; small occasions for the loss of patience, or of purity of thought; small sparks to kindle pride or vanity; small excuses for sloth and self-indulgence; in short, petty opportunities to forget that we are not our own, and to allow ourselves in what is not according to the will of God. Yes, the nets *are* spread upon the path. The Christian who purposes to walk with God must look at the fact, and remember that they are there. And it is no small humiliation to remember how often our own hands have had to do with the weaving of these nets. Very often our past has been busy preparing them for our present; let that

449

thought warn us not to construct entanglements for tomorrow by spiritual slackness today.

And then, near the net, though out of sight, there stands the fowler. The great organizer of the forces of evil is there, the personal enemy ever on the watch to spread his snare for the soul.

Now, what shall we do with these things? Much is to be done, I do not forget it, which lies within the reach of our own thought and will. Much net-like difficulty may be precluded by common precautions taken in a Christian spirit, by avoidance at times of place, and company, and sight, and book, which has a plain tendency to mischief. But when we come to the inmost heart and depth of the matter we have after all to own that our deliverance, our "bringing out," will be a sadly imperfect thing if we look no higher for it than to our own action or caution. Temptation in its essence goes deep as the very springs of the will; deliverance, to be deliverance indeed, must go as deep. And in this respect there is only one effectual method. Wonderful, paradoxical, direction and prescription! *"Mine eyes are ever toward the Lord."*

What surprising imagery this is! Let not the Christian think that no effort is to be made, no earnest thought bent upon the feet and the net. But a yet "more excellent way" [1 Cor. 12:31] is needed to give efficacy to the effort and self-examination. It *is* a paradoxical secret, but it is a perfectly true one; if you want to get clear of the net which is entangling you, do not study its meshes; *look up* "unto the Lord." He is the Deliverer. He understands the net and the way out of it better than you do. Tempted Christian, entangled in the net of your own mistakes—there stands your Deliverer. He is not yourself. He is not an idea, a principle, an abstract truth. He is Jesus Christ.

What is the harassment, the net, in your path? Is it vanity? Is it pride? Is it ill-temper? Is it waste of the talent of time? Such nets are cunningly woven. They are formidably strong. They are a sore burden to drag, even for a mile along the road. Then make the revealed experiment of committing them to the Lord; He is able to deliver you from every net that Satan's industry and experience can weave. Make trial of Him, and you will find that the net is not so much plucked away as dissolved away from about your feet. His secret strength will so take possession of the heart given up to Him that you shall walk at liberty, treading on the net, finding the secret of His power.

43

When Life Is Too Difficult to Bear

And the angel of the Lord came again the second time, and touched him,
and said, Arise and eat, because the journey is too great for thee—
1 Kgs. 19:7

This verse occurs in one of those great scenes of Scripture which photograph themselves on the thought and on the soul. Elijah in his strength had triumphed on Mount Carmel, and lorded it as more than king and nation, in his Master's name. But now comes the contrast; we see a man frightened, helpless, utterly discouraged, scared away by a mere message from the scene of this glorious victory. That message was a strange piece of evil insight on the part of Jezebel. She must have divined that the strong man would be *weak with reaction;* so she launched her threat, in all its impious daring, on the very morrow of the victory; and behold—Elijah feared, arose, and fled. Down through Israel, down to the utmost southern edge of Judah (thinking, perhaps, that the house of Jehoshaphat would not effectually protect him from their kinsman Ahab); onward, onward he goes, into the deep wilderness, shrinking from even the presence of his servant, till at last he lies down in the exhaustion of despair.

It is a *teaching* picture, drawn for our learning. Elijah was a giant in spiritual strength, BUT he was so only in his God. In himself, he was, like every other man save but One, mortal, sinful, ready to halt and fall. And this, we seem to gather, he had been tempted to forget. Listen to his groan beneath the juniper: "I am not *better than my fathers*" [v. 4]. Who had told him that he was? Does not this show us what had been the whisper of the tempter into the ear of self-love? The subtle enemy had drawn him out of strength into weakness, because out of God into self-esteem. So still it is, when the Christian, however greatly used for God, listens to the falsehood which exalts himself. He takes then the surest path to total defeat, to deepest mortification. Again and again the Lord shows His people that it is so. When they are weak, then they are strong, BUT when in themselves they seem strong, then they are weak.

But there is another side to the picture. Look from the servant, prostrate and despairing, to the Almighty and all-tender Master. He who is never weak entered into the weakness of His servant. He whose sympathy is measured by His eternity understood Elijah, and did not cast him off. He was patient with Him, and wonderfully tender. He felt for the exhausted frame and harassed nerves. And He saw to it that Elijah first received the blessed gift of sleep, and then not only sleep but food. The "cake baken on the coals, and the cruse of water," were the Lord's provision. He who had lifted Elijah so far aloft in spirit never forgot that he was in the body. "He knew his frame, and remembered that he was dust."

Again, we have here a parable of the grace of God in the Christian life. "The journey is too great for thee." Yes, Elijah was *to walk* from Beersheba to Horeb; a little today, a little tomorrow, through the grim wilderness of Paran. How was he to go! He was already tired out. Vain now was the iron will and the indomitable resolution. He needed a revival of strength from outside; and his Lord gave him, accordingly, something better than his own resources. The Angel brought him angels' food, and he had enough meat. He had but to rise, and eat, and behold he could do the impossible; he could get to the Mount of God.

We too have a journey to travel, a hill to reach. We are not yet there, but on the way; not yet in the street of gold within the gate, but on the path of the pilgrimage—which is indeed one of piece with its end, for both road and end are Jesus Christ, BUT the experience is widely different in the two. And the journey, do you not sometimes feel that it is too great for you? You think of next year, of next week, of tomorrow. "How shall I persevere, how shall these feeble feet ever reach the courts above? I shall one day perish by the enemy's hand; the journey is too great for me." Yes, but your Lord also knows it, and He says to you, "I understand it all; I bid thee go, not in your strength but mine. I bid thee, first, not walk but feed"; "arise and eat"; and the Lord Himself is the living food. You remember the sixth chapter of John, and that great discourse where the true "Angel of the Covenant" seems to stand by all His people and to say, "The journey is too great for you; arise and eat," "he that eateth me shall live by me" (v. 57). Faith is the lips and the throat by which that food is taken. But the power is not in lips or throat; it resides in the wonderful food. It is His part to make thee strong. Jesus Christ, unseen but ever with thee, in thee, is thy life. Wholly trusted, He can give victory and triumph, so that the traveler shall not merely drag his feet to the end of the journey, but "shall walk and not faint," and shall stretch a strong hand out to others, leading them to the heavenly meat. And at last he shall climb the hill, not with feet, but on wings.

The journey of *life* is too great for thee. So, too, is the journey of *death;* not indeed in its length, but in its depth of unutterable change. It is but a step, but it is through a cloud, thin but awfully opaque. It is not distance but difference that makes *that* path too great for thee. But it is not too great for Him who is the Bread of life which cometh down from heaven, and who must ascend again thither with all that feed on Him. "My flesh and my heart faileth; the journey is too great for me; Thou knowest it, O my Master, but Thou art the strength of my heart, and my portion forever. Thou wilt guide me, and then receive me with glory."

44

The "Valleys" of Life

*The Syrians have said, The Lord is God of the hills, but He is not God of
the valleys—1 Kgs. 20:28*

You remember the incident to which these words belong. It was
that remarkable time when God visited in mercy His stricken Israel,
not long after the great drought which ended with the sacrifice on
Carmel. The Syrians invaded the country, just when the Hebrew
forces were reduced to zero, and everything seemed ready to be
swept away. It was an awful moment, not only as being dreadful in
itself, but as coming after a time of sin, judgment, and mercy, and
then (after Elijah's flight) a time of failure again. Yet even then the
Lord remembered His people, and put His power upon their side,
and they won a glorious victory in Him. The victory came in two
parts. The first battle was on the highlands of Israel. The Syrians
seem to have thought that Israel's national God was a mountain
Spirit, and that if they only could get their enemies to meet them on
the broad plain of Jezreel, where Israel had often been defeated before, they would carry all before them; the mountain God could not
help His tribes upon the level ground! Then the Lord sent His
prophet to say that He was jealous for His glory; His enemies should
feel that He was as strong below as above; down in the plain Israel
should triumph in Him.

I see in this history a word to us in regard to the hills and valleys,
not of Palestine, but of life. Human life has its hilltops, alike in nature, and in grace. Whatever of itself tends to uplift or gladden us,
and make us feel strong, is one of life's hills. There is the hill of

youth, with its glorious possibilities and boundless hopes; there is the hill of strength and health, when we begin day by day with a buoyant enjoyment of our work; there is the hill of success; there is the green flowery hill of a happy home. In spiritual things there is the hilltop of "first love," the hilltop of a glad discovery of our Lord. There is the hilltop of the Lord's Day and of the House of God; there is the hilltop of the Holy Table, spread, spiritually, on the utmost heights aloft. Now of all these hilltops the Lord is God. Hours of brightness and joy, natural as well as spiritual, belong to Him. He claims to be present in our sunshine quite as much as in our shadows; and the sunshine is safe as He can make them if we walk on them with Him.

But life has its valleys as well as its hills. And of these too there are many sorts. Life sinks into a dark pass sometimes, in great anxieties, or bitter disappointments; or it becomes an "Achor," in which you are convinced of sin, as Israel was in Achan's woeful case. The Lord takes you down there, to show you to yourself. He puts His finger on the sins of tongue, or temper, or spirit, or deed. He makes past iniquities awfully real to you, till you cry out, "What shall I do to be saved?" [see Acts 16:30]. Or He leads you through a valley of tears, as some dear one is taken from your side, and the shadow of death is upon you; or He brings you to that Valley of Humiliation, of which the *Pilgrim's Progress* speaks, and into which most of us find it (as Christian found it) hard to go down. Or—and this is what the history speaks of most pointedly—life looks to you not so much like a deep valley as like a broad, open plain, hot and featureless, where the land is flat and the air is faint. Your life seems full of uninteresting duties, things of the earth, earthy, and you have to plod on from hour to hour with no positive helps to your Christian life, and, perhaps, exposed to actual opposition in the way of your walk with God.

But now, God is the God of the valleys. In the passage before us He makes it the great point that He *is* the God of the valleys. The hills may be taken for granted, BUT He is jealous for His glory in the lowlands, the dangerous plains where the fatigue is, and the hot air, and the malaria of the marsh, and where also the Syrians hope to bring their forces best into action. What does the valley represent to you and to me? Is it imaged to us by the valley? It belongs to the

Lord. That strait pass where you know not how to turn, into which He seems to have shut you up, it belongs to Him; if you have made a covenant with Him, He will keep it with you even there. He is the God of the valley of Achor, into which your treachery towards Him, and your defeat because of it, have brought you; He can meet you even there; such a valley is often a great opportunity for divine mercy. Or is your "valley" the open plain of common life and plodding hours, the "secular" things which you are obliged to do? The Lord is the God of these also. Read the many words in Paul's Epistles addressed to Christian slaves. They had to do precisely the same outward duties after their conversion as before; nevertheless they were to find that God was the God of the plain; He could glorify it into a scene of triumph; it could all be done as "unto Him." If God made the Christian bondservant of those days more than a conqueror, can He not do the like for you? Tomorrow, when we are not in the sanctuary of God, but in the shop, or in the study, or in the daily round of most ordinary life at home, we shall find Him the God of the valley, and we shall find it good to be there. Then, when the plain slopes down into that last valley which leads to the river's brink, He will be the God of that valley too. He will lead you all the way across, till you come to the Highlands of the other side, where you shall live aloft forever with the God of the Heavenly Hills.

45

Trust God and Nothing Else

So Gehazi followed after Naaman—2 Kgs. 5:21

Our first Lesson this morning is chiefly occupied with the story of Naaman. That story is one of the most striking in the whole Bible, as an illustration of gospel truth. In itself it is extraordinarily full of life and vivid interest, as we read of the little girl, the Israelitish captive, made the means of guiding her Syrian master to the divine remedy for his disease; and then as we read of the perplexity and fear of the ungodly Hebrew king, who saw nothing but political treachery when Naaman came with his money and his letter; and then in the grand figure of Elisha, the more than kingly prophet, rebuking his own king for unbelieving fear, and afterwards, without fear or favor, prescribing to Naaman the plain, prosaic, humiliating cure of a sevenfold bath in Jordan. Naaman's vehement offense at first, and then his frank obedience, and cure, and gratitude, and faith—all come before us as things which we seem rather to see than to read of; so powerful is the absolute simplicity of the Scripture story.

But there is another story in the chapter, the story of Gehazi; and it is to this that I ask your earnest attention now. It is full of teaching, of reproof, and warning, and "instruction in righteousness" [2 Tim. 3:16].

What do we know of Gehazi? We read of him in three main passages; and the first is chapter 5:12, where he is named as a servant, or personal attendant, of Elisha; just as Elisha had served Elijah, and Joshua had served Moses. He had lived for years in an air of holi-

458

ness, and truth, and self-denial; he had walked with the pure—should he not be pure? With the holy—should he not be holy?

Up to that time, apparently, he *had* maintained a pious appearance; otherwise Elisha, so zealous for God's honor, would scarcely have kept Gehazi so near him.

Nevertheless, when Naaman turned away, Gehazi—just fresh from the miracle—thought only of the money that Elisha had declined. He instantly framed an ingenious lie, actually using the Lord's name in the matter: "As the Lord liveth, I will take somewhat of him" [v. 20]. He took full advantage of Naaman's utter lack of suspicion. He accepted on false pretenses about seven hundred pounds worth of property; hid it in the tower, or storehouse; and went in to look Elisha in the face, with a fresh lie ready as his screen. We all know his bitter punishment. Alas, we do not know whether it worked repentance, and whether, though his "flesh" was "destroyed," his "spirit" shall be found "saved in the day of the Lord" [see 1 Cor. 5:5].

Gehazi's case speaks aloud to every one of us who has ever had the least consciousness of the dark power of inbred sin; it warns us *never* to trust anything less than the very reality of God's own grace to overcome it. Yes, it speaks to us one by one, and bids us to beware. "Beware, O hearer of the gospel? No outward ordinances ever yet shut out the deceitfulness of sin. The will and thought can run riot in the sanctuary of God; yea, at the Table of the Savior. No holy connections ever yet shut out the deceitfulness of sin. It is possible to despise and reject and exclude the Lord even when you daily see Him glorified in the lives of His people; even when those people are your heart's own beloved."

What shall we do? Is it all meant to teach us to despair? No, brethren; the very opposite. It is meant, if it may be, to drive us from false refuges to the everlasting arms, to the sure refuge, to the Almighty influence, even to the Lord Jesus and to the Spirit of our God. It is to warn—but also to invite us with love divine. It is to say to the soul that knows its sin a little, but not its Savior: Trust nothing else, nothing less than a real coming, your very self, to Christ. Ask nothing else, nothing less, than a real visitation of the Holy Spirit, to expose and to subdue your iniquities, by making plain to you your Redeemer's preciousness. Use every means indeed, BUT mistake none of them for the fountain. Acquaint yourself with Him, and you shall *not* "be hardened by the deceitfulness of sin" [Heb. 3:13]. And it says always, to the very end, to the awakened and believing, "Take heed. No past experience, no present privilege, no service to Elisha, nor to Elisha's Lord, will ever do to keep down the traitor and keep out the enemy. Daily—now as ever, and so to the end—you must clasp your Lord's right hand, you must take home your Lord's presence, you must welcome your Lord's indwelling, which alone can overcome the deceitfulness of sin. To the end of the day, as in its morning hour, you must be washed, you must be sanctified, only in the name of the Lord Jesus and by the spirit of our God."

46

The Christian's Aims, Limits, and Possibilities

We aim at nothing less than to walk with God all day long; to abide every hour in Christ; to love God with all the heart, and our neighbor as ourselves; to live, and that in no conventional sense, "no longer to ourselves, but to Him who died for us and rose again" (2 Cor. 5:15).

We aim to yield ourselves to God" as the unregenerate will yields itself to sin, to self; to have "every thought brought into captivity to the obedience of Christ" [see 2 Cor. 10:5]. In the region of outward life our aim is to break with all evil, and follow all good. It is never, nevermore to speak evil of any man; never to lose patience; never to trifle with wrong, whether impurity, untruth, or unkindness; never in any known thing to evade our Master's will, never to be ashamed of His name. This is our aim, not in any conventional sense, such as to leave us easy and tolerably comfortable when we fail. Not so; God forbid. Failure when it comes across this aim will come with the pang of a shame and disappointment which we shall little wish to feel again. It will be a deeply conscious discord and collision; it will be the missing of a divine smile, the loss of "the light of the king's countenance" [Prov. 16:15]. The Christian's aim is bound, absolutely bound, to be nothing less than this—"Let the words of my mouth, and the meditation of my heart, be acceptable in thy sight, O LORD, my strength, and my redeemer" [Ps. 19:14]. We are absolutely bound to put quite aside all secret purposes of moral compromise; all tolerance of besetting sin, for the sad reason that it is

461

besetting. With open face we behold the glory of the Lord, and ask to be changed at any cost, all around the circle of life, into the same image. We cannot possibly rest short of a daily, hourly, continuous walk with God, in Christ, by the grace of the Holy Ghost.

But I come to speak briefly of the *limits.* I mean, of course, not limits in our aims, for there must be none, nor limits in divine grace itself, for there are none, but limits, however caused, in the actual attainment by us of Christian holiness. Here I hold, with absolute conviction, alike from the experience of the Church and from the infallible Word, that, in the mystery of things, there will be limits to the last, and very humbling limits, very real fallings short. To the last, it will be *a sinner* that walks with God. To the last will "abide in the regenerate" that strange tendency, that "mind of the flesh," which eternal grace can wonderfully deal with, but which is a tendency still. To the last, the soul's acceptance before the Judge is wholly and only in the righteousness, the merits, of Christ. To the last, if we say we have no sin, we deceive ourselves [1 John 1:8]. In the pure, warm sunshine of the Father's smile shed upon the loving and willing *child,* that child will yet say, "Enter not into judgment with Thy *servant"* [Ps. 143:2]. Walking in the light as He is in the light, having fellowship with Him, and He with us, we yet need to the last the blood of Calvary, the blood propitiation, to deal with sin.

Then, lastly, come up into view the sacred *Possibilities* of the matter. It is possible, I dare to say, for those who will indeed draw on their Lord's power for deliverance and victory, to live a life—how shall I describe it? A life in which His promises are taken as they stand, and found to be true. It is possible to have affections and imaginations purified through faith, in a profound and practical sense. It is possible to see the will of God in everything, and to find, it, as one has said, no longer a sigh, but a song. It is possible in the world of inner act and motion to put away, to get put away, *"all* bitterness, and wrath, and anger, and evil speaking" [Eph. 4:1], daily and hourly. It is possible, by unreserved resort to divine power, under divine conditions, to become strongest, through and through, at our weakest point; to find the things which yesterday upset all our obligations to patience, or to purity, or to humility, an occasion today, through Him who loveth us and worketh in us, for a joyful consent to His will and a delightful sense of His presence and sin-annulling power. These are things divinely possible. And, because they are His work, the genuine experience of them will lay us, must lay us, only lower at His feet, and leave us only more athirst for more. May I ask each reader of these pages to pause here with the heart question, "How high goes my own conscious aim, and what, as to the possibilities of grace, are my personal expectations?" And will he add a prayer? "Thou, Lord, who knowest my heart, all its desire and all its need, show me what Thou art able to do with it, and do what Thou art able; through Jesus Christ. Amen."

47

"Take Your Burdens to the Lord"

Hezekiah received the letter from the hand of the messengers and read it;
and Hezekiah went up unto the house of the Lord and spread it out before
the Lord—Is. 37:14

Since David's time God's chosen people have seen sadly many
"changes and decays." They have been misled under Solomon by
earthly splendor and power. They have been dislocated under Re-
hoboam into two hostile sections, and the hope of the old political
power and prestige of David is gone forever. And now the northern kingdom, so long the seat of open idolatry, is swept away by the
Assyrian, and the narrow bounds of Judah are entered and occupied by the legions of Nineveh. The arrogant invader has already
sent across the country from Lachish a detached force to summon
Jerusalem. They have uttered their contemptuous invitations to surrender, and the king, as he hears what has been said, has "rent his
clothes and covered himself with sackcloth" [2 Kgs. 19:1], and has
sent to Isaiah, and received from him a brief answer of good hope.
But the storm gathers again. Hezekiah receives this time, from the
same or similar terrible couriers, sent now from Libnah, not a
speech but a letter. And it is this letter that this week's meditation
pertains to. It is a very searching test of peace and faith to open
some letters. Certainly it was so for Hezekiah when in that dark
time he undid Sennacherib's epistle and "read it," read it over with
his own eyes. It was sad reading. It was a coarse and insolent assertion that Hezekiah's God was a deceiver. Not that He was a nonen-
tity; that was not the heathen's line of thought. Jehovah was in his

eyes a god, one of the miscellaneous pantheon of the nations, merely on the level of the tutelary power around him, the gods of Gozan and Haran, and of the Hittites at Sepharvaim on the great river. *They* had gone down before the Assyrian and his gods, and so would the god of small and feeble Judah go down also.

Let us not forget the tremendous trial of faith involved in such words spoken at that time. Assyrian paganism then, to every eye but that of faith, was a power enormously greater than that of Judah and its worship. In science and culture, as well as in military weight and force, Assyria was to Judah somewhat as Germany now would be matched against Portugal [pre-World War I]. All the conditions of the case, in the order of nature, made that letter look like the sure and certain announcement of an inevitable and most terrific ruin.

But Hezekiah does not sit down to lament and to despond. He feels the savage wound; he feels it in the depth of his soul. But he takes it straight to the Divine Healer. Without one hint of delay, the narrative tells us that he "went up into the house of the Lord, and spread it before the Lord." He had "spread it" once already before his own eyes, to read the syllables traced by Sennacherib's scribe. Now he spread it out again, and, as it were, presented it to his unseen King, that He too, with full and special attention, might see, word for word, what the heathen autocrat had been saying about Him.

As he holds it out to those eyes, he speaks with reverent freedom to those ears—he owns that the facts of the letter are true; the pagan *has* destroyed the nations, and burned their gods. But he repudiates the inference. These gods are no gods at all. Now let Jehovah deign to show Himself what He is—the Supreme, the Eternal, the Creator; "that all the kingdoms of the earth may know that Thou art Jehovah, God, even Thou only" [see 2 Kgs. 19:19; Is. 37:30].

We do not read that any mystic voice of music, or of thunder, answered Hezekiah from within Solomon's sanctuary. But a supernatural reply did come, through human agency. A messenger soon reached the king from the house of Isaiah, and brought another writing in his hand. It was Jehovah's dictated response to Sennacherib's epistle, promising the deliverance which "that night" was wrought by the Angel of Death in the vast camp at Libnah.

Such was Hezekiah's communication with God that critical day in the Temple court. What do we see in it, as a message to ourselves? We see an example, vivid and most noble in its aspect, of the way in which the believing Christian is to "cast his care upon the Lord" [1 Pet. 5:7], to "make known his requests" [Phil. 4:6] at dark and perplexing times. Does not the case answer to a great deal in the experience of Christians called to meet the real duties and difficulties of "this troublesome world"? The trying *letter* we may occasionally receive is but an instance of numberless possible trials which we are to "spread before the Lord." Take them all to Him. Take the book that has troubled your faith, take the temptation that has so easily and so successfully beset you, take the anxious phenomena of Church, of State, of World, of Family, which come before your mind's eye like threatening letters from the powers of evil, full of omens of defeat; and spread them out before Him who understands how to meet them, every one, with solutions and acts of deliverance beyond all your hopes. And do not forget *where* Hezekiah carried the letter and spread it before the Lord's eyes; "into the Temple of the Lord" [Luke 1:9]. The true archetype to the Temple of old is nothing less than our incarnate Lord Jesus Christ, the veritable, the historical, the objective "Man, Christ Jesus"; "Image of the Invisible God," yet actual Man; as truly a figure of history as Augustus, or Charlemagne, yet also One with the Eternal Father above all time; as truly our Human Friend as ever a mother was to her little child, yet also our Sacrifice for sins and, in the literal fact of His Resurrection, Conqueror of death. He is Altar, Sacrifice, Ark, Shechinah, Temple. We must take the troublesome letter, the bewildering book, the anxious event, the serious state of things, to God in Him. We must spread it out before God in truths and blessings. And so we shall await the answer in peace, and see the thing we dreaded trodden down already under the feet of our faithful God.

48

Nehemiah's Fellowship with God

Then the king said unto me, For what dost thou make request? So I prayed to the God of heaven—Neh. 2:4

It is a story of "silent providence" which we have before us in the book of Nehemiah. Not one miracle is recorded in it, nor in its companion book of Ezra. But not the less impressive, therefore, is the teaching of those books on the possibility and the blessing of direct fellowship with God.

"So I prayed to the God of Heaven." Here is our point for study. We have here before us a human heart in sudden and instantaneous communion with God. Nehemiah speaks in our presence to his heavenly Master, asking for guidance at a moment of crisis in his path. And his act of communion with God is full of instruction for us, in its character, its circumstances, and its conditions.

Its Character—It was as brief and as *ejaculatory* as possible. It took place between a question and its answer. "'For what dost thou make request?' 'If it please the king, and if thy servant have found favor in thy sight, that thou wouldest send me unto Judah, unto the city of my fathers' sepulchers, that I may build it. . . . So it pleased the king to send me, and I set him a time" [vv. 5, 6].

Nehemiah's prayer must have been the work of moments; not so long as a minute; for a minute makes a long and embarrassing interval in a conversation, however intimate and free; and this conversation was very far from being such. It was a prayer, for certain, offered in silence. Even as a matter of policy, Nehemiah would scarcely have made his anxiety (which was great; see v. 31) prominent to the

467

king's mind, as an audible petition to his God would have made it. And anywise, such praying aloud would have been a dangerous anomaly. In a moment, in silence, the petition was formed, presented, attended to, and answered.

Let us also learn the art of such quick communications with the Throne. We are invited to them by the assurance of more than instantaneous *attention;* "Before they call, I will answer, and while they are yet speaking, I will hear" (Is. 65:24).

Its Circumstances—It is the banqueting-hall of the enormous palace of the Persian, in the festal hour, before the great king and his queen; the splendid representatives of the vast world-power which at that moment held in absolute vassalage, as in the hollow of its giant hand, the People of the Covenant. Everything around him would go to make Nehemiah "look not at the things unseen but at the things seen" [1 Cor. 4:18], and to direct his whole thought, whether for hope or despair, upon the human forces around him and their earthly magnificence and mastery.

But it was otherwise with Nehemiah. As truly as Moses before him, "he endured, as seeing Him who is invisible" [Heb. 11:27], and as holding fellowship with Him. The Persian Empire and its emperor vanishes from between Him and his God, and leaves the air clear for the soul's instantaneous cry, and for the silent answer to it.

If we are "found in Him," we shall find ourselves as free to hold fellowship with Him in the most crowded and the most distracting scene of secular existence, so it be our duty to be there, as in the upper chamber, or the twilight field. Free, silent instantaneous— the communication shall be real indeed.

Its Conditions—Here let us refer back to the first chapter of Nehemiah's simple book. What do we see there? We see the same man in fellowship with God *behind the scenes.* And that was no casual or lightly intermitted process of fellowship. He "sat down and wept, and mourned certain days, and fasted, and prayed before the God of Heaven" [Neh. 1:4]; pouring out a confession and a petition full of the details of the woe, and sin, and need. His soul was in antecedent contact, conscious and ample, with his God; therefore he was ready to touch Him so instantaneously in the moment of his crisis.

The message to us is self-evident. It is our first and continual duty to seek our eternal Friend, persistent, humbly, fully, in all the detail of confidence, behind life's curtains.

Then, when we have to walk in front of them, "before the sons of men" [Ps. 31:19], we shall not be taken by surprise; we shall know how, in an inner secrecy, and with a blessed certainty, to "make our requests known to God" [Phil. 4:6].

49

Never Alone

I am the Almighty God; walk before me, and be thou perfect—Gen. 17:1

These were the Lord's words to Abraham when Abraham was ninety-nine. It was a time of sore trial to his faith. The years rolled on, and he was childless still. Yet the hope of the world depended upon the child of the promise yet unfulfilled. Then came this message; the Lord appeared and spoke; how, we know not, only we know that it was revelation, not reverie; not Abraham's idea, but God's own utterance to his spirit. The Master spoke to the servant, and led him away from his anxieties, above them and beyond them, to himself, the Almighty God, or (to render *El Shaddai* more exactly), the all-resourceful God, the all-sufficient God; a word including all power, but giving life and tenderness with it besides. And withal He led him away to the peaceful thought of a quiet service under the Master's eye, carried on in a single-hearted fidelity. "Walk before Me, and be thou perfect," perfect in thy will to walk. This would be the best possible secret for a peaceful trust in his master's promise.

We will not now consider further the case of Abraham, though it will deepen our thought on the text to remember the circumstances under which it was spoken. I take the words now as one of those great Scriptures which we may lawfully study apart and in themselves. I take it as the text for some simple meditations upon the walk of the servant of God.

Here we have before us both thoughts—the servant and the walk. The word "walk" speaks for itself, and the word "servant" lies hidden

470

in the phrase, "Walk *before me,*" which gives us the idea of the life-work carried on in a sovereign presence under a "great Taskmaster's eye." It is not, "Walk *with* me," nor again, "Walk *in* me," as in that wonderful word of Paul's, "As ye have therefore received Christ Jesus the Lord, so *walk ye in* Him" [Col. 2:6]. It is "Walk *before* me." The phrase is not infrequent in the Scriptures. Long years afterwards Abraham used it to Eliezer, speaking with the happiness of a clear conscience before God; "The Lord before whom I walk" [Gen. 24:40]. Later again, Jacob, at the end of his days, recalling the holy past, speaks of "Him before whom my fathers, Abraham and Isaac, did walk" [Gen. 48:15]. In the Prophets and in the Psalms it occurs again and again: "I will walk before the Lord in the land of the living" [Ps. 116:9]; "in the light of the living" [Ps. 56:13]. Everywhere its bearing appears to be the same; it is the thought of a surrendered life lived in the presence of its Possessor.

So here we have that great truth of the Scriptures, that redeemed man is the servant of his God, not in the sense of hiring and contract, not in the sense of duty rendered on a terminable arrangement, nor, again, of a service done merely because it is personally agreeable to the doer. No; in Scripture almost invariably the idea is connected with bondservice; the man *belongs,* and is therefore at the disposal of his Possessor; his Master has all rights over him, and he has none against his Master. "Bought with a" mighty "price," he is altogether "not his own" [1 Cor. 6:19, 20].

"Servant of God." It is a glorious word, so glorious that Scripture often reserves it for the very greatest of the saints. Moses, who knew God face to face, is distinctively called "the bondservant of God." The Apostles, inmost friends of God Incarnate, delight to call themselves, "bondservants of Jesus Christ." Shall we not covet the same title, or rather love it, for it is already ours? "Yes, Lord, I am not only Thy worshiper, Thy adherent, the reciter of the creed of Thy glory, the bearer of the name of Thy people. I am personally Thy property, I walk before Thee, Thou Almighty One, as Thine own,"

Such self-surrender seems, perhaps, a forbidding thing from outside, BUT try it, and it will prove far different from within. From without, it is like the gray, rocky wall of some stern castle, to be entered only through the guarded door. But you enter, and the castle is a palace, and its garden is a paradise, and the Master walking in it trans-figures Himself into your most tender Friend. But you must enter in to know; you must accept the service to find it "perfect freedom."

Meanwhile, this great truth never stands alone. The servant of God, His absolute property, is never merely His servant. He also is always His "son that serveth Him" (Mal. 3:17).

But now we come to the word "walk." It is a metaphor very fre-quent in Scripture. A concordance will show you this at a glance. What does it mean? It means life viewed in its active occupations; not so much as a journey (though this thought is not absent) as a scene of duties in which the worker moves from hour to hour, to and fro, and in and out. The servant is at work in his Master's domain. Un-hasting, he is yet unresting, looking always for the next thing to do. His loins are girded, he is not loitering, nor dreaming; he *walks* be-fore his Master's face. He does this anywhere and everywhere. In his most solitary hour and in his most public hour, in the home, in the shop, in the field, on the journey, in the collage, he walks, ready for the Master's will, "before the master's face."

"Walk before me, and be thou perfect," be thou single-hearted. The words carry a double message straight to our lives; a message of searching, and also of holy joy. First they say, "Christian, you are never alone for a moment; in the most secret spot, in the most se-cret thought, you are never alone; you are followed about as surely by that present sight and hearing as you are followed about by the air you breathe and by the ground you tread."

> Set God before thee; every word
> Thy lips pronounce by Him is heard;
> Oh! couldst thou realize that thought,
> What care, what caution would be wrought!

Yes, let it bear on the use of your tongue, on the use of your time, on the use of your example; you are never out of sight or out of hearing of the Holy One, to whom you belong. Let the whole weight of that fact tell upon your soul. Do not live with your back to your Master; meet His eye with a look which says, "I know that I am Thine, and that Thou art here."

But then the same thought comes with its blessing and its joy. Whose gaze and hearing is it that follows you about? Is He indeed "an austere man," standing in the shadows with a cold eye bent on you while you are toiling in the sun? No, this everlasting Observer is the everlasting Friend, to whom you are infinitely dear. Yes, infinitely, for you are a member of His dear Son. He sticketh closer than the noblest brother; He is immeasurably your kindest Friend. You are not only near Him, you are in Him, by union with His Christ; that union which is not only a majestic arrangement, but an embrace, close and tender beyond your thought. So walking before Him, you are indeed, in a sense most sacred, never alone. In the deepest loneliness, never alone; under the heaviest discouragements, never alone; toiling in a cold mist of circumstances, yet never alone. You live, you bear, you work, in the sweet secret place of an everlasting union; one with Him who does indeed entirely own you, but takes an interest untold in you, His property; delights in your nearness to Himself, and holds you by His own right hand.

50

"Walk in the Light"

If we walk in the light, as He is in the light—1 John 1:7
Come ye, and let us walk in the light of the Lord—Is. 2:5

You remember how the verse which forms my first text ends; "We have fellowship one with another, and the blood of Jesus Christ, His Son, cleanseth us from all sin." That is to say, where there is this walk in the light, there the Lord and His servant indeed have communion together; and then (a promise specially needful where a "walk in the light" brings even the specks of defilement into view) the atoning blood avails evermore for the disciple's acceptance, and procures evermore for him the gift of the promised Spirit to subdue his iniquities.

"If we walk in the light." What is the special suggestion of that phrase? It sets before us two main conceptions; a walk in the light as to illumination, and a walk in the light as to joy.

(1) To walk in the light is to live, move, and act as those who see things around them as they are, instead of under the veils and overshadowing of self-deception and self-will. In this connection take special note of the words, "as He is in the light." How is God in the light? In this respect, that He sees all things exactly as they are, without a mist, cloud, refraction, or distortion. He sees His own eternal Being just as He is; His own infinite glory is present to Him as the most absolute of facts, necessary, infinite, all beautiful and all good.

Again, the Father sees the Son just as He is. "No one knows the Son but the Father" [Matt. 11:27]. It demands an infinite insight fully to understand Christ. The deepest sighted believer here, to whom the Lord Jesus is most precious, has but touched from the shore the waters of His glory; only to the Father's infinite sight that infinite ocean is all known.

Again, God sees sin just as it is, and as no other eye can see it. He sees it as the "abominable thing that He hates" [see Jer. 44:4], the harsh and horrible discord with His will. To Him it is no "fall upward," no painful process of development, as some would take it now to be. It is never anything but condemnable, whether it be sin manifest and outrageous, or sin silent and quite in secret.

Again, thanks be to Him, He sees the atoning Sacrifice just as it is. To Him the "bleeding glories" of Calvary are seen as infinitely and forever satisfying and pleasing; "worthy" indeed in His eyes is "the Lamb that was slain" [Rev. 5:12], perfect and eternal before Him is the redemption wrought out by the blood of the Cross. And He sees the power of His Spirit and the possibilities of His grace just as they are. He sees in their wonderful fullness the deliverance, rest, and power laid up in Christ, to be given to faith by the Spirit's touch.

Now, if we are to "walk in the light, *as He is in the light,*" we see thus in measure what this means. We are to step as it were into the Lord's field of vision, and to accept with willing eyes His light upon things as they are. We are called to a walk in which, as to Him, there are not concealments and no reserves. We are called to see, at whatever cost of humiliation, our unutterable need, our tremendous contrast to the holiness of God; while on the other hand we are to behold, in some measure, "with open face . . . the glory of the Lord" [2 Cor. 3:18].

(2) Here let me take up my second text, and pass on the loving appeal of the Lord's great prophet: "Come, and let us walk in the light of the Lord." Come, friends and brethren, and look away from everything to Jesus Christ. Here is a something with which to walk and to work in the warm light, shed from the face of the Son of God. Behold the Christ, the Lamb, the Risen One, the Ascended, the Coming Jesus; who shall say what the Father sees Him to be? Infinitely great He is to the Father's heart, loved by Him before the foundation of the world, so that whatever is in Him is quite close to that heart, fully within that love. Oh, come then, and in the light of the Lord behold "the King in His beauty" [Is. 33:17], your Savior

and your God. The truest joy ever given to the human heart is in the sight of Christ Jesus, and all that He can be for you, as your very own. Christ is the light of Heaven, and when the soul steps out into that light and walks in it, receiving for its very self's need the blessed Person and all He is, then it has on earth the light of Heaven.

And what will it be when the light in which we walk passes, as it will pass, into the everlasting day? Here we see not all things, even in the light He gives. Of Scripture itself it has been well said that it is a lamp rather than a sun. But the day will come when the sun will rise, and the path will be found to have passed into the golden street of the City, where "the Lord God giveth light" [Rev. 22:5], and "the Lamb is the light thereof" [Rev. 21:23]. Then you will look around and see indeed; "in Thy light we shall see light" forever [Ps. 36:9].

Heaven is no dream. And it is not reached by dreaming. It is reached by a walk in the light, in the light of the conviction of the God of holiness, in the light of His blessed glory in the face of Jesus Christ.

51

The Christian Walk

This I say therefore, and testify in the Lord, that ye henceforth walk not as other Gentiles walk, in the vanity of their mind—Eph. 4:17

"Walk, not as others." So I read our text, in its most general application. Its first message was, of course, to the Ephesian converts in the midst of the heathen, in that city of idolatry and of iniquity. We, by God's mercy, dwell in a land of Christian light; and let us not forget the mercies of that fact. Unspeakable is the difference between heathendom and even nominal Christendom; none can tell the restraining and moderating power in the world's life of pervading Christian ideas and Christian witness. So the text cannot mean to us in all its details what it meant to the Ephesians.

Nevertheless, this message, in its heart and center, is still the same. For what does the Apostle in effect call on them to do? To live, in the Lord's Name, *above public opinion;* to take a line of their own against it, just so far as it might be against the will of God.

And this, remember, was an appeal, not to exceptional and eminent Christians, but to the Christian. Had the man come, just as he was, to Christ, to find in Him pardon and life? Then, of course, and at once he was Christ's, for service and obedience; he was bound to walk at his Master's orders, "not as others."

And this is for us today. In England, as in Ephesus, we are saved, if saved at all, to belong and to obey; as those who are "delivered from this present evil world" [see Gal. 1:4], in the tyranny of its unhallowed thoughts and ways. Under all differences, we have this in

477

common with the Ephesians; the world is around us, and we are to walk "not as others."

But now we pause to ask what the text does *not* mean. Not for a moment does it mean that we are to take a line of our own for the sake of contrariety. That is not the spirit of the gospel. The gospel is essentially a power which amalgamates, and leads to kindly concessions, where right and wrong are not concerned. It gives a death-blow to self-conceit, and so smoothes many an angle in human communication. The gospel is the noblest school of courtesy, for it leads us to esteem others better than ourselves. It is an education in sympathy, and in the power to take other people's points of view. It makes a man sensitive to the rights of others, and willing to consider even their prejudices with respect.

But if so, if this is what the precept does not mean, what does it mean? It means such union with the Lord that the line of His will shall always be our rule. Let those who take another line around us be ever so many, and let them be ever so influential; our part is, in union with Him, not lightly to judge them, certainly not to anathematize them, but indeed not to walk their way.

Is your lot cast among those who think little or think scorn of religion, who utterly neglect God's Word, or take up with the last fashionable attack upon it; who despise His sacred Day, that sweet garden of rest and holiness which He has fenced for man's benefit, and whose fences man is now so busy treading down? Walk not as they walk. With quiet firmness take a line of your own, in obedience to conscience and to the Lord. Do you find yourself among those who in some sense profess religion, but reconcile it, alas, with practices that are not of trust and of love—with unkind words, with dishonest enterprise, with self-indulgent sloth? Walk not as they walk; take the Lord's line, if you bear the Lord's Name. Let Him lift you above the stress and power of that rough, turbid stream, the world's opinion, which will be far too strong for you if you trust yourself in it out of Him.

If by the world we mean, not merely so many multitudes of people, but people whose principles and practice are not governed by God, then necessarily the world, however it may be veneered, is never hallowed. It does not get educated into holiness; its maxims and standards are not those of the Lord Jesus Christ, and you, Christian man, must be prepared not to walk its way.

How shall this be done? Here is a strong stream; who shall swim against it? Here is a vast crowd sweeping downward; who shall walk up through it the other way? You are called to do it, and in that very call you know there lies the promise of the possibility. And the possibility is explained close to our text, where Paul tells us why "others" walk as they do. It is in the vanity of their minds, with a darkened understanding, alienated from the life of God. Such is the secret of their gravitation downward. Then you and I are to be lifted upward by the opposites to these conditions; by union with the life of God in Christ; that union which is realized in loving communion with the Lord; by eyes opened to our Savior's glory, as we look for it in His Word, and apply what we see to life. So will the mind lose its "vanity," and receive the holy strength and weight of a Christian will.

"It is not in us." Man of strong will, thank God for your strength, but use it only in Him. That strong lever, if you make *yourself* the fulcrum, may only quicken your motion the wrong way. Man of weakest will, take your weakness to the Mighty One; you shall find His strength becoming yours. You shall find it possible humbly, but invincibly, to walk not as others; you shall live as one who does not mount the tribunal to judge them, but judges this rather, that for him the will of God is the law of life.

If we would "serve our own generation by the will of God," before we "fall on sleep," we must not be the slaves of our generation; we must come to Christ and yield ourselves to Him, and be ready, in His Name, and by His strength, and for His sake, to "walk not as others."

52

Walk Accurately

See then that ye walk circumspectly—Eph. 5:15

The Greek word rendered "circumspectly" may be more closely and simply rendered "accurately." The thought given is that of painstaking attention to details, under a sense of their importance; a remembrance, not only in general but in particular, of the duties of the Christian's walk.

Approaching the text, let us notice its connecting word; "See *then.*" This points us, of course, to what has gone just before; and what was this? It was the Christian's duty to seek to exercise an influence for God in the dark world around him, from which, on the other hand, he was carefully to separate himself in spirit. He was to be a ray of light that should penetrate this darkness, and should both reprove it for its evil and attract out of it one and another of its victims. But in order to be this he must himself be consistent; he must be "light in the Lord" [Eph. 5:8]; not in general only, but in detail; he must *"accurately"* walk. The text therefore has to do with Christian conduct as it tells upon others, and not merely as it is right in itself, or as it is good for the doer. It refers to that all-important fact, that the saved man is saved not only for himself, but for others too; that his Rescuer "plucks him from the burning," not only not to be lost, but to be shaped into an implement; he is intended to have an influence, and to tell. This is a truth for all who are true. In one way or another, every believer is called to "tell" for Christ, even if it be in the humblest and the homeliest way. If he is watched by only two or three human beings, he has there an opportunity of "telling," and he is to take it. It is a solemn double call; on the one hand, never to advertise himself, never to pose as superior in goodness; on the other hand, always to remember the responsibility and the privilege of influence and example.

"See then that ye walk accurately." My brethren, remember the all-importance of consistency in order to witness—that witness which we must all bear, more or less by lips, more and more in life. Let us be covetous, let us be ambitious, of such a life as that, a life of witness in and through consistency. What nobler hope can we have than to leave, when we pass away, a track like that behind us; a memory which shall say to those who care to think of it, that it evidenced the reality of Christ?

Paul bids us soar to the skies in our aims, but come down, in the fulfillment to the pathway upon earth, with its step by step, its patient going on, its attention to the next thing and the next, if that end is to be attained.

Are we seen to walk "accurately" in matters of considerateness? In common Christian life, I dare to say, the word "considerateness" covers nine-tenths of consistency. Witness for Christ is woefully spoiled when that is forgotten. Does the Christian student at college give way, for example, to indolence on the Lord's day? Does he cause needless trouble by rising late, and wanting his meal late too; reckless of what this means to those who must bring it to him? He is walking very "inaccurately" if so, and his inaccuracy discredits every good word from his lips, and every text upon his walls. There are two things to which every Christian is called, as he is the Lord's servant and not his own master; he is called to *take* trouble, and he is called to *save* it; to be a *carer* for others, in unselfish readiness to help them, to be a *sparer* of others, as to what he asks them to do for him.

Again, are we found to walk "accurately" in the tone and manner of our life? Are we careful not to be men of moods, uncertain in temper, changeful from day to day as to the spirit in which friends or attendants find us? Do not let matters of this sort drift. Do not dream that self can take care of self. Remember also that there is no promise that even grace will do the work of self-discipline. Grace is infinitely necessary that we may be able to discipline ourselves, but we, by grace, must *use* grace, in watching and in prayer; we must *think* as well as believe, if we would walk "accurately."

Are we accurate about the brightness and chastened cheerfulness of Christian life? A really gloomy Christian walks "inaccurately"; his steps are out of all consistency with those of the Lord of light and love. Let us seek for what He can give; a spirit bright with the pure gladness of "leisure from itself," a certainty of peace with God, a certainty of the Presence of the Eternal Friend, which must liberate, and elevate, and if I may so say, naturalize our happiness, and must keep our sympathies open to the joys as well as the sorrows around us.

Remember, as we close, the sacredness of the "reason why" for this constant duty. It is to be done not for our own glory, but altogether because we belong to Christ. You have come to His feet for mercy and for life; you have held up your hands to be clasped within His hands in surrender as His vassal. Your life is annexed by Him, and *what is His* can never be unimportant. True, you feel yourself, in yourself, to be as insignificant as you please, but in and for your Lord you are not insignificant, you are *significant.* You are a sign, a signal, by which others may be directed, or misdirected, as to Him. Shall we not discipline ourselves in a watchful conformity to His will, so that we may be true tokens and straight lines?

1906

THE END